THE WORLDS OF RENAISS

Angus Gowland investigates the theory of melancholy and its many applications in the Renaissance by means of a wide-ranging contextual analysis of Robert Burton's encyclopaedic *Anatomy of Melancholy* (first edition 1621). Approaching the *Anatomy* as the culmination of early modern medical, philosophical, and spiritual inquiry about melancholy, Gowland examines the ways in which Burton exploited the moral psychology central to the Renaissance understanding of the condition to construct a critical vision of his intellectual and political environment. In the first sustained analysis of the evolving relationship of the *Anatomy* in the versions issued between 1621 and 1651 to late Renaissance humanist learning and early seventeenth-century England and Europe, it corrects the prevailing view of the work as an unreflective digest of other authors' opinions, and reveals the *Anatomy*'s character as a polemical literary engagement with the live intellectual, religious, and political issues of its day.

ANGUS GOWLAND is Lecturer in Intellectual History at University College London.

IDEAS IN CONTEXT 78

The Worlds of Renaissance Melancholy

IDEAS IN CONTEXT

Edited by Quentin Skinner and James Tully

The books in this series will discuss the emergence of intellectual traditions and of related new disciplines. The procedures, aims and vocabularies that were generated will be set in the context of the alternatives available within the contemporary frameworks of ideas and institutions. Through detailed studies of the evolution of such traditions, and their modification by different audiences, it is hoped that a new picture will form of the development of ideas in their concrete contexts. By this means, artificial distinctions between the history of philosophy, of the various sciences, of society and politics, and of literature may be seen to dissolve.

The series is published with the support of the Exxon Foundation.

A list of books in the series will be found at the end of the volume.

THE WORLDS OF RENAISSANCE MELANCHOLY

Robert Burton in Context

ANGUS GOWLAND
University College London

CAMBRIDGE
UNIVERSITY PRESS

CAMBRIDGE UNIVERSITY PRESS
Cambridge, New York, Melbourne, Madrid, Cape Town,
Singapore, São Paulo, Delhi, Tokyo, Mexico City

Cambridge University Press
The Edinburgh Building, Cambridge CB2 8RU, UK

Published in the United States of America by Cambridge University Press, New York

www.cambridge.org
Information on this title: www.cambridge.org/9781107403017

First published 2006
First paperback edition 2011

A catalogue record for this publication is available from the British Library

ISBN 978-0-521-86768-9 Hardback
ISBN 978-1-107-40301-7 Paperback

Contents

Acknowledgements *page* ix
Conventions xi

Introduction 1
The 'Letter to Damagetes' 8

1 The medical theory of melancholy 33
The nature and status of medical inquiry 35
Medicine and humanist philosophy 40
Body and soul 43
Neo-Galenic occultism 50
The *Anatomy* and the medical theory of melancholy 54
Division and definition 56
Causes, symptoms, prognostics, cures 72
Medical occultism in the *Anatomy* 85

2 Dissecting medical learning 98
The humanist critique of medicine 100
Medicine and Christian humanism 122
Knowledge and its uses 135

3 Melancholy and divinity 139
England and Europe 141
English theology and ecclesiastical politics 143
University theological dispute 151
The intellectual complexion of Laudianism 154
Religious melancholy 158
Orthodoxy and controversy 161
War and religion 166
The English Church 169
Predestination and despair 174
Humanism and the early Stuart Church 192
Spiritual politics in the *Anatomy* 203

4 The melancholy body politic 205
Psychology and politics 206
Jacobean theories of monarchy 212
Court and counsel 219
Dissecting the body politic 223
The politics of melancholy 240

5 Utopia, consolation, and withdrawal 246
The philosopher and the commonwealth 253
Melancholy and utopia 261
On misery and consolation 266
Satire and philosophy 275
Democritus Junior 287

Conclusion: Robert Burton's melancholy 295

Bibliographies 302

Index 329

Acknowledgements

My greatest debt is to Quentin Skinner. He first encouraged me to read Burton, oversaw my study on him from its inception, and has provided inspiration, encouragement, and kind support for a number of years. I would also like to thank the examiners of my doctoral dissertation – Peter Burke, from whose encyclopaedic knowledge I have benefited greatly, and Warren Boutcher, whose acuity and advice have been very influential upon my approach to the *Anatomy.* I am grateful to Peter Stacey, with whom I have enjoyed many absorbing conversations on Renaissance philosophy; and to Richard Serjeantson, whose generously shared erudition has been of much assistance. Other friends and colleagues to whom warm thanks are due include Valentina Arena, Geoff Baldwin, Malcolm Bowie, Brendan Bradshaw, Cathy Curtis, Hannah Dawson, Lauren Kassell, Richard Luckett, Iain McDaniel, Peter Mack, Claire Preston, Peter Schröder, Jeremy Schmidt, David Sedley and Nicholas Tyacke. Richard Fisher has been an extraordinarily patient and supportive editor.

I would also like to acknowledge the Fellows of King's College, Magdalene College, and Christ's College in Cambridge, and the members of the Department of History at University College London, all of whom have provided hospitable and stimulating environments assisting the development of this work. Ivan and Mary Schröder's generosity with books has been remarkable; my parents Richard and Alison have been a constant source of support and encouragement. My deepest gratitude is to my wife Ingrid, whose conversation and loving patience – along with my son Conrad – have sustained me throughout.

Conventions

Bibliographies. These are lists of the primary and secondary sources I have quoted, and make no claim to be comprehensive guides, either to the ever-increasing literature on *The Anatomy of Melancholy* or to the more general themes discussed in this study. For a useful guide to publications relating to the *Anatomy* printed before 1988 see Joey Conn, *Robert Burton and 'The Anatomy of Melancholy': An annotated bibliography of primary and secondary sources* (Westport, Conn., 1988). In the bibliographies of printed primary sources and footnotes I list anonymous works by their title. All references to journal numbers in the bibliographies of secondary sources are given in arabic form.

Classical names and titles. In both the text and the bibliographies, Greek and Roman writers are referred to in their most familiar single-name form. Greek titles have been translated into English, but all other titles are given in their original language.

Dates. I follow my sources in using the Julian Calendar when citing those written or published in Britain, and the Gregorian when citing those written or published on the continent of Europe after 1582.

Gender. I have attempted to maintain gender-neutral language where possible, but when quoting sources which clearly do not I have not altered their sense.

References. I follow the author-date system, and give references in arabic numerals to chapters from individual texts and to parts of multi-volume works. I have generally given section and chapter headings (as well as page numbers) of texts which have multiple editions to facilitate cross-referencing. As an exception that runs throughout, references to the text of *The Anatomy of Melancholy* are generally given in the main body of the text when they are to single passages of text, but in the footnotes when they are to more than one passage. When referring to the formal divisions of the *Anatomy* ('Partitions', 'Sections', 'Members', 'Subsections') I have capitalised these to indicate their reference to the apparatus of the book. All references to the *Anatomy* are to the recent critical edition (Burton 1989–2000 in the bibliography below) and give the volume number, page, and line number of this edition. When referring to the three volumes of the editors' commentary, line numbers are no longer possible and I just give volume number and page. With the exception of references to the prefatory satire (pages 1–112 of the critical edition), to enable cross-referencing between this study and other editions of the *Anatomy*, I have parenthetically indicated the location of references whenever these pertain to new Partition, Section, Member, and Subsection numbers. For example, (1.217.21–3 [1.2.1.1]) refers to volume 1, page 217, lines 21 to 23, located in Partition 1, Section 2, Member 1, and Subsection 1. When referring to additions or modifications to the editions of the *Anatomy* published between 1621 and 1651, however, I also use the author-date system, as in the following instance: Burton 1632, p. 697; or 3.401.32–402.15 (3.4.2.1).

Transcriptions. I have generally preserved original spelling, capitalisation, italicisation, and punctuation in my quotations, but I have normalised the long 's', expanded contractions, corrected obvious typographical errors, and made modern orthographical alterations – such as changing 'u' to 'v' in English sources, and *vice versa* in Latin – when I have deemed it helpful for clarity.

Translations. When quoting from classical sources I have generally followed the translations provided by the Loeb Classical Library when available. When quoting early modern sources all translations are my own, unless otherwise indicated. I have occasionally referred in brackets to modern translations of classical texts after references to early modern editions of these texts, and to modern editions of early modern texts, for the potential assistance of those without access to the same editions.

Introduction

Surveying the world outside his study in Christ Church, Oxford, at the end of the year 1620, Robert Burton diagnosed an epidemic of melancholy. It was now, he thought, 'a disease so frequent . . . in these our daies, so often happening . . . in our miserable times, as few there are that feele not the smart of it'. Since it was 'a disease so grievous, so common', he claimed to 'know not wherein to do a more generall service, and spend my time better, then to prescribe means how to prevent and cure so universall a malady, an Epidemicall disease, that so often, so much crucifies the body and minde' (1.110.9–19). Burton cited a range of neoteric philosophical and medical authorities to support his diagnosis. Whilst examining the spleen and its role in generating hypochondriacal melancholy in the 1552 edition of his *De anima*, Philipp Melanchthon had written that there were so many cases of this disease it was pointless to count the sufferers.[1] Later in the century André du Laurens had concluded his chapter on the same species of melancholy by noting its frequency 'in these miserable times', and pointing out that 'there are not many people which feele not some smatch thereof'.[2] 'This disease is most frequent in these days', agreed Girolamo Mercuriale, in the chapter on melancholy in his *Medicina practica* of 1601.[3] The same diagnosis was supported by Giulio Cesare Chiodini, who asserted in his *Consultationes* of 1607 that 'in our times scarcely anyone can be found who is immune from its contamination'. Melancholy, according to Chiodini, had not

[1] Melanchthon 1552, sig. F2: 'Exempla adeò crebra sunt, ut hic nomina eorum recitare nolum, quos vidimus hoc morbo laborare.' This observation was not present in the 1540 edition.

[2] Du Laurens 1599, p. 140.

[3] Mercuriale 1617, I.10, p. 55: 'Sed istud satis est intelligere, hanc affectionem esse temporibus nostris frequentissimam, ut propter hoc pertineat ad culturam ingeniorum vestrorum diligenter curationem hanc intelligere.'

only spread throughout the population; it was, as he put it, the 'fountain of almost all other diseases' afflicting his society.[4]

The Anatomy of Melancholy was written as a response to a perceived epidemic of the disease. But earlier in the book's preface, Burton gave a different account of his reasons for writing. This was that he was himself afflicted by the disease, but considered writing about it to be a beneficial enterprise: 'I write of Melancholy, by being busie to avoid Melancholy' (1.6.29–30). How could writing about something be construed as a means of avoiding it? Having raised the question, the answer which he immediately supplied was in accordance with the Senecan maxim 'Otium sine literis mors est et hominis vivi sepultura',[5] that the activity of writing was a 'playing labor' to counteract the danger of the 'idlenesse' that caused and exacerbated the condition (1.6.30–7.5). But why write about melancholy rather than another, more light-hearted subject? Because, as he confessed, he felt an overwhelming need to 'scratch where it itcheth', and 'could imagine no fitter evacuation' of his melancholic 'Impostume' than to investigate the nature of the affliction (1.7.18–20). As he continued, it became clear that he intended this activity of 'scratching' – an appropriately physical metaphor for a lifelong writing enterprise – to have a psychologically therapeutic effect. His purpose was 'to ease my minde by writing', and his strategy to accomplish this was to 'expell *clavum clavo*, comfort one sorrow with another, idlenes with idlenes', and 'make an Antidote out of that which was the prime cause of my disease'. (1.6.29–30, 7.16–17, 23–5). This was turning melancholy against itself, apparently a kind of literary-poetic 'homeopathy' working on the principle of *similia similibus curantur* and in obvious tension with conventional Galenic 'allopathy' based on the contradiction of opposites.[6] It was for his own benefit, though he was careful to remark that he 'would helpe others out of a fellow-feeling' by spending his 'time and knowledge . . . for the common good of all' (1.8.6–10). He had an illustrious predecessor in Cicero, who had famously written the *Consolatio seu de luctu minuendo* 'after his Daughters departure' (1.7.31–2), and had offered a vision of philosophical writing in retirement

[4] Chiodini 1607, consultatio 98, p. 232: 'Affectus melancholicus, maximè verò qui flatulentus, & Hypochondriacus vocatur, adeo nostris temporibus frequenter ingruit, ut quemadmodum nullus ferè ab eius labe immunis reperitur, ita propria natura omnium quasi morborum, omnium penè Symptomatum occasio existat, id quod in omnibus, at praesertim in illustrissimo.'

[5] Seneca 1917–25, DCCCII.3, vol. II, pp. 242–3. On the Stoic conception of writing as spiritual exercise see Hadot 1998, pp. 48–51.

[6] See Blok 1976, pp. 139–46.

that would simultaneously relieve the *animi aegritudo* of the author and serve the commonwealth.[7]

How exactly did Burton envisage the literary transformation of the 'disease' into its 'Antidote'? The answer is in the character of the book's contents, which were presented as an investigation, not of the author's own melancholy, but rather of the diverse forms of melancholy in the world surrounding him. It is this sustained involvement with the condition of the contemporary environment which allows us to speak of Burton's vision of the world as melancholy, and which distinguishes his treatise from both the conventional medical writings of the era and the self-exploratory project of Montaigne.[8] In his eschewal of inwardness there was, perhaps, an Augustinian rejection of the *amor sui* involved in introversion for the sake of self-knowledge rather than the discovery of God – recall Pascal's castigation of Montaigne's 'sot projet . . . de se peindre'.[9] But Burton had a practical psychological rationale. In the main treatise of the *Anatomy*, it was emphasised that although the melancholic would be inclined to indulge restless thoughts, he was not to be allowed to 'please himselfe' in solitariness with 'private and vaine meditations', as this would only exacerbate his psychological turmoil (1.392.24–393.31 [1.3.1.2]; 2.109.12–15 [2.2.6.2]). Sufferers from the disease were advised to resist the temptation to revel in the 'fond imaginations' brought by 'this delightsome melancholy', and instead 'divert' their 'thoughts' away from the conditions that had led to their personal affliction (2.101.15–102.31 [2.2.6.1]). Burton made the point that the melancholic should 'never bee left alone or idle . . . least hee abuse his solitarinesse', and to this end, he told his readers that they should 'set him about some businesse, execise or recreation, which may divert his thoughts', otherwise his restless imagination would 'melancholize, and be carried away instantly, with some feare, jealousie, discontent, some vaine conceipt or other'. (2.106.19–107.7 [2.2.6.2]).

Given this conception of the diseased imagination's tendency to 'worke upon it selfe', we can see why, in Burton's view, it would have been counterproductive to engage in introspection. Provoked by a desire to relieve his melancholy, and having gained knowledge of its effects from his own '*melancholizing*' (1.8.2–6), he chose to investigate the forms of the disease that he perceived elsewhere, to 'comfort one sorrow' – his

7 Cicero 1933, I.4, pp. 10–13.
8 On Burton's use of Montaigne's *Essais* see Dieckow 1903, pp. 92–115.
9 Pascal 1976, p. 322.

own – 'with [that of] another'. His fundamental self-therapeutic procedure was therefore not homeopathic introversion but allopathic diversion, which he hoped would 'ease' his own melancholy. By constructing an elaborate vision of the melancholic world, he was giving in to his compulsion to 'scratch where it itcheth' but avoiding the temptation to 'melancholize' upon himself. This negative view of melancholic self-reflection extended even to his conception of the effects of reading about the disease in the *Anatomy* itself. In the third edition (1628), he warned that the propensity of the melancholic to 'misapply' everything he experienced to himself was such that anyone afflicted with the disease would be well advised to omit 'the Symptomes or prognostickes in this following Tract' in case 'hee trouble or hurt himselfe' unnecessarily.[10] Readers were left to wonder whether the author included this because of the mixed reception of earlier versions of the book, which, he claimed, had led to his being 'honoured by some worthy men' but 'vilified by others'.[11]

Even if the *Anatomy* was written to provide its author with relief from his own condition, Burton wanted his readers to consider his 'chief motives' to be the 'generalitie of the Disease, the necessitie of the Cure, and the commodity or common good that will arise to all men by the knowledge of it' (1.20.26; 23.9–10, 19–24). We should see the aims of the author with respect to himself and his readership as united by a shared concern to assist the alleviation of melancholy.[12] The goal to be attained was tranquillity, which appeared throughout the book as the opposite of the anxiety that characterised the experience of the disease. However, as I aim to show in this study, Burton's conception of his own melancholy was inextricable from his perception that the early modern world was suffering from the same condition. Insofar as the *Anatomy* was the written enactment of its author's search for tranquillity, it was simultaneously an attempt to address the absence of tranquillity in that world – to understand its variety of kinds, causes, and symptoms, and discover means of its remedy.

***

[10] Burton 1628, p. 17; or 1.24.7–14. See also Burton 1624, p. 161, or 1.387.5–7 (1.3.1.2); Burton 1628, p. 174, or 1.387.20–3 (1.3.1.2); and Burton 1632, p. 183, or 1.387.20–1 (1.3.1.2). This idea was echoed in Shaftesbury's *Characteristicks* (1711): Cooper 1999, vol. II, p. 143.

[11] Burton 1628, pp. 10–11; or 1.14.26–15.5. Cf. 1.9.11–13.

[12] See Heusser 1987, Vicari 1989, and Miller 1997.

Robert Burton was born on 8 February 1577 in the village of Lindley, Leicestershire, into a well-established landed gentry family.[13] Robert was the second son of Ralph Burton and Dorothy Faunt; we know very little of his five sisters and three brothers, with the notable exception of William. Like his younger brother, William Burton put his humanistic education to good use, authoring an unpublished Latin play, *De amoribus Perinthii et Tyanthes* (1596), translating the Greek of Achilles Tatius into *The most delectable and pleasaunt History of Clitophon and Leucippe* (1597), and proceeding to acquire fame in antiquarian circles largely as a result of the publication of *The Description of Leicestershire* (1622). In this work, William recorded his great admiration for his uncle and godfather Arthur Faunt, one of a number of Catholics on Dorothy's side of the family, as 'a man of great learning, gravity and wisdome'.[14] Faunt had attended Merton College in Oxford in the 1560s before becoming a Jesuit, after which he published a number of works of controversial theology and mingled freely as an intellectual exile in the court circles of Counter-Reformation Europe.[15] He seems likely to have had an influence on William's religious leanings, since the latter enthusiastically anticipated, and subsequently endorsed, the Laudian programme to restore the 'beauty of holiness' to the English Church by refurbishing his own chapel at Lindley in 1623.[16] (This feature of the Burton family heritage has been overlooked by modern scholarship on *The Anatomy of Melancholy*,[17] but the religious values represented by Arthur Faunt may well have been a significant background factor in shaping the spiritual sympathies it expressed.) William Burton also recalled in *The Description of Leicestershire* that after being deprived of the office of Lieutenant General of Leicestershire by the Earl of Huntingdon in 1588, Arthur's brother Anthony 'fell into so great a passion of melancholy, that within a short time after hee dyed', and took the opportunity to advertise the family wares: 'What the force, power, and effect of Melancholy is, I referre the Reader to the *Anatomy of Melancholy*, penned by my brother *Robert Burton*.'[18]

Robert Burton was schooled in Sutton Coldfield and Nuneaton, before matriculating from Brasenose College, Oxford, in 1593. There is an

[13] For most of the extant biographical details see Nochimson 1974.
[14] Burton 1622, pp. 106.
[15] Burton 1622, pp. 105–6.
[16] See Cust 2004–5.
[17] For example, in Nochimson 1974, p. 87.
[18] Burton 1622, p. 105.

unaccounted pause in his university career, which has prompted speculation that at this time he suffered some kind of illness, and possibly visited the astrological physician Simon Forman in London for treatment of melancholy.[19] However, after his election to a Studentship at Christ Church in 1599 – it is impossible to know why Burton changed college, though it is interesting to note that Brasenose had a reputation for producing 'godly' preachers[20] – he proceeded under the tutorship of John Bancroft, the future bishop of Oxford, to receive his BA in 1602, his MA in 1605, and finally his BD in 1614. Two years later, he was appointed to the benefice of St Thomas in Oxford, and after another two years was granted his licence to preach. Around this time, he served for three years as Clerk of the Oxford Market. In 1624, he acquired another living as Rector of Walesby in Lincolnshire, which he was apparently forced to resign in 1631 when his patron, the Countess Dowager of Exeter, turned it over to Lionel Cranfield, Earl of Middlesex. In 1633 or 1634, he was preferred to the more substantial Rectorship of Seagrave in Leicestershire with the support of the county aristocrat George, Lord Berkeley. His new patron had been made a Knight of the Bath in 1616 when Charles became Prince of Wales after the death of Prince Henry, and although he would not be active in the Civil War, his royalist sympathies are suggested by his impeachment in the Commons for high treason in September 1647. Burton's family partially held their manor in Lindley from the Berkeleys, and George had also possibly been tutored by Burton at Christ Church. It was perhaps significant that it had taken over a decade for Burton's dedication of the *Anatomy*, first made in 1621, to achieve its desired effect.

Burton's first literary production was a Latin pastoral comedy, *Alba*, which was performed before James I at Christ Church on 27 August 1605. It seems not to have gone down well. One observer, Philip Stringer, called the play 'very tedious', and reported that 'if the Chancellors of both Universities had not intreated his Majesty earnestly, he would have gone before half the Comedy had been ended'.[21] It is now lost, but the costume and props lists indicates that it involved classical-mythological figures, kings, nymphs, hermits, satyrs, morris-dancers, a magician, an old crone, and a dozen live white doves.[22] In the following year, Burton began his second work, the Latin comedy *Philosophaster*, which he revised

[19] See Evans 1944, p. 7, and Traister 1976.
[20] Richardson 1972, pp. 58–63. On Brasenose see Dent 1983, p. 167.
[21] Quoted in Nochimson 1974, p. 97.
[22] Boas and Greg 1909, pp. 249–50, cited in Nochimson 1974, p. 98.

and corrected in 1615. This satirised the various 'Philosophasters' to be found in the university life of 'Osuna' – a thinly disguised Oxford – and its characters included a Jesuit magician, 'Polumpragmaticus'; his sidekick, 'Equivocus'; a mathematician, 'Lodovicus Pantometer'; a sophist, 'Simon Acutus'; and a grammarian, 'Pedanus'. As these names indicated, and as the epilogue confirmed, the purpose of the play was to ridicule contemporary scholarship and provoke reform: 'Fremat, frendat licet. / Unus et alter laesus. Bonus quisque dabit / Iam renovatae plausum Academiae. / Longùm efflorescat Osuna Academia.'[23] This anticipated one of the themes of the *Anatomy*, and we can see a prototype of Burton's satirical-encyclopaedic authorial *persona* of 'Democritus Junior' in the wandering scholar 'Polumathes', who delivered the lament 'Divites plures, paucos doctus, sapientem neminem.'[24] We do not know exactly when he began the composition of the *Anatomy*, but given the size of the book it was presumably several years before its first publication in 1621. He continued to work on it up to his death in January 1640, producing new editions of ever-increasing length in 1624, 1628, 1632, and 1638. A version with a relatively small number of the author's final additions and modifications was published posthumously in 1651.

Very few details concerning Burton's life at Oxford have survived, but this is more than compensated for by the rich mine of information about his interests preserved in the form of his large personal library.[25] As well as being librarian at Christ Church from 1626 onwards, he was an avid collector of books and all kinds of printed material in genres that ranged from theology, history, medicine, politics, literature, geography, astronomy, and astrology to mathematics, agriculture, law, and descriptions of marvels. The range of intellectual interests this reflects was not unusual in itself, since this was the age in Oxford, and indeed in England, where achieving a reputation for 'general', encyclopaedic learning was held to be one of the greatest triumphs of a humanist's career.[26] But comparing his library to others of the era, he appears to have been particularly interested in information about the contemporary world, as over three-quarters of his books of history and literature were concerned with the sixteenth or seventeenth centuries, and like many of his contemporaries he regularly indulged himself by purchasing news pamphlets.[27] His active reading

23 Burton 1977, p. 226.
24 Burton 1977, p. 195.
25 See Kiessling 1988.
26 See Casaubon 1999 and Feingold 1997, p. 218.
27 Osler 1926, p. 187; Kiessling 1988, p. 371.

practices – also typical amongst humanists of this period – are suggested by the annotations that can be seen in about one-fifth of his volumes. As one would expect, works dealing with melancholy are heavily annotated, and copious reference lists on a range of subjects that were discussed in the *Anatomy*, as well as quotations, anecdotes, poems, proverbs, and paradoxes, can be found scribbled in the pages, flyleaves, and blank pages of many books.[28] Some of his notes reveal a reader who was very far from being disengaged. Burton's response to George Carleton's dismissal of judicial astrology near the beginning of his *Ἀστρολομανία: The madnesse of astrologers* (1624) was to ask in a marginal comment, 'What alreadie?' 'Mentitur' was his more blunt reaction to John Eliot's claim, in *The survay or topographical description of France* (1592), that the population of Paris was 'many millyons'.[29] His library acts as a strong testament to the fact – which we shall see confirmed by the contents of the *Anatomy* – that he was a critical reader, engaging with his books and looking to use and transform their contents for his own purposes. The currently prevalent image of Burton as a naïve and occasionally careless compiler of other authors' views cannot remain.[30]

THE 'LETTER TO DAMAGETES'

Burton's response to the contemporary world was largely determined by a combination of moral-philosophical and spiritual commitments, and in seeking to understand the way these were manifested in the content and form of the *Anatomy* we need first to examine his choice of *persona* as 'Democritus Junior'. The title-pages of the six editions of the work published between 1621 and 1651 concealed the author's identity behind this pseudonym, notwithstanding the inclusion of several clues elsewhere in the book.[31] Six of the seven parergic components accompanying the main text – the illustrated frontispiece and its expository 'Argument', the dedication to Lord Berkeley, the poems 'Democritus Junior ad Librum suuum' and 'Heraclite fleas...', and the admonitory 'Lectori malè feriato' – referred to Democritus Junior, and the first pages of the

[28] Kiessling 1988, pp. xxxxiii–iv.

[29] Kiessling 1988, p. xxxiii.

[30] See, for example, the views expressed in Bamborough 1989, p. xxvi; Vicari 1989, p. 193; Pigeaud 1992, p. 221; and cf. the comments on Montaigne scholarship in Friedrich 1991, p. xxix. For a recent suggestion that Burton was an 'active' reader see McCutcheon 1998, p. 74.

[31] See Burton 1621, sig. Ddd3^{v}, and the hints at 2.61.12–13; 2.61.17–18, d; 2.61–31–2, k; 2.66.21–5, p (2.2.3.1). From the third edition onwards, Burton's portrait and coat of arms appeared on the illustrated frontispiece.

satirical preface provided substantial detail concerning the 'reason of the Name' Burton had assumed (1.6.12). Few modern readers have failed to register the high degree of importance that must be given to this pseudonym, and its literary-satirical associations have been well illustrated.[32] But its philosophical aspects have been almost totally ignored. The satirical connotation of the laughing figure of Democritus was in fact an aspect of his moral-philosophical identity. It is by attending to this dimension of 'Democritus Junior' that we may recover the 'truth' Burton avowedly delivered whilst speaking 'in jest'.

The prefatory satire 'Democritus Junior to the Reader' was an extended adaptation of the pseudo-Hippocratic *Letter to Damagetes*, an apocryphal tale in which the philosopher Democritus proved to the physician Hippocrates that the world was universally suffering from madness.[33] The *Letter* was well known in European humanist circles, especially after its inclusion in Fabio Calvo's Latin translation of the Hippocratic *corpus* issued in 1525, though Burton was virtually unique in using it in such substantial detail. His adaptation bore all the hallmarks of the manner in which humanists had long sought to apply classical texts to the contemporary world.[34] In the first place, he employed the trope of *similitudo temporum* – based on the axiom that the essentials of human nature never change (1.39.2–12) – to update the message of the *Letter* for the contemporary world. Indeed, it was his opinion that Democritus's assessment of 'the World in his time' was even more relevant to 'this life of ours' than it had been to his own age (1.37.14, 20). More important, however, were the philosophical aims of 'Democritus Junior to the Reader'. Its core argument was rooted in the moral psychology found in the pseudo-Hippocratic text, an eclectic configuration of Cynic, Epicurean, and Stoic ideas. As we shall see in later chapters, Burton extensively exploited the intellectual resources of this text as a platform for addressing contemporary political issues. To begin to understand his position, we must first look at his re-telling of the *Letter*, whose importance was signalled by his decision to insert it '*verbatim* almost, as it is delivered by *Hyppocrates* himselfe' one-third of the way into the preface (1.33.6–7).

In Burton's account, which began by supplementing information about Democritus contained in the *Letter* with details taken mainly from

[32] See Holland 1979; Jehasse 1980; Rutten 1992, pp. 181–6.

[33] Hippocrates 1990, XVII, pp. 73–93.

[34] For the reception history of the *Letter to Damagetes* see Rütten 1992; on Burton's use of the text see Rütten 1993.

Diogenes Laertius, the renowned philosopher was a citizen of the Thracian town of Abdera, to which place he had been summoned as 'their Lawmaker, Recorder or Towne-clearke'. Eventually, however, he took off to 'a Garden in the Suburbs' to devote himself 'to his studies, and a private life',[35] only occasionally visiting the harbour to '*laugh heartily*' at what he saw there (1.3.1–5). His laughter was provoked by the ridiculousness of the 'whole life' of the Abderans, who for their part were convinced that Democritus had succumbed to madness, and summoned the famous physician Hippocrates 'that he would exercise his skill upon him' (1.32.33–33.4). On meeting Democritus alone in his garden, '*with a Booke on his knees*' and '*cutting up severall Beasts*', Hippocrates discovered that he was investigating the causes of madness and melancholy, and expressed his admiration at Democritus's 'happinesse and leasure' – in contrast to his own life consumed by necessary 'domesticall affaires' (1.33.10–24). At this, Democritus 'profusely laughed', explaining the cause of his mirth to be 'the vanities and fopperies of the time', seen especially in the absence of virtue and variety of passions that dominated men, made them miserable, and produced ridiculous 'behaviours' that 'expresse their intollerable folly' (1.33.24–34.2).

Hippocrates initially countered Democritus's case that men were 'as disordered in their mindes, as *Thersites* was in his body' with the idea that their actions were compelled by necessity, and excused by the uncertainty of human knowledge of the future (1.34.21–6). But the philosopher expanded his argument. Mankind was deserving not of pity but of laughter because it failed to 'consider the mutability of this world', sought 'superfluities, and unprofitable things' beyond that which had been provided by 'Nature', succumbed to 'Avarice, Envy, Malice, enormious villanies, Mutinies, unsatiable desires, Conspiracies, and other incurable Vices', and generally 'know not themselves' (1.35.7–36.3). Such was the vanity, hypocrisy, and passionate madness of humanity, Democritus concluded, 'why should I not laugh at those, to whom folly seemes wisdome, will not be cured, and perceive it not?' (1.36.3–37.8). The scene ended with a critical reversal of the Abderans' diagnosis. According to Hippocrates, 'the World had not a wiser, a more learned, a more honest man, and they were much deceived to say that hee was mad' (1.37.9–13).

Two general features of this fable are indispensable for understanding its role in the *Anatomy*. First, although Burton recorded Democritus's

[35] Cf. Hippocrates 1995, XVII.2, pp. 74–5 (=Hippocrates 1525, p. 713).

fame as 'a generall Schollar' with expertise in divinity, medicine, politics, mathematics, and the natural world (I.2.15–22), he was portrayed as essentially a moral philosopher concerned with the ethical status of human irrationality, and particularly 'perturbations and tranquillity of the minde' (I.35.9). What the fable enacted, then, was a transferral of authority from medical science, represented by Hippocrates, to moral philosophy and psychology, represented by Democritus (in chapter two, we shall see that this had repercussions upon the status of the medical knowledge investigated in the main treatise). In the second place, a central theme of the fable was the relationship between the philosopher and the political community. Democritus had retired from a life of political activity in the service of Abdera to a private life of wisdom accomplished in studious solitude; in Latinate terms, the *Letter* seemed to endorse the claims of the *vita contemplativa* against those of the *vita activa*. But if this withdrawal signified contempt for human society, it did not entail total disengagement. The philosopher's ethical responsibility dictated that the physical detachment of withdrawal should enable the perception and diagnosis of the world's ills, guaranteeing clarity and integrity in the observer's viewpoint. Withdrawal was the condition required for moral and political critique. In chapters three to five I explore the ways in which Burton engaged in this type of activity in the *Anatomy*.

Before proceeding further, we need to establish the philosophical credentials of the figure of Democritus in more detail. In terms of classical dogma, the Democritus of the *Anatomy* as well as the *Letter* incarnated a range of Greek ethical themes. Most obviously, Democritus exhibited many Epicurean features. His renunciation of political activity and social life accorded with the notorious Epicurean injunction to 'live unknown' (Λάθε βιώσας).[36] His dishevelled appearance and 'neglect' of diet (I.33.12, 37.11–12) indicated a simple lifestyle that could have been that of an Epicurean sage, though they also suggested a Cynic or Stoic appreciation of poverty as a sign of contempt for worldly values.[37] There was perhaps also a reference to the Garden in Democritus's choice of location, an impression that was strengthened in the *Anatomy* by the image of the walled community depicted on Burton's frontispiece. More importantly, the message of Democritus accorded with his appearance.

[36] Usener (ed.) 1887, fr. 551, p. 327.
[37] Diogenes Laertius 1925, X.130–2, vol. II, pp. 654–7. Cf. Hippocrates 1995, XVII.2, pp. 74–5 (= Hippocrates 1525, pp. 712–13).

The world was sick, deluded by irrational values and beliefs. Mankind suffered, perpetually subject to diseases and mental perturbations, because it gave full rein to boundless and 'empty' desires and refused to live self-sufficiently according to nature. The highest good in this world was apparently ἀταραξία, the Epicurean goal of absence of bodily pain and 'tranquillity of the minde' (I.35.9, 36.II). The philosopher's remedy was the harsh reproof effected by condemnation and contemptuous laughter.[38]

Neither the pseudo-Hippocratic Democritus nor 'Democritus Junior' was a purely Epicurean creation, however.[39] Many of the salient features of both could equally have been derived from the Cynics' advocacy of self-sufficiency and shamelessness in criticising the vices and desires of humanity, as had been illustrated by the lives of Diogenes – to whom Burton compared himself (I.5.22)[40] – and the perpetually scoffing Menippus.[41] Some of these themes could also be attributed to the Pyrrhonian Sceptics, for whom the contrast between the worldly life of perturbations and false ethical beliefs on the one hand, and the simple life of philosophically attained ἀταραξία on the other, was fundamental.[42] But the Stoic features in the Democritus of the *Letter* were most significant for Burton, particularly his denunciation of the gamut of human passions as vicious and destructive of health and happiness,[43] which was derived from the core Stoic belief that the root cause of human suffering was irrationality (I.36.4–6). This also probably determined Democritus's conception of wisdom as based upon recognition of 'the mutability of this world' (also an Epicurean tenet), and his vision of virtuous living rooted in knowledge and control of the self in contrast to the 'fickle and unconstant' life of vice (I.35.13–36).[44] Although Democritus's claim to occupy 'some high place above you all' echoed the κατασκοπιά of the

[38] For these themes see especially I.33.27–32; I.34.5–7, 20–2; I.35.21–3, 30; I.36.5–II, 17–18, 30. Cf. Hippocrates 1995, XVII.5–XVII.7, pp. 80–3, 84–5 (= Hippocrates 1525, p. 713) and XVII.4, XVII.7–9, pp. 80–1, 84–9 (= Hippocrates 1525, pp. 714, 718–19); and Diogenes Laertius 1925, X.85, vol. II, pp. 614–15.

[39] As asserted in Barbour 1998, pp. 63–73.

[40] See also the reference to Diogenes in Burton 1621, p. 4, removed in the third edition.

[41] Diogenes Laertius 1925, VI.99, vol. II, pp. 102–3.

[42] See also Hippocrates 1995, XVII.9, pp. 90–1 (= Hippocrates 1525, p. 719), omitted in Burton's version. On Democritus as an 'honorary Sceptic' see Diogenes Laertius 1925, IX.72, vol. II, pp. 484–5.

[43] See I.33.27–34.I; I.34.20–I; I.35.29–30, 32–3; I.36.9–14; I.36.29–37.I and Hippocrates 1995, XVII.4–9, pp. 80–91 (= Hippocrates 1525, pp. 714–16).

[44] Cf. Hippocrates 1995, XVII.7–8, pp. 84–7 (= Hippocrates 1525, pp. 715–16) and XVII.10, pp. 90–1 (= Hippocrates 1525, pp. 719–20), not in Burton's version.

Cynics, the assumption of a cosmic perspective was strongly associated with Stoicism. Seneca's justification of this radical alteration of consciousness in the *De brevitate vitae* mapped directly on to the arguments of Burton's Democritus, just as it had to those of Langius in Justus Lipsius' *De Constantia* (1584). It was 'necessary to leave the ground' to free ourselves from our bodily passions, live virtuously, and obtain knowledge of life and death.[45] 'Democritus Junior' *qua* satirist may have been Cynic, but his laughter at humanity signified the distanced contempt for the external world and the vagaries of fortune commended in Democritus by Seneca in the *De ira* (1.4.21–4).[46] The intended priority of the Stoic over the Epicurean, Cynic, or Sceptical aspects of the philosophical position of 'Democritus Junior' was confirmed when Burton compared himself as 'a Collegiat Student' to '*Democritus* in his Garden', being 'sequestred from those tumults and trobles of the world', and (quoting Daniel Heinsius) '*tanquam in speculâ positus*... in some high place above you all, like *Stoicus Sapiens, omnia sæcula, præterita presentiaque videns, uno velut intuitu*' (1.4.17–21).

Burton's emphasis on the Stoic identity of 'Democritus Junior' set the scene for his fundamental moral-psychological contention about melancholy, madness, and virtuous rationality. The argument proper began inconspicuously with a slight modification made by Burton to the Democritus fable. It has rarely been noted that the episode related in the *Anatomy* differed from the original in that it dealt not just with madness, as in the pseudo-Hippocratic text, but madness and melancholy.[47] According to the *Letter to Damagetes*, when Hippocrates first approached Democritus, the latter was writing 'A treatise on madness' [Περί μανίης].[48] In Fabio Calvo's authoritative Latin translation of the Hippocratic *Corpus*, the source used by Burton, Democritus's book was 'de furore, & insania, maniave'; but in the *Anatomy* its 'subject' was stealthily extended to cover 'Melancholy and madnesse' (1.6.2–3).[49] Burton named the physiological object of Democritus's anatomical

45 Seneca 1928–32, XIX.2, vol. III, pp. 350–1; Lipsius 1595, II.26, p. 125. On the 'view from above' see Hadot 1995, 228–50, and Hadot 2002, pp. 206–7.

46 See Seneca 1928–35, II.10.5, III.6.3, III.37.3, vol. I, pp. 186–7, 268–9, 342–3. See also Ficino 1975, LXI, XXVIII, vol. II, p. 78, vol. IV, p. 48. For discussion see Jéhasse 1980 and Ménager 1995, p. 65.

47 The notable exception is in Holland 1979, pp. 186–8. See also Rütten 1993, pp. 37–9.

48 Hippocrates 1990, XVII.2–3, pp. 75–7.

49 Hippocrates 1525, p. 714; see Burton's comments 3.285.26, v (3.3.1.2) and 3.1.430.f (1.4.1.1). At 3.1.33.0, he misquoted his source as writing '*De furore, mania, melancholia*', when the original had only 'de insania' (Hippocrates 1525, p. 714).

investigations '*atra bilis* or melancholy' (I.6.5–6), but the Greek text had only χολῆς, and Calvo's edition 'fellis, bilisve' – that is to say, 'gall or bile', but not specifically black bile.[50]

At first glance, Burton appears to have made this modification in order to manufacture ancient authority for his treatise on melancholy, anchoring it in the humanist tradition of *imitatio* (I.6.9). But his elision of madness and melancholy also initiated a Stoic moral argument, justifying an extensively defined concept of melancholic madness and sanctioning an interchangeable usage of terms describing mental disease throughout the book. In the most important moral-philosophical passage of the preface, he asked, 'who is not a Foole, Melancholy, Mad?', and proceeded to explain that

> Folly, Melancholy, Madnesse, are but one disease, *Delirium is a common name to all. Alexander, Gordonius, Jason Pratensis, Savanarola, Guianerius, Montaltus,* confound them as differing *secundùm magis & minùs*; so doth *David, Psal.* 75. 4. *I said unto the Fooles, deale not so madly,* & 'twas an old *Stoicall* paradox, *omnes stultos insanire,* all fooles are mad ... Who is not touched more or lesse in habit or disposition? If in disposition, *ill dispositions beget habits, if they persevere,* saith Plutarch, habits either are, or turne to diseases.' Tis the same which *Tully* maintaines in the second of his *Tusculanes, omnium insipientum animi in morbo sunt, & perturbatorum,* Fooles are sick, and all that are troubled in mind ... And who is not sick, or ill disposed, in whom doth not passion, anger, envie, discontent, feare & sorrowe raigne? Who labours not of this disease? (I.25.8–22)

Here the medical and scriptural arguments, employed in a somewhat dubious fashion, were supports for the central contention contained in the fourth Stoic paradox that 'all fooles are mad'. As Cicero had related in the *Tusculanae disputationes*, passions were vicious because they were irrational judgements about the world, and virtue resided in *ratio*. They were accordingly unnatural, unhealthy dispositions of the soul, and were accurately described as 'perturbations' or psychological 'diseases'. To be foolish, to experience passion or to reason incorrectly, was literally to be mad, or to suffer psychological derangement: '*omnes stultos insanire*'.[51] In Burton's account, even if the incidence of a passion was only temporary, if unchecked its innate tendency to become a settled form of behaviour

[50] Hippocrates 1525, p. 714 and Hippocrates 1990, p. 79. At I.33.0, Burton quoted Calvo's text as 'fellis bilisque', i.e. gall and bile rather than black bile.

[51] Cicero 1927, III.4, pp. 242–3. See also Cicero 1942, IV, pp. 278–83, and Horace 1929, III.2, pp. 152–81.

would ensure that the 'disease' prevailed in the soul.[52] The sufferer of 'passion, anger . . . feare & sorrowe' was unequivocally 'sick'.

Burton's argument about melancholy and madness therefore ran along Stoic lines, as follows: since 'all fooles are mad', and since passions were evidence of foolishness, then those suffering from melancholy, itself a passionate condition of fear and sorrow, were essentially madmen. From this perspective, there could never be any categorical distinction between melancholy – however conceived, in a strict medical-pathological sense or otherwise as a fleeting moment of sorrow – and madness. 'So that take Melancholy in what sense you will', he wrote, 'properly or improperly, in disposition or habit . . . discontent, feare, sorrow, madnesse, for part, or all, truly, or metaphorically, 'tis all one' (I.25.31–4). The positive correlate of this argument, on Aristotle's authority, was that 'to be wise & happy are reciprocall tearmes' (I.63.19–20). The psychologically disturbed and foolish melancholic was thereby presented as the depraved antitype of classically figured happiness, an incarnation of the necessary coincidence of misery, ignorance, and moral turpitude (I.63.32–3). This was the core of the moral-psychological case against the world presented by Democritus Junior with exuberance in the remainder of the preface.

Although this was a classical argument, Burton took care to present it as being in accordance with Christian spirituality. Drawing on Pauline theology and the teachings on wisdom in Ecclesiastes, he described melancholic madness as a condition of sinfulness (I.25.35–26.I). Elsewhere, he used three spiritual arguments to elaborate his denunciation of contemporary morality. The first, which recalled Erasmus's employment of Augustinian precepts in the *Moriae encomium*, was a denunciation of intellectual pride ('*Prov.* 3. 7. *Be not wise in thine owne eyes*' [I.60.10–11]), a sin rooted in the perverted passion of self-love, and 'an ample testimony of much folly' (I.61.2).[53] The second was the equation of sinfulness and foolishness, established by reference to Psalm 107:17 ('Fooles . . . by reason of their transgressions' [I.61.6]) and glossed with the Stoic conclusion, 'If none honest, none wise, then all Fooles' (I.61.13–14). The third was the patristic doctrine that in the soul of postlapsarian man the will had been perverted, dethroning reason from its position of mastery in the soul and making him resemble a beast

[52] Cf. Lipsius 1644, III.20, pp. 354–60.
[53] See Augustine 1984, XII.6, XIV.13, pp. 477, 571–4.

enslaved by a multitude of passions: 'all men are carried away with Passion, Discontent, Lust, Pleasures', confuse 'vertues' and 'vices', and therefore 'more then melancholy, quite mad, bruit Beasts and void of all reason' (1.61.27–30; 62.11–18).[54] Again, this was compatible with the Stoic equation of passion and error (1.62.5–6). The patristic flavour of 'Democritus Junior to the Reader' was equally apparent in its use, perhaps indicative of a further debt to Erasmus, of *contemptus mundi* to satirise human society (1.26.18–21). The 'Monastique' life (1.4.18) was simultaneously the classical *vita contemplativa* and the patristic rejection of worldly affairs. Contempt of the world, particularly of its moral evaluations, was established as the spiritual position from which the Democritean message could be delivered.

What this Christian-Stoic conflation of melancholy with madness permitted Burton to do was to expand the scope of contemporary arguments about the epidemic of melancholy. He could now claim that whilst the disease in its medical sense was widespread (1.110.9–19), in its deeper moral-spiritual sense it was universal. Having freed himself from the constraints of medical doctrines about melancholy, he could establish the collective melancholic madness of humanity by surveying its viciousness, sinfulness, and foolish susceptibility to passions: 'Who labours not of this disease?'

***

The *Anatomy* opened, then, with a classical moral-psychological diagnosis of universal melancholy. Early modern perceptions of the prevalence of the disease may have been rooted in a real increase of its incidence, though whether this was truly the case is a question that now lies beyond the domain of reliable historical inquiry.[55] What is clear is that the diagnostic significance of the disease expanded in the sixteenth century, not in terms of its intrinsic medical-theoretical content, but in the extent to which it was deemed useful in a range of intellectual and cultural contexts. As Burton's work accurately testifies, this was substantially due to a growth of interest in psychology, especially in the passions of the soul, which encouraged a particular type of viewpoint in which it became

[54] See Augustine 1984, XIII.13–14, XIV.11, pp. 523, 568–71.

[55] The issues in the following three paragraphs are discussed in more detail in Gowland 2006. For the peak of learned medical interest in melancholy in the later Renaissance see Diethelm 1971, pp. 32–49, 164–206.

possible to see widespread melancholy in the population at large. The contents of many of the psychological writings of this era reflected their origins in a longstanding concern in humanist moral philosophy and literature with the effects of mortality, sickness, and misfortune on the soul. They were also bound up with the broad preoccupation observable in a wide range of Italian humanist works with the interior as the locus of authentic spirituality.[56] They were further shaped by the Protestant and Catholic reform movements, which ensured that this increased attentiveness to psychological health became confessionalised, politicised, and visible in the public domain.[57]

As this suggests, neither the 'ecological niche'[58] in which melancholy flourished, nor perceptions of its widespread occurrence, was a purely intellectual phenomenon. Inquiries into the passions were inquiries about the occlusion of reason and the breakdown of psychic harmony in the individual, but they were also, implicitly or explicitly, about the disintegration of the harmony in society. Writers like Burton, who were preoccupied by the moral-spiritual search for freedom from the destructive inner tyranny of perturbations, presented this search as a response to a perception of turmoil afflicting the external world, which was itself labelled as a domain where psychological conflicts were being played out on a grand scale. Early modern investigations of the passions, in other words, were rooted in a particular kind of response to events in contemporary Europe, and were socially and politically significant. This was reflected by the frequent employment in moral-psychological discourse of metaphorical language mapping external macrocosmic conflict on to the internal microcosm – passions were 'seditious', the cause of 'Civil dissension' in the soul, and so on.[59] This was a perspective that derived substantively from the classical association of virtuous rationality with political harmony and of vicious passions with lawlessness. Accordingly, the common perception that post-Reformation Europe was spiralling downwards into chaos with the onset and progressive spread of warfare across the continent found its learned humanistic expression in the diagnosis of widespread psychological disorder, the

56 See Trinkaus 1940 and Levi 2002, esp. pp. 2–3, 7–9, 16.
57 See particularly Delumeau 1965, 1977, 1978, 1988, and 1990. See also Bossy 1985 and Taylor 1989, pp. 127–42, 184.
58 I am borrowing this phrase from Hacking 1998.
59 See, for example, Du Vair 1598, p. 41; Reynolds 1640, pp. 273, 97; Charron 1620, I.18, pp. 74–7.

triumph of passion over reason on the macrocosmic scale. This was Burton's viewpoint, where the 'lamentable cares, tormentes, calamitys & oppressions' brought by the conflicts plaguing Europe were described as the products of irrational passion, a devilish 'fury' designed to satisfy only fallen humanity's 'lust and spleen', and therefore the unmistakable sign of '*Mundus furiosus*, a mad world'.[60]

Of course, neither the perceived 'epidemic' of melancholy nor the late humanist preoccupation with the passions is simply reducible to a concern with the political and religious conflicts developing after the Reformation. The increased concern with the disease was partly stimulated by contemporary perceptions of the rise in the incidence of witchcraft and demonic possession, particularly since learned occultist authors had incorporated ideas about melancholy into the surrounding controversies.[61] It also fed into the commonplace moralistic belief in 'the licentious loosenes of [the] times'.[62] But Burton was not the only member of the early modern learned community for whom discoursing on the passions and on melancholy served to express anxieties that were provoked and shaped by these conflicts. The *Anatomy*'s concern with the passions of the soul and their role in determining the moral and spiritual rectitude of mankind served to present the book to its readership as a contribution to European humanist moral philosophy, which had been characterised from the mid-sixteenth century onwards by a notable increase in the publication, translation, and circulation of Hellenistic moral psychology. As the rising popularity of continental neo-Stoicism demonstrates, these intellectual resources were increasingly being employed to resolve moral and political problems provoked by an era seen to be dominated by vicious conflict and bloodshed, and particularly to offer means of attaining inner strength and tranquillity in the face of external chaos.[63]

Burton's interest in the soul supplied his discourse on melancholic perturbations with another dimension that concerned the status of human knowledge. Meditation on the effects of the passions on postlapsarian understanding had been a longstanding preoccupation of philosophical writers on psychology and epistemology, and it would

[60] Burton 1632, p. 30; or I.41.23–45.2.
[61] See, for example, James I and VI 1603b, sig. A2^{r}; Cotta 1616, sig. A3^{v}, 60, 66. Cf. Jorden 1603, sig. A3^{r} and Lipsius 1595, II.25, p. 65. I explore this issue in more detail in chapter one.
[62] Du Vair 1598, sig. A5^{r-v}.
[63] Neo-Stoicism is addressed in chapters four and five below.

continue to be discussed in learned circles throughout the seventeenth century.[64] What was effected in the *Anatomy* was an extraordinary confluence of these moral, political, and intellectual perspectives, a scholarly dissection of the destructive effects of melancholic passions on the individual, on the external world and on the encyclopaedia of knowledge. At the same time, however, this 'dissection' served as the vehicle for a very particular philosophical purpose.

***

'Democritus Junior to the Reader', as had been indicated by the subtitle of the book, was meant to guide its readership by 'conducing' them to see the truth of the *Letter to Damagetes* exemplified in its pages. How did this work? The answer is to be found in the way in which Burton's manipulation and application of the message of the *Letter* in the preface furthered a distinctively humanistic intellectual agenda. Here the key figure was Erasmus. The famous Dutch humanist had provided a template for Burton in the form of the *Moriae encomium*, which had employed a satirical *persona* similarly constructed out of Stoic, Cynic, and patristic materials. Interest in the satire was not unusual. As the young John Milton observed in 1618, in an oration delivered at Christ's College, Cambridge, 'there is in the hands of everyone that most clever *Praise of Folly*, a work not by a writer of the lowest rank'.[65] Burton acknowledged the debt with frequent references to the work throughout.[66]

Erasmus had inspired in the learned communities of northern Europe a spiritualised model of philosophical erudition, characterised by the fusion of the elevated classicism of earlier Italian humanists with a moralised conception of piety that eschewed the systematic pursuit of abstract doctrines of God – the famous *philosophia Christi*. He had inherited and developed the longstanding humanist polemical goals, denouncing the arrogant, futile, and contentious curiosity of the so-called 'scholastic' inquiry that had long dominated theology faculties in universities across the continent, and calling for a reorientation of human learning towards the attainment of spiritual and moral virtue through the interpretation of scripture and classical texts. It was to support this agenda that Burton reinterpreted the *Letter to Damagetes* in his preface, where

64 See Harrison 2002.
65 *Prolusion* VI, quoted in Porter and Thomson (eds.), 1963, p. 99.
66 On Burton's use of the *Moriae encomium* see Colie 1967.

'Democritus Junior' repeatedly derided the scholastic pursuit of what contemporaries classified as *philosophia speculativa*, and prioritised its opposite, the *philosophia practica* concerned with the health of the virtuous and godly soul.[67]

To see the distinctively Erasmian humanism at work in Burton's prefatory satire we should begin, appropriately enough, with one of its paradoxes. This was that 'Democritus Junior' permitted no exceptions to his classification of the 'whole world' as melancholic and mad. If only 'Mounsieur *no-body*' could 'goe free' from his judgement (1.107.10) then this included not only the reader ('Thou thy selfe art the subject of my Discourse' [1.1.31]) but the author himself. This cast doubt upon the reliability of his message (1.112.10–22),[68] partly for amusing effect, but like the whole of the preface it was rooted in a serious intellectual position – Burton wanted his readers to apply the Horatian dictum '*Quamvis ridentem dicere verum quid vetat?* one may speake in jest, and yet speake truth' to everything in his 'Satyricall Introduction' (1.111.18–19). By the time he concluded his diatribe with this paradox, 'Democritus Junior' had established that 'Philosophers and Schollers' had no claim to wisdom and were not to be trusted: 'those superintendents of wit and learning' may well have been 'honored' as 'Minions of the Muses', but in reality they were 'acute and subtile Sophisters', prone to foolish and ridiculous disputes, who 'have as much need of Hellebor as others' (1.100.16–22).

Like Erasmus, Burton diagnosed the problems afflicting contemporary society as being bound up with a crisis of learning and pedagogy, and its portrayal drew upon the traditional humanist critique of scholasticism by focusing on philosophers' failure to put their knowledge to good use. On the authority of a number of humanists including Erasmus and Vives, 'Schoole divinity' was derided as 'a vast Ocean of *Obs* and *Sols*... A labyrinth of intricable questions, unprofitable contentions', and so labelled '*incredibilem delirationem*' (1.101.8–14). When he turned to 'humanity', whose 'followers' had 'cract their skonce' with '[m]uch learning', it became clear that he was concerned with the practical moral failure of devotees of wisdom, including those who had cultivated and

[67] In this study I am using the terms 'humanism' and 'scholasticism' to describe Burton's agenda in the senses established in Schmitt 1983, pp. 17–18, and Grafton 1991, pp. 34, 39, 41–2. This is not to suggest that the opposition captures the complexity of early seventeenth-century intellectual culture, where the two types of inquiry are frequently intertwined and in many cases indistinguishable.

[68] On the paradoxical image of 'Nobody' see Calmann 1960.

propagated the *studia humanitatis*, to apply their learning to their own persons. 'Rhetoricians' were criticised for their ability to 'perswade other men what they will . . . move, pacifie, &c.' but inability to 'settle their owne braines' and conduct themselves with the ethical propriety appropriate to one who delivers 'faire speeches' (1.101.19–102.4). A similar charge was brought against those 'supercilious Criticks, Grammaticall triflers, Notemakers', and 'curious Antiquaries', who sought out 'all the ruines of wit . . . amongst the rubbish of old writers' and spent their time arguing about '[w]hat cloaths the Senators did weare in *Rome*, what shooes, how they sate, where they went to the close stoole', rather than studying the gospel. They 'doe no body good' (1.102.17–103.11).

According to 'Democritus Junior', every discipline was damningly beset by an unbecoming contentiousness. Behind this lay the passion of pride. Each scholar in every field ridiculously 'sets up the flagge of his owne peculiar science' against the others (1.102.14–15). This failing made plain the wholesale failure of philosophers to derive practical moral benefit from the intellectual pursuit of wisdom. As Burton concluded in the second edition, 'they are a kinde of mad men, as *Seneca* esteemes of them, to make doubts & scruples, how to read them truly, to mend old Authors, but will not mend their own lives'.[69] Supporting the earlier expression of patristic *contemptus mundi* and denigration of worldly wisdom (1.25.28–32.13), this critique of the scholarly prioritisation of speculative, intellectual pursuits over the practical cultivation of virtue harked back to the ideal of Christian folly. The bid for Erasmian *auctoritas* was made with the remark that 'generally wee are accounted fooles for Christ, 1. *Corinth.* 14' (1.27.4), and the paradoxical inclusion of the satirical art in the ridicule: 'I neede not quote mine Author, they that laugh & contemne others, condemne the world of folly, deserve to be mocked, are as giddy-headed, and lie as open as any other. *Democritus* that common flouter of folly, was ridiculous himself' (1.101.3–6).

This humanist polemical position was essential for the enterprise of the *Anatomy*, in the first instance because, as Burton made clear, it coloured his attitude towards medicine. The earliest sign of his discontent with the condition of medical knowledge was placed a short way into the preface, where he was concerned to justify himself against 'the greatest exception' that his readers could have taken at his labours, namely 'that I being a Divine, have medled with Physicke' (1.20.5–6). His strategy was first to explain that he had been 'desirous to suppresse my labours' in Divinity on

[69] Burton 1624, p. 59; or 1.103.11–14. See similar remarks at 1.29.30–2.

account of the current flood of 'Commentators, Treatises, Pamphlets, Expositions, Sermons', written by the 'forward and ambitious' and such 'that whole teemes of Oxen cannot draw them' (1.20.32–21.1).[70] He proceeded by charging this proliferation of writing in divinity with the further degradation of the 'Queene of Professions', which had lapsed into bitter 'controversie' and mad preoccupation with 'so many duplications, triplications, & swarmes, & swarmes of Questions', so that 'with this tempest of contention, the serenitie of charitie is over-clouded'. But he next observed that 'there be too many spirits conjured up already in this kinde, in all Sciences' (1.21.1–15), and it was medicine that illustrated the pervasiveness of scholastic error. 'Tis a generall fault ... in phisicke', as he related the view of the Danish Paracelsian Petrus Severinus, where days were spent '*in unprofitable questions and disputations*, intricate subtilties ... *leaving in the meane time those chiefest treasures of nature untouched, wherein the best medicines for all manner of diseases are to be found*' (1.21.21–5). 'These motives', he announced, 'at this present, have induced me to make choice of this Medicinall subject' (1.21.27–8).

The humanistic prioritisation of the practical cultivation of a simple, non-theological, moral-spiritual virtue, rooted in scripture and classical philosophy, over the speculative search for metaphysical truths, dominated the way in which the diverse materials, medical and non-medical alike, were collected and presented in the *Anatomy.* To see how this was so, we must attend to Burton's reasons for composing the book as a *cento.* He explained his choice of the quotational method in a section that was initially in the 'Conclusion' of 1621, but subsequently relocated (some readers had perhaps failed to grasp the point) to the beginning of the preface in expanded form in the second and third editions. Here he emphasised that he was not to be understood as simply reproducing other authors' words in the manner of a commonplace book. His authorial message was to be detected from the way in which he was presenting his material. It was a piece of characteristically elegant wit that this was itself expressed through quotations.

I have only this of *Macrobius* to say for my selfe, *Omne meum, nihil meum,* 'tis all mine and none mine. As a good hous-wife out of divers fleeces weaves one peece of Cloath, a Bee gathers Wax and Hony out of many Flowers, and makes a new bundle of all ... I have laboriously collected this *Cento* out of divers Writers ... The matter is their most part, and yet mine, *apparet unde sumptum sit* (which *Seneca* approves) *aliud tamen quàm unde sumptum sit apparet*, which

[70] Burton's attitude towards patronage is explored in chapter five.

nature doth with the aliment of our bodies, incorporate, digest, assimulate, I doe *conquoquere quod hausi*, dispose of what I take. I make them pay tribute, to set out this my *Maceronicon*, the method onely is myne owne, I must usurpe that of *Wecker è Terentio, nihil dictum quod non dictum priùs, methodus sola artificem ostendit*, we can say nothing but what hath beene said, the composition and method is ours onely, and shewes a Scholler . . . Though there were many Giants of old in Physicke and Phylosophy, yet I say with *Didacus Stella, A Dwarfe standing on the shoulders of a Giant may see farther then a Giant himself*; I may likely add, alter, and see farther then my Predecessors. (I.II.4–12.4)

The important messages of the *Anatomy* were therefore to be found in the way in which Burton saw fit to 'incorporate, digest, assimulate' and 'dispose of' them. This would reveal the ways in which he had decided to 'add, alter, and see farther then' the authors whose words he had borrowed – in other words, his commentary.

The point of writing in *cento* form was to express one's own argument ventriloquistically through the words of others. As such, it represented the vertiginous apex of humanist *imitatio*, carrying such strong valuation of ancient wisdom that for Hobbes it exemplified 'learned madness'.[71] Like the *cento* itself, the practice of employing quotations to construct a sense not originally present in the material being quoted was classical in origin, but the manner in which one was able or entitled to express oneself through others' words had been of great literary and philosophical concern to humanists from Petrarch onwards.[72] There was also an obvious parallel between the humanistic activity of compiling a commonplace book and the construction of a *cento*, since both were founded on the possibility that piecing together other authors' words could result in originality through a process of creative 'digestion'. In Burton's rendition of the endlessly cited Senecan topos, it was to write as 'a Bee gathers Wax and Hony out of many Flowers, and makes a new bundle of all' (I.II.6–7).[73]

How did the *cento* serve as the vehicle for Burton's commentary, and by extension his intellectual agenda? One of the reasons for the apparent eccentricity of the *Anatomy* to the modern eye is that its subject matter is

[71] Hobbes 1994, p. 63; Hobbes had given Burton a copy of his 1629 translation of Thucydides (Kiessling 1988, entry 1601). For an overview of the Renaissance *cento* see Tucker 1997, pp. 267–75.

[72] For the key classical sources see Plutarch 1961, IX.I, pp. 218–27, and Seneca 1917-25, XVI, XXXIII, vol. I, pp. 107, 233, 237, 239. For further discussion see Friedrich 1991, pp. 378–9. Cf. also Erasmus 1986, p. 145.

[73] See Moss 1996, pp. 101–15, 138–9; Goyet 1996, pp. 441–98. Cf. Montaigne 1603, I.25, III.12, pp. 61, 64, 71, 629, and Goyet 1987, p. 30.

commonly thought to be scientific, and indeed the book advertises itself on its title-page as containing knowledge that has been, at least partially, 'medicinally' analysed. However, citations of authority were ubiquitous in medical works of the period. This was in large part because humanist theorists from Lorenzo Valla onwards had developed an expansive conception of dialectic that came to infiltrate much of the scientific output of the later Renaissance. Incorporating the rhetorical argumentation found in Cicero and Quintilian alongside the logical tools of Aristotle, the 'new' humanist dialectic had paved the way for the admission of arguments from uncertain but generally accepted commonplaces or maxims, and particularly from authority, into logically respectable discussions in a diversity of disciplines, medicine included.[74] In many places Burton's work exemplified this model of humanistic science, presenting non-apodictic, dialectical arguments that weighed the opinions of ancient and neoteric authorities and had recourse to the *opinio communis doctorum* to adjudicate in controversy. But the *Anatomy* was a *cento*. Its argumentation was based on the citation of authority to the near-total exclusion of the other, more logically respectable methods appropriate to humanist dialectical science such as induction or reasoning from analogy. We should not presume that this indicates Burton's incompetence in logic – according to Anthony Wood he had 'made considerable progress' in this discipline whilst at Brasenose College[75] – but rather his typically humanistic scepticism with regard to the utility of its 'needlesse Sophismes' (1.364.22–3 [1.2.4.7]). Whilst this *cento* yielded loosely scientific knowledge through the accumulation of authoritative quotations, in the final analysis it was, as Thomas Fuller put it, 'a booke of Philology' – that is to say a work of textual interpretation.[76]

As with the other great humanist *cento* of the era, Justus Lipsius's *Politicorum sive civilis doctrinae libri sex* (1589), the *philologia* of the *Anatomy* was both self-expressive and imbued with practical philosophical purpose.[77] Both goals were expressed through the rhetorical and dialectical 'body' of the book, which presented itself simultaneously as an expressive revelation of the author's melancholic '*malus Genius*'

[74] See Jardine 1983; Maclean 1984 and 2002; Jardine 1991, pp. 105–6; Mack 1993; and Serjeantson 1998, pp. 60–102, esp. pp. 82–8. I address the scientific status of medicine in more detail in chapter one.

[75] Wood 1815, p. 652.

[76] Fuller 1662, p. 134. See also Wood 1815, vol. II, p. 652.

[77] See Lipsius's claim, 'ego e Philologia Philosophiam feci', quoted in Morford 1991, p. 137. Cf. Montaigne 1603, I.25, pp. 64, 68.

(1.7.21) – 'I have laid my selfe open (I know it) in this treatise, turned mine inside outward'[78] – and an anatomisation of the scholarly knowledge of the melancholy that prevailed in the world. Crucial to the latter goal was the moderately sceptical stance suggested by the *cento* format, which in Burton's hands communicated a distinctive commentary on the limitations of the speculative aspects of the knowledge it surveyed. Notwithstanding its medical-scientific topical skeleton and its periodic employment of technical Galenic analytical procedures, the expansive and impassioned investigation of melancholy was characterised by the author as being in essence infinitely complex, particular, and uncertain. This was appropriate to the domain of human affairs. In the terms of classical humanist rhetoric, the knowledge 'opened up' to its audience was being delivered in a fashion that was only probable or plausible.[79] As we shall see in detail in chapter two, Burton was conscious of the epistemological ramifications of his quotational method, and made devious use of them to expose the irreconcileable conflicts and 'hairsplitting' between different authorities, leave disputes suggestively unresolved, and ultimately withhold his own view.

In this way the *Anatomy* reflected its author's insistence that he had 'digested' his quotations and turned them to his 'purpose' to constitute a new, sceptical textual meaning (1.19.20). Positive arguments from authority became arguments from lack of real authority, or arguments from the proliferation of uncertain authorities.[80] Although Burton claimed his 'method' was entirely his 'own', this type of argumentation had a sixteenth-century provenance. It had been employed to display the shortcomings of worldly wisdom in Gianfrancesco Pico della Mirandola's *Examen vanitate doctrinae gentium et veritatis Christianae disciplinae* (1520), in Cornelius Agrippa's immensely popular *De vanitate et incertitudine scientiarum invectiva* (1526), and most famously in Montaigne's 'Apologie pour Raymond Sebond', where the varied dogmas of ancient philosophical sects were juxtaposed to prove the sceptical point that humans were capable of attaining only plausible

[78] Part of this phrase first appeared in Burton 1621, sig. Ddd^r; or 3.469.17. It was subsequently relocated to 1.13.7–8.

[79] See Aristotle 1967, I.2.14, pp. 24–7; Cicero 1930, pp. 10–109; Cicero 1942, II.5, pp. 312–15; Cicero 1949, I.29.44, XIX.73, pp. 82ff., 438–9; and Quintilian 1920-2, II.17.39, V.7, V.11.43–4, vol. I, pp. 342–3, vol. II, pp. 168ff., 296–7.

[80] See Huarte Navarro 1594, p. 161; Wright 1971, pp. 300–9; and Bacon 1906, I.4.5–7, pp. 31–4.

opinions about nature.[81] Burton had read these three authors, and it was significant that he referred to Agrippa's *De vanitate* to support ridicule of the 'absurd tenents' and 'prodigious paradoxes' of philosophers (I.100.24–5; 157.18 [I.I.2.9]). However, the targets of his scepticism – the profusion of futile 'duplications, triplications, & swarmes of Questions' – were more explicitly associated with the traditional humanist critique of scholastic *philosophia speculativa* than those of his predecessors.

In his Latin comedy *Philosophaster* (1615), Burton had ridiculed the scholastic logic exemplified by the syllogistic demonstration as a form of futile sophistry that depended on 'retia sermonum', tricks of speech.[82] A similar message was delivered by the *Anatomy* with more subtlety, through a form of argumentation that caricatured the methodology – most famously exemplified in the *Sententiae* of Peter Lombard and Thomas Aquinas's *Summa*, and still found not only in many learned works of Burton's era but also in the disputations required for Arts degrees[83] – whereby *quaestiones* were addressed through the exposition of *auctoritates* and the raising of *objectiones*, with the matter being resolved in the *resolutio* or *determinatio* with the statement of the *auctoris opinio* or *judicium*. What was demonstrated throughout Burton's work was that the existing learned discussions of *quaestiones* about melancholy had in many cases only produced a morass of conflicting *auctoritates*, the result being an unresolvable 'tempest of contention' (I.21.13–14) to which the addition of authorial opinion would be futile. The satirical point punctuating the investigation of melancholy was to show the manner in which pervasive 'scholastic' habits had corrupted contemporary learning with impractical contentiousness, intellectual pretension, and curiosity. Such vices could be effectively purged from the life of the philosopher and the encyclopaedic *corpus* by means of ridicule.[84]

There were limits to Burton's scepticism. It was not the product of a self-consciously dogmatic revival, but rooted in the longstanding Christian contempt for worldly wisdom. It was also, crucially, only the negative counterpart to a positive intellectual agenda to communicate the

81 Pico Della Mirandola 1969, vol. II, p. 738; Agrippa 1575, fols. 5^r, 140^r–154^r; Montaigne 1603, II.12, pp. 252–352. I address this aspect of Burton's argumentation in chapter three below.

82 Burton 1977, I.2, pp. 34–5.

83 See Binns 1990a, pp. 5–7, 357–9.

84 On this conception of satire see Heinsius 1629, p. 54. See also the translator's introduction to Agrippa 1575, sig. ¶.iii.

knowledge of *practica* deemed useful for the cultivation of moral and spiritual virtue.[85] There were resonances of Academic scepticism in his method, both in the probabilist emphasis on the opinionative nature of the knowledge he discussed,[86] and in the periodic suspension of authorial judgement concerning its truthfulness – it is worth recalling that the *Moriae encomium* had recommended the sect as 'the least assuming of the philosophers'.[87] But the account of the limited human capacity for knowledge in the *Anatomy* was directly derived from patristic accounts of the detrimental effects of the Fall on the human powers of rational understanding.[88] Burton could not have been clearer that the origins of the confused and debased condition of the melancholy that afflicted all humanity were to be traced to the sin of Adam (1.121.5–128.29 [1.1.1.1]). However, he also held that although postlapsarian man's will and rational faculties were corrupt, there was a 'decayed Image of God, which is yet remaining in us' (3.355.6–7 [3.4.1.2]). This indicated a belief that human beings retained some of their prelapsarian intellectual capacities, even if only weakly. The radical Calvinist position was virtually impossible to reconcile with a Christian humanist belief in the possibility of gaining moral and spiritual benefit from pagan philosophy.[89] What was effected in the *Anatomy* was not an exhaustively sceptical rejection of human learning, but its humbling where appropriate, and its reorientation in accordance with holy doctrine and ancient moral wisdom where possible.

Burton therefore assumed the position of a moderately sceptical humanist looking to turn everything he found in the course of his learned investigation to his particular purpose, either to discredit domains of knowledge that had become intolerably encumbered with the effects of speculative contentiousness, to derive practical benefits in the cause of moral and spiritual virtue, or, where possible, to do both at once. His authorial posture was constructed accordingly, as that of a detached philosopher amusedly, in places wearily, leafing through his books in 'idle' leisure, and occasionally recording his own opinion as one amongst many others (1.7.4–5; III.24–5). This image was supported by his

85 On extra-institutional scepticism in this period see Jardine 1987, pp. 92–3.

86 According to Jardine 1983, dialectical citation had been associated with Academic scepticism by Valla; but Valla's adherence to this position has been challenged in Mack 1993, p. 109.

87 Erasmus 1986, p. 118.

88 See Augustine 1984, XXII.22, p. 1067.

89 On the parallel views of Keckermann and Alsted see Hotson 2000, pp. 66–77, and Stone 2000, p. 67.

incorporation of a number of conversational rhetorical characteristics throughout the scholarly analysis of the *Anatomy* that were appropriate to the informality of the *sermo.*[90] This was most evident in his habitual adumbration of quotations with parenthetical comments, occasionally of a derogatory nature, which instantiated the leisurely claim that he 'writ with as small deliberation as I doe ordinarily speake' (1.17.16–17) – as in his typically sardonic ridicule of Pomponazzi: '*Pomponatius* justifies in his Tract (so stiled at least) *De immortalitate Animæ*' (3.404.31–2).

Two more interconnected features of Burton's philosophical aims and compositional methods were important to the character of this erudite *cento.* As we have seen, the satire of 'Democritus Junior to the Reader' announced a model of inquiry privileging the pursuit of moral-spiritual virtue through *philosophia practica* over and against the futile curiosity of *philosophia speculativa.* As well as signalling a moderate humanistic scepticism, this justified an eclectic and anti-dogmatic approach to the intellectual materials being presented and discussed. There were limits to this inclusivity. As we shall see, Burton was careful to distance himself from extreme occultist, openly heretical, or dangerously atheistic pagan works, though he delighted in relating their contents. However, his opposition to philosophical sectarianism, often through association with scholastic contentiousness, had again been foreshadowed in *Philosophaster*, and it was manifested throughout the *Anatomy* in its author's willingness to pick and choose from the full range of available works, ancient, medieval and neoteric.[91] These works could be found across the entire range of learned inquiry in early modern Europe. As the genuinely encyclopaedic contents of Burton's book made clear, discourse on the concept of melancholy had become ramified across a wide range of Renaissance disciplines, reaching into the territories not only of medicine, but theology, moral philosophy, natural philosophy, history, and even geography.

The remarkable range of the knowledge non-dogmatically revealed and discussed on every page of the *Anatomy* exemplified a trend towards extreme philosophical eclecticism that was rapidly gathering pace in late sixteenth and early seventeenth-century European philosophy.[92]

[90] See Gowland 2000, esp. pp. 6–7.
[91] See 1.266.31–3 (1.2.3.8) and Burton 1977, 1.2, pp. 31–2.
[92] See Blair 1997, pp. 107–15; Kelley 1997, p. 14 and 2001.

As Burton's exasperation at the size of the 'Catalogue of new bookes' appearing 'this year' and indeed throughout 'all this age' made clear (1.10.23–5), this was partly a product of the proliferation of scholarly material across the continent stimulated by a burgeoning book trade. In some this stimulated ambitious synthetic enterprises, such as Johann Heinrich Alsted's *Encyclopedia septem tomis distincta* (1630). However, Burton's reaction to this 'vast *Chaos* and confusion of Bookes' (1.11.1–2) seems to have been close to despair. It is plausible to see the *Anatomy*'s growing intellectual pessimism – which will form one of my preoccupations throughout this study – as stemming from a perception that the problems of resolution and synthesis provoked by the eclecticism of the era were insurmountable except through recourse to some form of scepticism.

As an encyclopaedic *cento* the *Anatomy* displayed an erudition that was both genuinely up to date and genuinely European, and it was significant that the scholarly resources Burton drew upon were largely the products of the Latinate intellectual culture that continued to remain prominent in the universities of the era both across the continent and in England.[93] The contents of the *Anatomy* strongly indicated its author's adherence to the notion of a *respublica literaria* of European humanists.[94] In this respect, its roots were once again to be traced back to Erasmus, not only to the sixteenth-century success of his pedagogical programme for the attainment of Latin literacy, but also to its accompanying ideal of the autonomous, impartial, and cosmopolitan humanist scholar devoted to the education of Europe.[95] But Burton's work was undertaken at a time when this Latinate culture had an increasingly confident rival in the form of vernacular humanist enterprise, manifesting itself in original literary and philosophical productions as well as translations and adaptations of works from Latin and other European languages.[96] The *Anatomy* was of course written in the vernacular, and its author typically translated or paraphrased his Latin quotations throughout. By making a huge range of elite scholarly discourse available to a new type of audience, it presented itself as work both for posterity and for an immediate domestic audience,

[93] See Binns 1990a.

[94] See Schoeck 1984, and the reference to 'Reip. literariæ bonum' in Burton's preface to Rider 1612, sig. ¶4^{v}. On the *respublica literaria* in the later Renaissance see Waquet 1990, Burke 1999, and Miller 2000.

[95] See Jardine 1993.

[96] See Boutcher 1996 and Loewenstein 1996.

effectively bridging the venerable European *respublica literaria* and early Stuart vernacular culture.[97]

However, there were signs that Burton was uncomfortable with aspects of vernacular humanism. This was evident in his insistence in the preface that he had been compelled against his wishes to write in the vernacular by the ignorant commercial realities of the contemporary publishing environment.

It was not mine intent to prostitute my Muse in *English*, or to divulge *secreta Minervæ*, but to have exposed this more contract in *Latin*, If I could have got it printed. Any scurrile Pamphlet is welcome to our mercenary Stationers in *English*, they print all,

——— cuduntque libellos
In quorum foliis vix simia nuda cacaret;

But in *Latin* they will not deale; which is one of the reasons *Nicholas Car* in his Oration of the paucity of *English* Writers gives; that so many flourishing wits are smothered in oblivion, ly dead and buried in this our Nation. (1.16.9–18)

This now seems disingenuous. It is difficult to imagine the *Anatomy* without its author's pithy and occasionally witty vernacular translations. However, Lipsius's Latin *cento* had brought him fame in learned European circles, and Burton's fondness for the conjunction of economical elegance and scholarly credibility in Latin manifested itself in various places in the book, particularly at the end of the 'Digression of the Misery of Schollers' (1.324–327.26 [1.2.4.1]). That he had some telling uneasiness about the unlearned nature of his potential audience was suggested by his decision to deliver his diatribe against 'unclean intercourse' in his discussion of therapies for love melancholy in Latin (3.206.31-207.19 [3.2.5.2]). He also withheld what one must presume to be a not unrelated cure for jealousy, being 'not willing to publish' for some unspecific 'reasons' – hinting coyly that 'if you be very desirous to know it, when I meet you next, I will peradventure tell you what it is in your eare' (3.329.20-4 [3.3.4.2]). In fact, Burton's preference to use Latin translations of originally vernacular European works, even when English versions were available, indicated that he both cherished the early sixteenth-century ideal of the Latinate *respublica literaria* and had an aversion to the increasingly evident association of 'practical' humanist vernacularism with the world of court-centred diplomatic politics.[98]

97 For these aspects of Latin and vernacular writings see Binns 1990a, pp. 1–2.

98 This aspect of vernacular humanism is emphasised in Boutcher 1996. On 'practical' humanism see Grafton and Jardine 1986, pp. 161–200.

This was evident in his referral to the Latin translations of authors such as Castiglione and Botero, both of whom were available in English and had become popular in political and commercial circles, but which Burton used for purposes that were presented as appropriate within a self-consciously impartial intellectual inquiry, and carefully absorbed to a traditional humanistic discussion.[99] This pointed to an author who was ill at ease with the mingling of day-to-day politics with the fruits of scholarship. Although he made copious use of the King James Bible, it also set him at odds with the changing religious associations of the English vernacular, which had once underpinned an Elizabethan ideology of the Protestant nation but was gradually becoming appropriated by puritan pietistic discourse.[100]

Burton's task of transmitting the learning and values of the European *respublica literaria* in the *Anatomy* was reflected not just by its intellectual sources – in its 'anatomy' of knowledge – but by the geographical scope of its analysis – its 'anatomy' of the world. He saw the different forms of melancholy as prevalent not just in England, but in Europe generally, and he consistently located issues that were of domestic significance within a broader continental, and in some cases global, context. This meant, not that his most pressing concerns were not shared by his early Stuart contemporaries, but that the nature of his response to these concerns was determined by his engagement with continental scholarship. It was also shaped by an accompanying conviction that the spiritual and political fate of the European *corpus Christianorum* would be ultimately indivisible upon national or confessional grounds. In this sense the *Anatomy* reworked the Christian humanist vision for the seventeenth century. The great problem, however, was that Burton's world was rapidly losing what little resemblance it still had to that of Erasmus, More, and Vives, and the long-term divisive political and religious effects of Reformation and Counter-Reformation were progressively eroding the credibility of their

[99] Burton referred, not to Sir Thomas Hoby's translation of *The Courtyer* (London, 1561), but to Bartholomew Clerke's *De curiali sive aulico libri quatuor* (London, 1593), which had first been published in 1571; his copy was heavily marked (Kiessling 1988, entry 310). He referred to Georg Draudius's Latin translation of Botero's writings, the *Tractatus duo: prior de illustrium statu & politia, libris X. Posterior de origine urbium, earum excellentia, & augendi ratione, libris III* (Ursel, 1602), although owning a copiously annotated copy of Robert Peterson's 1606 translation of the *Delle cause della grandezza delle città* (Kiessling 1988, entry 199). For Burton's uses of Castiglione and Botero see chapters one and four respectively.

[100] I explore Burton's disapproval of puritan casuistry and sermons in chapter three.

vision.[101] It is in this conflict – between Burton's cherishing of the ideal of a harmonious, politically unified, and spiritually virtuous Europe underpinned by humanist erudition, and his steadily fading hope for its realisation – that I believe we can find the historical dynamic that generated and shaped his concern with melancholy.

[101] On the fate of Erasmian humanism in England see Porter and Thomson 1963, McConica 1965, and Trevor-Roper 1987, pp. 40–119, 186–99.

CHAPTER 1

The medical theory of melancholy

It is evident from even the most cursory browse through *The Anatomy of Melancholy* that much of Burton's labour in writing involved investigating and assessing the ever-increasing mass of medical works that had established the disease as one of the most serious forms of mental affliction of the era. Insofar as part of his aim was to divulge learning in a manner that would be of practical benefit to his readership, it is imperative to view the *Anatomy* as an encyclopaedic compendium of classical, medieval, and early modern medical knowledge about melancholy, and in this respect the book was an unrivalled success. However, whilst the *Anatomy* offers a vantage-point from which the contours of medical knowledge can be viewed, we should avoid the presumption that Burton provides us with a straightforward vision of this field in the early seventeenth century. His purpose was not to compile other authors' opinions disinterestedly, but to present them in a fashion that furthered moral and spiritual goals. Admittedly, in many respects he had no desire to depart from contemporary medical orthodoxy. But what was the role of his exhaustive exploration of the medical teachings about melancholy in his larger humanist project?

Here I shall investigate the way in which the *Anatomy* presented the resources of the continental neo-Galenic medical community as a pragmatic intellectual-therapeutic response to the author's perception that melancholy had reached epidemic proportions in his society. Burton's most obvious purpose in digesting and translating the medical texts dealing with the disease was to disclose learning that could be of therapeutic utility to both his English audience and himself. As its genuinely encyclopaedic inclusiveness suggests, it was central to this project that it should display the entirety of the existing range of scholarly knowledge about melancholy. A large part of what I present in this chapter will be concerned with the central medical and psychological teachings that shaped Burton's investigation, with a view to showing its learned character. The utility of the book to the 'common good of all' depended upon its visible erudition. The detail of his account of melancholy also provided the medical-scientific structure for his response to the religious and political problems of his contemporary environment, as we shall see in later chapters.

What I intend to show here and in the following chapter is that what Burton offered to his audience was not a disengaged encyclopaedic textbook that summarised existing medical-scientific ideas, though it could be used as such. Rather it was conceived as a useful exploration of medical learning that would guide its readership through the whole *corpus* of knowledge on a route that was morally, spiritually, and philosophically correct. This was not a straightforward task, and was not without internal tensions. Most obviously, the exhaustive scholarly intention that gave rise to the medical analysis of melancholy indicates a therapeutic pragmatism that at times sat ill at ease with the concern for moral and spiritual rectitude. Yet Burton's medical investigation showed far more than would have been expected from an enthusiastic amateur. As we shall see, he did more than demonstrate a grasp of the logical procedures espoused by early modern learned physicians and unsurpassed mastery of the medical territory on melancholy. Throughout the book he concerned himself with the activity of purging the encyclopaedic 'body' he revealed of its moral and theological errors, and also of what he took to be its obvious – and in most cases, generally agreed – scientific fallacies.

Equally importantly, what Burton did *not* do was to take it upon himself to adjudicate upon every controversial point he encountered. This reflected not just sceptical detachment on the author's part (the subject of the following chapter), but also a particular conception of medicine that suited the agenda he had announced in 'Democritus Junior to the Reader'. Here the key to understanding the role of medical discourse in Burton's writing lies first of all in the contemporary vogue for a conception of medicine as an 'art' – productive of health, and attentive to particulars and the role 'experience' in diagnosis and treatment. This provided Burton with a means of bestowing scientific credibility upon his humanistic *philosophia practica*, at the same time as buttressing his case against scholastic speculation. What we see in the *Anatomy*, then, is a treatise that absorbed medical learning into a humanist philosophical enterprise. Negatively, it discredited physicians' use of scholastic techniques and their reliance on over-systematised doctrine and general rules, and ridiculed the curiosity about matters beyond human capacity that had disfigured the discipline and led it astray from its divinely appointed therapeutic origins. Positively, it provided a skeleton of probable scientific doctrine, from kinds and causes to prognostics and cures, around which the medical pragmatist could operate both effectively – by attending to the particularity of the individual pathological instance, and to the dictates of experience – and in accordance with moral-theological rectitude.

To demonstrate the scientific and humanistic identity of Burton's analysis of the medical theory of melancholy, it is important to establish the character and basic doctrinal content of the medical scholarship of the period, when this is considered not just as a source of authoritative discussion and doctrine, but also as a branch of learning with a broadly agreed set of methodical procedures and discursive conventions that established and shored up its disciplinary status.[1] It will also be necessary to address the occasionally fraught relationship between humanist philosophy and medicine, by attending to some of the ways in which Burton's predecessors had attempted to harmonise the idea of physic as a divine gift with the suspiciously pagan, not to say atheistic, implications of its overt veneration of ancient doctrine and tendency towards materialist explanations. To this end, I begin this chapter with a brief survey of the disciplinary character of early modern learned medicine, considering the long-running debate over its scientific or artistic status, and then present some fifteenth- and sixteenth-century attempts to bring it into line with Christian dogma. This is followed by another outline, this time of the central neo-Galenic doctrines of body and soul, and the infiltration of these by occultism, which are essential to an understanding of the medical theory of melancholy. We can then proceed to an analysis of the version presented in the main treatise of the *Anatomy*.

THE NATURE AND STATUS OF MEDICAL INQUIRY

Just as Burton's choice of subject matter responded to one of the prevalent medical and psychological concerns of the era, so his textual method of approaching it was ostensibly drawn from the existing conventions of scholarly medical investigation. Throughout the second half of the sixteenth century and well into the seventeenth, despite the growing recognition of the utility of direct observation, and particularly of anatomical dissection as a means to acquire authoritative knowledge of the human body, learned medicine in Europe remained a predominantly text-based discipline. The revelation of new information about the

[1] See Maclean 2000, esp. pp. 66–7, 336, 339.

human body by practical anatomy was almost always accommodated within the existing Aristotelian-Galenic framework of explanation, and only rarely provoked a questioning of that framework. Even the most radical anatomy teaching in the Italian universities in this era involved the dissection of corpses alongside the exposition of the works of Galen.[2] Contemporary readers of Burton's book would not have been surprised to see him investigate the disease of melancholy primarily through the exposition and interpretation of texts.

The definitive characteristics of medical learning were addressed directly in this period through discussion of the traditional problem of whether medicine, often through direct comparison with law, was *scientia* or *ars*. The majority of medieval and early modern university discussions concluded with the observation that it was both science and art: science, insofar as it was based on the demonstrable knowledge of natural philosophy, but art insofar as this knowledge was applied for the production of health. Medicine was thus frequently divided into scientific *theoria*, understood to encompass the domain of physiology and the natural-philosophical principles that underlay medicine obtained by the *physicus*; and artistic *practica*, which incorporated everything pertaining to medical practice, and which was implemented by the *medicus*. But there was no consensus on the question.[3] In the Aristotelian terms that predominated in early modern university faculties, medicine usually qualified as a science on the basis of its employment of logic. Although there was a significant degree of slackness in much learned medical argument – notably in the uncertain domain of semiotic conjecture – a loosely scientific conception of the discipline could be credibly advanced on account of its aspiration to identify causes, one of the central characteristics of apodictic demonstration.[4] This view was supported by the logical procedures of the *quaestio* method, in which the accordances and discordances between authoritative doctrines were analysed through reasoning from first principles towards universally valid conclusions. Although the format was becoming progressively unfashionable in general philosophical inquiry, many academic medical discussions continued to be structured

[2] See Nutton 1988b and Siraisi 1997, p. 95.

[3] See, for example, the discussion in Huarte Navarro 1594, pp. 173–9. For the spectrum of learned opinion see Kristeller 1956 and 1976; Maclean 1992, pp. 22–9, and 2002, pp. 70–6; McVaugh 1990, pp. 74–7; Siraisi 1987, pp. 226–38, 1990b, pp. 174–6, and 1990c, pp. 219–20.

[4] See Maclean 2000, pp. 238, 248, 250, and 2002, pp. 73, 103, 121–3, 146–7, 163–4, 288–91, 335.

in this way well into the seventeenth century,[5] and, as Andrew Willet's *De animæ natura et viribus quaestiones quaedam* (1585) demonstrates, it persisted in England in the field of psychology.[6] Typically, the employment of *quaestiones* reflected a 'scholastic' vision of a unified field of timeless philosophical knowledge, primarily constituted through the exposition of and commentary on authoritative works with a view to their ultimate synthesis.[7] It was common for a neo-Galenic physician to discuss and attempt to reconcile the teachings of Hippocrates, Aristotle, and Galen, along with those of Avicenna, Rhazes, and Alexander of Tralles, but also of contemporary authors such as Andreas Vesalius, Jean Fernel, and André du Laurens.

The scientific conception of medical discourse could be buttressed in other ways. It could be anchored in the critical role given to λόγος in the discovery and treatment of disease in the Hippocratic texts, and in Galen's assertion of the necessity of logically demonstrative techniques to the formation of doctrine.[8] Arguments from authority for the scientific basis of medicine, however, also drew upon medieval sources, commonly Avicenna's *Canon* or the justifications of 'philosophical medicine' in the extensive series of *quaestiones* produced by the School of Salerno.[9] This view was exemplified by a subgenre concerned purely with the reconciliation of contradictions in and between authoritative texts, exemplified and inspired by the *Conciliator* of Pietro d'Abano, and seen in sixteenth-century works such as Girolamo Cardano's *Contradicentium medicorum liber* (first ed., 1545), Jacques Peletier's *De conciliatione locorum Galeni, sectiones duae* (1560), and Francisco Vallés's *Controversiarum medicarum et philosophicorum libri decem* (1582).[10] Some recognised that the conciliatory project would benefit from the excision of accumulated, unauthorised error – often attributed to the ignorance of vulgar, unlearned 'empirics' – from the *corpus* of received knowledge. This was the purpose of Laurent Joubert's compilation of *Erreurs populaires au fait*

[5] See, typically, Arnald of Villanova 1585, cols. 1849–74; Vallesio 1582, *passim*; Du Laurens 1599, p. 91; Manardi 1611, IX.2, p. 186; Mercuriale 1617, I.6, I.10, I.16, pp. 21, 22–5, 40–5, 48–50, 85; Ferrand 1990, pp. 240, 298, 322, 354.

[6] See Binns 1990a, pp. 207–9.

[7] See Grant 1978; Schmitt 1983, pp. 16–18, 50; Maclean 1992, p. 117; Siraisi 1987, pp. 23–4, 221–93, 1990a, p. 76, and 2001, pp. 140–56.

[8] Hippocrates 1839–61, vol. VI, p. 278, and 1962, II.26, pp. 12–17; Galen 1991, I.3.14–15, I.4.3, pp. 16–17.

[9] See Avicenna 1608, I.I.I.I, vol. I, p. 1; Lawn 1963 and 1993; Ottosson 1984.

[10] See especially Cardano 1667, vol. VI, p. 297, and Vallesio 1582, p. 2. For discussion, see Maclean 1980, p. 44, and 2002, pp. 58–9; and Siraisi 1997, pp. 43–69.

de la médecine et regime de santé (1578), a treatise that was reprinted several times and issued in Latin translation as *De vulgi erroribus* (Antwerp, 1600).

Despite their conspicuously scholastic trappings, however, many early modern medical texts incorporated ideas and methods suggesting that medicine was more properly described as an art. This view could be based authoritatively upon the description of the medical τέχνη in the Hippocratic *Aphorisms* and *On Ancient Medicine*, Aristotle's *Nicomachean Ethics*, Galen's *Ars parva*, or the pseudo-Galenic *Introductio, seu medicus* and *Definitiones medicae*.[11] As the sixteenth century wore on, medicine was increasingly being described as primarily an art, whose practical purpose – the production of health – depended less on demonstrative reasoning and synthesis of the *quaestio* than on the physician's observation and 'experience'.[12] This is partly attributable to the recognition that ancient Greek authors had given sense data a role alongside reason in the discovery of knowledge, but it was also due to the rising popularity in learned circles of the methods found specifically in the Hippocratic *corpus*. From this point of view, seen most famously in the works of Cardano and later of Thomas Sydenham but evident in a wide range of medical output, the Hippocratic eschewal of systematic theorising from first principles in favour of the detailed discussion of individual case-histories and aphorisms provided an impeccably authoritative alternative to Aristotelian methodology. By directing attention towards the individual pathological instance, this approach underscored the diversity and particularity of nature. Rather than being deposited timelessly in authoritative texts, medical knowledge was to be gained by gathering together individual case-histories, and interpreting them through reason and conjecture in the light of accepted doctrine.[13] This constituted the task of the physician as the application of diagnostic and therapeutic principles to a non-uniform domain of cases that continually threw up exceptions to general rules. It was a vision of the discipline in which *practica* took priority over *theoria*.[14]

[11] Hippocrates 1931, I.1, pp. 98–9, and 1962, I.9, pp. 12–13. Aristotle 1934, III.3.8–11, pp. 136–7; Galen 1528b, fols. 4^{r-v} and 1821–33, vol. XIV, pp. 674–89.

[12] On the status of 'experience' in learned circles see Dear 1995, esp. pp. 11–31; Pittion 1987, pp. 107–8; Siraisi 1981, pp. 118–37, 314–17, and 1997, p. 45; and Wear 1995, p. 170.

[13] On conjecture see Galen 1831–3, vol. XIX, pp. 3–4, cited in Ferrand 1990, p. 267. On the integration of particular cases to general explanations see Altomari 1559, I.1, p. 6.

[14] For discussion of these trends see Daston and Park 1998; Findlen 1994; Maclean 2000 and 2002, pp. 22–3, 32–5, 77, 114, 164, 169; Nutton 1989; Siraisi 1997, pp. 119–45, and 2001, pp. 226, 287–327; Smith 1979; and Wear 1995, pp. 157–8.

Some of those conceiving and propagating an image of medicine as an art in this way, like Cardano in some of his works, also exhibited an awareness of the historical conditions influencing authoritative texts and hence of the development of medical knowledge across the centuries. Alongside the increasingly evident utility for physicians of burgeoning sub-fields such as anatomy, botany, alchemy, and other experimental forms of occult natural philosophy, this brought the suggestion that there might be cases in which ancient or medieval diagnoses and treatments would need revision in the light of neoteric experience.[15] It was a typically humanistic paradox that the Hippocratic *corpus* was both construed as the repository of a *pristina medicina* and used to generate a vision in which the present could surpass the past; and although the impact of this tendency should not be overstated – only rarely did it displace the atemporal citation of authorities with antiquarian discussion of historical origins – one may observe in the later sixteenth century a growing awareness of the possibility of progress and innovation amongst university-educated physicians.[16]

Here I would like to denote these two conceptions of medicine as 'scholastic' and 'humanist' respectively. In the former, medicine was a broadly scientific discipline characterised by continuity with its medieval heritage, most notably in its incorporation of logical techniques designed for the resolution of authoritative knowledge. In the latter, it was primarily an art, with a definitive practical purpose, tailored towards a variable object, and (for some) characterised by historical development. We should remember that the majority regarded medicine as both science and art, and also that – as the complexity of Cardano's oeuvre demonstrates – the visions expressed by many medical authors do not fit neatly into either category. Nearly all learned physicians acknowledged that they were duty bound to combine reason and experience with authority in some manner, and that the ultimate goal of their enterprise, although in large part concerned with the theoretical understanding of causes, was therapeutic. But if there was no propaganda war, there was divergence on the status of the discipline. From the 'humanist' point of view, a large proportion of the early modern medical scholarship found in the *Anatomy* was problematically continuous with its putatively scholastic heritage. By contrast with ethics and politics, in medicine there had been

15 See Siraisi 1997, pp. 15, 19, 45 and Maclean 2002, pp. 77, 209–10, 229–32.

16 See Siraisi 2000, pp. 15–26, 2001, pp. 157–83, 325 and 2003; Maclean 2002, pp. 23–4, 104.

no self-conscious break with the past. What I shall be referring to as the neo-Galenic synthesis may have been rooted in ancient Greek doctrine, but it had grown in an accumulative manner and incorporated many medieval teachings. As well as yielding generalised diagnoses and therapies that were logically grounded but insensitive to the variable nuances of the particular case, many medical texts paraded a timeless conception of knowledge and inquiry, in which the task of the scholar was centrally constituted as the harmonisation of the doctrines of different authorities through techniques of conciliation. In these ways, the conflict of views concerning the character of medicine mapped directly on to the traditional polemical opposition of humanism to scholasticism.

MEDICINE AND HUMANIST PHILOSOPHY

Early modern neo-Galenic medicine possessed a significant degree of disciplinary autonomy, but like its ancient predecessor it had, at least in theory, a close relationship with ethics and theology. This derived substantially from the widespread acknowledgement of the two-way relationship between the body and the soul, which – especially after the storm of controversy which followed the publication in 1516 of Pietro Pomponazzi's *De immortalitate animae* – was the subject of intense speculation amongst philosophers as well as physicians throughout the early modern era. On the one side, as the Spanish physician Juan Huarte Navarro recorded in his *Examen de ingenios para las ciencias* (1574), this relationship was determined by the Galenic idea '[t]hat the maners of the soule, follow the temperature of the body'.[17] On the other, as Juan Luis Vives wrote in the third book of his influential *De anima et vita*, and equally in accordance with ancient doctrine, 'Affectus enim rationem corporis non recipiunt modò, sed præstant.'[18]

Although the sixteenth-century understanding of the mutual dependence of body and soul had been filtered through the heritage of medieval physiological and psychological theory, it was directly associated with the teachings of antiquity, and in particular with the writings of Plato and Galen. The Aldine publication of Galen's detailed analysis of the relationship between soul and body in the *De placitis Hippocratis et Platonis* (1525) was frequently cited and discussed by humanists on the

[17] Huarte Navarro 1594, pp. 21–2. [18] Vives 1555, p. 152.

subject,[19] but it was Plato who provided in the *Charmides* the most pithy injunction that the physician should treat the soul as well as the body in order to address 'the whole' of man.[20] This idea resonated throughout early modern theory and practice, where the concept of a medicine that combined physiology and psychology – the latter, when concerned with the passions, entering into the domain of moral philosophy – was tailored to the cure of the body and soul together. Medicine could thereby be integrated to the conception of the *prisca sapientia* of the ancients and assume a central place in the Renaissance encyclopaedia. As Galen himself had insisted, in order to become 'true followers of Hippocrates', physicians must 'know all the parts of philosophy, the logical, the physical, and the ethical'.[21]

The greatest obstacle to the integration of Renaissance moral philosophy, theology, and orthodox learned medicine was the association of both Galenism and Aristotelian natural philosophy with atheism. The impious image of medical learning was successfully exploited in the later sixteenth century by Paracelsus and his followers, though they drew upon longstanding distrust of learned physicians – hence the medieval saying, 'Ubi tres medici, duo athei.' The cliché of the irreligious university-trained physician had attained intellectual credibility on account of the widespread medical veneration of a pagan author – Galen – who had more than once displayed a materialistic tendency to reduce the soul to its 'temperature' or mixture of qualities. This was buttressed by the linkage of Galenic psychology with the materialism sometimes thought to be entailed by Aristotelian hylomorphism (which implied that the soul and body are inextricable aspects of the form and matter of the living being), and more seriously with the suspicious doctrines of Averroës.[22]

There were options available to later Renaissance humanists who wished to present a spiritually legitimate medicine, all of which relied on the integration or identification of philosophy, including physiology and psychology, with theology. One model had been constructed by Italian Neoplatonists such as Marsilio Ficino, Domenico Benivieni, and Cardano, who drew upon an image of Christ as a spiritual healer with

[19] See Nutton 1988a, pp. 286ff., and Nutton 1990, pp. 143–7. Burton cited the *De placitis* at 2.6.5–6.

[20] Plato 1927, pp. 18–21 (156d–157a); see Du Laurens 1599, p. 107, and Burton's citations at 1.247.12–13; 2.100.7–9; 2.109.22–4; 3.49.32; and 3.75.19–23. See also Plato 1914, pp. 548–9 (270c).

[21] Galen 1997, III.59.63, pp. 33–4.

[22] See Michael 2000.

magical powers to elevate an occultist ideal of the physician as magus. Ficino's masterpiece, the *Theologia Platonica de immortalite animarum* (1482), which had reconciled the Platonic theory of soul to Christianity (in the process refuting Averroism), represented an important alternative to the Aristotelian-Galenic synthesis dominant in university medical circles.[23] Another influential rebuttal of the atheistic implications of Galenic medicine had been delivered by Philipp Melanchthon, who met the charge head-on in his *De anatomia* and *De anima*. Melanchthon synthesised Lutheran theology, neo-Galenic medical *theoria*, and the psychological teachings of Aristotle (as well as Plato and Cicero) to argue that the body and soul were both created by God and were together the subject of divine grace; by addressing the nature of the soul through the operations of the body, he was able to demonstrate that the manifestations of psychic dysfunction were physically pathological and spiritually sinful, and that the manifestations of sinfulness could themselves be physical.[24] This offered physicians and moral philosophers a model for understanding and treating disorders in which Christian ethics were inseparable from medical doctrine, and which provided ammunition for combating the Paracelsian separation of neo-Galenism and Reformed orthodoxy. It was not until the following century, with the publication of the medical writings of Daniel Sennert and the Calvinist encyclopaedias of Bartholomaeus Keckermann and Johann Heinrich Alsted that the most controversial occultist doctrines were credibly presented in a form that was harmonious with both Aristotelian-Galenic and Christian dogma.[25]

In truth, the gap between medicine and Christianity had never been as unbridgeable as some perceived, and one did not need to be a fully fledged disciple of Ficino or Melanchthon to combine the two. According to scripture, medicine was the gift of God (Ecclesiasticus 38:4), and there were theoretical parallels between Galenism and Christian doctrine. Galen's praise of the divine craftsmanship of the human body gelled with a religious conception of physiology, and patristic authors from St Jerome to Isidore of Seville had used pagan medical psychology in their moral theology. Moreover, Galen's conviction that the decay of the divinely crafted organism was inevitable could be easily be translated into the Christian axiom that sickness was a punishment for original sin and so

[23] Siraisi 2001, pp. 233–4 and 244ff.

[24] See Nutton 1990, p. 147, and 1993, pp. 12, 21; Kusukawa 1995, esp. pp. 91–2, 98–9; and Michael 2000, pp. 163–5.

[25] See Hotson 2000.

a consequence of the Fall of man.[26] Disease could therefore be interpreted, and treated, as a moral and spiritual as well as a physiological defect even without recourse to the Neoplatonic or Philippist syntheses. In the neo-Galenic medicine of the later sixteenth century, the mutual dependence of body and soul provided grounds for the interweaving of physic and religion from causes to cures, where the combination of spiritual and medicinal therapy was deemed desirable and, in certain cases, indispensable. Successful treatment depended not only on the knowledge and skill of the physician, but on the will of God and (in the Reformed tradition) his bestowal of grace.[27] Effective medical *practica*, no less than *theoria*, could therefore possess a spiritual basis – hence the large number of early modern physicians who were also divines.

BODY AND SOUL

In keeping with the notion that the *medicus* drew upon the natural-philosophical knowledge of the *physicus*, it was commonplace for neo-Galenic physicians to assert that knowledge of disease must be preceded by knowledge of both body and soul (for this reason Burton offered a 'Digression of Anatomy' in the first Partition of his book [I.139.18–19 (I.I.2.I)]).[28] The edifice of early modern learned medicine was founded on a functional understanding of human anatomy, supported and refined through techniques of logical argumentation.[29] As we have seen, however, this did not mean that the physician was required to possess knowledge of the physical body only. Since the body both affected and was affected by the operations of the soul, pathology required understanding of psychology. Conversely, as both Melanchthon and Vives had underlined in their treatises *De anima*, divines and moralists needed to comprehend physiology in order to understand the workings of the soul, since these – being mediated via thought, imagination, will, and emotion – were knowable only through their operations in the body. Following this principle, I shall first outline the doctrines of body and soul structuring the neo-Galenic understanding of the disease of melancholy, before proceeding to Burton's presentation of the theory itself.

[26] Galen 1997, XIX.840, p. 69. The *loci* are Luke 13:4–5, John 9:1–3, Acts 12:23, and Augustine 1984, XXII.22, p. 1067.
[27] For example, in Lemnius 1576, fol. 14^{r}.
[28] Cf. Bright 1586, pp. 47–8.
[29] See Nutton 1991, p. 17, and Siraisi 1990a, p. 86. Cf. Galen 1969, VII.4, p. 43.

The medical orthodoxy was largely formulated in the medieval era as a combination of ideas originating in the Hippocratic *corpus*, the biological and psychological works of Aristotle, and the writings of Galen. However, the dominant synthesis up to the middle of the seventeenth century had been developed in late antiquity by Byzantine encyclopaedists and in the medieval era by Latin translators and Arabic authors, who had influentially systematised the Hippocratic-Galenic and Aristotelian traditions.[30] To begin: according to the Hippocratic texts, the healthy body was the product of an equilibrium in the mixture (κρᾶσις) of the four bodily humours (χῡμοί) which nourished the body – blood, phlegm, yellow bile, and black bile.[31] Since each humour was either hot and moist (blood), hot and dry (yellow bile), cold and moist (phlegm), or cold and dry (black bile), a healthy humoral κρᾶσις resulted in an even balance of the elemental qualities of heat, coldness, wetness, and dryness throughout the parts of the body. An excess or defect in the amount of the humours, an imbalanced or 'disordered mixture' (δυσκρᾶσία), upset the equilibrium of qualities and caused disease. Aristotle added the idea that heat was imbued with life-giving and health-preserving properties, particularly aiding digestion.[32] Incongruities between the Hippocratics and Galen on the number and character of humours were later ironed out by Avicenna, who in the *Liber canonis* listed four primary and four secondary humours. Both were to be found in good and bad kinds, the former being absorbed into the substance of the body to provide nourishment, and the latter being 'superfluities', which, if not naturally excreted, would cause damage.

For Galen, the Hippocratic notion of a mixture of qualities as primarily a function of humoral κρᾶσις was the principal causal factor in health or sickness.[33] The three principal parts of the body sustained by the humours, 'concocted' (i.e. transformed by digestive heat) out of nutriment,[34] were the brain, the heart, and the liver; and these, according to the Platonic doctrine followed by Galen, were the seats in the body of cognitive, vital, and nutritive psychological activity respectively.[35] A concomitant of this process was that each bodily part had its own

[30] See Ullmann 1978, Ballester 1995, and Siraisi 1987.

[31] Hippocrates 1978, p. 262.

[32] See Aristotle 1936b, II.8, II.11, III.13, pp. 117, 135, 201, and 1961, II.2, pp. 122–9.

[33] Galen 1997, VII.876, I.3.519, 521, pp. 87, 206, 207. Cf. Lemnius 1576, fol. 33^{v}. On Galen's humoral scheme see Siegel 1968, pp. 206–7, 216.

[34] Galen 1997, IX.807, p. 169; Galen 1821–33, I.6, vol. I, p. 470.

[35] Plato 1929, pp. 180–7 (69d–71d) and 1930–5, vol. I, pp. 372–405 (434d–441c); Galen 1978–84.

individual κρᾶσις, and the part's performance of its natural function was dependent upon this mixture being appropriate to its natural requirements.[36] Since Galen's was a functional physiology, disease was broadly defined as any impairment of the body's constitutive organs' natural activities.[37] A disease could therefore be localised in the body through the excessive accumulation or putrefaction of a humour in a certain part, upsetting its mixture.

For Galen as for Aristotle and the Hippocratics, then, each living body was a mixture of hot, cold, wet, and dry, and health consisted in the 'good proportion' of these qualities throughout the parts of the body, considered in relation to the requirements of each bodily faculty and biological genus.[38] In order to classify types of unhealthiness and disease, he divided human bodies into nine classes of temperament or complexion, four of which were constitutionally 'ill-balanced' in a simple sense (determined by an excess of one of the four qualities), four in a composite sense (determined by an excess of hot and wet, hot and dry, cold and wet, or cold and dry), and one 'well-balanced mixture' which was optimum for health.[39] The complexion predisposed to particular diseases and forms of behaviour, both of which were closely associated with its qualitative character. The ideal complexion was rarely, if ever, found. Nearly every human body was 'ill-balanced' to some extent, but there was an approximate health in the relatively stable imbalance of a temperament when the bodily faculties operated unimpaired.[40]

After Avicenna's description of the primary and secondary humours, there were usually said to be eight varieties of temperate and eight distemperate complexions.[41] But the Arabic interpreters of Galen also investigated health in the Aristotelian terms of vital heat, and combining the two approaches led to the advent of the concept of 'radical moisture' (*humiditas substanciale*), the correct level of which was considered crucial to the maintenance of the vital heat in the body.[42] As both hot and moist, blood became the principal material cause of radical moisture and vital heat, and so for medieval and early modern physicians the most healthy

36 Galen 1997, II.6.629–30, p. 258.
37 Galen 1991, I.5.4, II.1.1–5, pp. 22, 40–1, and 1997, I.3.519, VI.547, II.4.609, pp. 206, 219, 248–9.
38 Galen 1997, I.1.509–10, VI. 547–8, pp. 202, 220.
39 Galen 1997, I.8.559, p. 225.
40 Galen 1997, I.9.566–67, III.4.676, pp. 229, 280.
41 Avicenna 1608, I.1.1.1, vol. 1, pp. 11–13.
42 Avicenna 1608, I.1.1.1, vol. 1, p. 12; cf. Lemnius 1576, fol. 7v.

complexion was the 'sanguine' type.[43] The melancholic complexion, in which black bile was preponderant, was the least healthy, since the coldness and dryness of the humour were opposite to heat and moisture.[44] Medieval writers also developed the ancient theory of the complexions or temperaments into a behavioural characterology based on the four primary humours. Instead of being psychic by-products of the mixture of qualities, complexions were determined directly by the humours. There were now four simple temperaments. The sanguine was associated with a psychological 'good temper', happiness, and light-heartedness. The superabundance of hot and dry yellow bile (or 'choler') predisposed to anger and 'hot-headed' behaviour. The cold and moist phlegm led to a passive and apathetic psychological complexion. Finally, the preponderance of cold and dry black bile produced a fearful, sad, and lethargic complexion.[45]

Despite the schematic character of this system, it was axiomatic for Galen and his followers across the centuries that individual complexions were impermanent, and that the mixtures upon which they were based were constantly fluctuating. Not only did the qualities in the body change or destroy one another over time – moisture was always being destroyed by heat, for example; a wide variety of external factors influenced the κρᾶσις through the alteration of qualities.[46] The most prominent of these in Galen's writings came under the heading of regimen, and were associated with the authority of Hippocrates: diet, evacuation of bodily substances, environment and climate, exercise, sleep, and the passions of the soul.[47] Medieval and early modern neo-Galenists, who likewise emphasised the possibility of the pathological or therapeutic alteration of the humoral balance and internal qualities,[48] classed these regimental factors as the six 'non-naturals', and these became fundamental to orthodox diagnosis and therapy.[49]

As the last in this list of factors indicates, health and disease were not simply physiological concepts. Ancient Greek writers typically posited a relationship between the body and soul that was direct, and specifically

43 Du Laurens 1599, p. 85. See also Lemnius 1576, fols. 86^{v}, 88^{r}. See Klibansky, Panofsky, and Saxl 1964, pp. 13, 61–2.

44 Lemnius 1576, fol. 135^{r}. Cf. Vives 1555, p. 150.

45 See the typical account in Wright 1971, pp. 64–5.

46 Galen 1997, I.2.516–17, II.4.604, II.366, pp. 205, 246, 374.

47 Galen 1997, XXIII.367, p. 374; ibid., IX.884–5, pp. 91–2; and Galen 1821–33, I.8, vol. VI, pp. 40–1.

48 Bright 1586, pp. 85–6; Lemnius 1576, fols. 4^{v}–5^{v}, 84^{r}, 127^{v}.

49 See Rather 1968, Jarcho 1970, and Niebyl 1971.

manifested in the ways in which emotions both influenced and were caused by the predominance of somatic qualities.[50] But Galen gave this subject the most sustained and influential treatment, emphasising the ways in which bodily conditions determined mental and psychological states. In the treatise subsequently translated into Latin as *Quod animi mores corporis temperamenta sequuntur*, he offered the following formula: 'The faculties (δυνάμεις) of the soul depend on the mixtures (κρᾶσεις) of the body.'[51] But the soul was not just a 'slave to the mixtures of the body',[52] the soul *was*, in part, the body's κρᾶσις – 'this is actually what the mortal part of the soul is, the mixture of the body'.[53] Having established this principle (which, as later commentators recognised, threatened the immortality of the soul), Galen argued that the 'natural activities [of the soul] are liable to impairment from the mixture of the body', and quoted *Timaeus* 86e–87a to the effect that the humours could 'cause all kinds of diseases of the soul, great and small, few and many'.[54]

Galen also followed the Hippocratics and Aristotle in stating that the bodily qualities inclined the soul to certain corresponding affections or emotions, which were processes associated with qualititative change in the body.[55] These were primarily caused by physiological operations,[56] but they also altered the body. He wrote that 'excess of all affections of the soul . . . will change the natural composition of the body', and described both the 'drying' process set in motion by anxiety and leading to disease, and the detrimental effects of passions on the proper functioning of the heart.[57] Moreover, the passions arising from the irrational parts of the soul hindered the proper functioning of the rational soul (the κρᾶσις of the brain) by interfering with its lines of communication with the rest of the body. In this scheme, passions were properly, and non-metaphorically, classified as diseases affecting the functioning of the organism.[58]

50 Hippocrates 1839–61, VI.5.5, vol. V, p. 316, and IX, vol. V, pp. 488–91; Aristotle 1961, II.4, pp. 136–9, quoted in Galen 1997, VIII.793, p. 162.

51 Galen 1997, I.767, p. 150.

52 Galen 1997, III.779, p. 155, referring to cases of melancholy.

53 Galen 1997, III.774, IV.782, pp. 153, 157. Cf. Galen 1978–84, IX.9.6–14, vol. II, pp. 598–601.

54 Galen 1997, V.785, VI.789, pp. 158–9, 160.

55 Galen 1997, VIII.804, p. 167.

56 Galen 1821–33, II.9, vol. VI, p. 138.

57 Galen 1997, II.4.604, p. 246, XXIV.371, p. 376; 1978–84, II.7, vol. I, pp. 152–7; and 1997, III.742–3, pp. 292–3, XII.473–4, p. 335.

58 Galen 1978–84, V.I.I–3.32, vol. I, pp. 294–313; cf. Galen 1997, I, pp. 100–27, analysed in Hankinson 1993, p. 207.

Just as physiological health required a median state between the excess of qualities in the body, psychological health was a condition in which the soul was held midway between all excessive affections.[59]

Humanists commonly associated the interaction between body and soul with the teachings of Hippocrates, Plato, and Galen,[60] but the orthodox explanation was heavily indebted to medieval theorists who had extended the classical understanding of the πνεῦμα, the subtle material 'spirit' in the heart which mediated body and soul.[61] Arabic authors developed Galen's doctrines about πνεῦμα by interpolating a third type, πνεῦμα φῦσικόν or 'natural spirit', so that each of the Platonic/Aristotelian parts of the soul (cognitive, vital, and nutritive) had a corresponding 'spirit' to act as a go-between in its functions in the body. Animal spirits or psychic πνεῦμα were posited in the brain, mediating the activities of cognition, perception, and the nervous system; vital spirits were located in the heart, from where they pervaded the whole body, mediating the vital functions; and natural spirits were positioned in the liver, mediating the processes of nutrition and growth. According to Avicenna, all three types originated from a single *spiritus*, the immediate material cause of the body.[62] Early modern writers followed suit by describing the *spiritus* as not just the conveyer of natural heat and radical moisture throughout the body, but also the agent communicating the activities of the soul. As Levinus Lemnius explained, it was the 'ruler and director' of all the soul's actions in the body.[63]

Theories drawing on these doctrines to describe the beneficial or detrimental physiological effects of emotions were widespread in neo-Galenic medical works. According to the orthodox understanding, the enhancement of vitality accompanying joy not only expanded and heated the heart, but also stimulated an increase in the quality and quantity of the *spiritus* there produced, resulting in a health-inducing surge of the spirits upwards to the head and outwards to all the bodily parts. Conversely, the contraction of the heart in fear hindered its production of *spiritus* and provoked an inward and downward movement of the spirits, damaging the functions and therefore the health of all the outlying bodily parts. But whereas for Galen passions were primarily physiological phenomena, medieval and early modern faculty psychology was

[59] Galen 1997, II.1.576, pp. 232–3.
[60] See, for example, Ficino 2001–, XIII.4, vol. IV, pp. 190–1.
[61] Aristotle 1961, II.4, III.3, pp. 140–1, 230–1.
[62] See Harvey 1975, pp. 16, 23; Siraisi 1987, pp. 29, 338.
[63] Lemnius 1576, fols. 7^r–8^r, and 7^r–19^v generally.

essentially Aristotelian in its emphasis on the primacy of apprehension (in the rational soul) and appetite (in the sensitive soul) in stimulating emotions. The emotions were thus movements of the soul, not of the body.[64] This became the orthodox understanding of emotion in medical and psychological texts, where the movements of the soul's appetites in the brain were said to be communicated via the animal spirits to the heart, enabling a corresponding movement of the spirits throughout the body.

The emotions were also thought to affect the body's production of humours and spirits, and so have the potential to upset the healthy balance of the organism. In the *Theologia Platonica*, for example, Ficino identified four motions of the *phantasia* in the rational soul – desire, pleasure, fear, and pain – that 'entirely dominate the body, since they alter it in every way'.[65] Generally speaking, the advent of an emotion in the soul created a surge of its qualitatively corresponding humour to the heart. In order to respond to the physiological requirements of the 'hot' emotion of anger, for example, the heart attracted hot and dry choler from the seat of its production in the gall; this humour then rose to heat and excite the brain and impair reason. In joy, a rush of warm and moist blood humour to the heart enabled the increased production of vital spirits, which then spread throughout the parts of the body to improve their functions. In fear or sadness, black bile was attracted from the spleen. This humour contracted the heart, which drew in and imprisoned the blood and spirits from the rest of the parts, depriving them of the vital heat and moisture necessary for healthy functioning, and cooling and drying the whole organism. The blood around the heart, thus cooled and dried, would degenerate into more black bile, which then spread outward through the body with a multitude of damaging consequences. On the occasion of an emotion, then, the body was altered, at least temporarily, to the physiological complexion with which that emotion was associated.[66] Avicenna had explained in addition that by affecting the properties and characteristics of the spirits, the emotions had the power to facilitate or hinder the functioning of the mental faculties.[67]

[64] See Gardiner, Metcalf, and Beebe-Center 1937, p. 115.

[65] Ficino 2001–, XIII.1, vol. IV, pp. 114–15.

[66] Wright 1971, pp. 65, 83. On the physiology of specific emotions see Melanchthon 1834–60, vol. XIII, p. 127 (= Melanchthon 1552, sig. P3); Vives 1555, p. 152; Lemnius 1576, fol. 128^r; Wright 1971, p. 105; La Primaudaye 1618, pp. 455, 497.

[67] Avicenna 1608, I.4–9, vol. II, pp. 335–8.

NEO-GALENIC OCCULTISM

Despite exhibiting broad continuity with the medieval understanding of body and soul, early modern medical teachings were distinguishable from their predecessors by their frequent incorporation of occultist ideas, which had contentious implications for the orthodox neo-Galenic synthesis.[68] The most important of these for our purposes related to the influence of the cosmos and diverse occult qualities and causes on the body, the concept of sympathy, and the mysterious workings of *spiritus* and the imagination.

In the first place, learned physicians commonly acknowledged the existence of 'hidden' or 'secret' qualities deemed to be manifest only through their effects.[69] Hidden qualities and causes were widely credited, and growing interest in the topic was reflected in the proliferation of compendia of occult natural 'secrets' in the second half of the sixteenth century, such as Cardano's *De secretis* (1562) and Johannes Jacob Wecker's *De secretis libri XVII* (1582).[70] More conspicuously problematic for physicians was the parallel rise in speculation about the operations of magical divination and incantation, miracles, and demonic spirits. (Such phenomena were technically preternatural, but they entered the domain of medical *practica* insofar as they affected body or soul.) The contentious character of occult inquiry in natural philosophy and medicine is most visible in debates over the deceptive capacity of demons, where claims for the authenticity of divine omens were dismissed as either forgeries manufactured by intermediary spirits or instances of superstitious divination.[71] Controversy also followed the works of authors influenced by Ficino's strain of occult philosophy and astral medicine. This was the case for Jean Fernel's *De abditis rerum causis* (1548), which detailed a wide range of occult pathogens, and formulated a theory of disease of the 'total substance' requiring explanation and treatment outside of the neo-Galenic framework of qualitative therapy.[72] But although Fernel had his critics, most agreed that there were preternatural exceptions to the rule that pathological causes should be regarded as natural.[73] Even staunch

68 On contemporary critics of occultism see Vickers 1992.

69 See, for example, Cardano 1663, vol. V, pp. 539–40, 546–7, citing *Philebus* 533d–534a.

70 See Eamon 1994.

71 See Daston 1991, pp. 101ff.

72 Fernel 1567, II.10–13, 17–18, pp. 93–110, 122–33; cf. the discussion in Argenterio 1558, pp. 157–8.

73 See Siraisi 1987, pp. 348–9, and 1997, pp. 149–73; Maclean 2000, pp. 232–4. Cf. Burton's usage at I.203.21–5 (I.2.1.5).

rationalists like André du Laurens admitted that some pathogens were seemingly occult.[74]

Occultist tendencies were also apparent in two learned medical concepts based on the Stoic notion of cosmic harmony. The first of these, the idea of 'sympathy' (*consensus*), had been popularised by Girolamo Fracastoro in his *De sympathia & antipathia rerum* (1546), and defined by Fernel as 'an affection against nature passed on by the corruption of another bodily part'.[75] Also suggesting occult means by which the body could affect the soul or *vice versa*, sympathy appealed to neo-Galenists partly because it could help account for the apparent spontaneity of diseases affecting the whole body (diseases by 'universal sympathy').[76] The second concept was that of *spiritus*, which was elaborated through reference to the ancient understanding of πνεῦμα as the active binding force effecting correspondences between astral and earthly bodies. According to Ficino, who in the third book of the *De vita* gave the neo-Galenic doctrine of the subtle *spiritus* a cosmic-theological dimension, because of its astral associations the *spiritus* was the bearer of magical capacities. This idea entered medical literature via authors like Fernel, but the supernatural qualities of *spiritus* were also useful for those in search of a theological basis for physiological theory. In the 1552 edition of his *De anima*, Melanchthon described the operations of the Holy Spirit in the body, which mingled with the vital and animal spirits and imbued them with a *divina lux*. Conversely, he claimed, the Devil could also interfere with the spirits, impeding the judgement and producing madness.[77] The direct relationship between the Holy Spirit and the bodily spirits was asserted in similar terms by Lemnius.[78]

The other putative locus of supernatural activity was the imagination, which since antiquity had been deemed a fallible power capable of altering the composition of the body.[79] This notion was given detailed attention in medieval psychology, where the powers of common sense (*sensus communis*, or *phantasia/imaginatio*, located in the anterior ventricle of the brain) and imagination (or the 'estimation', *virtus aestimativa*, located in the middle ventricle) were said to bridge material

[74] Du Laurens 1599, pp. 98–9.

[75] Fernel 1567, I.4, p. 179: 'Συμπάθεια affectus est contra naturam parti alterius vitio impertitus.'

[76] See, for example, Du Laurens 1599, pp. 88, 128, 140.

[77] Melanchthon 1834–60, vol. XIII, pp. 88–9 (= Melanchthon 1552, sig. K5).

[78] Lemnius 1576, fols. 25^{r-v}.

[79] Aristotle 1961, VI–VIII, pp. 456–71.

objects and the immaterial soul.[80] Since the common sense (directly) and imagination (indirectly) were related to the material world and were both sensitive faculties, they were considered vulnerable to external influence and interference, and it proved a short step from this conception of susceptibility to the formulation of occult powers. Avicenna had suggested that through its dealings with the material 'forms' of the universe it had the capacity to perform operations outside the body,[81] and in the fifteenth and sixteenth centuries the deceptive and occult powers of the imagination were frequently discussed by philosophers and physicians.[82] For Ficino and other Neoplatonists, it was the faculty by which the 'lower', non-intellectual soul was affected by astral forces and was accordingly the medium for cosmological magic.[83] Some orthodox medical writers theorised the imagination as the instrument of malign diabolical interference in the body, and it was also conceived as a faculty with the power directly to induce and cure certain types of disease – either, as Avicenna had suggested, through occult means, or else indirectly through its capacity to affect the passions of the soul.[84]

Finally, the occultist study of astrology both permeated the orthodox medical tradition and formed the basis for the most significant challenge to that tradition. The relationship between astrology and medicine had been indisputably authorised by the writings of the Hippocratics, for whom health depended upon harmony between the human body and the cosmos. In Hippocratic theory, blood tended to predominate in spring, yellow bile in summer, black bile in autumn, and phlegm in winter; the movements of the cosmos across the seasons therefore had an integral role in a successful prognosis.[85] This scheme was very commonly reproduced in early modern medical works, and the intertwining of astrology with *theoria* and *practica* became ever tighter with the incorporation of Arabic teachings associating seasons with specific planets, the humanist study of works such as Ptolemy's *Tetrabiblos*, and the pervasive influence of Neoplatonism.[86] The recognition of the legitimacy of astrology by those

[80] See Harvey 1975 and Olivieri 1991, pp. 66–70. Burton summarised the scheme at 1.152.7–35 (1.1.2.7).

[81] See Avicenna 1508, IV.4, fol. 20^{v} and ff. Burton referred to this passage at 1.254.26 (1.2.3.2). See also Avicenna 1546, fols. 100^{r-v} and 1608, I.1.6.5, vol. I, p. 75.

[82] For instance, in Du Laurens 1599, p. 74.

[83] Ficino 2001–, XII.4, XIII.2, XIII.4, vol. IV, pp. 50–3, 150–61, 190–7.

[84] See Pittion 1987, p. 124, and Siraisi 1987, p. 283.

[85] Hippocrates 1978, pp. 265–6, and 1990, XV, p. 71.

[86] For example, see Lemnius 1576, fols. 87^{r-v},136^{r}–136^{v}.

such as Melanchthon and Cardano also sanctioned the construction of astrological horoscopes predicting the course of health and disease, which were routinely used as prognostic instruments by popular astrological physicians.[87] Challenge to the deterministic elements of astrology came most famously from Giovanni Pico della Mirandola in his *Disputationes adversus astrologiam divinatricem* (1493), and in the following century from Reformed authors asserting the priority of divine Providence over astral governance. But a moderate position in which the stars were able to incline but not compel qualitative change in earthly bodies was assumed by many authors of this period.[88] Although the strictest neo-Galenic rationalists opposed the idea that the planets exerted influence by occult means, it was common to adopt Pico's position (which itself harked back to Rhazes) that they could affect man through the manipulation of heat, light, and motion. This entailed not a rejection of astrology, but rather its naturalisation.[89]

Astrology was also central to the only serious challenge to the dominance of the neo-Galenic learned medical orthodoxy in the sixteenth century, presented by Paracelsus's medical-spiritual system. According to Paracelsus, the sixteenth century heralded an era of violence, irreligion, vice, and new diseases, all of which called for a revolutionary new type of medicine that would be totally identified with theology. We need not trouble ourselves here with the details of his elaborate fusion of mystical and chemical ideas: Burton was chiefly interested in Paracelsianism as a source of controversy rather than of doctrine. It is worth noting, however, that notwithstanding the scientific posture adopted by the critics of Paracelsus, the conflict between neo-Galenists and Paracelsians was not so much one between rationalism and occultism in modern terms, as one between different conceptions of the power and extent of supernatural forces acting on and within the human body. Many writers sympathetic to the more intellectually respectable influence of Neoplatonism, such as Thomas Browne, appeared to straddle the two groups.[90] Rational and occult concepts intermingled in both the neo-Galenic and Paracelsian medical traditions.

[87] See MacDonald 1981 and 1996, and Kassell 1998.

[88] See Calvin 1561, sigs. Aiiii–Bi, Bv.

[89] Pico's argument is analysed in Siraisi 1987, pp. 283–5, 288. Cf. Rhazes 1973, p. 524.

[90] See Browne 1977, I.34, p. 103. But cf. Scaliger 1607, CI, p. 349, and Bacon 1906, II.10.2, II.11.3, pp. 127, 138.

THE *ANATOMY* AND THE MEDICAL THEORY OF MELANCHOLY

We are now in a position to approach the early modern theory of the disease of melancholy,[91] and through this the medical content of Burton's *Anatomy*. As I noted above, the overwhelmingly textual basis of the investigation of melancholy in the *Anatomy* (the medical aspect of what Fuller referred to as its 'philology') was consonant with the methodology of orthodox neo-Galenic university-based medicine in the early seventeenth century. In Oxford, although the second and third decades of the century saw a series of benefactions to the university for lectureships and readerships in science, including the Tomlins readership in anatomy in 1624, the texts of the Hippocratics and Galen were not displaced from the centre of the curriculum until the 1640s.[92] That Burton chose to explore melancholy through the exposition of other books, then, in no way categorises him as exceptional – either as an eccentric bibliophile clinging to a world of decaying humanism, or as a traditionalist opponent of a nascent 'new science'. The text-based method of the *Anatomy* in no way detracted from the book's medical-scientific credibility, which in this respect was unimpeachable in the terms of its age. Nevertheless (as I noted in the introduction) there were important respects, relating both to presentational style and philosophical substance, in which Burton's method of investigation was strikingly unconventional. This should not be forgotten, but in what immediately follows I shall overlook these for the sake of clarity and extract the medical account of melancholy, before returning to them in the next chapter.

The principle that the age and the validity of an idea were positively related was central to the enterprise of recovering the *prisca sapientia* of the ancients, and it followed that in the early modern body of accumulated knowledge about medical matters the most authoritative doctrine was to be found in the texts of the Hippocratics, Aristotle, and Galen. However, although early modern readers found influential discussions of melancholy in the short pseudo-Hippocratic treatise *De atra bilis agitatione melancholiave* and in the third book of Galen's *De locis affectis*, both of these drew on teachings previously elaborated – in particular by Rufus of Ephesus in his Περὶ μελαχολίας, now

[91] In early modern writings the term 'melancholy' could refer to the disease, the complexion, or the humour black bile. In the following account I have attempted to keep them distinct.

[92] On science and medicine at Oxford before 1640, see Frank 1973, pp. 207–11, 239; Sinclair 1974, p. 373; Tyacke 1978; Webster 1975, pp. 115–29; and Valadez 1974, pp. 397–406.

preserved only in fragments – and were relatively brief. Consequently, although the framework in which the early modern understanding of melancholy was located was that of the orthodox Hippocratic-Galenic and Aristotelian synthesis, a number of other, now less well-known authors came to the fore in the formation and elaboration of the central ideas about the disease. In what follows, I shall provide an outline of Burton's medical account of melancholy and interrogate the principal means by which he presented it as a survey and exploration of the early modern medical theory as it had accumulated across the centuries.

Burton's account was encyclopaedically inclusive, ranging across a huge number of writings on the disease, as well as on topics that in his view had a bearing on it. The character of the works he used was significant. Although many were ancient or medieval, many were neoteric, and his activity of continuously expanding the book with the appearance of each new edition enabled him to present a view of the scholarship that was noticeably and self-consciously up to date. Moreover, with one or two notable exceptions, the vast majority of the medical texts he quoted and commented upon had been produced in Latin by continental neo-Galenists, and this gave genuine substance to his claim to be making the higher reaches of knowledge exchanged between the learned in European university circles accessible to his domestic readership in the vernacular. He also drew conspicuously upon the logical conventions of neo-Galenic method to order what was in its basic content a relatively uncontentious but intellectually respectable analysis of the disease. However, notwithstanding his posture of caution with regard to medical-scientific conventions, at some points in the book – notably in his treatment of the subjects of erotic and religious melancholy – his particular moral and theological concerns prompted him to expand the scope of the existing medical understanding in ways that would become highly significant for the character of his overall enterprise.

At the same time, Burton assessed the therapeutic utility and moral-spiritual rectitude of the learning he was divulging. Here it was critical that the manner in which he presented this learning indicated an identifiably Hippocratic conception of medicine as an art, which through attention to particulars and appeals to experience would present the best opportunity to produce health. For one advantage of his approaching medicine as *ars* rather than *scientia* was that he no longer needed to concern himself with accommodating the authoritative statements of pagan authors to the ethical and spiritual problems raised by his investigation. Instead, recognition of the all-pervasiveness of 'exceptions' on the basis of particularity and experience made possible a coherent position for the author-physician in which each authoritatively sanctioned 'rule' could be shaped – or even abandoned – in accordance with the extra-medical requirements of the moral philosopher and theologian. Galenic doctrine could be deemed applicable in a case where it conformed with Christian principles, and rejected as inapplicable where it did not. Being free of the generalising, quasi-scholastic dictates of the systematic pursuit of medical 'science' through rigorous conciliation, Burton could give free rein to his broader humanistic quest for rectitude in matters of body and soul. This position also provided him with a stance appropriate to the theologically dangerous territory of occultist medicine. After addressing the medical method applied to melancholy in the *Anatomy*, and the learned content of the account to which it gave rise, I shall therefore end by looking at the way in which Burton's conception of the medical art enabled him to explore the problematic issues raised by the infiltration of the scholarly orthodoxy by occultism.[93]

DIVISION AND DEFINITION

Two aspects of Burton's method were fundamental in establishing the medical-scientific credibility of the *Anatomy*. The most conspicuous technique employed throughout the book to organise and interpret material was *divisio*, which was highly effective when applied to an extensive and unwieldy subject matter. Division was a well-known instrument of early modern dialectic, but its main significance in the *Anatomy* stemmed from its ancient association with medical theory.[94] Indeed, the famous synoptic tables of the book, which provide vivid visual illustration of Burton's implementation of division – appropriate to an 'anatomy' – simply reflect a practice that had long been conventional to scholarly medical publications, and was not a sign of direct Ramist influence.[95] In orthodox medicine, the utility of διαίρεσις or *divisio* was generally attributed to its ability to assist the physician's task of comprehending the complex and multifaceted entities – bodies,

[93] The following account is particularly indebted to Starobinski 1960; Klibansky, Panofsky, and Saxl 1964, pp. 3–123; Siegel 1971; Neugebauer 1979; and Jackson 1986. Useful studies of early modern theories include Babb 1951, Jobe 1976, Veith 1976, Schleiner 1991, Alet 2000 and Brann 2002.

[94] For Hippocratic διαίεσις see Plato 1914, pp. 548–9 (270c–d).

[95] This is discussed in Gowland 2000, pp. 22–7. See generally Maclean 2002, pp. 60–1, 143–4.

diseases, humours, spirits, and so on – which he was charged with treating, permitting him to make inferences about them that were rationally informed.[96] In the sense, therefore, that it enabled the rational ordering of the potentially (or practically) infinite particulars of medical subject matter, heavy dependence on division was the characteristic of an 'art' which, according to Porphyry's definition, was *de infinitis finita scientia* and concerned with the presentation of probable data. More particularly, it was used to distinguish between genera and species, wholes and parts, accidents and properties, and the divergent meanings of words.[97] For all disciplines division also had a well-recognised pedagogical utility, exemplified by Burton's tables, insofar as the division of wholes into parts enabled the organisation of material from any discipline for easy digestion. According to Jean Bodin, analysis through *divisio* was 'praestas illa docendarum artium magistra'.[98]

Perhaps most importantly in medicine, for neo-Galenists as for Galen, division into genus and species was the logical procedure that led to the knowledge of diseases.[99] It was therefore the means by which one could arrive at a definition of disease, which was deemed central to any medical-scientific investigation. In Aristotelian method, definitions were statements of essence (οὐσία), i.e. the formal cause.[100] This was the approach taken by Galen, who explained in the *De methodo medendi* – a work that had enormous influence on early modern medical theory and practice[101] – that the discovery of an essence depended upon an agreed common conception (κοινὴ ἔννοια), and that definitions of essence served as the first principles or axioms of medical science.[102] In the case of disease, the essence was the disposition impeding the activity of a bodily part, and this disposition was the object of therapy.[103] In neo-Galenism, the theoretical centrality of essential definition to the understanding and treatment of disease was supplemented by the Aristotelian suggestion that definition was achievable through the four 'predicables', namely *genus*, *species*, *proprium*, and *differentia*, with the addition of *accidens* made by Porphyry.[104]

96 On the medical utility of logic generally see Bartholin 1628, fol. 3r.
97 See Maclean 1992, pp. 73–4, 111–14, and 2002, pp. 103, 121–3, 128–37, 140–5, 204.
98 Bodin 1566, p. 15.
99 Galen 1821–33, II.7, vol. VIII, p. 612.
100 Aristotle 1936b, I.1, pp. 12–13.
101 See Bylebyl 1991.
102 Galen 1997, I.806–7, p. 53; Galen 1991 I.3.13, I.4.6, I.5.2–10, pp. 15–16, 18, 21–4.
103 Galen 1991, I.5.1–4, II.1.3, II.3.10, pp. 21–2, 40–1, 46.
104 See Maclean 1992, pp. 103–14, esp. 105–6, and 2002, pp. 144–5. Cf. Galen 1528b, fol. 4r.

Burton routinely employed *divisio* as the primary means of logical-scientific investigation. This kind of division was explicitly involved throughout the anatomical digression at the beginning of the first Partition, the physiological Subsection of which was also the only part of the main treatise that omitted discussion of scholarly controversy (perhaps because like Vesalius he considered it to be epistemologically more secure than its psychological counterpart). When anatomising the parts of the body, he implemented the Hippocratic division of parts into 'contained' and 'containing' (1.140.15–16 [1.1.2.2]), and, within 'containing' parts, applied the orthodox ancient medical distinction between 'similar' and 'dissimilar' parts (1.142.4–5 [1.1.2.3]). Division into genera and species was employed to explore the different kinds of madness and melancholy throughout the book; and as for the *divisio* of the causes of melancholy, Burton's readers were assaulted with a barrage of Galenic and scholastic-Aristotelian distinctions, which forcefully asserted the logical-scientific nature of the enterprise in hand: 'primary', 'universal', 'precedent', 'efficient', 'outward', 'adventitious', 'remote', and 'accidental' were all opposed to 'secondary', 'particular', 'antecedent', 'material', 'inward', 'innate', 'continent', and 'immediate' causes.[105] Other important divisions were between natural, supernatural, and preternatural causes (1.172.4 [1.2.1.1]; 1.205.6–7 [1.2.1.6]), necessary and non-necessary causes (1.211.7–9 [1.2.2.1]), and causes working in substance or accident (1.211.24). He also divided symptoms into universal and particular (1.381.15 [1.3.1.1]), of body and mind (1.381.31, 3.139.4 [3.2.3.1]), and cures were either general or particular (2.1.16–17 [2.1.1.1]). It is worth noting, however, that the notable lack of scholastic-Aristotelian classificatory language in the third Partition – a vague exception may be found at 3.58.17 (3.2.2.1) – suggests that he considered a large proportion of its erotic and religious subject matter to be less appropriate to this type of analysis. The repetitive use of division constituted a large part of the scientific structure of Burton's anatomisation of the subject of melancholy, and its absence in certain parts of the work was significant.

Most important to Burton's medical-scientific task was his use of division as the means to arrive at an essential definition, and in this sense *divisio* was at the base of his account of the theory of melancholy

[105] See 1.172.2–3 (1.2.1.1); 1.199.15–16 (1.2.1.4); 1.203.20–3 (1.2.1.5); 1.211.25 (1.2.2.1); 1.327.27–328.8 (1.2.4.1); 1.372.2–7 (1.2.5.1); 1.378.13 (1.2.5.4); and 1.380.3 (1.2.5.5). On causal topics in dialectic see Carbone 2003, III.12–18, pp. 350–68; in learned medicine, see Maclean 2000, pp. 240–1, and 2002, pp. 262–4.

(cf. I.139.16 [I.I.2.I]). According to the traditional Hippocratic-Galenic view largely followed by early modern physicians, melancholy was one of the species of the genus madness (*delirium*). In ancient Greece, the word μελαγχολία typically designated a mental abnormality which might or might not be accompanied by fear and sorrow, and, as Jacques Ferrand pointed out in his *De la maladie d'amour ou melancholie erotique* (1623), μελαγχολᾶν meant for the Greeks 'to be out of one's mind'.[106] The other two species of *delirium* were frenzy (or phrenitis) and mania. This threefold division of madness was commonly reproduced in the medical literature of the era.[107] Conventionally, frenzy was an acute disease, yielding the symptoms of delirium and fever, and mania was a chronic disease, resulting in fierce and prolonged delirium but no fever. The disease of melancholy was also chronic and without fever. Accordingly, Burton divided '*Dotage*; Fatuity, or Folly' into phrenitis (I.132.13–16 [I.I.I.4]), mania (I.132.30–1), and melancholy. Melancholy and mania were both distinguished from frenzy by Burton because they were 'without an ague' (I.132.17–18), and mania was said to differ from melancholy because it caused raving 'farre more violent then *Melancholy*' and was 'without all feare and sorrow' (I.132.31–133.2). These distinctions derived from the Hippocratics, but they had been authoritatively elaborated by Soranus of Ephesus, Galen, and Avicenna.[108]

In dividing melancholy from mania and frenzy, Burton was laying the groundwork for an essential definition of the melancholic disease. His next task was to distinguish between the natural periodic occurrence of emotions associated with melancholy, such as sadness, and the pathological condition of melancholy – a problem compounded by the fact that in Hippocratic-Galenic theory, black bile was present in every human body, and each complexion was continually in flux. It was a short and erroneous step from this position to the conclusion that when anyone was fearful or sad they were necessarily also pathologically 'melancholic'. To solve this difficulty, Burton had recourse to the Aristotelian distinction between disposition and habit. A disposition, in this view, was a certain

106 Ferrand 1990, p. 235. The terminological confusion is discussed in Hippocrates 1962, p. lviii; Klibansky, Panofsky, and Saxl 1964, pp. 15–17; Rosen 1969, p. 93; and Jackson 1986, pp. 4–5.

107 See Du Laurens 1599, pp. 81, 87–8; Manardi 1611, XVII.I, p. 315; Ferrand 1990, p. 256; Mercuriale 1617, I.15, I.16, pp. 76, 84. For exceptions see Ficino 1985, VIII.3, p. 158 (followed in Valleriola 1588, p. 196), and Paracelsus 1996, pp. 152–3.

108 Caelius Aurelianus 1950, pp. 561–3; Galen 1528a, fol. 19r, and 1976, III.7, p. 83; Avicenna 1608, III.I.4.15, III.I.4.18, vol. I, pp. 487–9.

quality or 'character', very susceptible to change, such as heat or cold, sickness or disease; habits, on the other hand, were settled dispositions, 'the formed states of character in virtue of which we are well or ill disposed in respect of the emotions', and so manifested in stable predispositions which were either moderate or excessive.[109] Burton translated this Aristotelian theory into neo-Galenic terms, so that a habit was broadly equivalent to a complexion or temperament (for some early modern writers, habits affected the psychic faculties by regularising the motions of the animal spirits in the brain),[110] whereas a disposition corresponded to a temporary humoral imbalance or emotional response entailing a deviation from the natural complexion.[111] Accordingly, he defined melancholy in disposition, from which 'no man living is free', as 'that transitory *Melancholy*, which goes & comes upon every small occasion of sorrow, need, sicknesse', and other 'melancholic' emotions which were 'any wayes opposite to pleasure' (I.136.12–17, 19–20 [I.I.I.5]). Melancholy in habit was, by contrast, 'a setled humor . . . not errant but fixed' (I.139.9–12). Whilst it was important to note that according to the ancient theory 'it falleth out oftentimes that these *Dispositions* become *Habits*' (I.138.15–16; cf. I.25.14–16), he dealt with the potential ambiguity arising from 'melancholy' by employing the topic of *aequivocatio* and dispensing with 'melancholy in disposition' as an 'Æquivocall and improper' usage (I.136.17).[112]

Burton next implemented the topic of etymology, or the division of a word into its component parts: 'The *Name* is imposed from the matter, and Disease denominated from the materiall cause: as *Bruel* observes, Μελαγχολία, *quasi* Μέλαινα χολή, from black Choler' (I.162.6–8 [I.I.3.I]).[113] However, Galenic method also required essential definition, constituted by a description of the pathological disposition impeding the functioning of a bodily part. Accordingly, Burton employed the predicables concerned with definition – genus, species, *proprium*, *differentia*, and *accidens*. After a brief discussion of the various ancient, medieval, and neoteric definitions available to him, he offered a definition that drew on some of the key contemporary continental

109 See Aristotle 1934, II.5.1–2, pp. 87ff., and 1938, VIII, pp. 62–5.
110 See, for example, Vives 1555, p. 121.
111 For a similar implication see Argenterio 1558, pp. 179–80; cf. Galen 1997, II.6.604–7, pp. 246–7.
112 On equivocation see Aristotle 1966, I.18, pp. 324–5.
113 See Du Laurens 1599, p. 86; Manardi 1611, IX.2, p. 183; Mercuriale 1617, I.10, p. 39.

medical authorities of the *Anatomy* – Ercole Sassonia, Eliano Montalto, and André du Laurens. It appeared in the first edition as follows:

> The *summum genus* is *Dotage*, or *Anguish of the minde*, saith *Areteus, of a principall part, Hercules de Saxoniâ* addes, to distinguish it from Cramp and Palsie, and such diseases as belong to the outward Sence and motions (*depraved*) to distinguish it from Folly and Madnesse (which *Montaltus* makes *angor animi* to separate) in which, those functions are not depraved, but rather abolished, (*without an ague*) is added by all to sever it from *Phrensie*, and that *Melancholy*, which is a pestilent Fever. (*Feare and Sorrow*) make it differ from *Madnesse* (*without a cause*) is lastly inserted to specifie it from all other ordinary passions of *Feare and Sorrow*. Wee properly call that *Dotage*, as *Laurentius* interprets it, *when some principall facultie of the minde, as Imagination, or Reason is corrupted, as all Melancholy persons have*. It is without a Feaver, because the humor is most part colde and dry, contrary to putrefaction. *Feare* and *Sorrow* are the true Characters, and inseparable companions of *Melancholy*, as hereafter shall be declared.[114]

The genus, of which melancholy was a species, was 'dotage' (*delirium*). Its *propria* were the impairment of a principal internal faculty of the mind (such as reason or imagination), and the emotions of fear and sorrow. It was differentiated from frenzy by being without fever; from cramp, palsy and diseases affecting the outward senses (like sight or hearing) by being an impairment of an internal mental faculty; from mania by being an impairment (or depravation) but not destruction of a mental faculty; and from natural emotions of fear and sorrow by being without outward cause. In the second edition of 1624, completing the topical scheme, Burton revised his definition and made fear and sorrow technically non-essential accidents rather than 'true Characters'.[115]

Because of its tangled presentation Burton's definition of melancholy may at first seem unwieldy, but it can easily be summarised as 'a species of *delirium* involving an impairment of a principal internal mental faculty, usually accompanied by groundless fear and sorrow', and was broadly conventional. As we have seen, the classification of melancholy as a species of *delirium* had an ancient heritage, and the other aspects of his definition were the product of an accumulation of medical theories across the centuries. Galen had defined melancholy in the *De locis affectis* as a species of mental disease without fever and producing fear and sorrow, in which he had been followed by Paul of Aegina in the seventh

114 Burton 1621, pp. 46–7; or 1.163.2–17 (1.1.3.1).
115 Burton 1624, p. 30; or 1.163.14–17 (1.1.3.1).

century.[116] In orthodox early modern medical works, definitions of melancholy were in general agreement, and usually involved *delirium*, the absence of fever, and the symptoms of fear and sadness.[117]

We saw above that Burton used Du Laurens's definition of dotage, as the depravation of 'one of the principall faculties of the minde, as imagination or reason', in order to specify that melancholy entailed the corruption of an internal mental faculty.[118] He elaborated on this with discussion of the topic of the 'affected part', which had been made authoritative in medical pathology by Galen's widely read treatise *De locis affectis*. Again, the account outlined in the *Anatomy* was congruent with Hippocratic-Galenic convention, whereby the primary organ affected in melancholy was the brain, though the heart, as the seat of emotions, was sometimes said to be affected secondarily (I.163.21–164.10 [I.I.3.2]),[119] and other bodily organs could also be damaged through sympathy (I.164.12–13, 16–19). More particularly, Burton followed Sassonia and Alberto Bottoni, both of whom had specified that within the brain it was the apprehensive powers of the internal senses (of which the imagination was one) which were directly affected. This performed the task, crucial for a Christian physician, of preserving the essence of the immortal rational soul from the stain of depravation. As Du Laurens had explained, if the rational soul appeared to be touched, this was only through its accidental qualities: the reason could fall into error in melancholy, but only because it was misinformed by a corrupted imagination.[120] As Burton stated his position in the second edition, the depraved imagination in the anterior ventricle of the brain was at the root of melancholic *delirium* (I.164.20–165.6).[121]

116 Galen 1976, III.7, III.10, pp. 83, 93, cited in Ferrand 1990, p. 235; Paul of Aegina 1567, III.14, col. 424 (= Paul of Aegina 1844–7, vol. I, p. 383). The pseudo-Galenic *Definitiones medicae* specified that 'Melancholia passio rationi officiens cum cordis difficultate, & cum nutricatione eorum, quibus maxime vesci delectantur. Gignitur autem sine febre: huic abnoxijs multa bilis, eademque nigra stomachum laedit, adeo, ut vomitus sequatur' (Galen 1528b, fol. 19v (= Galen 1821–33, CXLVII, vol. XIX, p. 416); considered authentic and quoted in Victorius 1574, p. 101).

117 See for example Bright 1586, p. 1; Du Laurens 1599, pp. 86–7; and Mercuriale 1617, I.10, pp. 39–40.

118 See also Platter 1602–3, I.3, vol. I, p. 98 (= Platter, Cole, and Culpeper 1662, p. 27).

119 Hippocrates 1839–61, VI.8.31, vol. V, pp. 354–57, and 1978, pp. 248–9; Manardi 1611, IX.2, pp. 182, 185; Mercuriale 1617, I.10, pp. 41–4.

120 Du Laurens 1599, pp. 74, 82.

121 Burton 1624, p. 31, or I.165.4–6 (I.I.3.2), revising I.164.26–165.4. Similar accounts are in Du Laurens 1599, p. 87; Mercuriale 1617, I.10, pp. 39, 41, 84; and Ferrand 1990, p. 260.

Burton's definition of melancholy was fundamental to the medical theory of the first and second Partitions of the *Anatomy*, but two points required clarification before its basis was complete. The first was the physiological 'matter' of melancholy (I.166.8–168.9 [I.I.3.3]). As the etymology of the disease indicated, its physiology derived its principal characteristics from the humour black bile. This was the case in most of the medical literature from antiquity to early modernity, and the centrality of ideas about black bile – usually considered viscous, earthy, sedimental, cold and dry, and the most noxious of the humours[122] – to theories of the disease of melancholy made the condition an archetypal *exemplum* of a humoral imbalance yielding strong psychological symptoms.[123] When not in excess, black bile had a role to play in the natural functioning of the body, aiding digestion and nourishing bodily parts such as the bones and spleen.[124] There was, however, a second, 'unnatural' kind of black bile which had unequivocally toxic effects, generated out of combusted humours and later known as 'adust melancholy'.[125] In Avicenna's scheme of 'good' and 'bad' humours, the theory of combustion was fused with that of the four humours, unnatural black bile originating from burnt yellow bile, blood, phlegm, or natural black bile. It was therefore possible to speak of natural and unnatural kinds of 'choleric melancholy', 'sanguine melancholy', and 'phlegmatic melancholy', as well as pure melancholy derived from either non-adust or adust black bile. The characteristics of each melancholic condition were understood to be influenced by the humour out of which the adust melancholy had arisen.[126]

Early modern neo-Galenic medical writings generally conformed to this system, and Burton's account was no exception (I.141.18–19 [I.I.2.2], 145.17–20 [I.I.2.4], 166.24–7 [I.I.3.3]). Black bile caused disease either when it was in excess, when it induced a cold and dry distemperature in bodily parts, leaving a deposit of corrupt dregs – when not successfully purged by the spleen – which pervaded the body; or

[122] Galen 1529, fols. 1^r–16^r; Galen 1821–33, II.7, III.3, vol. VII, pp. 202–4, 222, vol. XVI, II.27, pp. 299–301; and Galen 1997, II.4.604, II.6.642–3, III.4.679, pp. 246, 264–5, 281–2. See also Argenterio 1558, p. 158, and Mercuriale 1617, I.10, p. 42.

[123] See Galen 1997, V.788, p. 160. Cf. Aristotle 1936a, pp. 106–7.

[124] Galen 1968, IV.15, V.4, vol. I, pp. 232–5, 255. See also Galen 1963, II.9, pp. 203–15.

[125] Galen 1976, III.9, pp. 88, 90 (cf. Galen 1952, II.9, pp. 209–13); Aëtius 1567, II.2.9, cols. 251–2.

[126] Avicenna 1608, I.I.4.I, vol. I, pp. 22–3, and III.I.4.18, vol. I, p. 489; Bernard of Gordon 1617, II.19, p. 250.

when it was immoderately heated, which not only produced adust black bile but also resulted in dark, noxious vapours rising to the brain, causing fear (in the same manner as external darkness) and other deleterious symptoms.[127] As Burton summarised, black bile caused disease by 'offending' either 'in *Quantity* or *Qualitie*' (I.166.23–4).[128] In his *De anima*, Melanchthon had also described how the mixture of black bile with other humours produced different kinds of melancholic condition.[129] Burton explained along the same lines that the effect differed 'according to the mixture of those naturall humours amongst themselves, or foure unnatural adust humours, as they are diversly tempered and mingled'. When the melancholic mixture was generally cold, the symptoms of insanity were mild, but when hot, 'much madnesse followes with violent actions'. Yellow bile in the melancholic mixture produced furious 'choleric' madness, whereas the presence of blood resulted in excessive gaiety and 'sanguine' laughter (I.166.26–167.2).

The structure of the medical-scientific account of melancholy in the *Anatomy* was completed by the enumeration of the basic species of the disease, first according to the somatic location of the damage effected by black bile, and more extensively, in the third Partition, dealing with 'love melancholy', according to its erotic or religious nature. The traditional division of melancholy along the former lines was into three distinct species, a scheme sometimes said to be derived from Rufus of Ephesus, but made authoritative by Galen in the *De locis affectis* and subsequently found in Byzantine, Arabic, medieval, and early modern medical works including the *Anatomy* (I.169.22–7, 36 [I.I.3.4]).[130] The first was 'head melancholy', involving a local accumulation of black bile in the brain, in either its natural cold and dry forms or its hot and dry adust forms, and accompanied by predominately mental symptoms which depended on the nature of the distemperature. The second, 'melancholy of the whole body', occurred when the bloodstream and

127 See Galen 1528a, fols. 67^{r-v} (= Galen 1821–33, II.7, vol. VII, pp. 202–4) and 1976, III.10, p. 93; Constantinus Africanus 1536, pp. 280–1 (= Ishâq ibn 'Imran and Constantinus Africanus 1977, pp. 108–9); Avicenna 1608, III.I.4.18, vol. I, p. 488.

128 Cf. Lemnius 1576, fols. 142^{v}–143^{r}; Bright 1586, 1–2, 102–3, 161.

129 Melanchthon 1552, sig. K5 (= Melanchthon 1834-60, vol. XIII, p. 85). See also Ficino 1985, VIII.3, p. 158; Paracelsus 1996, p. 180; Bright 1586, pp. 111, 110–16.

130 Rufus of Ephesus 1879, pp. 358–9, discussed by Burton at I.168.17–18, and Galen 1976, III.9, pp. 89–94. See further Oribasius 1567, col. 122; Alexander of Tralles 1567, cols. 162–3 (= Alexander of Tralles 1933–6, vol. II, p. 223); Constantinus Africanus 1536, pp. 284–5 (= Ishâq ibn 'Imran and Constantinus Africanus 1977, pp. 106–7); Avicenna 1608, III.I.4.18, vol. I, p. 489; Du Laurens 1599, pp. 88–9; and Ferrand 1990, p. 236.

consequently all the parts of the body became affected by black bile; it was particularly associated with the dysfunction of the attractive power of the spleen, resulting in mental and somatic symptoms, including a darkening of the skin. In the third, 'hypochondriacal melancholy', the upper abdominal area known as the 'hypochondrium' (comprising the spleen, liver, gall, bladder, and uterus) was said to be affected. The symptoms of this species of melancholy included flatulence and digestive disorders – hence it was sometimes known as 'windy melancholy' – as well as psychological disturbance resulting from dark and cloudy vapours rising to the brain, which, following Galen's account in the *De symptomatum causis* II.7, were understood to have been produced by the heating and evaporation of black bile that had putrefied in the hypochondrium.[131] Before concluding, however, Burton took note of the practical impossibility of the task of disentangling these different species of melancholy, not only from each other, but also from other diseases which were 'so often intermixt' (I.170.3–8). Many reputable ancient and neoteric writers had expressed this kind of opinion.[132]

The theory of love melancholy, to which the third Partition of the *Anatomy* was entirely devoted, also had ancient roots, though its systematic formulation was a medieval accomplishment.[133] Sexual love had a long and venerable philosophical association with both madness and melancholy: it had been categorised as a psychological disease in *Phaedrus* 265a–b, where Plato had distinguished between 'pure' and 'impure' forms of eros, and the literary productions of dramatists and poets from Sophocles to Lucretius and Ovid strongly reinforced the idea of erotic desire as a kind of pathological delirium.[134] But most important for medieval and early modern physicians was Aristotle's account of how 'anger, sexual desire, and certain other passions, actually alter the state of the body, and in some cases even cause madness'.[135] According to the Aristotelian theory of erotic passion, with the sight of a beautiful person

131 See also Galen 1976, III.10, pp. 92–3, and 1997, II.5.615, pp. 251–2; Constantinus Africanus 1536, pp. 280–1 (= Ishâq ibn 'Imran and Constantinus Africanus 1977, pp. 88–9).

132 See Aëtius 1567, II.2.9, cols. 250–1, citing Rufus; Avicenna 1608, III.1.4.19, vol. I, p. 489; Melanchthon 1552, sig. K5 (= Melanchthon 1834–60, vol. XIII, p. 84); Montalto 1614, IV.21, pp. 295–6.

133 The following discussion is especially indebted to Lowes 1914, Beecher and Ciavolella 1990, and Wack 1990.

134 Sophocles 1957, I.446, p. 89; Lucretius 1976, IV.1069, pp. 358–9; Ovid 1979 and 1984, III.33–570, vol. I, pp. 148–61.

135 Aristotle 1934, VII.3.7, pp. 388–91.

the imagination generated a phantasm in the soul, creating a sensible appetite capable of overpowering the rational faculties, heating and expanding the πνεῦμα mediating body and soul, and thereby distorting perception and cognition.[136] This broadly correlated with patristic accounts, based on Platonic psychology, which attributed to original sin the pathological incapacity of the rational powers of the soul, unaided by Christ, to overcome sexual love (and indeed all its passions).[137]

The pathological species of love melancholy, however, had not been designated in ancient Greek or Roman medicine.[138] It was in fact Rhazes, Haly Abbas, and Avicenna who merged the ideas of inordinate erotic desire as madness, and madness as melancholy, preparing the ground for the subsequent conflation of love melancholy with other forms of melancholy. In Latin commentaries on these authors, this species of melancholy assumed the name *amor hereos*.[139] For the detailed explanation of the condition, medical writers such as Arnald of Villanova, Bernard of Gordon, and Dino del Garbo employed a combination of Aristotelian psychology and Galenic physiology to show how erotic desire upset the temperamental balance of the body and soul, and how, as Arnald put it, 'violent and obsessive cogitation upon the object of desire' resulted in the corruption of the perceptual faculties of the brain. In brief, *amor hereos* was a condition in which the phantasm – generated by the imagination (or *phantasia*) from a visual sense image or visual *species* received by the eye – of the object of desire became permanently fixed in the internal senses of imagination and memory, obsessively focusing all conscious activity on and around this phantasm, and eventually causing a general mental and physical breakdown.[140] The phantasm of the desired object (the image of a 'good' fixed in the mind, as opposed to a real object deemed 'good' by the faculty of estimation) became the only goal present to the consciousness of the lover, who was thus gripped by a powerful form of melancholic delirium manifested by the unending

136 Aristotle 1934, IX.4.4–V.2, pp. 532–9; Aristotle 1961, II.4, III.3, pp. 140–1, 230–1; Aristotle 1936b, I.1, II.4, III.10, pp. 14–17, 84–95, 190–1. Cf. Aristotle 1923, II.4, pp. 118–19.

137 See Clement of Alexandria 1867–9, II.20, vol. II, pp. 60–71; cf. Aquinas 1952–62, I.2.82.3, vol. I, pp. 377–8.

138 But see Galen 1976, VI.5, p. 184, and Aretaeus 1856, p. 300.

139 Avicenna 1608, III.1.4.23, vol. I, p. 494; Constantinus Africanus 1536, I.20, p. 18. See Lowes 1914, and Beecher and Ciavolella 1990, pp. 70–2, 75–6.

140 Arnald of Villanova 1585, cols. 1525–6; Bernard of Gordon 1617, II.20, p. 255; Valesco da Taranta 1516, fol. 19^r.

hallucinatory pursuit of an image lodged inside the brain.[141] This fixation was known as the *complexio venerea*, and became the basis of an account of erotic delirium which characterised this species of melancholy in medieval medical writings. The result was that its symptomatology and therapy became, in many cases, almost identical with those of melancholy traditionally conceived.[142]

Medieval writers had also Christianised the Arabic theory by associating the condition with the impure form of desire subsequent to the Fall (*amor concupiscentiae*), which patristic authorities had contrasted with the chaste prelapsarian love accessible to humanity only through Christ (*amor amicitiae*).[143] Subsequently the same division was elaborated by Leone Ebreo and Ficino in the Platonic terminology of the 'two Venuses' (*Philebus* 186a–b) – one earthly, the other heavenly – which structured the expansive 'Eros and Anteros' literary tradition exemplified by Giovan Battista Fregoso's *Anteros, sive tractatus contra amorem* (1496).[144] This perspective tallied with the Augustinian valuation of *caritas* – the chaste love that flowed from human *amor Dei* – as the spiritual basis of the Christian community in this world,[145] which in turn provided theologians and physicians with authoritative means of distinguishing between love that was virtuous and healthy and that which was sinful and pathological. When the *quaestio* 'An amor sit morbus?' was affirmatively determined at Oxford in 1620, then, it was in the faculty of medicine, not theology.[146]

By the early seventeenth century, it had become commonplace in learned medical circles to acknowledge and discuss the species of love melancholy. Indeed, the disease received lengthy analysis by the physician Jacques Ferrand in his *Traité de l'essence et guérison de l'amour ou melancholie erotique* (1610), which was revised in 1623 under the title of *De la maladie d'amour ou melancholie erotique*, and issued in 1640 in English translation by Edmund Chilmead of Christ Church. Like Ferrand, in the third Partition of the *Anatomy* Burton offered the account of love melancholy which fused Aristotelian and Galenic with patristic and Neoplatonic doctrines. As in the first Partition, he first established

141 Arnald of Villanova 1585, cols. 1525–6; le Chapelain 1982, II.8.48, pp. 284–5.
142 See Constantinus Africanus 1536, I.20, p. 18, and le Chapelain 1982, III.60, pp. 304–5.
143 See Bernard of Gordon 1617, II.20, p. 257; cf. Avicenna 1608, III.1.4.23, vol. I, p. 494.
144 See Nelson 1958, pp. 78–80; Beecher and Ciavolella 1990, pp. 11, 91–2; Wack 1986; and Cherchi 1994.
145 Augustine 1984, XIV.9, pp. 561–6, esp. 563–4.
146 See Sinclair 1974, p. 372.

his Galenic credentials with the topics of definition and affected part, defining love in general as 'a desire of enjoying that which is good and faire' (3.9.20–1 [3.1.1.2]), and noting that it affected not only the heart, but also the rational faculties in the brain and the appetitive faculties in the liver (3.16.14–22 [3.1.2.1]). This definition was then elaborated with the Neoplatonic division between the 'two Venuses', which combined classical ideals of beauty with Christian ideas of spiritual and moral perfection to denounce 'vulgar', selfish, earthly love.[147] The structure of his inquiry also incorporated two further *divisiones* taken from the Neoplatonist Leone: the first was a tripartition of love into natural, sensible, and rational kinds; and the second was a further Aristotelian subdivision of rational love (including the human love with which he was concerned [3.16.9–10 (3.1.1.2)]) relating to its objects as they were '*Utile, Jucundum, Honestum*, Profitable, Pleasant, Honest' (3.16.24–5 [3.1.2.1]). In the case of the first two categories of objects, Burton wrote, excessive love was vicious and so caused melancholy (3.17.8–22.24), and the same ensued when love attracted by honest objects was defective (3.28.11–12 [3.1.2.3]). More specifically, '*Heroicall*, or Love melancholy' related to excessive desire for the subdivision of pleasant objects of 'rational' love (3.20.27–8; 3.22.18–20 [3.1.2.2]). By contrast, the Christian virtue of charity, a properly ordered and psychologically healthy love whose object was 'compounded of all these three', was further distinguished from pagan friendship on the grounds that the latter did not 'proceed from a sanctified spirit . . . and a reference to God' (3.29.11–12, 23–4 [3.1.3.1]), and described in proper Augustinian fashion as 'true love indeed, the cause of all good to mortall men, that reconciles all creatures, and glewes them together in perpetuall amity and firme league' (3.31.30–2).

In this part of the book, Burton displayed a far larger degree of independence from orthodox medical theory than in the first two Partitions, choosing to give priority to poetic authorities in accordance with the ancient commonplace that poets were experts on the subject (3.193.3 [3.2.3.1]).[148] This gave his discussion a distinctly lighter and even non-medical appearance. Such independence was also marked by his innovative designation of the passion of jealousy as 'a bastard branch, or kinde of Love Melancholy' (3.273.15–16 [3.3.1.1]). Jealousy had occupied a prominent position in conventional medical discussions – Ferrand,

[147] See 3.10.17–21, 3.11.33–12.14 (3.1.2.1); 3.22.30–1 (3.1.2.3); 3.39.10–12 (3.2.1.1); 3.226.23–5 (3.2.5.3). Cf. Ferrand 1990, p. 225.

[148] See, for example, Valesco da Taranta 1516, fol. 19v.

for example, had devoted a chapter to the question of 'Whether jealousy is a diagnostic sign of love melancholy'[149] – but Burton's reasoning here derived from the idea that it was a necessary but destructive accompaniment of love. Here he drew upon a debate conducted in Italian Neoplatonic and Petrarchan revivalist circles as to whether jealousy could coexist with love, and explicitly followed Benedetto Varchi and Torquato Tasso in insisting on their inseparability (3.273.13–14).[150] His account then followed the analytic-topical pattern found throughout the *Anatomy*, from definitions (3.273.23–30), equivocations (3.274.1–277.20), and different kinds and objects affected (3.277.25–280.18), to causes, symptoms, prognostics, and cures. This was in many respects a recapitulation of his treatment of *amor hereos*, essentially based on the neo-Galenic conception of the destructive effects of excessive passions on the body and mind.

The last type of melancholy Burton identified in the final Section of the *Anatomy* was religious. Again, its theory had classical roots in the Greek classification of melancholy as a species of madness, which permitted its association in the first place with the Platonic idea of divine fury, and subsequently with notions of supernatural inspiration and demonic interference.[151] Because the principal symptoms of melancholy were fear and sorrow, the theory of the disease also became intertwined with medieval teachings concerning spiritual despair drawn from the patristic theory of *acedia*.[152] However, as Burton indicated at the beginning of the Section, his formal designation of religious melancholy as a disease with distinctive diagnostics and therapeutics was contentious and largely innovatory, having only very recent general parallels in the writings of Sassonia and Felix Platter (3.330.6–331.12 [3.4.1.1]). As in the analysis of love melancholy, detailed physiological and medical-psychological explanations of the processes involved in religious melancholy are generally conspicuous by their absence.[153] The same goes for medical authorities: Avicenna received only two mentions in the Section, neither of which referred to his medical teachings

149 Ferrand 1990, pp. 301–2.

150 See Cherchi 1992, pp. 123–32. Cf. le Chapelain 1982, 1.371–400, pp. 146ff. and Ferrand 1990, p. 301.

151 Amongst the important *loci* are Aretaeus 1856, pp. 299, 304 and Plato 1966, 464–5 (244a–b). For discussion see Heyd 1995 and Brann 2002.

152 See Wenzel 1967, esp. pp. 30–1, 47–67, 186, 191–4; and Brann 2002, pp. 52–6, 142–4, 223–4.

153 For some exceptions see 3.330.23–6 (3.4.1.1); 3.387.39–388.30 (3.4.1.3); 3.411.24–29 (3.4.2.3); and 433.11–34 (3.4.2.6).

(3.330.15; 370.6–15 [3.4.1.3]). Burton's approach here instead derived from the philosophical and theological discussion of love at the beginning of the third Partition, and specifically from his striking insistence that the human propensity towards the disease in general was caused by a defect of charity (3.33.14–38.20 [3.1.3.1]).

Religious melancholy was the subspecies of love melancholy in which the human desire naturally attracted by the beauty of the divinity had become pathologically defective or perverted (3.332.5–337.7 [3.4.1.1]). It was thus constituted in fundamentally Augustinian psychological terms as a corruption of *amor Dei*, and the charity that flowed from it, into *amor sui*. Whereas those who were 'truely enamored' were motivated by 'the love of God himselfe', Burton said that this subspecies of the disease was prevalent because 'We love the world too much: God too little, our neighbour not at all, or for our owne ends' (3.337.3–12). He then initiated a further division – the religious-political implications of which we shall explore in chapter four – by denoting in Aristotelian (or perhaps Theophrastan) fashion the 'two extreames of *Excesse* and *Defect*', which manifested themselves respectively in 'Superstition' and 'Impiety', or in 'Idolatry and Atheisme' (3.337.24–7). He was careful to clarify that he did not mean that there could be 'any excesse of divine worship or love of God', but rather that it was possible to be 'zealous without knowledge, and too sollicitous about that which is not necessary' (3.337.27–32).

Before proceeding, we should note two difficulties that remained in the early modern medical conception of melancholy. The first is the very fine and sometimes non-existent distinction between the melancholic complexion and the melancholic disease. In theory, the complexion was innate whereas the disease was adventitious, and the two also differed in the degree of symptomatic affliction. But the close associations between them derived not only from the identity of their dominant psychological symptoms (i.e. fear and sadness), but also from the fact that the melancholic by temperament was predisposed to the disease through a constitutional preponderance of black bile in the body. In part, this was because in the authoritative writings of Galen the disease of melancholy was not properly distinguished from the effects of an excess of black bile, but in general it is easy to see that the conception of the natural toxicity of the humour in medical writings eroded the boundary between the theoretically healthy 'stable imbalance' of a complexion and the condition of disease. Although Du Laurens was at pains to uphold the distinction between those who had healthy 'melancholike constitutions' and those who were truly 'sicke, and such as are pained with the grief which men call melancholie',[154] Burton apparently confused the two by describing melancholy in 'Habit' as 'a Chronicke or continuate disease, a setled humour' (I.139.10–11 [I.I.I.5]).

A second point of difficulty derived from the association of melancholy and madness. Melancholy was commonly classified as a species of *delirium*, but the characteristics of the different species of this genus overlapped. In antiquity, the belief that black bile was at the source of insanity led to the strong association of melancholy and mania. For Galen, the humour could cause severe delusion by attacking the central nervous system.[155] In Aretaeus's description of mania, some patients were said to be more 'melancholic' (μελαγχολικοι), and others more 'deranged' (ἐκμαίνουται); he concluded that 'melancholy is the commencement and a part of mania'.[156] Alexander of Tralles had stated that 'in effect, mania is nothing other than an exaggeration of the melancholic state taken to an extreme savagery', and Avicenna had argued that when the symptoms of melancholy included violence and convulsions the disease changed its character and was properly called mania.[157] Some ancient authors dissolved the distinction between melancholy and mania, or madness generally, altogether. Cicero translated μελαγχολία as *furor* on the grounds that the latter term connoted psychic convulsion better than 'atrabiliousness', and in his *De medicina* Celsus described melancholy as 'a kind of mania' (*genus insaniae*).[158] Melancholy had also been directly associated in the Hippocratic *corpus* with epilepsy and other nervous diseases like apoplexy, mania, and blindness.[159]

This confusion of melancholy and madness – in its different species, or in general – was noted by several early modern commentators.[160] Typically, though, the problem was given its most extensive analysis by

[154] Du Laurens 1599, pp. 84–6. See also Platter 1602–3, I.3, vol. I, pp. 118–20 (= Platter, Cole, and Culpeper 1662, pp. 32–3).
[155] Galen 1976, III.9, pp. 86–8.
[156] Aretaeus 1856, p. 299.
[157] Alexander of Tralles 1567, col. 165 (= Alexander of Tralles 1933–6, vol. II, p. 226); Avicenna 1608, III.I.4.18, vol. I, p. 488: 'Quumque melancholia componitur cum rixa, & saltu, & [scintillis,] permutantur, & nominatur mania.'
[158] Cicero 1927, III.5.11, pp. 236–9; Celsus 1953–61, III.18.17, vol. I, p. 299.
[159] Hippocrates 1839–61, VI.8.31, vol. V, pp. 354–7, discussed in Constantinus Africanus 1536, pp. 289–90 (= Ishâq ibn 'Imran and Constantinus Africanus 1977, pp. 130–3); and Hippocrates 1978, VI.56, p. 231. See also Galen 1976, III.9, pp. 86–8.
[160] Altomari 1559, I.7, p. 74; Du Laurens 1599, p. 88; Mercuriale 1617, I.10, pp. 43–44, and I.16, p. 84; Ferrand 1990, pp. 232, 235, 264.

Burton, who noted that '*Madnesse, Phrensie*, and *Melancholy* are confounded by *Celsus*, and many Writers'. 'Others', he continued,

> ...leave out *Phrensie*, and make *Madnesse* and *Melancholy* but one Disease, which *Jason Pratensis* especially labours, and that they differ onely *secundùm majus* or *minus*, in quantity alone, the one being a degree to the other, and both proceeding from one cause. They differ *Intenso & remisso gradu*, saith *Gordonius*, as the humor is intended or remitted. Of the same minde is *Areteus*, *Alexander Trallianus*, *Guianerius*, *Savanarola*, *Heurnius*, and *Galen* himselfe writes promiscuously of them both, by reason of their affinity, but most of our neotericks doe handle them apart, whom I will follow in this treatise. (I.132.21–30 [I.I.I.4]; cf. I.168.13–15 [I.I.3.4])

Later in the same Subsection, however, he effaced the distinction in describing 'demoniacall ... obsession' as 'the last kinde of madnesse or melancholy' (I.135.31–2). As we shall see in the following chapter, he did not always keep his promises to the reader, in this case for good reason.

CAUSES, SYMPTOMS, PROGNOSTICS, CURES

Having defined melancholy and located it in the scheme of human anatomy and pathology, Burton continued by implementing the received Hippocratic-Galenic division of disease into causes, symptoms, prognostics, and cures throughout the first and second Partitions. To commence his analysis of causes, he made the claim to be using the method made authoritative by Galen, according to whom in the *De methodo medendi* 'those cures must be unperfect, lame, and to no purpose, wherein the causes have not first beene searched' (I.171.16–19 [I.2.I.I]). The investigation of causes was essential to Galenic diagnosis,[161] and emphasis on the necessity of their knowledge (even on a conjectural basis) to successful treatment was the hallmark of neo-Galenic rationalism. To elaborate this approach, Burton then quoted Fernel – for whom knowledge of causes was '*a kinde of necessity*' to the demonstrative scientific method required by medicine and all natural science[162] – and contrasted the method of the 'Empericks' which 'may ease, and sometimes helpe, but not throughly roote out' disease (I.171.22–3). Burton was well aware that the Empirical neglect of reasoning was inimical to Galenic method, and the Methodical disregard

[161] Galen 1821–33, I.I, vol. XI, pp. 1–6.

[162] Fernel 1567, I.II, p. 185: 'ita & medicis, qui omnia in corporis commoditatem usúmque referunt, in primis necessaria est causarum quæ morbos effecerunt observatio, sine neque morbos præcavere curare licet'.

of experience was considered equally foolhardy. Accordingly, he had Galen's injunction confirmed by 'the common experience of others' (1.171.17–18), implying that his method would be based on an authentically Galenic combination of rational theory (λόγος) and experience (εμπειρία) gained from clinical observation.

Also Galenic was Burton's enumeration of a multiplicity of causal factors involved in diagnosis, signalled by his warning of the 'variety' of causes (1.171.26), but best illustrated by the second and third parts of the 'Synopsis of the first Partition'. For Galen, the causes of health or disease were 'natural', 'non-natural', or 'counter-natural'.[163] In orthodox early modern medical literature, 'natural' causes in the body (*res naturales*) were generally seven, comprising the elements, the complexions, the humours, the spirits and natural heat, the faculties and functions, and the generative capability. The 'non-naturals' (*res non naturales*) were six, comprising the group of external factors we noted above: diet, retention and evacuation, climate, exercise, sleeping and waking, and the passions of the soul. 'Counter-natural' causes were broadly translated as 'supernatural' or 'preternatural' causes. Burton initially followed this scheme, progressing 'downwards' from supernatural (1.171.13–199.11 [1.2.1.1–1.2.1.3]) to natural (1.199.12–210.23 [1.2.1.4–1.2.1.6]) and then non-natural causes (1.211.1–327.26 [1.2.2.1–1.2.3.15]).[164] Subsequently, he followed the Galenic sequence of causes, from the immediate or predisposing cause (*causa evidens*), through the inducing cause (*causa antecedens*), to the conjunctive cause (*causa continens*). Although the use of Aristotelian causal terminology was not rigorous in the *Anatomy*,[165] these were divided into two groups, being evident and accidental causes (1.327.27–371.31 [1.2.4.1–1.2.4.7]) and antecedent or continent causes (1.372.1–376.18 [1.2.5.1–1.2.5.2]).

In his symptomatology and analysis of prognostics Burton did not have recourse to this technical jargon, but he retained a similar degree of methodological awareness and adherence to learned medical tradition. According to the sixth book of the Hippocratic *Epidemics*, close scrutiny of the signs of disease in the patient, involving the noting of discordances and concordances amongst these until the essential symptoms of the condition could be reliably distinguished, was integral to a successful diagnostic judgement.[166] In Hippocratic and Galenic medicine, the

[163] Siegel 1973, pp. 220–30.

[164] Cf. 1.211.8–9, 19–23 (1.2.2.1), and Bright 1586, p. 25.

[165] See, for example, 1.203.20, 245.22. Cf. Argenterio 1558, pp. 94–101.

[166] Hippocrates 1839–61, VI.3.12, vol. V, pp. 298–9.

diagnostic process initiated by symptomatology was completed by prognosis, and so was seen to be essential to the τέχνη of the physician.[167] The investigation of prognostics had been defined by the foundational Hippocratic *Prognostics* as the contemplation of signs predictive of the future course of disease, addressing its length and progress towards either recovery or death.[168] Both symptomatology and prognostication, therefore, were dependent on the physician's interpretation of a diversity of pathological signs and their subsequent integration into an orderly scheme via rational method.

At the beginning of his analysis of symptoms of melancholy, Burton emphasised the difficulty of his enterprise in the terms of the Hippocratic-Galenic tradition, noting the semiological chaos presented by this disease, which hindered the physician's task of making clear-cut diagnostic distinctions. Melancholy, he wrote, created a 'diversity of melancholy signes . . . as the causes are diverse, so must the signes be, almost infinite' (1.381.22–5 [1.3.1.1]). Nevertheless, he continued the attempt to impose order by implementing a division of somatic and mental symptoms, and within this, a further division of general and particular symptoms (1.381.15; 30–31). Following a tradition established in the medical literature by Galen's *De symptomatum causis*, he ended the Section with an analysis of their immediate physiological and psychological causes (1.418.18–428.7 [1.3.3.1]). In his survey of prognostic signs, the division was between a collection of 'good' signs presaging a return to health, and a host of 'bad' ones leading to madness or death (1.428.11 [1.4.1.1]). Insofar as it here consisted of the ordering of theoretically infinite materials, his symptomological and prognosticative 'art' was clearly the production of *de infinitis finita scientia*.

Burton's presentation of treatments for melancholy was methodically 'reduced' in the same way, the diversity of 'severall' cures being grouped according to the traditional Greek scheme of dietetics (or regimen), pharmacy, and surgery (2.18.5–25 [2.1.4.3]).[169] The theoretical principles underpinning his discussion of these kinds of cure were, once again, those of Galenic medicine, in which the goal of the study of symptoms and prognostics was the understanding of appropriate medical therapy.[170]

167 See Galen 1969, VII.4, p. 43.

168 Hippocrates 1978, pp. 170, 185. For a commentary see Cardano 1663, vol. VIII, pp. 581–806.

169 See Celsus 1953-61, vol. I, pp. 6–7; Galen 1997, XXIV. 848–9, XXXIII.869–70, pp. 73, 84; and Avicenna 1608, I.4.1.1, vol. I. p. 195.

170 Galen 1976, II.10, p. 67, and VI.5, p. 182.

It was a characteristic feature of this tradition, derived from the theoretical basis of the Hippocratic *corpus* and the logical treatises of Galen, that medical treatment should be based on demonstrable reason.[171] More specifically, the particularities of therapy, being rooted in the theory of the elemental qualities and humoral complexions, were determined by the principle that *contraria contrariis curantur.*[172] As Galen summarised in the *Ars medica*, the cure of disease depended on the removal or counteraction of the pathological cause, so 'the fundamental and general aim of healing is to introduce the opposite of that which is to be destroyed'.[173]

The identification of the primary cause of melancholy with a view to its removal by means of treatment by contraries was also required by Rufus of Ephesus, and subsequently in the overwhelming majority of medical literature on the disease.[174] Following this tradition, Burton's therapeutic recommendations generally involved the counteraction of the cooling and drying effects of black bile by means of various techniques to warm and moisten the body, thereby offsetting the pathogenic humoral disequilibrium of melancholy. In fact, his text was specifically organised to facilitate the removal of regimental pathological causes, the structure of the survey of dietetic cures directly mirroring that of his analysis of 'non-natural' causes. However, despite the broad Galenic rationalism of his detailed account of treatments, for him this approach provided a necessary but not sufficient basis for an effective cure, which (like that of Cardano) required the patient to have confidence in the physician (2.14.18–19; 15.23–4 [2.1.4.2]). This psychological 'softening' of Galenic rationalism was derived from the Hippocratic principle of the necessity of the active role of the patient in successful therapy, and, insofar as confidence related to the condition of the soul, it had later been formally included in the category of 'non-natural' factors that could determine health or sickness.[175]

If these therapeutic axioms are clear, however, the notion of a cured condition is less so. For although in Galenic therapeutic terms a 'cure' consisted of the destruction of a pathological cause through the manipulation of the bodily qualities, the physiological theory of humoral

[171] Hippocrates 1839–61, vol. VI, pp. 26–7.

[172] See Hippocrates 1978, II.22, p. 209; Galen 1991, II.4.17, p. 52, and 1997, I.2.514–15, p. 204. For a typical restatement see Lemnius 1576, fol. 47r.

[173] Galen 1997, XXVIII.380, p. 381. See also ibid., IX.329–30, p. 356.

[174] Rufus of Ephesus 1879, pp. 457–9; cf. Bright 1586, pp. 242–5.

[175] Hippocrates 1978, I.11, p. 94; I.1, p. 206. See Maclean 2002, p. 96.

complexions did not allow for the real existence of a perfectly balanced and healthy state. Whether a patient was technically 'cured' in the terms of ancient and early modern medicine, then, depended not on his or her self-evident return to a condition of perfect health, but rather on the recognisable eradication of the specific functional impairment which defined the disease – with the likely possibility of a relapse due to one's humoral complexion, or even the continued existence of another pathological condition.[176] Indeed, in neo-Galenic medicine there was also an intermediate category, known as the *neutrum*, that lay between sickness and health – one might be partly healthy and partly sick, for example, or sometimes healthy and sometimes sick.[177] This had serious implications for the treatment of melancholy, which, being addressed to a disease directly derived from a complexion, was typically geared towards temporary alleviation through regimen rather than permanent and absolute 'cure' in the modern sense of the word. Here was one reason why Burton was reluctant to present any medical measures as permanent remedies for melancholy, however effective they may have been in the short term. As he wrote, medicine 'must needs ease, if not quite cure' the disease (2.266.2 [2.5.3.2]). It was also why, at the end of the book, he exhorted those with a propensity to melancholy to continual vigilance over their health (3.445.33–446.5 [3.4.2.6]).

Turning from method to content, the account presented in the *Anatomy* fell squarely within the orthodox Latinate medical tradition that predominated in continental and English university medical circles of the era. Although much of the substance of Burton's medical analysis can be easily found in other neo-Galenic works, it is notable in two related respects: first, for its attentiveness to the interaction of physiology and psychology in every part of the disease, from causes to cures; and second, for its periodic but very strong emphasis upon the moral aspect of this interaction.

The first of these is most apparent in Burton's detailed delineation of the processes in melancholy whereby psychological disturbance could be provoked by somatic factors. Black bile was the most important material cause, but other diseases and localised distemperatures could also lead to melancholy (1.373.23–376.14 [1.2.5.1]).[178] In his account of love melancholy, physiological stimuli to erotic desire, such as the natural

[176] See Siraisi 1990a, pp. 136–7, 1997, p. 35, and 2001, pp. 182–3; Wear 1995, p. 173.
[177] For a study see Joutsivuo 1999.
[178] See Hippocrates 1839–61, VI.8.31, vol. V, pp. 354–7, and 1978, VI.56, p. 231; and Mercuriale 1617, I.10, p. 45.

'temperature and complexion' or the non-natural excessive retention of seed, were classed as secondary or predisposing causes (3.59.24; 60.25–32 [3.2.2.1]).[179] As well as being causes of melancholy, apparently groundless fear and sorrow were its most prominent symptoms,[180] and Burton added an innovative gloss to the traditional account whereby sorrow and melancholy 'beget one another and tread in a ring' (1.256.19–21 [1.2.3.4]). In his explanation, which supplemented that of Galen in *De symptomatum causis* II.7 with its elaboration by later commentators, the passions of fear and sadness were produced by noxious fumes rising out of black bile, affecting the heart by darkening the vital spirits, and disturbing the mental faculties by obscuring the animal spirits in the brain (1.418.26–419.27 [1.3.3.1]).[181] Stemming from fear, sorrow, and damaged mental faculties was a host of what could now be described as paranoid emotional states: fear of death, suspiciousness, timidity, misanthropy, and suicidal tendencies (1.385.4–395.17 [1.3.1.2]).[182] The peculiar irritability of melancholics' imaginations made them prone to psychosomatic disease (1.387.3–24; 387.36–388.3), to oscillation between extreme states of joy and sadness, and to impaired judgement and hallucinations (1.391.18–393.31; 402.7–403.9; 3.148.9–19 [3.2.3.1]).[183] Another symptom was licentiousness, since, as well as being stimulated by the overactive imagination, the sexual appetite was 'tickled' by the hot vapours released by adust black bile (1.382.15 [1.3.1.1]; 420.25 [1.3.3.1]).[184]

A potentially contradictory set of mental symptoms with a material basis stemmed from the tension between the widely discussed pseudo-Aristotelian theory of genial melancholy (which I shall revisit later in this chapter) and the Galenic emphasis on the damage wrought on the brain's

179 See Galen 1976, VI.5, VI.6, pp. 184–5, 197; Bright 1586, pp. 80ff.; Huarte Navarro 1594, pp. 142–3; Mercuriale 1617, I.10, p. 45; Ferrand 1990, p. 248.

180 Hippocrates 1978, VI.23, p. 229, cited in Galen 1976, III.10, p. 93. The ambiguity of *Aphorisms* VI.23 was pointed out in Cardano 1663, vol. VIII, p. 491; but cf. Avicenna 1608, I.2.1.1, vol. I, p. 77.

181 Galen 1821–33, II.7, vol. VII, p. 202. For later elaborations see Bright 1586, pp. 100–4, 107–8, 161, and Mercuriale 1617, I.10, pp. 40–1, 48–9.

182 See Rufus of Ephesus 1879, pp. 455–6; Galen 1821–33, III.1, vol. XVIIa, p. 213, and 1976, III.10, p. 93; Avicenna 1608, III.1.4.19, vol. I, pp. 489–90; Montalto 1614, IV.21, p. 293.

183 See Rufus of Ephesus 1879, p. 355; Aristotle 1934, VII.7, pp. 416–17, and 1957, XXX.1, pp. 160–9; Galen 1976, III.10, p. 93; Constantinus Africanus 1536, pp. 288–9 (= Ishâq ibn 'Imran and Constantinus Africanus 1977, pp. 124–9); Alexander of Tralles 1567, col. 165 (= Alexander of Tralles 1933–6, vol. 2, pp. 230–1); Ferrand 1990, pp. 269, 278–9.

184 See Ferrand 1990, pp. 250–1.

functions by black bile.[185] Citing Dürer's *Melencolia I*, Burton wrote that melancholics were 'of a deepe reach, excellent apprehension, judicious, wise and witty'; but qualified this by adding that though they were 'of profound judgement in some things . . . in others, *non rectè judicant inquieti*' (1.391.21–8 [1.3.1.2]; cf. 1.383.3–4 [1.3.1.1], 400.9–16 [1.3.1.3]).[186] Elsewhere, he referred to Du Laurens's interpretation of the pseudo-Aristotelian *Problems* XXX.1, where the symptom of prophetic ability or 'melancholic inspiration' caused by black bile had been authoritatively asserted (1.400.10–16 [1.3.1.3]; cf. 1.427.19–428.7 [1.3.3.1]).[187] Many of the symptoms of love melancholy also exemplified the influence of the body on the soul, particularly those associated with the *complexio venerea*. These included an exclusive focusing of attention on the object of desire (3.154.7–9; 156.15 [3.2.3.1]), mental alienation (3.160.16), deranged and deluded perception of the perfect beauty of the object (3.164.3–170.9), and excessive loquaciousness about this beauty (3.168.25–169.7).

A large proportion of the therapies for melancholy were devised to counteract the physiological and psychological effects of black bile. Dietetic or regimental therapies, Burton recorded, 'comprehend those six non-naturall things' (2.19.5 [2.2.1.1]), and typically involved the manipulation of the primary qualities. Since the condition usually involved a cold and dry distemperature, as Giovanni Manardi had summarised the principle, it 'therefore requires treatment with heat and moisture'[188] effected by methods such as temperate sleep, exercise, or bathing.[189] Melancholic passions could also be tranquillised, and fixed ideas dispersed, by evacuative coitus – a therapy that had long been prescribed for erotic melancholy to counteract the overabundance of seed and displace the phantasm of the desired object from the memory

[185] But see the association of dryness with intelligence in Galen 1821–33, III.1, vol. XVIIa, p. 213, and 1997, IV.781–2, V.786–7, pp. 156–7, 159; cf. Burton's remark at 1.422.3–4. For reconciliations see Ficino 1576, I.5, p. 498; Lemnius 1576, fol. 148r; Huarte 1594, pp. 59, 84–5; Mercuriale 1617, I.10, p. 40; and Burton's approach at 1.421.27–8 (1.3.3.1).

[186] See Aristotle 1936b, pp. 310–11, cited in Mercuriale 1617, I.10, p. 48.

[187] See Aristotle 1957, XXX.1, pp. 162–3; Rufus of Ephesus 1879, p. 456; Ficino 2001–, XIII.2, vol. IV, pp. 162–5; Agrippa 1533, I.60, p. 78; Huarte Navarro 1594, p. 98; Mercuriale 1617, I.10, pp. 46–7, 49.

[188] Manardi 1611, IX.2, XVII.1, pp. 185, 316–18: 'Facta igitur egritudo calidis humidis indiget.'

[189] Galen 1976, III.10, p. 94; Constantinus Africanus 1536, p. 293 (= Ishâq ibn 'Imran and Constantinus Africanus 1977, p. 184); Avicenna 1608, III.1.4.20, III.1.4.24, vol. I, pp. 490, 494; Arnald of Villanova 1585, col. 1531; Hippocrates 1525, pp. 693, 695; Du Laurens 1599, pp. 106, 114–16; Mercuriale 1617, I.10, p. 54.

(2.28.3–33.4 [2.2.2.1]; 3.242.21–243.21 [3.2.5.5]).[190] Pharmaceutical remedies for the disease generally worked either by modifying the qualitative somatic disposition – the function of humectant alteratives – or by decreasing the quantity of the offending humour – effected by 'diminutives', the most celebrated and dangerous of which was black hellebore (2.231.1–235.7 [2.4.2.2]; 241.11–16 [2.5.1.3]).[191] When all else failed, the perilous diminutive surgical therapy of phlebotomy removed black bile directly from the bloodstream (2.237.1–33 [2.4.3.1]).[192] This was also appropriate for the most serious cases of love melancholy, as it quelled the surge of blood and animal spirits which accompanied excessive desire (3.206.21–30 [3.2.5.1]).

Burton paid close attention to the ways in which the movements of the soul altered the body. This is apparent in his lengthy discussion of the final non-natural cause, the passions of the soul (1.246.18–327.26 [1.2.3.1–1.2.3.15]), which adhered to the Aristotelian principles of medieval faculty psychology and the neo-Galenic idea that the emotions aided or impaired the humoral balance by affecting the spirits. Hence the inherently unreliable imagination, 'mis-conceaving or amplifying' sense-data (1.249.6 [1.2.3.1]), distorted perception, exacerbated passions, and disturbed the spirits and humours (1.249.12–31). The emotions most responsible for causing melancholy – in accordance with the Hippocratic *Aphorisms* VI.23, which dominated early modern medical coverage of this question – were sorrow and fear, which cooled and dried the body and particularly the brain (1.257.13–260.13 [1.2.3.4–1.2.3.5]).[193] Other passions such as shame, 'immoderate pleasures', and general discontents and anxiety, as well as factors that induced passions such as 'Terrors and Affrights' (1.333.5–12 [1.2.4.3]) and poverty (1.350.2–3; 354.22 [1.2.4.6]), could also cause melancholy by similar means, since they ultimately led to misery and fear (1.261.1–268.18 [1.2.3.6–1.2.3.8]).[194] By sending the spirits rushing outwards from the heart, immoderate anger could also lead to melancholy (1.268.21–2, 25–6 [1.2.3.9]). In the 'Digression of the Misery of Schollers' Burton also famously expounded

[190] See Lucretius 1975, IV.1068–72, pp. 358–9; Rhazes 1544, IX.11, pp. 354–5; Bernard of Gordon 1617, II.20, pp. 258–9; Ficino 1576, III.11, pp. 544–5.

[191] Rufus of Ephesus 1879, pp. 323–5, 359–60, 387–8, 457–8; Avicenna 1608, III.1.4.20, vol. I, pp. 491–2.

[192] Rufus of Ephesus 1879, p. 358; Galen 1976, III.10, pp. 90–1; Avicenna 1608, III.1.4.24, vol. I, p. 494; Du Laurens 1599, pp. 123–4.

[193] Hippocrates 1978, p. 229. See also Rufus of Ephesus 1879, pp. 455–6; Celsus 1953–61, II.7.19, vol. I, p. 125; Huarte Navarro 1594, p. 59; Ferrand 1990, p. 248.

[194] See Galen 1976, III.7, pp. 82–4, and Mercuriale 1617, I.10, p. 45.

the theory that excessive love of learning caused the disease, drawing on the idea – traceable to the Hippocratic *corpus* and the *Timaeus* but influentially elaborated by Ficino – that mental exertion consumed the animal and vital spirits, cooling the blood and rendering body and brain melancholic (1.302–304.2 [1.2.3.15]).[195] He also noted that astrological factors as well as idleness and solitude were at work in this syndrome (1.303.1–2, 21–2; cf. 1.243.1–245.23 [1.2.2.6]).

In his account of love melancholy, Burton again employed medieval Aristotelian psychological theory to explain the workings of '*Heroicall*' love in body and soul. Thus, the sight of a beautiful object (3.65.13–90.13 [3.2.2.2]) generated the passion of love in the heart through the agency of the eye (3.77.9–10), and since in the soul of fallen man '[t]he sensitive faculty most part over-rules reason' (3.16.18 [3.1.2.1]; cf. 3.49.19 [3.2.1.2]), this passion could become inordinate. 'Heroicall Love' was therefore 'a passion of the braine, as all other melancholy', in which 'both imagination and reason are misaffected, because of his corrupt judgement, and continual meditation of that which he desires' (3.57.31–58.10 [3.2.1.2]). Medical detail was generally sparse in this part of the book, and the neo-Galenic account of the manner in which strong passions upset the qualitative balance of the body and depraved the mental faculties was simply assumed, but a Latin marginal note explained that the faculties of estimation and imagination were corrupted by the fixation of the form of the desired object in the brain.[196]

The range of the effects of the soul on the body were also evident in the categories of symptoms, prognostics, and therapies. In love melancholy, for instance, many symptoms were by-products of the psychic disturbance caused by erotic desire, which in turn upset the body's regimen.[197] This was the case for 'paleness, leanenesse', and 'drinesse' (3.139.5, 10–11 [3.2.3.1]),[198] hollow-looking eyes [3.139.6–8],[199] blushing and sweating

[195] See Hippocrates 1839–61, VI.5.5, vol. V, pp. 316–17; Plato 1929, pp. 238–9 (87e–88a); Ficino 1576, I.4, pp. 496–7. See also Rufus of Ephesus 1879, p. 455, and Constantinus Africanus 1536, p. 284 (= Ishâq ibn 'Imran and Constantinus Africanus 1977, pp. 104–5).

[196] '... est corruptio imaginativæ & æstimativæ facultatis, ob formam fortiter affixam, corruptumque judicium, ut semper de eo cogitet, ideoque rectè melancholicus appellatur. Concupiscentia vehemens et corrupto judicio æstimativæ virtutis' [3.58.z [3.2.1.2]].

[197] See Hippocrates 1839–61, VI, vol. V, pp. 266–357.

[198] See Galen 1821–33, III.12, vol. VII, p. 952; Constantinus Africanus 1536, I.20, p. 18; Arnald of Villanova 1585, cols. 1528–9; Ferrand 1990, p. 275.

[199] Oribasius 1567, VIII.9, col. 123; Paul of Aegina 1567, III.17, col. 426; Avicenna 1608, III.1.4.23, vol. I, p. 494; Ferrand 1990, pp. 269, 276–7.

(3.143.10–20; 159.9), variable pulse (3.142.12–143.3),[200] sighing (caused by preoccupation with the object of desire in the imagination and memory [3.139.15]), and excessive thinness (a consequence of distraction and its attendant insomnia [3.139.21-4]).[201] The same relation structured the prognostics of the disease, where the heating effect of the passion of desire in the body was said to lead to an inflammation and drying of the brain, inducing a state of mania (3.198.2–5 [3.2.4.1]). Death was brought about either through suicide, here the specific prognosis of despair from unfulfilled desire (3.199.15–18), or through murder, which was the circumstantial result of the abnormal behaviour brought about by excessive passions and mania distorting the mental faculties (3.200.18–201.10).[202] In the curative category, a number of non-natural measures were designed to increase vital heat in the melancholic by inducing pleasure, as in Burton's recommendations of 'change of ayre and variety of places' (2.64.19, 25 [2.2.3.1]) and moderate 'recreative' exercises of both body and mind (2.67–96.1 [2.2.4.1]; 238.18 [2.5.1.1]; cf. 3.202.3 [3.2.5.1]). Here, providing the therapeutic counterpart of the pathology of scholarly melancholy, he singled out study as a means of raising vital heat, diverting anxiety, counteracting idleness, and refreshing dull spirits (2.84.16–95.4 [2.2.4.1]).

The critical importance attributed to psychological therapies in the *Anatomy* is evident in the extensive 'Consolatory Digression', which provided theological and moral-philosophical arguments to rectify the passions. Other medical authors had made similar recommendations, though never in comparably detailed or substantial fashion. I shall be returning to this aspect of Burton's work in chapter five, but here we should note his separate analysis of the arguments and practical strategies suitable for the treatment of love melancholy, which were designed to act on the faculties affected in the *complexio venerea* by dislodging the fixation on the desired object, dissipating hallucinations, and generally 'turn[ing] Love to hate' (3.207.24–209.3 [3.2.5.2]; 211.17–215.14; 229.33–240.12 [3.2.5.3]).[203] Properly ethical persuasion could also be used to correct the false and deluded judgement of beauty which

200 See Galen 1821–33, vol. XIV, pp. 630–5, revised in Avicenna 1608, III.1.4.23, vol. I, p. 494. See also Vallesio 1582, III.13, pp. 132–4, which Burton appears to have misread at 3.142.15–17 (3.2.3.1).

201 Du Laurens 1599, pp. 94–6, 118; Ferrand 1990, pp. 276, 280.

202 Arnald of Villanova 1585, col. 1529; Bernard of Gordon 1617, II.20, p. 257.

203 For example, see 3.211.28–9, 214.u (3.2.5.2); cf. Avicenna 1608, III.1.4.24, vol. I, p. 494, and Arnald of Villanova 1585, cols. 1530, 1531.

(particularly in the Neoplatonic analysis) was at the origin of excessive erotic desire, thereby addressing the faculty of estimation directly.[204]

The manner in which Burton incorporated medical doctrines within a moral and spiritual framework is one of the subjects of the next chapter, but it is worth registering here that it was in the parts of the work that dealt with the effects of disease on the soul that his extra-medical judgements were most pronounced. The explanation of the causes of love melancholy, for example (3.65.9–132.17 [3.2.2.2]), was dominated by a moralised discussion of social factors inducing love that drew heavily on Heinrich Kornmann's *Linea amoris* (1610), and was paralleled in the medical literature by only the most eclectic works such as Ferrand's *Traité*.[205] As he made clear, he was here concerned to expound the 'Moralls' of his subject matter (3.118.7 [3.2.2.4]), which were organised around the Aristotelian ethical mantra that '[t]here is a meane in all things, this is my censure in briefe' (3.126.15–16 [3.2.2.4]). Similarly, Burton's coverage of the prognostics of pure melancholy ranged over their medical aspects and established the incurability of the condition when it was inveterate or habituated (1.429.9–10 [1.4.1.1]), before settling into a substantial discussion of the moral and spiritual status of suicide (1.430.25–438.27).[206] This moralising impulse led him elsewhere to place strict qualifications upon the kinds of therapy that could be recommended – for instance, he countenanced coitus only after marriage, which according to the conventional gloss on 1 Corinthians 7:9 remedied the concupiscence of postlapsarian man (3.243.21–7 [3.2.5.5]).[207] It also led him temporarily to abandon the orthodox neo-Galenic conception of erotic desire, which was exclusively pathological, in favour of a Neoplatonic or Petrarchan appraisal of the positive influence on the soul of pure or divine love in terms of its many 'good and graceful qualities' (3.182.20–1 [3.2.3.1]).[208] At another point, it even necessitated a linguistic switch, and the suspension of his project to digest and present the Latinate erudition of the European scholarly community to a wider

[204] See 3.218.13–15; 3.227.31–32; 3.220.14; 3.221.13 (3.2.5.3). Cf. Du Laurens 1599, pp. 122–3.

[205] Kornmann 1610, *passim*; Ferrand 1990, pp. 242–9.

[206] See Rufus of Ephesus 1879, pp. 355–6; Paracelsus 1996, p. 153; Du Laurens 1599, pp. 92–3; and Mercuriale 1617, I.10, p. 50. On the difficulty of curing the condition see Galen 1976, III.10, p. 91; Alexander of Tralles 1567, col. 165 (= Alexander of Tralles 1933–6, vol. II, p. 232); Aretaeus 1856, p. 476; and Du Laurens 1599, pp. 107–8, alluded to at 2.13.17–18 (2.1.4.1).

[207] See also Du Laurens 1599, p. 122, and Ferrand 1990, p. 334.

[208] See 3.182.29–195.22 (3.2.3.1); cf. Ficino 1985, VI.4, p. 112, and Shakespeare 1988, V.1.4–6, pp. 328–9.

domestic audience in the vernacular. The *Anatomy* reported in Latin the medical usage of herbal applications to the genitalia to suppress lust (3.206.31–207.18 [3.2.5.1]), perhaps because the 'vulgar' words for the genitalia were sometimes considered to excite the imagination, stimulating the passions and sexual appetite of one's readers in a way that Latin, the language of philosophers and learned physicians which directly addressed the understanding, did not.[209]

***

This was largely conventional in terms of content, but the exposition of the theory of melancholy in the *Anatomy* was not a straightforward or uncritical reflection of the orthodox medical teachings of the period. In the first place, although much of the technical logical apparatus that Burton employed to structure his analysis suggested a commitment to medicine as a scientific discipline with demonstrative aspirations, his core message told otherwise. Perhaps unsurprisingly given his frequent references to Cardano, he sympathised with the tendency to accord special status to Hippocrates, and explored its implications in a number of ways that not only coloured his conception of the medical art, but also placed in question the credibility of many of the works to which he referred throughout. The authority of Hippocrates was often invoked by the *Anatomy* to support an experiental particularism that modified and occasionally subverted the generalised explanations and prescriptions found in other neo-Galenic works.[210] This was especially evident in Burton's analysis of regimen, where pre-eminence was typically accorded to Hippocratic authority. After cataloguing dietary causes of melancholy at length (1.212.15–225.13 [1.2.2.1]), the *Aphorisms* was cited to introduce exceptional factors that undercut large parts of what had gone before. The point was that '[n]o rule is so generall which admits not some exeption', and that 'custome', which 'doth alter nature it selfe', 'somewhat detracts, and qualifies according to that of *Hippocrates.* 2. *Aphoris.* 50' (1.225.17–26 [1.2.2.3]). In fact, the multitude of exceptions presented by the foodstuffs consumed in different geographical regions that did not damage health, but 'which diet our Physitians forbid', proved that 'custome is all in all' and therefore that 'common experience' was decisive (1.227.12, 22–3). In the *Contradicentium medicorum*, Burton wrote,

209 See, for example, Huarte Navarro 1594, p. 46. Cf. Ovid 1979, pp. 202–3.
210 On the connotations of 'experience' see the studies cited in n. 12 above.

Cardano 'adviseth all men to keepe their old customes', and in the third edition Burton noted that this was 'by the authority of *Hippocrates* himselfe, *dandum aliquid tempori, ætati, regioni, consuetudini*'.[211] Although Burton had humanistic respect for Galen, in the face of the variety of individual human complexions, therapeutic particularism grounded in 'experience' repeatedly triumphed over neo-Galenic rational generalisation in the *Anatomy*. The discussion of dietary remedies again referred to the *Contradicentium*: 'when all is said *pro* and *con*... I conclude, our own experience is the best Physician' (2.27.3–10 [2.2.1.2]).[212] The same went for exercise, 'of which . . . ther be divers sorts, & peculiar to severall callings' (2.83.15–18 [2.2.4.1]);[213] and eventually for physic generally: 'Every man as he likes, so many men so many mindes, and yet all tending to good purpose, though not the same way . . . experience teacheth us every day many things' (2.225.16–19 [2.4.1.5]).[214]

Other aspects of the presentation of medical knowledge in the *Anatomy* drew on and propagated the agenda of Hippocratism. Burton's obvious fondness for detailed case-histories reorientated diagnosis and therapeutics away from generalities and towards particulars. Moreover, as we shall see in detail in the next chapter, at crucial points Burton articulated a view of the discipline grounded in the paradoxical historicism increasingly being found in learned medical circles, but employed it to place limitations on the efficacy of physic. For now, it is enough to see this Hippocratic approach as compatible with 'weak' sceptical probabilism. But this also encapsulated what many university physicians would have viewed as an appropriate balance of *ratio* and *experientia*. More importantly for the broader project of the *Anatomy*, Burton's use of aphoristic 'Instances and examples' assisted his navigation of a morally and spiritually secure passage through the hazardous and controversial territory of medical occulism that permeated the material he had undertaken to disclose. In this way, his vision of the medical art enabled him to retain the scientific credibility of his account of melancholy whilst clearing a space for the incorporation of his deeper concerns.

211 Burton 1632, p. 74 (1.2.2.3); cf. Vives 1964, vol. VI, p. 198.

212 See Cardano 1663, I.6, vol. VI, pp. 303–5. As Burton had shown at 1.228.6–11 (1.2.2.3), this accorded with *Aphorisms* 1.17. Cf. 2.27.6–7 (2.2.1.2) with Hippocrates 1978, II.38, p. 211, cited again at 1.228.16 (1.2.2.3).

213 See also Galen 1997, XXIII.366, XXV.372, pp. 373, 377.

214 See also 1.248.3–4 (1.2.3.1); 2.59.3–4 (2.2.3.1); 2.208.30–209.1 (2.4.1.1); 2.220.24–5 (2.4.1.4); 2.231.8 (2.4.2.2); 2.255.1 (2.5.1.5); 2.255.30–1 (2.5.1.6).

MEDICAL OCCULTISM IN THE *ANATOMY*

Insofar as it is an accurate presentation of the orthodox neo-Galenic theory of melancholy, the medical discourse of the *Anatomy* is also testament to the infiltration of occultist philosophy into the writings of the learned physicians of the era, seen in ideas that in some cases were at odds with the tenets of strict medical rationalism. We noted above that Burton used the concept of sympathy in his definition of melancholy, but he also discussed notions less fully integrated into the orthodox medical tradition. In his understanding, all supernatural causes were traceable to God, by whom all diseases were ultimately sent as a punishment for sin after the Fall (I.172.4–174.10 [1.2.1.1]). This was an idea often expressed in medieval and early modern medical works, and one of its purposes was to help dissipate the potential aura of atheistic materialism.[215] But Burton entered more contentious territory when he considered the preternatural role of 'Spirits and Divels' in causing melancholy by manipulating the imagination, in a long and tangled 'Digression of the Nature of Spirits, bad Angels or Divels' (I.174.11–195.21 [1.2.1.2]).

Though careful to maintain distance between his own views and many of the opinions recorded in this digression, Burton agreed on the basis of scriptural authority that such demons and spirits existed (I.175.9–13), and that apparently 'they can cause and cure most diseases' and 'deceave our senses' (I.180.1).[216] The explicit association between demonic possession and melancholy went back at least as far as the *Epitome medica* of Paul of Aegina, and Arabic medical texts discussed the matter in detail.[217] In early modern medical literature, the idea that devils interfered with the imagination was a commonplace,[218] and the role of the imagination thus corrupted was a theoretical crux in late sixteenth-century debates about witchcraft.[219] Demonic interference had also been associated with the passions (and therefore sin) by the early Christian Fathers, and this idea was central to much Christian teaching reiterated in the sixteenth century.[220] Given the direct relationship between humoral complexions and emotions in neo-Galenism, it is easy to see how the

215 See, for example, Du Laurens 1599, pp. 80–1.

216 See Augustine 1984, XXII.22, pp. 1067–8.

217 Paul of Aegina 1567, III.14, col. 425 (= Paul of Aegina 1844–47, vol. I, p. 383). See also Galen 1821–33, vol. XIX, pp. 699–720.

218 For example, see Du Laurens 1599, p. 100, and Guazzo 1929, p. 106.

219 See Anglo 1976 and Céard 1976. For Italian parallels see Brann 2002, pp. 3–10, 33–7, 153–88, 205–46, 342–6, 332–441.

220 For example, in Wright 1971, p. 85. See Wenzel 1967, p. 14.

notion that evil spirits stirred up passions via the humours became widespread. Black bile was proverbially said to be 'the Devil's bath' (*balneum diaboli*), the medium for demonic activity in the body. Evil spirits were thought to delight in stirring up this humour and exploiting its toxic effects on the mental faculties to induce sinful passions.[221]

The demonic preference for black bile was sometimes explained analogically on the basis of the dark and semi-excremental nature of the latter, though its cold and terrestrial nature also suggested sympathetic association with the Devil. Either way, those of a melancholic complexion were thought especially susceptible to possession or deception by evil spirits.[222] One of the most influential *loci* was in Avicenna's *Liber canonis*, where it was stated in a seemingly sceptical tone that if demons were indeed able to cause melancholy, then it was by altering the complexion so that black bile was in abundance.[223] In physiological terms, any factor engendering black bile in the body could be a cause of the melancholic disease;[224] if evil spirits could stir up black bile, then they could cause melancholy.[225]

In Burton's account, the Devil manipulated the part primarily affected in melancholy, namely 'the *Phantasie*... by mediation of humours', though he noted that 'many Phisitians are of opinion, that the Divell can alter the minde, and produce this disease of himself' (1.193.10–12). He then cited Avicenna's report of some physicians' belief '*quòd Melancholia contingat à dæmonio*' (1.193.13) (later misreading Avicenna's non-commital position [1.400.28–31 (1.3.1.3); 1.428.3-5 (1.3.3.1)]), and explained that 'thereupon belike this humour of Melancholy, is called *Balneum Diaboli*, the Divels bath' (1.193.28 [1.2.1.2]). Burton knew that this was tricky territory, and was reluctant to commit himself to an account that designated a single means by which this was accomplished, 'whether by obsession, or possession, or otherwise' (1.194.12).[226] The Devil was also able to induce melancholy indirectly, according to some of Burton's contemporaries, via witches and magicians. Noting that '[m]any

221 See Agrippa 1533, I.60, p. 78; Lemnius 1576, fol. 23^v; Wright 1971, pp. 330–1.

222 See Huarte Navarro 1594, pp. 92–3.

223 Avicenna 1608, III.1.4.18, vol. I, p. 489: 'Et quibusdam medicorum visum est, quòd melancholia contingat a dæmonio: sed nos non curamus, quum physicam docemus, si illud contingat a dæmonio, aut non contingat, postquam dicimus, quoniam si contingat a dæmonio [sufficit nobis], ut convertat complexionem ad cholera nigra: deinde sit cause illius [choleræ nigræ] dæmonium, aut non dæmonium.' On the uses of Avicenna in early modern demonology see Brann 2002, pp. 24, 211–12, 342–3.

224 As assumed in Bright 1586, p. 25. See also Hippocrates 1525, p. 692.

225 Guazzo 1929, p. 106.

226 On the epistemological issues at stake see Pittion 1987, p. 124.

deny Witches at all, or if there bee any, they can doe no harme', of which opinion were Johann Weyer and Reginald Scot, amongst others (1.195.33–196.6 [1.2.1.3]), Burton sided with the *opinio communis doctorum* (1.196.6–7) in arguing that with the aid of the Devil they could 'hurt and infect men and beasts' (1.197.10). Indeed, they were able to 'cure and cause most diseases, to such as they love or hate, and this of *Melancholy* amongst the rest' (1.198.18–19).

Elsewhere, however, Burton was disinclined to unnecessary occult explanations, and emphasised the psychological benefit of the naturalistic account of mental illness that had its authoritative precedent in the Hippocratic *On the Sacred Disease*. The best means of giving melancholic sufferers 'satisfaction', he wrote, was 'to shew them the causes whence they proceed, not from Divels, as they suppose, or that they are bewitched or forsaken of God . . . but from naturall and inward causes, that so knowing them, they may better avoid the effects, or at least endure them with more patience' (1.418.20–5 [1.3.3.1]). When he conceded the possibility of demonically induced symptoms, it was either with overt reluctance (1.426.21–3), or – in cases of prophetic inspiration – to steer a middle course between radical materialism reducing them 'wholly to the ill disposition of the humor' and Neoplatonic mysticism referring to 'a divine kind of infusion' (1.427.19–428.7; cf. 1.400.23–34 [1.3.1.3]). His position was therefore similar to the moderately sceptical but inclusive Thomas Browne, who held that 'the Devill doth really possesse some men, the spirit of melancholy others, the spirit of delusion others'.[227] What was critical here was the particularist argument that each case could differ, permitting the introduction of moral-spiritual rectitude as the criterion for adjudication. This is why Burton did not settle on either supernatural or rationalist-sceptical ground. Ultimately he insisted only on the indisputably orthodox point that any cases where melancholy could be said without doubt to be supernaturally induced were to be traced ultimately to divine permission (1.195.13–15 [1.2.1.2]).

Some of the magical ideas surveyed in Burton's exploration of melancholy had strikingly rationalistic associations, particularly those derived from the connection of the imagination and black bile with occult or demonic forces. Although medieval medical writers had generally avoided recourse to occult concepts, in retaining the Aristotelian psychological concepts of πνεῦμα, phantasm, and visual *species* to explain the mediation between the material world, body, and soul, they had

[227] Browne 1977, 1.30, p. 98; but cf. ibid., 1.11, p. 197.

preserved the intellectual basis that would subsequently provide the structure for early modern disquisitions on the power of images to effect real physiological changes in the body through the imagination. It thus became possible to conceive of images and magical incantations as having real efficacy through their emission or creation in the mind of visual *species*, received by the eyes, intensified by the mental faculties, and converted by the imagination into phantasms in the mind.[228] When coupled with the humanist revival of interest in ancient magical ideas and the growth of learned occultism, this psychological theory opened the floodgates for a series of controversies about the power of the imagination. In the digression 'Of the Force of Imagination', Burton followed Aristotle and Avicenna, and referred to Pomponazzi's *De incantationibus* (1520) to explain how this faculty could affect the physiology of the body, leading to either sickness or health (1.253.28–254.4 [1.2.3.2]).[229] Indeed, such was the power of the imagination that '[a]n Empiricke oftentimes, and a silly Chirurgian, doth more strange cures, then a rationall Physitian' (1.254.8–9). Even Weyer and Paracelsus agreed, as Burton reported, that it could also perform magical effects in an external body (1.254.22–8).[230] Elsewhere, he drew on the notion of black bile as *balneum diaboli* to explain that fear disturbed the imagination, which triggered a surge of the humour in the body and 'invites the divell to come to us' (1.260.10–13 [1.2.3.5]) – a teaching which also clarified how tempestuous weather could lead to melancholy through occult means (1.237.14–20 [1.2.2.5]).

In the sixteenth century, both the occultist attribution of disease to demonic spirits and meditations on the strange effects of the imagination were crystallised in the controversial subject of amatory magic, and these topics accordingly permeated early modern writings on love melancholy. Medieval physicians had largely discounted ancient doctrines of love magic, but their successors in subsequent centuries were more receptive, and focused particularly on the efficacy of diabolical witchcraft in manipulating the imagination to induce erotic melancholy.[231] In the *Malleus maleficarum* (1487–9), Heinrich Krämer and Jakob Sprenger had influentially illustrated how devils and diabolical witchcraft could induce the condition of *amor hereos*, either by stirring up lustful desires in a body with a melancholic disposition, or by conjuring up erotic phantasms

[228] See Wack 1992, pp. 15–16.
[229] As acknowledged in Bacon 1906, III.9.3, p. 126.
[230] See also Montaigne 1603, I.20, p. 44.
[231] Wack 1992, pp. 10–13, 16–19.

in the imagination and thereby tempting to sin at the same time as distorting the mental faculties.[232] In tandem, the reproduction in sixteenth-century natural histories of testimonies to the effect that certain objects possessed occult forces provided intellectual justification for humanists interested in charms and spells.[233]

In the final Subsection on the causes of love melancholy, Burton acknowledged that the 'last battering engins' used by those in the grip of lust to obtain the gratification of their desire were 'Philters, Amulets, Spells, Charmes, Images, & such unlawfull meanes', and finally aid from 'the Divell himselfe' (3.135.31–4 [1.1.1.4]). Although there is no doubting his commitment to the primary role of the imagination in the etiology of love melancholy, he was well aware of the parameters of the debates surrounding this territory and took care not to commit himself – either to the fully fledged occultism of figures like Agrippa (3.137.23–4 [1.1.1.5]), or to the sceptical views of those such as '*Erastus*, *Wierus*, and others, [who] are against it' and granted that 'such magical effects' could be performed only by 'the Divell himselfe' (3.137.28–31). However, we may suspect that he privately inclined to the latter position, since it paralleled his argument elsewhere, on the basis of testimonies from 'experience', that witches and magicians used charms, images, and amulets 'which generally make the parties affected, melancholy', but that these objects were manipulated by the Devil and had no occult efficacy in themselves (1.199.2–9 [1.2.1.3]).[234] It also tallied with his dismissal of similar remedies for love melancholy as 'absurd', 'Pagan, impious, irreligious . . . and ridiculous' (3.240.16–17, 28 [3.2.5.4]; 318.33–9 [3.3.4.2]). But even if this was where his own opinion lay, instead of resolving the controversy on amatory magic he chose to refer the curious reader to a number of demonological works including the *Malleus*, Agrippa's *De occulta philosophia*, Pomponazzi's *De incantationibus*, and Ficino's *Theologia Platonica* (3.138.30–3 [3.2.2.5]).

As in cases of demonically induced melancholy, God was also ultimately responsible for the astral causes of the disease. The *Anatomy* dismissed the radical critics of astrology, including Sextus Empiricus, Giovanni Pico della Mirandola, and others who (according to Burton) had argued that the movements of the cosmos had no influence on earthly affairs, and assumed a moderate position between astral

232 See Beecher 1992, pp. 51–4; Céard 1992, pp. 34–41; and Brann 2002, pp. 25–31, 134–42, 313–30.

233 Copenhaver 1991, pp. 383–4.

234 See the similar ambiguity in Ferrand 1990, pp. 340–1.

determinism and human free will. The admission that '*nam & doctis hisce erroribus versatus sum*' was appropriate to this problematic territory,[235] but he followed Melanchthon in asserting that God controlled the stars, which 'doe incline, but not compell . . . and so gently incline, that a wise man may resist them' (I.199.25–200.6 [I.2.I.4]).[236] This prepared the way for the Neoplatonic theory of melancholy established by Ficino, who in the third book of the *De vita* had fused ancient astrology with the pseudo-Aristotelian *Problems* XXX.I. Melancholics were here endowed with a range of characteristics that included unusual mental ability, and the predominant astral causes of melancholic complexions identified as the cold and dry Saturn and Mercury.[237] More particularly, the ascendance of Saturn at the time of nativity was considered by Neoplatonists, and also by some eclectic but generally orthodox Aristotelian natural philosophers like Melanchthon, to exert a malign influence on the complexion and thereby create a predisposition to the melancholic disease.[238] In the circles of strict Galenists, doctrines concerning Saturn and other astral causes of melancholy were rarely conceded, but they were equally rarely contradicted outright. At the extreme end of resistance to these ideas, the most self-conscious rationalists like Mercuriale referred to Pico's anti-occultist position – as we have seen, in reality a naturalistic compromise whereby the stars were permitted to affect man through the manipulation of natural qualities on earth.[239] Eclectic writers like Cardano, however, and professional practitioners like Richard Napier, had embraced astrological teachings openly and wholeheartedly.[240]

Burton was sensitive to the problems of theological and intellectual respectability that accompanied these occult matters, and supported his ostensibly surprising citation of Paracelsus that 'the true and chiefe cause' of melancholy is 'to bee sought from the Starres' with the more cautious approaches of more reputable '*Galenists* and Philosophers, though they not so stifly and preremptorily maintaine as much' (I.200.19–21). In the corresponding part of the analysis of love melancholy, he implied that

[235] This phrase first appeared in Burton 1628, p. 52. See also I.200.20–1 and 201.21–3 (I.2.I.4).
[236] Melanchthon 1834–60, vol. X, p. 714.
[237] Ficino 1576, I.4, III.2, pp. 496, 533, and I.5, pp. 497–8, generally. On genial melancholy see Klibansky, Panofsky, and Saxl 1964, Schleiner 1991, and Brann 2002, esp. pp. 82–149, 247–332.
[238] Melanchthon 1552, sig. K5 (= Melanchthon 1834–60, vol. XIII, p. 84); cf. I.200.21–2 (I.2.I.4).
[239] See Mercuriale 1617, I.10, p. 49.
[240] On Cardano's astrology, see Siraisi 1997 and Grafton 2000; on Napier, see MacDonald 1981.

'Physitians' (presumably extreme Galenic rationalists) did not recognise astral causes of this disease at all (3.59.23–4 [3.2.2.1]). Amongst those who did acknowledge this type of causation, however, were Melanchthon and the later fifteenth-century Neapolitan humanist Giovanni Pontano, whose *De rebus coelestibus* (1494) had detailed the effects of planetary conjunctions, and from which Burton quoted at length (1.200.25–201.12 [1.2.1.4]). The astrological causes of melancholy were chiefly the influences of Saturn, Mercury, and Mars, and could be revealed by a horoscope charting their position in the configuration of the heavens at the time of the sufferer's birth (1.201.1–3). Yet the credibility of astrological medicine remained questionable. Having cited more occultist authorities, he attempted to diffuse the anticipated resistance of his learned readership with the testimony of several 'Physitians, *Galenists* themselves', who conceded planetary influences upon 'this peculiar Disease', and who were supported by 'Instances and examples... amongst those Astrologian Treatises' (1.201.20–30). The latter, 'Hippocratic' point was crucial, as it compensated for the apparent rational-scientific defects of astrological theory. The assertion that Saturn caused melancholy remained unproved by reason, but his belief was grounded in the testimony of observation and experience. His position was thereby saved from the theologically dubious scepticism that denied the power of God to influence sublunary bodies through the manipulation of the cosmos.

As we saw, like many of his learned contemporaries Burton incorporated the Neoplatonic understanding of genial melancholy within his orthodox medical theory by arguing that although they were 'of profound judgement in some things, ... in others, *non rectè judicant inquieti*' (1.391.21–8 [1.3.1.2]). However, his reception of the occultist explanation for love melancholy proposed by Ficino and Baldassare Castiglione in the third book of *Il libro del Cortegiano* (1528), in which blood spirits were transmitted and received through the eyes so that they visually 'fascinated' or infected the lover, was comparatively positive – even if reported in a typically detached fashion ('as some thinke' [3.88.19 (3.2.2.2)]). In accordance with the medieval psychology that underlay theories of amatory incantation, but drawing explicitly on a Platonic notion of *eros* as a form of magical enchantment,[241] Ficino had described vulgar or 'bestial' love as a condition whose physiological precondition was the corrupting preponderance of black bile or burned blood humours

[241] See Plato 1925, pp. 178–9 (202e); cf. Burton's allusion at 1.80.20.

in the body.[242] This condition, Ficino wrote, was involuntarily generated in its victims by an exchange of subtle blood spirits or vapours, which were emitted and received by means of rays or 'darts' containing these vapours exiting and entering through the eyes.[243] As Burton articulated the theory, drawing on Ficino and Castiglione, the stirring of desire in the agent's heart generated an upward motion of spirits to the eyes, and these emitted 'rayes' which, 'sent from the eyes, carry certain spirituall vapours with them, and so infect the other party, and that in a moment'. Since the spirits exchanged had been infected by the poisoning humours of the body, so, according to Burton's quotation of Ficino, '*the vapour of the corrupt blood doth get in together with the rayes, and so by the contagion, the spectators eyes are infected*' (3.88.19–25).[244] In this way, the lover's gazing resulted in a debilitating depletion of spirits of the agent as well as the depositing of poisonous spirits in the victim's veins, intoxicating the spirits and from there the whole organism: '*So the beames that come from the agents heart, by the eyes infect the spirits about the patients*,[245] inwardly wound, and thence the spirits infect the blood' (3.88.29–89.1).[246] When lovers exchanged blood vapours they were also transmitting images (in the form of phantasms) of themselves contained in these vapours, leading to a state of psychological estrangement similar to the *complexio venerea* (3.90.1–5).[247] This theory had also been central to Kornmann's account in the *Linea amoris*.[248]

The final kind of occultist doctrine found in orthodox medicine well beyond the seventeenth century, and given significant attention in the *Anatomy*, was in the domain of pharmaceutical therapy. Although the efficacy of some drugs was given an explanation through the theory of qualitative change, it was a common feature of ancient, medieval, and early modern medical texts that certain medicaments were simply declared to be effective treatments, without reference to this theory or anything resembling an explanation.[249] Galen had admitted that the operations of some substances – certain foods, poisons, even amulets – on

[242] Ficino 1985, VII.12, p. 168. For the classical roots of this idea see Galen 1821–33, vol. XVIIb, pp. 25ff.; Aristotle 1953, IV.30, pp. 132–3, and 1957, XXX .1, p. 159.
[243] Ficino 1985, VII.4, p. 159.
[244] See Ficino 1985, VII.4, p. 160.
[245] See Castiglione 1994, p. 277.
[246] See Ficino 1985, VII.4, p. 160. Cf. also ibid., VII.4, p. 161, with Burton's rendition at 3.89.4–17 (3.2.2.2).
[247] See Ficino 1985, II.8, p. 57; Castiglione 1994, p. 277.
[248] Kornmann 1610, III, pp. 58ff. Burton cited Kornmann's 'five degrees of lust' at 2.65.9–12 (3.2.2.2).
[249] Wear 1995, pp. 159–60, 173.

the body could be investigated only empirically, and understood by reference to the occult notions of their hidden properties and 'total substance'.[250] And as noted above, the sixteenth-century growth of philological study of the natural histories of antiquity encouraged the belief in humanist circles in the powers of objects and substances which were beyond the bounds of human perception and comprehension. Typically, in his discussion of herbal remedies Burton simply stated their empirical (or folkloric) effectiveness without explanation,[251] and ridiculed the idea that compound pharmaceuticals could be justified on an Aristotelian-scientific basis: 'Let the best of our rationall Physitians demonstrate and give a sufficient reason for those intricate mixtures' (2.224.3–4 [2.4.1.5]). There was no sudden change in his argumentation – or rather the lack of it – when he turned to the explicitly occult remedies of precious stones, metals, minerals, and amulets advocated by Paracelsus and his followers (2.219.4–222.28 [2.4.1.4]; 251.10–27, 254.5–255.5 [2.5.15]), approved by authors of less controversial reputation like Ficino and Cardano on the grounds that they could harness astral forces, but rejected by some medical authors like Ferrand.[252]

Just as he showed a sceptical tendency towards occultist ideas elsewhere in the *Anatomy*, there were signs here that he was not sympathetic to such remedies. Discussing the apparently benevolent power of gold, he hinted that it might be the product of pleasure derived from the accumulation of wealth rather than the secret 'vertue' of an occult quality (2.221.15–21 [2.4.1.4]), and was unequivocal that those 'medicines are to be exploded, that consist of words, characters, spells, and charmes, which can doe no good at all, but out of a strong conceit, as *Pomponatius* proves; or the Divells policy, who is the first founder and teacher of them' (2.255.2–5 [2.5.1.5]). More generally, his habitual practice was to discuss such measures whilst signalling their questionable status with 'many' anti-occultist (and specifically anti-Paracelsian) Galenists such as Thomas Erastus (2.219.6–10, 221.15–27 [2.4.1.4]). Ultimately, however, his preferred strategy was to withhold his own opinion about the general efficacy of allegedly magical therapies, proclaiming in the copy of 1632

[250] See Copenhaver 1991, pp. 330–1.

[251] See 2.217.21–218.16; 2.218.32–219.3 (2.4.1.3); and 2.260.24–261.16 (2.5.3.1).

[252] See Paracelsus 1996, pp. 179–80; Ficino 1576, III, pp. 531–72; Cardano 1663, vol. II, pp. 552–69; Ferrand 1990, p. 346. Cf. Platter 1602–3, I.3, vol. I, p. 157 (= Platter, Cole, and Culpeper 1662, p. 43).

that he would 'let experience determine' the issue in each instance.[253] In this case, suspension of judgement indicated a tendency, not towards rationalist empiricism, but towards a scepticism longstanding in learned occultism concerning the possibility of comprehending the secrets of the natural world – and also towards the acceptance of the reality of such phenomena on an experiential but strictly non-rational basis. This is well attested by an anecdote inserted in the second edition of 1624, where he revealed the decisive role of his humanistic respect for learned *auctoritas* in provoking a reassessment of an occult therapy:

Being in the country, in the vacation time, not many yeares since, at *Lindly* in *Lecestershire* my fathers house, I first observed this Amulet of a Spider, in a nutshell lapped in silke, &c. so applied for an Ague by my mother. Whom although I knew to have excellent skill in Surgery, sore eyes, aches, &c. and such experimentall medicines, as all the country where shee dwells can witnesse, to have done many famous and good cures (& still doth) upon divers poore folks that were otherwise destitute of helpe: Yet among all other experiments, this me thought was most absurd & ridiculous, I could see no warrant for it. *Quid Aranea cum febre?* for what Antipathy? till at length rambling amongst authors (as I often doe) I found this very medicine in *Dioscorides* approved by *Matthiolus*, repeated by *Aldrovandus cap. de Aranea lib. de insectis*, I beganne to have a better opinion of it, and to give more credit to Amulets, when I sawe it in some parties answer to experience.[254]

The status of occult doctrines and therapies in the *Anatomy* is complex. In some parts of the work, Burton was unquestionably dismissive either of their scientific efficacy or of their theological rectitude. In others, he was receptive, particularly when apparently occult effects could be authoritatively traced to divine agency or grounded in 'experience' by what he counted as reliable testimony. In nearly every case, however, his discussion was accompanied by an epistemological anxiety that was appropriate to a controversial territory that had been infiltrated by varieties of scepticism. On the one hand, in Burton's Oxford – as in most other universities in this period – adherence to, or interest in, occult or magical doctrines did not detract from a humanist's intellectual respectability in any straightforward way.[255] Yet he was also typical in demonstrating awareness of the distinction between naturalistic and occultist concepts, as shown by his conscious employment of the terms

[253] Burton 1632, p. 376; or 2.220.24–5 (2.4.1.4).
[254] Burton 1624, p. 324; or 2.254.20–255.1 (2.5.1.5).
[255] See Feingold 1984.

'occult', 'secret', 'magical', 'natural', and 'rational', usually in a sense that broadly accorded with modern usage.[256]

When Burton encountered conflicts between explicitly occult or rational doctrines, he generally employed any of three strategies, two of which were determinative but not conciliatory. The first was to side with the *opinio communis doctorum*, a dialectical technique that was common in humanist scientific investigation. The second was to steer a middle way between what he presented as the extremes of full-blown occultism of figures such as Paracelsus or Agrippa, and the radical rationalism found in the writings of neo-Galenists such as Mercuriale or Erastus. In such cases Burton made no attempt to harmonise what were clearly incompatible doctrines, but – and here there was a strong parallel with the approach taken by Marin Mersenne in his *Quaestiones celeberrimae in Genesim* (1623), a work which Burton used extensively in the Section on religious melancholy from the second edition onwards – instead offered a theological resolution of controversy avoiding the Scylla of magical superstition and the Charybdis of atheistic naturalism. That he was able to carry out this strategy without contradicting many of the medical authorities, in whom both extremes were detectable, was largely due to the flexibility afforded by his conception of the medical 'art' that produced *de infinitis finita scientia* through the ordering of particulars on an experiential basis.

Burton's third strategy was to detail conflicting issues but leave controversies unresolved, and the frequency with which this occurred in the book largely constituted its idiosyncratically disharmonious but inclusive, encyclopaedic character. As we shall soon see, this had implications for his conception of the limits of medicine, but it is important to emphasise that such comprehensive eclecticism would have been for his humanist contemporaries an admirable sign of what Meric Casaubon extolled as the scholarly virtue of 'generall learning'.[257] Burton was described in just these terms as a 'general read scholar' by Anthony Wood, and it was for the 'variety of much excellent Learning' in the *Anatomy* that he was praised by Thomas Fuller.[258] We can also say plausibly that his intellectual agenda was more pragmatic than dogmatic, and, if he was unconvinced by the justifications behind certain occult ideas, he included them in his survey in the knowledge of the limitations of his own understanding.

[256] On this terminology see Cardano 1663, vol. II, p. 537.
[257] Casaubon 1999, esp. pp. 13–33.
[258] Fuller 1662, p. 134; Wood 1815, vol. II, p. 652.

Ironically, perhaps, such pragmatism was authentically Galenic. As Galen wrote, commenting on the Hippocratic *Regimen in Acute Diseases*, 'If the diagnosis of disease, and the prognosis of its future course do not lead to the discovery of the best cure, they are pointless; but if they do, they are useful.'[259]

***

Burton's account of melancholy, through the course of its definitions, causes, symptoms, prognostics, and cures, provided an accurate, exhaustively detailed, and unquestionably erudite survey of the understanding and practical therapy of the disease that was current in early modern learned medical circles. With regard to the characteristics of the theory, what is most striking from a modern perspective is its relatively stable nature across the centuries, from the Hippocratic *corpus* and Rufus of Ephesus onwards – despite such secondary-level modifications as the doctrines about vital and animal spirits, and the controversial incorporation of occultist concepts.[260] The *Anatomy* testifies to this remarkable stability, which not simply is attributable to the generally undisputed status of neo-Galenism in institutionally sanctioned medical theory and practice, but was the result both of the restoration of Greek medical texts by humanist philologists, and of the endeavours of learned physicians in reconciling contradictions and reintegrating the teachings of these works to the existing synthesis. The fact that Burton was able to include the doctrines of the Hippocratics and Galen alongside Avicenna and Du Laurens in his exploration of melancholy, frequently discussing contradictions but rarely being faced with obviously fundamental intellectual incompatibilities, was due to this intertwining and interaction of humanistic and scholastic endeavour in early modern university-based medical study. Equally importantly from the point of view of Burton's immediate intentions is the fact that the *Anatomy* made a body of European Latinate knowledge, constituted textually through the range of ancient and neoteric agreements and conflicts, available in the English vernacular in a form that did not sacrifice its intellectual credibility. On these counts, it constituted a significant achievement in Renaissance medical writing and publishing.

We have seen, however, that the book was more than an encyclopaedic textbook for practitioners or curious individuals otherwise unable to

[259] Galen 1821–33, I.2, vol. XV, p. 421.
[260] See Jackson 1986, pp. 46, 78–9, 95.

access the rarefied discourse of learned medicine. Burton's task was to investigate and present the knowledge of melancholy in a form that furthered a humanistic philosophical agenda. The *Anatomy* drew on a distinctive contemporary vision of the medical art and put it to use, as a vehicle for a conception of knowledge in which therapeutic pragmatism – understood in terms that threatened effectively to subordinate the pursuit of physiological health to the requirements of moral-psychological and theological rectitude – became the decisive factor in determining whether it should be accepted. In this respect, it was far from being a neutrally 'scientific' treatise in the modern sense of the term. However, as we shall see in later chapters, it was essential to Burton's polemical religious and political goals that he could draw on a theory of melancholy to provide ammunition that was credibly 'scientific' in the early modern understanding.

All this fulfilled a positive part of the task announced in 'Democritus Junior to the Reader' – namely, to present an understanding of the medical theory of melancholy that could be accommodated by and could contribute to the philosophically paramount enterprise of the melancholic's attainment of virtuous, happy tranquillity. In the next chapter, I shall address the ways in which the investigation of melancholy in the *Anatomy* performed the function of its negative counterpart in the preface, insofar as it delivered an explicitly satirical commentary on 'scholastic' aspects of contemporary medical learning and practice, and thereby completed the distinctive humanist undertaking of the construction of a genuinely moral and practical medical art stripped of its vain speculative curiosity.

CHAPTER 2

Dissecting medical learning

Despite the massive accumulation of medical learning in the *Anatomy*, Burton's authorial persona was not that of a physician but of a philosopher-divine, interested in and knowledgeable about medicine but with no pretence of being a practitioner. Indeed, he insisted that his book should not be used as a source of medical knowledge that could bypass the need for expert guidance. In the Subsection entitled 'Physitian, Patient, Physicke', he cited François Valleriola's warning against amateur self-medication, that '*without exquisite knowledge*' for anyone '*to worke out of bookes is most dangerous*', and related the example of 'a friend of mine' who upon 'finding a receipt in *Brassavola*, would needs take Hellebor', and who would have perished 'had not some of his familiars come to visite him by chance' (2.17.7–19 [2.1.4.2]). This was an appropriate health warning for a text that was aimed beyond the rarefied circles of the learned medical community, but it also reflected the manner in which Burton presented himself as an expert not in medicine but in philosophy and divinity. He was, as he wrote in the preface, 'by my profession a Divine, and by mine inclination a Physitian', having studied 'the Theoricke of Physicke ... not with an intent to practise, but to satisfy my selfe, which was a cause of the first undertaking of this Subject' (1.23.5–10). This was an encyclopaedic investigation, as the book's subtitle indicated, of the medicinal, historical, and broadly philosophical aspects of melancholy. Here the challenge is to see how these related and interacted to produce Burton's humanistic version of 'Democritean' physic.

Burton's choice of subject matter and the method by which it was handled was justified, he wrote, by the 'agreement' between the professions of medicine and divinity, particularly concerning a disease that was 'a common infirmitie of Body and Soule ... that hath as much need of a Spirituall as a Corporall cure' (1.22.22–3, 31–3). This was not an unusual argument, but it is worth pausing over its terms. The divine and the 'physitian', he wrote, 'differ but in object . . . One helpes the vices and passions of the Soule, Anger, Lust, Desperation, Pride, Presumption, &c. by applying that Spirituall Physicke; as the other use proper remedies in bodily diseases . . . A Divine in this compound mixt Malady, can doe little alone, a Physitian in some kindes of Melancholy much lesse, both make an absolute cure' (1.22.25–23.3). Here was a humanistic, non-theological conception of divinity as therapy of the passions, indistinguishable in its concern and practical effect from moral philosophy, and so the psychological counterpart of conventional physic.

How did Burton combine medicine with divinity and moral philosophy in his analysis of melancholy? For all the apparent simplicity of his Philippist-sounding argument for the benefits of being 'a whole Physitian' versed in 'Spirituall' as well as 'Corporall' matters, his appraisal of the status of medicine was far from straightforward. There are three strands in his position. We have already seen one of these, namely, the employment of key 'Hippocratic' themes clearing space for the incorporation of moral and spiritual judgements, and also, in places, tending to subsume medical materialism within the priorities of the philosopher-divine. I am here concerned with the remaining two, both of which directly involved the ethical aspects of medicine. In the first place, in tension with much of the learning presented in his wide-ranging investigation of the theory of melancholy, Burton adopted a stance towards medical knowledge and practice that was pointedly critical, and in places unequivocally contemptuous. The *Anatomy* called for the reorientation and downgrading of the goals of medicine as they had been conventionally conceived. The first part of this chapter situates this aspect of the book within the humanist tradition satirising medicine, and addresses the the question of how this influenced the way in which knowledge was divulged to its readers throughout.

The remaining component of Burton's position was manifested in his sensitivity to the harmony or disjuncture of the ethical and medical dimensions of melancholy. In this respect, his account of the relationship between melancholic body and soul was notably dependent upon the reconciliation of neo-Galenism with Reformed theology and spiritual ethics accomplished by Melanchthon in his *De anima*. However, in the final analysis, as we shall see in the second part of this chapter, the perspectives of divinity and moral philosophy on disease in Burton's work were not so much integrated into as elevated above those of medicine, in accordance with a traditional humanist prioritisation of practical over speculative philosophy. Had it been otherwise, the pseudo-Hippocratic fable would have lost its central point, which was to demonstrate the superiority of moral wisdom over medical science in matters of health through the triumph of Democritean wisdom over Hippocratic expertise.

One of the distinctive features of Burton's writing in the *Anatomy* was that intertwined with a sophisticated but largely conventional neo-Galenic investigation was a critical, satirical commentary on the shortcomings of contemporary medical-scientific knowledge and practice. This formed an integral part of its author's philosophical project. It is not that there is a serious, 'basic' medical-scientific discourse in the *Anatomy* that is decorated with ludic literary-satirical trimmings. And equally, it is not that the work is essentially satirical or ironic, and so not to be taken seriously. Rather, what Burton aimed to communicate by a variety of means was a body of knowledge that was both disciplined – framed by sceptical limits, stripped of speculative pretensions, and brought into line with moral and spiritual virtue – and also, as we shall see in subsequent chapters, of practical religious and political utility.

Such is the continuity in the *Anatomy* between medical discourse and discourse on medicine that in many places it is practically impossible to discern the difference between the two. In fact, their intersection occurred precisely at the points where Burton considered contemporary medicine to be at its most vulnerable. Conflicting diagnostic or therapeutic claims and potentially suspicious occult doctrines were repeatedly handled in 'Hippocratic' fashion, through appeals to experience and the particularity of cases, and were rationalised by references to the historical origins and development of the medical art. But that his purposes in emphasising the importance of experience, particularity, and history extended beyond a conventional advocacy of the practical therapeutic benefit to be gained therein becomes clear when we treat his critique of the origins, development, and limits of medical practice as a serious enterprise in its own right.

THE HUMANIST CRITIQUE OF MEDICINE

Humanist criticisms of medical learning and practice had medieval antecedents, but typically followed the example of Petrarch in the *Invectiva contra medicum* (1355). Petrarch's vituperation was primarily *ad hominem*, directed against an anonymous papal physician rather than 'against medicine or true physicians' – which were divine gifts 'devised to aid our mortal bodies'[1] – but his discontent flowed from contempt for 'the infamy of today's physicians, whose modern errors have extinguished her ancient glory'.[2] The detail of his case in the *Invectiva* reflected the polemical anti-scholastic agenda later elaborated at length in the *De sui ipsius et multorum ignorantia* (1371). This was clearest in his citation of reliance upon syllogistic and other 'vain and empty' forms of logic as proof of the abandonment of practical therapy in favour of speculative contentiousness,[3] and of the uncritical obsession with Aristotle and Averroës as a sign of ignorance and atheistic inclination.[4] It was also evident in his attacks on the misinterpretation and abuse of classical authors rather than on those authors themselves. It was not Galen who required correction, but his 'great host of unlearned and garrulous successors'; and it was not the Father of Medicine who was blameworthy, but 'the detractors and adversaries of Hippocrates' who had perverted their inheritance.[5] This position implied the dual possibility of a recoverable *pristina medicina* and a historically developing body of knowledge,[6] but its main thrust was to discredit contemporary medicine as an immoral and base mechanical art serving the body rather than the soul, whose greedy practitioners had decorated themselves with superficial erudition.[7] As things stood, 'thousands of people are in danger', their health being 'governed by the factious, divergent, and uncertain authority of physicians' who 'kill while declaiming, arguing, and shouting'.[8]

Many of Petrarch's concerns about the scholastic shortcomings of medicine were reiterated or developed by subsequent generations of humanists.[9] In the sixteenth century, the message that the knowledge used by physicians was a body of divergent and uncertain opinion was forcefully delivered by Gianfrancesco Pico della Mirandola in his sceptical *Examen vanitate doctrinae gentium et veritatis Christianae*

1 Petrarch 2003, I.19, I.26, I.40, II.71, pp. 16–17, 20–1, 30–1, 56–7.
2 Petrarch 2003, I.42, pp. 32–3. See also ibid., II.71, pp. 54–5.
3 Petrarch 2003, II.65, II.75, II.81, II.82, II.86, II.89, II.92, III.101, III.117, III.145, III.159, III.162, IV.162, IV.177, pp. 50–1, 58–9, 64–5, 66–7, 68–9, 72–3, 74–5, 82–3, 84–7, 92–3, 94–5, 122–3, 132–3, 136–7, 140–1, 150–1.
4 2003, II.85, III.109, pp. 68–9, 88–9. Cf. ibid., IV.194, pp. 164–5.
5 Petrarch 2003, I.17, I.26, pp. 16–17, 20–1.
6 Petrarch 2003, I.23, pp. 18–19.
7 Petrarch 2003, I.13, II.75, II.98, III.110, pp. 12–13, 60–1, 64–5, 78–9, 88–91. For the opposition to medicine to ethics see, for example, I.14, II.53, III.149, III.153, III.160, pp. 12–15, 40–1, 124–5, 130–1, 134–5.
8 Petrarch 2003, I.8, pp. 8–9.
9 See Maclean 1980, pp. 28–9; Nutton 1981, pp. 15–16; Siraisi 1990b, p. 176, 1990c, pp. 221–2, 224–8, 1997, pp. 14, 28–9, and 2001, pp. 172–4. Cf. the criticisms in Bacon 1994, pp. 302–3, and Galilei 1967, p. 113.

disciplinae (1520), which demolished the claims to certainty traditionally made for physiology by exposing its basis in an intrinsically contradictory mass of ancient doctrine.[10] A few years later in the *De vanitate*, Cornelius Agrippa assembled a comparably vigorous, if facetious, account of the corrupt uncertainty permeating medical theory and practice throughout the centuries. According to Agrippa, the history of medicine was one of sectarian antagonism, fraudulent and futile claims to rational *scientia*, and the killing of patients.[11] Later in the century this was also the conclusion of Montaigne, who in his essay 'Of Experience' derided the endless 'variety of medical arguments and opinions' and meditated at length on the problem of applying division to the unlimited particularity of human life.[12] In Montaigne's critique of medical epistemology, the infinity of signs that learned physicians acknowledged as the basis of the medical art undermined the credibility of their semiological procedures. What was revealed, in Florio's rendering, was their 'doubt and ignorance . . . and so many false prognostications of their arte'.[13] Neo-Galenic rationalism was downgraded accordingly: 'Experience in her owne precinct, may justly be compared to Phisicke, unto which, reason giveth place.'[14]

Many humanist critiques had constructive purposes. When the Petrarchan case against the scholasticism of medicine was restated by Juan Luis Vives in the *De causis corruptarum artium* (1531), it incorporated a vision of educational and professional reform. Physicians were over-reliant on Aristotle, Averroës, and the disputational methods derided in the *In pseudodialecticos* (1520), and exhibited contentiousness, greed, and careerist 'cupiditas gloriæ', but Vives's response was to propose a humanist programme of intellectual and moral education. Being based on clear and accurate translations of the works of Galen and Hippocrates, this would purge the profession of its medieval and un-Christian errors, and reorientate it towards its divinely sanctioned therapeutic duty.[15] Similarly, one of the purposes of the *De vanitate* was to call for a stripped-down, empirical, and non-theoretical medicine that would be centrally constituted by the administration of a purified pharmaceutics. Here at least, Agrippa was in agreement with those medical humanists

10 Pico Della Mirandola 1969, I.16, vol. II, pp. 791–802.
11 Agrippa 1575, fols. 142r–154r. Cf. the admission in Bright 1586, p. 268.
12 Montaigne 1603, III.13, p. 407.
13 Montaigne 1603, II.37, III.13, pp. 407, 635.
14 Montaigne 1603, III.13, p. 642. For the relationship between medical experience and dogmatic scepticism see Sextus Empiricus 1621, I.34, pp. 48–50.
15 Vives 1964, V.2, vol. VI, pp. 198–203.

who were recovering and restoring ancient works of pharmacological botany.[16]

In the following century, for Francis Bacon in *The Advancement of Learning* (1605), medicine was 'a science which hath been . . . more professed than laboured, and yet more laboured than advanced; the labour having been, in my judgment, rather in a circle than in progression'. In Bacon's view, the deficiency of medicine was to be traced partly to the neglect of the form of 'medicinal history' as exemplified in 'the ancient and serious diligence of Hippocrates, which used to set down a narrative of the special cases of his patients'. It had also failed to strike the appropriate balance between, on the one hand, the necessary attendance to particulars derived from 'the traditions of experience' and associated with 'empirics', and, on the other, the 'methods of learning' gleaned from rational philosophical inquiry. Here was an overlap between Baconian scientific reform, the humanist critique of scholastic neo-Galenic *theoria*, and the call for a return to Hippocratic origins.[17]

***

Burton had already registered in 'Democritus Junior to the Reader' that it was discontent with the current state of the profession that had 'induced me to make choice of this Medicinall subject', its 'generall fault' being manifested in futile contentiousness over 'intricate subtilties' (1.21.21–8). In the main treatise, the substance of Burton's views on this subject are revealed only towards the end of his account of the pure form of melancholy, in the penultimate Section of the second Partition. Here he began his argument by noting how 'many cavill' at '*Pharmaceutice*, or that kind of Physicke which cureth by medicines', as 'unnecessary, unprofitable to this or any other disease' (2.208.6–10 [2.4.1.1]). The discussion became progressively critical as its subject expanded into the subject of the shortcomings of physicians in general, whom 'some thinke . . . kill as many as they save, & who can tell . . .?' (2.209.3–4). As if prompted by this satirical *topos*, Burton proceeded to unleash a bitter vituperation against medicine, rearticulating the traditional case made by humanist critics of the discipline.

It was significant that this critique was provoked by the consideration of pharmaceutics, since it had been the perceived shortcomings of this branch of medical *practica* that had especially agitated Agrippa in the *De vanitate*.

[16] See Siraisi 1990c, p. 227.

[17] Bacon 1906, II.10.3–4, II.10.8, pp. 121–2, 124–5. See also Bacon 1994, I.70, pp. 78–80.

There was indeed no coincidence in the fact that here the *Anatomy* followed this part of Agrippa's work in its main thrust, since Burton cited it at several important points. Agrippa had taken his cue for the denunciation of medical sectarianism across the centuries from the *Prooemium* to Celsus's *De medicina*, a portion of text that was influential in the development of sixteenth-century scepticism and where the positions of the various medical sects (*empirici*, *methodici*, and *logici* or *dogmatici*) were surveyed and attacked for their multiplicity and equal justifiability.[18] Burton likewise cited Celsus, alongside the elder Pliny, on the historical origins of medicine,[19] and went on to express a view of the discipline as both *filia temporis* and shot through with pagan error and sectarianism. This was how it ran in the first two editions of the *Anatomy*:

> It is no art at all, as some hold, the beginning, practice and progresse of it, all is naught, full of imposture, incertainty, and doth generally more harme then good. The Divell himselfe was the first inventer of it: *Inventum est medicina meum*, said *Apollo*, and what was *Apollo* but the Divell? The *Greekes* first made an Art of it, and they were all deluded by *Apollo's* sonnes, Priests, Oracles... *Æsculpaius* his son had his temples erected to his Deity, and did many famous cures, but as *Lactantius* holds, hee was a Magitian, a mere Impostor, and as his successors, *Phaon*, *Podalirius*, *Melampius*, *Menecrates* (another God) by charmes, spells, and ministery of bad spirits, performed most of their cures. The first that ever wrot in Physick to any purpose, was *Hippocrates*, and his Disciple and Commentator *Galen*, whom *Scaliger* calls *Fimbriam Hippocratis*, but as *Cardan* censures them both, immethodicall and obscure, as all those old ones are, their precepts confused, their medicines obsolete, and now most part rejected. Those cures which they did, *Paracelsus* holds, were rather done out of their Patients confidence, and good opinion they had of them, then out of any skill of theirs, which was very small, he saith, they themselves Idiots and Infants, as are all their Academicall followers. The *Arabians* received it from the *Greekes*, and so the *Latines*, adding new precepts and medicines of their owne, but so imperfect still, that through ignorance of Professors, Impostors, Mountebankes, Empericks, disagreeing of Sectaries, envy, covetousnesse, and the like, they doe much harme amongst us.[20]

Besides its strikingly negative conception of the discipline in general, several aspects of this passage are notable. The first is the distinctively patristic emphasis on the theologically heterodox historical origins of the 'Art' in demonic delusion, and the willingness – surprising, in the

[18] Celsus 1953–61, vol. 1, pp. 2–41.
[19] This was added in Burton 1624, p. 296, or 2.209.17 (2.4.1.1), but see the references to Celsus at 2.212.29 (2.4.1.1); 2.224.20 (2.4.1.5); and 2.232.29–30 (2.4.2.2).
[20] Burton 1621, pp. 431–2; Burton 1624, p. 296; or 2.209.18–210.11 (2.4.1.1).

light of the clear debt of the *Anatomy* to orthodox neo-Galenism – to cite Paracelsus's assault on the 'Academicall followers' of the ancients in support of this. More important, though, is the light it sheds on the continuum Burton established between the Hippocratic revival propagated by Cardano and the longstanding humanist critique of medicine. The work used for the castigation of the 'immethodicall and obscure' writings of Hippocrates and Galen here was once again the *Contradicentium medicorum*, and when he continued to explain exactly how medicine was 'imperfect still', he crossed the evidently thin line between Hippocratic particularism and anti-medical satire with support from passages taken from the same author's *De sapientia* (1544) that ridiculed physicians' contradictory diagnoses and treatments and denounced their 'imposture and malice'.[21] He then explained another anecdote from Cardano concerning a Venetian physician routinely contradicted by his colleagues by means of Agrippa's damning principle that '*Omnis ægrotus, propriâ culpa perit, sed nemo nisi medici beneficio restituitur*' (2.210.19–25, o). The list of the faults of medical practitioners was rounded off with assertions that 'it is their ignorance that doth more harme', that 'their Art is wholly conjecturall', and that even '[t]he most rationall of them, and skilfull are . . . often deceaved'. Physicians' knowledge, in short, was 'uncertaine, imperfect, and got by killing of men'; it was little wonder that 'many diseases they cannot cure at all'.[22]

These were extraordinary arguments to be presented in what purported to be at least in part a medical treatise with practical therapeutic use. Even if they carried satirical intent – as in Agrippa's *declamatio*, or, for that matter, Erasmus's *Moriae encomium* – their significance should not be downplayed. Burton proceeded to offer an apparent retraction, but as it appeared in the first edition this was, if anything, more obviously facetious than what had gone before, being prefaced with the remark that 'I will urge these cavilling arguments no farther, lest some Physitian should mistake me, and deny me Physick when I am sick'.[23] The retraction, including an encomium that was laughably short given what had gone before, was partial – distinguishing 'the abuse from the use . . . *for necessities sake*' – and simply the scriptural qualification accompanying humanist criticism since Petrarch, '*The Lord hath created medicines*

[21] Burton 1621, p. 296; or 2.210.11–19 (2.4.1.1).
[22] Burton 1621, pp. 296–7 (2.4.1.1). Cf. Agrippa 1575, fols. 152^r–153^r.
[23] Burton 1621, p. 433; or 2.211.29–31 (2.4.1.1). On Burton's satirical palinodes see Renaker 1979.

of the earth, and hee that is wise will not abhorre them, Ecclus. 38. 1.'[24] Perhaps the best indication of Burton's insincerity here, though, can be found in the additions he made to this Subsection in subsequent editions, which amplified the satirical critique of medicine and undercut even the brief praise of the first edition. In the copy of 1624, he expanded his historical account of 'people [who] are still sound of Body and Minde, without any use of Physicke', with examples taken from Martianus Capella and the Flemish geographer Abraham Wortels (Ortelius),[25] buttressed his report of the opinion that 'Physitians kill as many as they save' with a quotation to this effect from Pliny,[26] strengthened his criticism of physicians' dependence on the unreliable semiology produced by pulses and urine with the remark 'I say nothing of *Criticke* daies, errours in Indications, &c.',[27] and recalled Petrarch's denigration of medicine as a lowly 'mechanical' art by reporting the view expressed in Xenophon's *Cyropaedia* that 'Physitians *were like Taylors and Coblers, the one mended our sicke bodies, as the other did our cloathes*'.[28]

Burton was less temperate in the third edition. 'How many murders they make in a yeare', he asked, '*quibus impunè licet hominem occidere*, that may freely kill folks & have a reward for it, for according to the dutch Proverbe, a new Physitian must have a new Churchyard; and who daily observes it not?'[29] He then elaborated his discussion of how medicine 'is no art at all, as some hold', by citing the *In aphorismorum Hippocratis libros medicae, politicae, morales, ac theologicae interpretationes* (1618) by the Genoese physician and polymath Pietro-Andrea Canonieri, which proved that it was 'not worthy the name of a liberall science ... because it is mercenary as now used, base ... a corrupt trade, no science, art, profession'.[30] Later in the Subsection he sharpened his criticism of the proliferation of conflicting medical 'Sectaries', 'which are as many almost as there bee diseases';[31] re-emphasised that '*Plus à medico quam à morbo periculi*, more danger there is from the Physitian, then from the disease';[32] again questioned 'if it be an art';[33] and added an

[24] Burton 1621, pp. 433–4; or 2.211.31–212.12 (2.4.1.1).
[25] Burton 1624, p. 295; or 2.208.12–17 (2.4.1.1).
[26] Burton 1624, p. 296; or 2.209.f (2.4.1.1).
[27] Burton 1624, p. 297; or 2.211.15–16 (2.4.1.1).
[28] Burton 1624, p. 297; or 2.211.27–9 (2.4.1.1).
[29] Burton 1628, pp. 335–6; or 2.209.6–9 (2.4.1.1).
[30] Burton 1628, p. 336; or 2.209.18–23 (2.4.1.1).
[31] Burton 1628, p. 336; or 2.210.10 (2.4.1.1).
[32] Burton 1628, p. 336; or 2.210.16–17 (2.4.1.1).
[33] Burton 1628, p. 337; or 2.210.32 (2.4.1.1).

Agrippan denunciation of practitioners as 'butchers, leeches, men-slayers; Surgeons and Apothecaries especially . . . though to say truth, Physitians themselves come not farre behinde'.[34] Finally, he included an unfavourable comparison of greedy contemporary physicians with their ancient pagan counterparts, alleging that the latter 'did not so arrogantly take upon them to cure al diseases, as our profesors doe, but some one, some another as their skill and experience did serve . . . not for gaine, but in charity, they made neither art, profession, nor trade of it'.[35]

The additions made to the qualifying retraction in the second and third editions hardly restored balance to these judgements. In 1624, straightforwardly enough, Burton reinforced the distinction between use and abuse by adding that '*aliud vinum, aliud ebrietas*, wine and drunkennesse are two distinct things'.[36] But in the light of what he had written before on its origins, his extended encomium of physic in the next edition was imbued with deep irony. Now he acknowledged it to be 'a most noble and divine science, in so much that *Apollo*, *Æsculapius*, and the first founders of it, *meritò pro diis habiti*, were worthily counted Gods by succeeding ages', and in contrast to other pagan deities '*Æsculapius* had his Temple and Altars every where . . . for the latitude of his art, deity, worthy, and necessity. With all virtuous and wise men therefore I honour the name, & calling.'[37] '*Æsculapius*' had only just been revealed as the son of 'the Divell' and, on the authority of Lactantius, 'a Magitian, a mere Impostor', so it is difficult to believe that Burton wanted to be taken seriously here. Clearly uninterested in sustaining any sincere defence of medicine, in the following edition he inserted a final sarcastic put-down of those before him who had: 'But of this noble subject how many panegyricks are worthily written? For my part, as *Salust* said of *Carthage*, *præstat silere, quam pauca dicere.*'[38]

Here was a rearticulation of the humanist critique of medicine that openly acknowledged its debt to both Cardano and Agrippa for its exposure of the dubious historical origins and development of a 'wholly conjectural' and fraudulent 'art', characterised up to the present day by greed, brutality, 'disagreeing of Sectaries', and uncertainty. But how were the elements of this critique reflected in the contents of the rest of the *Anatomy*?

[34] Burton 1628, p. 337; or 2.210.33–211.6 (2.4.1.1).
[35] Burton 1628, p. 337; or 2.211.22–7 (2.4.1.1).
[36] Burton 1624, p. 297; or 2.212.33–213.1 (2.4.1.1).
[37] Burton 1628, p. 338; or 2.212.1–9 (2.4.1.1).
[38] Burton 1632, p. 370; or 2.212.13–14 (2.4.1.1).

As his satirical narrative of the origins of medicine suggested, Burton recognised that knowledge had not been timelessly deposited in the works of the major authorities. Rather, with the historicist consciousness fostered by his typically humanistic interest in antiquarianism and philology, he conceived of it as the product of development across the centuries. As in the case of the writings of Hippocratic revivalists in medical circles, this was not without overlooking inconsistencies with his overall project – for instance, he did not choose to trouble himself with the problem of reconciling the notion of a classical *prisca sapientia* or the lionising of any ancient authority with a notion of intellectual progress over time.[39] Nevertheless, historical awareness surfaced periodically throughout the book. In his discussion of compound alteratives, he noted that 'in the infancy of this art' ancient physicians 'were content with ordinary simples', but now, '[a]s arts and sciences, so Physicke is still perfected amongst the rest . . . and experience teacheth us every day many things, which our Predecessors knew not of' (2.225.3–4, 17–19 [2.4.1.5]). A little later, he applied this argument by documenting in detail the history of the fluctuating therapeutic status of hellebore over the centuries (1.232.19–233.24 [2.4.2.2]). In addition to demonstrating consciousness of the internal contradictions of authoritative texts – there were, he remarked 'so many differences in *Galen*' (1.383.19 [1.3.1.1]) – he acknowledged that these texts had been incorporated into different explanatory systems in the hands of their various interpreters across time: '*Oribasius*, *Ætius*, *Avicenna*, have all out of *Galen*, but to their owne method' (1.11.26–7).

Although problematic, historicism was not wholly incompatible with medical inquiry conducted through the exposition and interpretation of texts, and the same can be said of the prioritisation of experience, individual case-histories, and particularism over systematic generalisation and logical argument that, as we have seen, characterised the medical analysis in the *Anatomy*. But in Burton's hands these themes were applied for the purpose of questioning the utility, and even the possibility, of comprehending the subject of melancholy.[40] Although the voluminous and contradictory material was organised and presented with a remarkable clarity, he never tired of suggesting that this was an impossible and perhaps futile task, repeatedly drawing attention to the shortcomings of his 'art' of producing *de infinitis finita scientia* by underlining the gulf

[39] On this issue see Muslow 2004. Cf. Hobbes 1996, p. 490.
[40] See similar scepticism in Huarte Navarro 1594, pp. 74, 153, 180.

between the ordered structure of his theoretical account and the chaos it was supposed to capture.

The idea that what Burton was presenting to his readership was not a straightforward account of melancholy of a kind that could be found in other medical works was arguably first communicated in the analysis of the soul in the 'Digression of Anatomy', where (in contrast to the preceding physiological discussion) he outlined the Aristotelian theory accepted in neo-Galenic circles whilst pointing to the 'many doubts' that 'arise' in the writings of various authors 'about the *Essence*, *Subject*, *Seat*, *Distinction*, and subordinate faculties of it' (1.147.19–20 [1.1.2.5]), and expounded the '[m]any erroneous opinions' prevailing about its rational part (1.155.8–9 [1.1.29]). In the following analysis of melancholy, he continued to note the erroneous contentiousness of the authorities on whom he was relying, on the question of the relationship between etymology and definition ('whether [black bile] be a cause or an effect, a Disease, or Symptomes, let *Donatus Altomarus*, and *Salvianus* decide, I will not contende about it' (1.162.9–10 [1.1.3.1]), on its 'severall Descriptions, Notations, and Definitions' (1.162.10–11), and on the 'difference' and 'doubt' concerning the affected part (1.163.21–2, 164.20–1 [1.1.3.2]).

It was, however, in his discussion of black bile that the controversial and dubious character of the literature on the disease became explicitly associated with the complex nature of the disease itself. 'Of the Matter of *Melancholy*', he began, 'there is much question betwixt *Avicen* and *Galen*', and referred to '*Cardans* Contradictions, *Valesius* controversies' and a host of others 'that have written either whole Tracts, or copiously of it' to show that like the ancients 'the Neotericks cannot agree' (1.166.9–15 [1.1.3.3]). What followed underlined the problematically diverse character of black bile, which was 'either *simple*, or *mixt*; offending in *Quantity* or *Qualitie*, varying according to his place, where it setleth . . . or differing according to the mixture of those naturall humours amongst themselves, or foure unnaturall adust humours, as they are diversly tempered and mingled' (1.166.23–167.2). As a consequence, '[t]his diversity of Melancholy matter, produceth diversity of effects', and this was inevitably mirrored in the conflicting 'difference' between authors on the subject (1.167.8–9, 168.4–5). Both were implicated together in the investigation of melancholic species: 'When the matter is divers and confused, how should it otherwise be, but that the Species should be divers and confused? Many new & old Writers have spoken confusedly of it' (1.168.11–13 [1.1.3.4]).

Here also was the associated recognition that medical analysis would necessarily involve the rational imposition of finitude upon infinitude. The species were 'infinite', and so were the symptoms, 'but they may bee reduced to three kindes, by reason of their seat, *Head, Body, and Hypochondries*' (1.169.1–10). Immediately, however, the technical uncertainty of this method of ordering infinites was underlined with the admission that this tripartition was recognised only by 'most of our new Writers', and that '*Th. Erastus* makes two kindes' whilst others 'againe make foure or five kindes' (1.169.10–17). Although on this occasion he sided with the *communis opinio*, i.e. the 'most received division' (1.169.22–3), it was not without warning that the three species 'are so often confounded amongst themselves' and 'intermixt with other diseases' that 'they can scarce be discerned by the most accurate Physitians' and 'the best experienced have been plunged' (1.170.3–70). This signalled that the medical knowledge revealed in the *Anatomy* was imperfect, by no means certain, and in many cases unreliable. He concluded the Subsection (and the Section concerned with the definition of melancholy) in the first edition by asking '[h]ow difficult a thing is it to treat of severall kindes apart; to make any certainty among so many casualties, distractions, when seldome two men shall be like affected *per omnia*?', but announcing that he would nevertheless 'adventure through the midst of these perplexities, and led by the clewe or thred of the best writers', attempt to 'extricate my selfe out of a labyrinth of doubts and errors'.[41]

By now, attentive readers – rather than the 'idle' ones he had excoriated in the parergon between preface and main treatise (1.114) – should by rights have known what to expect, yet Burton continued to emit knowing asides throughout his account to remind them of the shortcomings of what lay before them. The examination of causes began with the Galenic argument 'that those cures must be unperfect, lame, and to no purpose, wherein the causes have not first been searched' (1.171.18–19 [1.2.1.1]). But this was followed by a suggestion that the causes revealed were likewise 'unperfect'. As their discernment was 'a most difficult thing', '[h]e is happy that can performe it aright', and all the author could do was 'adventure to guesse as neere as I can, and rippe them all up . . . so they may the better be descried' (1.171.25–172.3). As with many such passages in the book, this could be simply a gesture of humility.

[41] Burton 1621, p. 54; or 1.170.30–171.11 (1.1.3.4).

However, it was peppered with indications that the author wanted his readers to realise the limitations of the knowledge being presented: the statement of extreme difficulty, which had by now become a commonplace of his exposition; a possible oblique allusion to the preface's argument that everyone suffered from misery, which implied that precisely no-one would be able to 'performe it aright'; the signal that what appeared was at three (perhaps four?) removes from the truth – 'I will *adventure* to *guesse* as *neere* as I *can*'; and a description of his discourse in the traditional satirical terms of 'ripping' up its objects – so that these 'may the better bee descried' in their imperfection.

The theme of the impossibility of ordering the infinitude of particulars, and more broadly of rationally comprehending melancholy, was developed in the discussion of symptoms, which began in the usual fashion by accurately pointing to the 'diversity of melancholy signes' acknowledged in the writings of medical authorities to the extent that they were 'almost infinite' (1.381.21–6 [1.3.1.1]). Actually, mental symptoms were truly 'infinite', and there were 'scarce of two thousand, that concurre in the same symptomes' (1.384.6, 395.32–3 [1.3.1.2]), leaving the author to 'adventure . . . to bring . . . some order' to 'a vast confusion and generality' (1.396.4–5). The same applied to 'peculiar' (i.e. particular) symptoms derived from temperamental causes, which were 'diversely varied' and 'infinite' (1.397.17–26 [1.3.1.3]). Appropriately enough for a reader of Montaigne, it was in the Subsection devoted to 'Symptomes from Custome' that Burton cast doubt upon any semiology purporting to order the circumstantial particulars of melancholy, which were such that 'as they write of heat and cold, we may say of this humour, one is *melancholicus ad octo*, a second two degrees lesse, a third halfe way'; the disease was 'super particular, *sesquialtera*, *sesquitertia*, and *superbitpartiens tertias*, *quintas*, *Melancholiæ*, &c. all those Geometricall proportions are too little to expresse it' (1.404.28–405.2 [1.3.1.4]). Although he continued the attempt to reduce signs to order, it was plain that he regarded the enterprise of collating symptoms into syndromes or significant groups – a procedure essential to the finite medical art – as impossible in melancholy. This is how he made the point in 1621:

> Who can sufficiently speake of these symptoms? or prescribe rules to comprehend them, they are so irregular in themselves, *Proteus* himselfe is not so divers, you may as well make the *Moone* a new coat, as a true character of a melancholy man . . . They are so confused, divers, intermixt with other diseases . . . who can distinguish these melancholy symptoms so intermixt with others, or apply them

to their severall kindes, confine them into method? 'Tis hard I confesse yet I have disposed of them as I could . . .[42]

The prognostics of melancholy, by contrast, were straightforward – they were 'either good or bad'. But he still managed to find contradiction in the literature on the topic (1.428.30, 429.15–17, 434.15–26 [1.4.1.1]), most suggestively on the lawfulness of melancholic suicide (1.434.27–438.27).

The theme of the limits of medical knowledge was resumed when Burton turned to cures. The Subsection 'Concerning Physicke' began conventionally enough by noting that 'there bee divers and infinite kindes' of medicine, '& those of severall natures, some good for one, hurtfull to another', and that therefore these were 'left to bee managed by discreet and skilfull Physitians, and thence applied to mans use'. This gave him the opportunity to describe the 'method, & severall rules of art' to order remedies 'for their particular ends', as being in the Hippocratic definition simply '*addition and substraction*' in a manner that 'ought to be most accurate' (2.17.31–18.4 [2.1.4.3]). But the reality did not live up to the ideal, since '[s]everall prescripts and methods I finde in severall men, some take upon them to cure all maladies with one medicine, severally applied'; the controversial Paracelsian '*Panacea, Aurum potabile*' exemplified the confusion 'of which I am now to speake', again of 'severall cures, severall methods, and prescripts' (2.18.5–17). The reader was prepared for what followed, namely a survey of the conflicting variety of therapies in the medical literature that also underlined the infinite, chaotic, and labyrinthine nature of a subject beyond the reach of human understanding.[43]

Two aspects of this commentary on the shortcomings of medical method are notable. The first is that it was defensible in the terms of contemporary neo-Galenic medical scholarship, and in a way satirically parasitical upon it. As we have seen, not only was the medical art conventionally characterised by the process of rationally ordering an infinitude of particulars, but learned writings on melancholy also frequently acknowledged that the disease was complex and variable, that it yielded an infinity of symptoms, and that it was extremely difficult to cure. Burton's emphasis on the problem of grasping melancholy in these terms derived from the Aristotelian principle, widely discussed in learned

[42] Burton 1621, p. 253; or 1.407.20–408.6 (1.3.1.4). See also 3.195.22–4 (3.2.3.1).

[43] See, for example, 2.213.4–5 (2.4.1.1); 2.223.9–10, 2.225.13–14 (2.4.1.5); 2.241.21–2 (2.5.1.3).

medical circles, that the intellect was incapable of comprehending infinites and that particulars could not be known with certitude, and applied it to the domain of human experience.[44]

To convey this directly, Burton had recourse to the rhetorical figure of ἀδύνατον, or stating the impossibility of expressing oneself adequately to the subject. In an enterprise formally committed to systematic analysis, what this communicated was an admission of defeat in an impossible enterprise, with fallen human reason fated to be frustrated by the unpredictable intricacies of melancholy at every turn. Here the *Anatomy* echoed the case against medicine that had been made by Montaigne in 'Of Experience'.[45] When in his second edition Burton undercut his own dietary prescriptions with the conclusion that 'our owne experience is the best Physitian . . . let every man observe and be a law unto himselfe', he may have been following Montaigne's essay when he continued by citing the opinion of '*Tiberius* in *Tacitus*', who 'did laugh at all such, that after 30 yeares of age, would aske counsell of others, concerning matters of diet: I say the same'.[46] Tiberius had been cited to the same effect by Montaigne to justify his view that 'reason giveth place' to experience in medicine.[47] By portraying melancholy throughout as the archetype of an infinitely confused disease, Burton signalled agreement with Montaigne's intimations about the limitations of reason in medicine, and drew a similar conclusion: that of all the arts promising health 'there is none [that] performeth lesse what they promise'.[48]

The second significant aspect of this commentary was that, like so many of the important features of the book, Burton expanded it considerably in the course of the editions published after 1621. In the second edition, he re-emphasised the variability of the mental symptoms of melancholy by noting that 'as in a River we swimme in the same place, though not in the same numericall water: and as the same Instrument affordes severall lessons, so the the same disease yeeldes diversity of symptomes', so that 'they be diverse, intricate, and hard to be confined' by method.[49] In the copy of 1628, this was prefaced with the observation

44 See Aristotle 1967, I.12.2, pp. 128–9, and cf. Bacon 1906, II.10.2, pp. 127, 129–30. On this principle see Maclean 1999, p. 303.

45 Montaigne 1603, III.13, p. 635. See also ibid., II.37, pp. 440–9.

46 Burton 1624, p. 204; or 2.27.9–14 (2.2.1.2). See also 3.112.28; 3.120.6–7; 3.123.17 (3.2.2.4); 3.232.16–17 (3.2.5.4); 3.245.15 (3.2.5.5).

47 Montaigne 1603, III.13, p. 642.

48 Montaigne 1603, III.13, p. 642. Cf. ibid., p. 633; Bacon 1906, II.10.3, p. 131, and 1994, I.70, pp. 78–80; and Burton 1977, II.3, V.4, pp. 70–3, 200–1.

49 Burton 1624, pp. 165–6; or 1.396.1–4 (1.3.1.2).

that 'there is in all melancholy *similitudo dissimilis*, like mens faces, a disagreeing likenesse still'[50] – an idea that referred to the semiological difficulty, acknowledged in contemporary medical scholarship, of 'learning truly to discerne between differing similitude and like differences'.[51] The third edition also included a new parallel between the bodies surveyed by the arts of politics and pathology, which served to illustrate the intractable problem of distinguishing between different kinds of the disease and point to the gulf between reasoned medical *theoria* and complex reality: 'I conclude of our melancholy Species, as many polititians doe of their pure Formes of Commonwealths, Monarchies, Aristocraties, Democraties, are most famous in contemplation, but in practise they are temperate and usually mixt, as the *Lacedæmonian*, the *Roman* of old, *German* now and many others'. Thus, '[w]hat Phisitians say of distinct Species in their bookes, it much matters not, since that in their Patients bodies they are commonly mixt'. It was, he reiterated, a condition marked by 'obscurity' and 'confused mixture' in causes and symptoms.[52] In 1628 he elaborated the sceptical conclusion of his discussion of customary signs, replacing his former statement that they were 'irregular' with a passage that memorably asked,

> . . . as *Eccho* to the painter in *Ausonius, vane quid affectas &c.* foolish fellow what wilt? If you must needs paint me, paint a voice, & a phantasticall conceipt, a corrupt imagination, vaine thoughts and different, which who can doe? The foure and twenty letters make no more variety of words in divers languages, then melancholy conceipts produce diversity of symptomes in severall persons. They are irregular, obscure, various, so infinite, *Proteus* himselfe is not so divers . . .[53]

The fourth edition further highlighted the disorder by suggesting that '[t]he tower of *Babel* never yielded such confusion of tongues, as this Chaos of melancholy doth variety of Symptomes'.[54]

What was most remarkable about Burton's meditations on the shortcomings of rational medical method in relation to understanding and treating melancholy, however, was the idiosyncratic manner in which they were reflected in his own procedures of investigation. For instance,

[50] Burton 1628, p. 180; or I.395.34–396.1 (I.3.I.2).
[51] John Cotta, *A short discoverie of the unobserved dangers of severall sorts of ignorant and unconsiderate practisers of physicke in England* (London, 1612), p. 17, cited and discussed in Maclean 2002, p. 137.
[52] Burton 1628, p. 36; or I.170.31–171.5 (I.I.3.4).
[53] Burton 1628, p. 188; or I.407.21–28 (I.3.I.4).
[54] Burton 1632, p. 190; or I.395.33–4 (I.3.I.2).

although he established the conventional neo-Galenic categories to structure his analysis, employment of the laconic '&c.' to 'end' discussions throughout the book implied that no method – and no human discourse – could ever grasp the infinite subject matter. More importantly, as we shall now see, the argumentative techniques of the *Anatomy* themselves drove home the limitations of medical reason, and implemented the humanist satirical agenda of 'Democritus Junior to the Reader', by ridiculing the uselessness of the 'scholastic' philosophical procedures that permeated early modern academic medical texts.

It has often been remarked that, deliberately or otherwise, Burton overwhelmed his readership with torrents of authoritative quotations, but the relationship between this aspect of the book and the methods employed in contemporary medical scholarship has never been properly addressed. Most of the medical investigation of the *Anatomy* was not unusual insofar as it was constructed around the exposition of the frequently contradictory positions of major authors on the subject in hand, and occasionally involved the author's expression of his own judgement in a controversy or siding with the *communis opinio doctorum*. However, given his claim to be writing for the 'common good', his heavy reliance on the exposition of problems through the commentaries of other authors (I.19.22–3) would have been regarded in learned medical circles as highly unsuitable for pedagogy, and pointed to a tension between his disclosure of a field of elite knowledge and the conventions internal to that field. More importantly, this type of argumentation, as he and his scholarly readers well knew, served only to establish what some saw as a worryingly weak form of plausibility – hence Montaigne's lament that '[i]t is not without some ill fortune, to come to that passe, that the multitude of believers . . . should be the best touch-stone of truth'.[55] Frequently he offered his opinion as one of many with no suggestion that *any* possessed superior justification, and periodically proclaimed a subject to be 'beyond the reach of humane capacitie' to qualify all the views that followed, including his own.[56] Unlike the vast majority of his erudite medical contemporaries, he typically left his own opinion obscure or unstated, and the conflicts between authorities unreconciled, by withholding a final determinative *resolutio*. The oscillation, then, between suspension of judgement and conventional resolutive intervention in

[55] Montaigne 1603, III.11, p. 613. On the weakness of argumentation from authority see Maclean 1992, p. 74, and 2002, p. 207.

[56] Burton 1628, p. 38; or I.174.18–19 (I.2.1.2). Cf., for example, Burton 1638, p. 46; or I.184.33–4 (I.2.1.2).

controversy generated a productive tension in Burton's authorial position. On the one hand, he was a distanced, ironic, and sceptical satirical commentator – a stance inherent in the *cento* form (1.110.27–32) – and on the other, he was a committed encyclopaedic investigator. In general, he committed himself only when he had to, either in order to produce or to adhere to a coherent structure of explanation that would permit him to continue his discourse with enough freedom to expatiate copiously, or else to conform to moral-theological orthodoxy.

Throughout the *Anatomy* Burton took palpable delight in reproducing part of the typical structure of scholastic disputation, citing authorities *pro et contra*, and then revealing sceptical detachment from what effectively became an unresolved two-sided argument.[57] This can be seen in many of the discussions where he withheld his own view and maintained an anti-dogmatic stance: for instance on the controversy between Averröes and Galen on the physiological cause of fear and sorrow ('it boots not') (1.418.28–419.27 [1.3.3.1]);[58] on the occult causes of melancholy in witches (1.204.15–205.2 [1.2.1.5]); on the benefits of diuretics for hypochondriacal melancholy (2.262.31–263.4 [2.5.3.1]); on the dogmatic conflict over the efficacy of occult therapies recommended by '*Paracelsus* and his Chymisticall followers' but controverted by Galenists (2.221.14–222.28 [2.4.1.4]); on marriage, whose virtues and vices had been typically emphasised by humanists and scholastics respectively, and a debate resolved with the remark that ''tis all in the proofe' (3.266.25–268.27 [3.2.5.5]); and on the crucial question of the therapeutic utility of the renowned hellebore (2.233.24–235.7 [2.4.2.2]). As he concluded the hotly disputed subject of chemical preparatives, the only appropriate response in the face of such contentiousness was to withhold judgement and carry on.

But what doe I meddle with this great Controversie, which is the subject of many Volumes? Let *Paracelsus*, *Quercetan*, *Crollius*, and the brethren of the *Rosy Crosse* defend themselves as they may. *Crato*, *Erastus*, and the *Galenists* oppugne *Paracelsus*, he brags on the other side, hee did more famous cures by this meanes, then all the *Galenists* in *Europe*, and calles himselfe a Monarch; *Galen*, *Hippocrates*, infants, illiterate, &c. . . . Thus they contend and raile, and every Marte write books *Pro* and *Con*, *& adhuc sub judice lis est*, let them agree as they will, I proceed. (2.243.26–244.12 [2.5.1.3])

[57] On the role of the two-sided argument in dogmatic scepticism see Sextus Empiricus 1621, fol. ¶2^{v}.

[58] Contrast the *resolutiones* in Du Laurens 1599, pp. 90–2; Ferrand 1990, pp. 240–1; Manardi 1611, IX.2, p. 183; and Mercuriale 1617, I.10, pp. 48–9.

That this aspect of Burton's writing derived from the established methods of learned medical investigation, and indeed partly reflected the conventional investigation of *controversiae* and *contradicentia* – where resolution through conciliation was not regularly exercised – is unquestionable. But in order to see the idiosyncratic satirical dimension of the absence of determination in the *Anatomy*, it is instructive to compare it with another humanistic medical treatise on melancholy, Jacques Ferrand's the *Traité de l'essence et guérison de l'amour ou mélancholie erotique* (first edition, 1610), as translated into English by Chilmead in 1640.

Some of the similarities between Ferrand's *Traité* and Burton's Section on 'Love Melancholy' are so striking that one modern critic, Falconer Madan, suggested that Burton was guilty of concealing his debt to Ferrand and perhaps of plagiarism. Although this is not impossible, there is no substantial evidence to support it.[59] In fact, the contrast between the two authors' expositions is far more important. Whereas Ferrand cited and quoted ancient and modern authorities and typically attempted to assimilate them within a discourse in which his own voice dominated and presided without a hint of irony, Burton composed a *cento* in which his quotations rivalled and frequently overwhelmed his authorial voice. As we have seen in the introduction, he was self-conscious about this method of composition. Both works, broadly speaking, were exercises in *philologia*, building up analyses of the subjects in hand through the compilation and comparison of textual opinions, but beyond this point they parted company.

In the first place, in accordance with the 'scholastic' conception of medicine, Ferrand's overriding methodological instinct was to employ argumentative strategies to reconcile conflicts between authorities and perspectives, to produce a *discordia concors* in which the question under discussion always found an answer. His treatment of dreams was typical, reconciling conflicting opinions on their origin through division into 'Naturall' and 'Divine' categories ('an easie matter'), continuing with Aristotle's refusal to 'acknowledge the Divine at all', but concluding that 'his authority is of lesse moment and force then that of *Moses*; which is also seconded both by *Hippocrates*, and *Homer*'.[60] Through a combination of logical argumentation, concession, and capitulation on the grounds of authoritative weight – and, if all else failed, by subdividing

[59] See Bensly 1909, p. 286, and Burton's pre-emptively defensive remarks at 3.60.k (3.2.2.1) and 3.206.w (3.2.5.1).

[60] Ferrand 1640, pp. 178–80 (= Ferrand 1990, p. 298).

the question to allow for both sides of the controversy to stand – Ferrand strove to achieve clarity through synthesis.[61]

At one level, Burton was concerned to produce a serious and informative analysis of the subject under discussion through *philologia*, and he, too, periodically employed conventional argumentative strategies – including comparison, capitulation, and reference to the *communis opinio* – that were designed to favour one view over another.[62] However, he repeatedly presented his text in a fashion that cast doubt upon the credibility of its scholarly investigation. Burton conducted an encyclopaedic survey of melancholy which incorporated ideas from conflicting intellectual traditions, but, in contrast to Ferrand, rather than attempting to reconcile them in his *cento*, he typically let his quotations speak for themselves and chose not to voice his own opinion or to resolve controversy. For instance, he noted that some 'deny the Divell can doe any such thing' as induce erotic melancholy, but simply told his readers, 'if you desire to be better informed, read *Camerarius*' (3.135.31–136.3 [3.2.2.5]). They were well advised to go elsewhere for answers, because Burton next plunged into the late sixteenth-century debate amongst physicians and demonologists on amatory magic, detailing the opposed opinions of Agrippa, Erastus, Weyer, and others without the slightest hint of adjudication (3.137.23–138.12 [3.2.2.5]). Having provided an authoritative spectrum of opinion – in which the category of 'naturall causes' ended up looking suspiciously magical even to the early modern eye – without betraying his position, the Subsection ended in typically ventriloquistic manner.

See more in *Schenkius observat. medicinal. lib.* 4. &c. which are as forcible, and of as much vertue, as that fountaine *Salmacis* in *Vitruvius*, *Ovid*, *Strabo*, that made all such mad for love that dranke of it, or that hot Bath at *Aix* in *Germany*, wherein *Cupid* once dipt his arrowes, which ever since hath a peculiar vertue to make them lovers all that wash in it . . . These above named remedies have happily as much power, as that bath of *Aix*, or *Venus* enchanted girdle . . . Read more of these in *Agrippa de occult. Philos. lib.* 1. *cap.* 50. *&* 45. *Malleus malefic. part.* 1. *quæst.* 7. *Delrio tom.* 2. *quæst.* 3. *lib.* 3. *Wierus*, *Pomponatius cap.* 8. *de. incantat. Ficinus lib.* 13. *Theol. Plat. Calcagninus, &c.* (3.138.15–33)

The ironic use of mythology and folkloric magic as a *determinatio* was here rounded off by one of Burton's favourite devices – to send his readership elsewhere. But these works would have done no more than

[61] See also Ferrand 1990, pp. 235, 240.
[62] For instance at 3.142.5–143.1 (3.2.3.1).

defer the resolution of the argument even further. The true function of this bibliography was to testify to the unimpeachable accuracy of his satirical 'dissection' of the debate; Agrippa, Kramer and Sprenger, Del Rio, Weyer, Pomponazzi, Ficino, and Calcagnini were the conflicting authors he had been citing all along, and so the effect of this 'conclusion', if we may call it that, was to point to his own account as a learned testimony of unreconciled – and probably unreconcileable – scholarly conflict.

In the 'Digression of the Nature of Spirits', we can see clearly how the successive accumulation of textual layers across different editions of the work expressed – and I would suggest contributed to – Burton's scepticism. In the first copy, the dissection of the authoritative conflicts concerning the contentious and 'very obscure' issue of 'the power of Divels' ran for just under fourteen quarto pages, but by the final posthumously issued edition of 1651 this had become seventeen and a half of the larger folio size.[63] From the start, he openly expressed doubts about many of the views he was recording, labelling them as not just 'opinion',[64] but 'paradoxes',[65] 'altogether erronious . . . to be exploded',[66] 'as vaine as the rest',[67] 'poeticall fictions . . . all false',[68] written by authors who 'to prove their assertions' should 'free their owne credits'.[69] He also made clear that this was terrain in which satisfactory *determinationes* were not to be found, concluding the thorny issue of how the Devil could cause melancholy with the remark that 'I will not determine, 'tis a difficult question',[70] and similarly labelling the controversy over the extent of demonic powers to similar effect 'hard to determine'.[71] As the digression expanded in the second edition, the tone of authorial incredulity towards the literature under discussion became more pronounced, as Burton undermined the views of the occult philosopher Johann von Heidenberg (Trithemius) with the phrase 'by what authority I knowe not',[72] and dismissed a wide range of teachings as 'most erroneous paradoxes . . . rejected by our Divines, and Christian Churches'.[73]

63 Burton 1621, pp. 57–71; Burton 1651, pp. 39–54 (1.2.1.2).
64 Burton 1621, p. 59; or 1.177.4 (1.2.1.2).
65 Burton 1621, p. 60; or 1.179.19 (1.2.1.2).
66 Burton 1621, p. 61; or 1.181.22–3 (1.2.1.2).
67 Burton 1621, p. 61; or 1.181.11 (1.2.1.2).
68 Burton 1621, p. 63; or 1.183.26–8 (1.2.1.2).
69 Burton 1621, p. 70; or 1.194.25–6 (1.2.1.2).
70 Burton 1621, p. 69; or 1.194.12–13 (1.2.1.2).
71 Burton 1621, p. 68; or 1.191.4 (1.2.1.2).
72 Burton 1624, p. 44; or 1.191.18–20 (1.2.1.2).
73 Burton 1624, p. 45; or 1.192.21–2 (1.2.1.2).

The 1628 version proceeded to employ the authoritative scepticism of Augustine to cast doubt upon the medical *ars* of ordering infinites ('I confesse I am not able to understand it, *finitum de infinito non potest statuere*'),[74] and punctuated the analysis with more sardonic asides pointing to the unreliability of the views being listed – 'This no doubt is as true as the rest', and so on.[75] In the copy of 1632, the sceptical aspect of the digression was tied to the ongoing critique of 'our subtile Schoolemen' and other contentious scholars, who were 'weake, drye, obscure, defective in these misteries',[76] and further dilated with more selections from the contradictory literature on the topic.[77]

This enterprise was continued in the 'Digression of the Ayre', where Burton made no pretence to be doing anything other than reporting a series of speculative questions he found raised by scholars concerning geography and cosmology. His principal conceit here was to imagine himself able to 'wander round about the world, mount aloft to those æthereall orbes and celestiall spheres' (2.33.12–13 [2.2.3.1]), and thus capable of testing the accuracy of contemporary reports and speculations about the earth and the heavens (2.34.10–11) – the implication being that these were opinions that lacked justification. In the first edition, this purpose was indicated by asides suggesting the disputed and unreliable status of the survey's quotations – 'And yet in likelihood it may be so' (2.34.22), 'Or whether that be true' (2.38.9), 'not as a truth, but a supposition' (2.50.12) – and underlined by the ironic recourse to '*Lucians Menippus*' to resolve controversy about the centre of the earth.[78]

Many of the additions made to this digression in the copies issued between 1624 and 1651 testify to Burton's increasing interest in the contemporary cosmological learning of the 'new science'.[79] But the main point communicated in all editions was the sceptical one that these views, however fascinating, were either unreliable or unverifiable products of speculative curiosity.[80] The second edition again used Lucian, to end the digression with derision of the 'curious controversies' conducted by

[74] Burton 1628, p. 38; or 1.174.18–25 (1.2.1.2).

[75] Burton 1628, p. 41; or 1.179.32–4 (1.2.1.2). See also ibid., p. 39; or 1.175.22 and 1.176.33–177.1 (1.2.1.2).

[76] Burton 1632, p. 39; or 1.174.20–3 (1.2.1.2).

[77] Burton 1632, p. 41; or 177.36 (1.2.1.2). For some later additions see Burton 1638, pp. 40–1; or 1.176.17–24 (1.2.1.2), and Burton 1651, p. 52; or 1.192.19–20 (1.2.1.2). See also Burton 1632, p. 503; 3.133.6–9 (3.2.2.5).

[78] Burton 1621, p. 321; or 2.41.25–7 (2.2.3.1).

[79] Browne 1952; Barlow 1973.

[80] See also 2.34.22; 2.37.28; 2.38.9; 2.40.16–22; 2.41.10–13; 2.41.25–27; 2.50.11–13; 2.51.10–11; 2.55.6–58.10 (2.2.3.1).

'Theologasters', 'Pagans... Hæreticks, Schismaticks, and some Schoolmen', and rubbed it in with the contrived humility of a confession that 'I am an infant, and not able to dive into these profundities, not able to understand, much lesse to discusse'.[81] As the digression expanded in subsequent editions, the gulf between truth and human opinion broadened with more Augustinian scepticism,[82] and extensive reports on geography and cosmology exemplifying how authors 'disagree amongst themselves, old and new, irreconcileable in their opinions'.[83] There were many other parts of the *Anatomy* that were less openly satirical or sceptical, but one of the functions of these two digressions was to bring the nature of Burton's scholarly enterprise clearly into relief. An integral feature of his purpose in writing was to reveal and comment on the uncertainty and unending *discordia* he found in his books, and this remained the same throughout.[84] As he concluded in the third edition, the propensity towards destructive contentiousness amongst scholars was such that '[s]carce two great schollers in an age, but with bitter invectives they fall fowle one on the other, and their adherents; *Scotists*, *Thomists*, *Reals*, *Nominals*, *Plato* and *Aristotle*, *Galenists* and *Paracelsians*, &c. it holds in all professions'.[85]

The distinctively 'melancholic' character of Burton's scepticism is well captured by the parallel between his conception of knowledge and his description of the disease's symptoms. 'What is most of our Philosophy', he asked,

> but a Labyrinth of opinions, idle questions, propositions, Metaphysicall tearmes... what is Astrology, but vaine elections, predictions; all Magicke, but a troublesome error, a pernitious foppery, Physicke, but intricate rules and prescriptions; Philology, but vaine Criticismes; Logicke, needlesse Sophismes; Metaphysicks themselves, but intricate subtilties, and fruitlesse abstractions? Alcumy, but a bundle of errors? To what end are such great Tomes, why doe wee spend so many yeares in their studies? Much better to know nothing at all, as those barbarous *Indians* are wholly ignorant, then as some of us, to be so sore vexed about unprofitable toies. (1.364.10–27 [1.2.4.7])[86]

[81] Burton 1621, pp. 328–9, 329–30; or 2.54.33–55.34; 2.56.1–24; 2.57.21–3 (2.2.3.1).

[82] Burton 1624, p. 212; or 2.41.10–11 (2.2.3.1); Burton 1638, p. 258; or 2.58.32–59.6 (2.2.3.1).

[83] Burton 1638, p. 257; or 2.57.25–30 (2.2.3.1). For new geographical material see, for example, Burton 1624, p. 210; or 2.37.28–38.3 (2.2.3.1). Many new passages were added to Burton 1638, pp. 241–58; or 2.33.23–55.23.

[84] See the sceptical asides at 3.14.14 (3.1.1.2); 3.120.27–8 (3.2.2.4); 3.122.16–17; 3.190.33–191.1 (3.2.3.1); and 3.290.33 (3.3.1.2).

[85] Burton 1628, p. 95; or 2.266.30–33 (1.2.3.8).

[86] Most of this passage was added to Burton 1624, p. 148.

This recapitulated the theme of philosophical *vanitas* from the preface (1.101.9–10), but the idea of the encyclopaedia as a 'Labyrinth of opinions, idle questions, propositions', was also mirrored in Burton's account of the 'labarinth of anxious and solicitous melancholy meditations' that afflicted melancholics, and more generally the 'labyrinth of errors' that was the world afflicted by melancholy (1.273.23 [1.2.3.10]; 2.85.21 [2.2.4.1]).[87] The implication of the metaphor was clear: the description of the melancholic symptoms of 'irresolution, inconstancy, vanity of minde . . . care, jealousie' (1.389.1–2 [1.3.1.2]) and 'suspition' could equally be applied to the knowledge of melancholy.[88] The labyrinthine discord, futility, and uncertainty of the philosophical *corpus* were themselves bound up with the prevalence of the disease.[89]

MEDICINE AND CHRISTIAN HUMANISM

How did these criticisms tally with Burton's moral-spiritual goals? The implications of the former were undoubtedly negative, but as with its humanist predecessors – the *De causis corruptarum artium* was cited on several occasions in the preface and main treatise[90] – its purpose was to delineate a space for an alternative approach. The message delivered by the tension between the content of the knowledge concerning disease and the sceptical method of its presentation was that it would only be through an apprehension of its limits, and recognition of its errors, that medicine could be properly administered. The Geneva edition of Sextus Empiricus issued in 1621 had asserted the value of scepticism for physicians and natural philosophers in precisely this way.[91] However, Burton's scepticism was not dogmatic but derived from his Christian humanism, and once again we find the key to his approach laid out in the preface to the *Anatomy*. What Democritus Junior ridiculed was scholarly contentiousness in all forms, but especially that which flowed from scholastic speculation on 'idle questions'; and what he advocated, following Erasmus, was a return to the practical cultivation of moral and spiritual virtue. Accordingly, what we find in the main treatise of the *Anatomy* is persistent mockery of *philosophia speculativa* – of medical-philosophical theory and the variety of therapies to which it gave rise – and a

87 For a political parallel see Vaughan 1626, pp. 85–6.
88 See also 1.390.28–9 (1.3.1.2); cf. 2.110.30–1 (2.2.6.2), and Browne 1981, p. 168.
89 On the metaphor of the labyrinth in the *Anatomy* see Starobinski 1962, p. 23.
90 See 1.64.33–4; 1.101.8; 1.102.27; and 2.99.6–9, t (2.2.5.1).
91 Sextus Empiricus 1621, fols. ¶2^{r-v}.

re-emphasis on the value of Christianised *philosophia practica*. Burton was consistent both in his association of speculative inquiry about melancholy with uncertainty and harmful contentiousness,[92] and in his prioritisation of its moral-philosophical and spiritual aspects. In this way the *Anatomy* formulated a distinctively Christian humanist analysis of the disease.

Much of what Burton undertook in the *Anatomy* could plausibly be viewed as an attempted synthesis of the theological, moral-philosophical, and neo-Galenic medical approaches towards melancholy.[93] The main treatise opened with a description of the Fall of man as the origin of all human affliction (1.121.6–128.29 [1.1.1.1]), and a typically Reformed Aristotelian identification of God as the first supernatural cause of the condition, the sender of all diseases as a just punishment for sin (1.172.4–174.10 [1.2.1.1]). More specifically, Burton gave a Philippist account of the passions which integrated Aristotelian faculty psychology, Christian theology, and orthodox Galenic medicine, locating their source in the 'depraved will' (1.160.22 [1.1.2.11]) and describing how they 'pervert the temperature of the body' (1.248.13 [1.2.3.1]). Certain passions, like envy and hatred, were sinful (1.263.5–9, 264.10–12 [1.2.3.7]), and idleness was associated with sloth (*acedia*), not only productive of agitation (1.239.7–8, 30–1 [1.2.2.6]) but a form of *tristitia* and so conducive to melancholy (1.238.25). In the analysis of cures for melancholy, there was a comparable concatenation of spiritual, moral-philosophical and medical teachings. He rejected magical or superstitious cures as unlawful (2.1.19–4.33 [2.1.1.1]; 2.8.1–11.14 [2.1.3.1]), advocated a combination of 'prayer and Physicke' (2.6.1 [2.1.2.1]), and also set out the requirement that the physician should be 'learned' and his medicine put 'in order' by method (2.11.32 [2.1.4.1]; 2.17.31–18.4 [2.1.4.3]). These stipulations were supplemented with the Hippocratic precondition that the patient had to be 'willing to be cured' and have confidence in the physician (2.14.18–19, 15.23–4 [2.1.4.2]).

When Burton came to the non-natural therapeutic category of the passions, he drew on the overlap between moral philosophy, theology, and medical psychology in this territory to give an extensive analysis of how the 'chiefest cure' of melancholy consisted in their rectification (2.99.20 [2.2.6.1]). In offering psychological therapies such as persuasion

[92] See also 1.295.16–18 (1.2.3.14), Burton 1977, 1.2, pp. 32–3.

[93] For these perspectives on melancholy in the Italian Renaissance see Brann 2002, esp. 47–8, 189–246, 303–8.

and deception to combat depression and hallucinations (2.112.2–7 [2.2.6.2]),[94] he opposed the radical strain of neo-Galenic rationalism – whose scorn of such techniques is illustrated by the mantra 'non enim verbis sed herbis aeger curatur'[95] – and adapted the implication of the Hippocratic *Aphorisms* I.1 to the humanist commonplace that rhetoric was necessary to tame unruly passions (2.106.18–19, 110.12–15).[96] The principle underlying his psychotherapeutic measures, found throughout the medical literature on melancholy from antiquity onwards, was that since such symptoms were psychologically caused, they could be psychologically rectified (2.110.21–3).[97] In this Section, the rectification of the passions was a medical-psychological enterprise, drawing on ethical doctrines and rhetorical techniques for their utility in counteracting 'cold' melancholic emotions (1.257.13 [1.2.3.4]).[98] The 'Consolatory Digression', by contrast, addressed the same problem from a moral-philosophical and spiritual point of view.

In fact, the integration of theology, moral philosophy, and medicine in the *Anatomy* was neither harmonious nor complete.[99] Although Burton detailed the physiological origins of melancholy, it is clear that he considered the most important causes of the disease to be psychological. Returning time and again to the *Charmides*, he was adamant that 'all the mischiefes of the Body, proceed from the Soule' (1.247.12–13 [1.2.3.1]; cf. 2.100.7–9 [2.2.6.1], 2.109.22-4 [2.2.6.2]), and that perturbations were 'the greatest of all' causes, 'most frequent and ordinary' (1.246.24–5 [1.2.3.1]). He gave this approach a theological grounding by insisting that after the Fall the passions are 'borne and bred with us' (1.248.5), a point elaborated with an Augustinian emphasis on the corrupt will as the root of perverted passions (1.255.30–256.6 [1.2.3.3]).[100] This was not an equally weighted alternative. Burton drew attention to the contrast between the aetiologies offered by neo-Galenic humoralism and moral philosophy or theology (1.248.16–17 [1.2.3.1]), and cited various sources,

[94] See Alexander of Tralles 1576, col. 165 (=Alexander of Tralles 1933–6, vol. II, pp. 231–2).

[95] Bartholin 1628, fol. 3^r. See Schmitt 1985, p. 14, and Maclean 2002, p. 104. But cf. 2.100.28–31, which twisted Galen 1821–33, I.8, vol. VI, p. 41, to sanction psychological therapy of melancholy; see also Galen 1997, I.899–900, p. 299, and Ferrand 1990, p. 306.

[96] Hippocrates 1978, p. 206. On rhetoric and the passions see Bacon 1906, II.18.1–5, pp. 167–71.

[97] See Rufus of Ephesus 1879, p. 459; Celsus 1953–61, III.18.17–18, vol. I, pp. 299–301; Avicenna 1608, III.1.4.20, vol. I, pp. 490, 492; Ficino 1576, III.22, p. 564; and Ferrand 1990, pp. 314, 316.

[98] For a survey see Jackson 1989.

[99] *Pace* Gardiner 1977, p. 384.

[100] See Augustine 1984, XIV.6, pp. 555–6.

including scripture, Augustine, and Vives's *De anima et vita*, strongly in favour of the latter viewpoint (1.248.18–27).[101] He devoted an entire Member to the passions as causes (1.246.17–327.24 [1.2.3.1–15]) and both a Member and a Section to their therapy (2.99.14–207.31 [2.2.6.1–2.3.8.1]). They were the 'the fountain, the subject, the hinges whereon [melancholy] turnes', which 'must necessarily be reformed' (2.100.18–19 [2.2.6.1]).

This was not necessarily in tension with the orthodox medical model of melancholy, which gave emotions an important role, and through them associated the disease with vices. It was also reasonably common for physicians to recommend moral-philosophical remedies for melancholic agitation.[102] But the same cannot be said of the way in which Burton's concern with the passions affected his use of medical-pathological categories. In the previous chapter we saw the strength of his grasp of technical Aristotelian-Galenic method and terminology, even if on occasion these were loosely applied, and that he was especially attentive to the definition of melancholy. However, despite criticising those who had 'confounded' madness and melancholy and announcing his intention to 'handle them apart' (1.132.21, 29–30 [1.1.1.4], 168.14–15 [1.1.3.4]), he frequently replicated this confusion. Madness improperly distinguished from melancholy initially entered the medical discourse somewhat inconspicuously, appearing in his citation of a case of witchcraft (1.198.26–8 [1.2.1.3]), but thereafter it resurfaced repeatedly in his analysis of 'Retention and Evacuation',[103] and subsequently throughout the main treatise.[104]

There are different ways of interpreting this confusion. By dissolving the distinction between the two conditions, Burton could have been reinforcing his portrait of the semiological chaos faced by the physician. Or he could have been writing in a deliberately 'muddy' rather than 'cleare' (1.18.10) fashion to score a satirical point against rigorous analytical distinctions in medical *theoria*.[105] However it is read, this technique permitted him to expand the territory of his investigation to

101 Augustine 1984, XIV.3, pp. 550–2.
102 For example, see Manardi 1611, IV.5, p. 39.
103 See 1.229.11; 1.230.2–5; 1.232.14; 1.233.2.
104 In the first two Partitions see, for instance, 1.234.5, 19, 25, u (1.2.2.5); 1.256.23–4 (1.2.3.4); 1.283.26–7 (1.2.3.12); 1.288.1, 28–9, 31, 33 (1.2.3.13); 1.298.20–3 (1.2.3.14); 1.303.6, 10 (1.2.3.15); 1.369.25 (1.2.4.7); 1.400.22, 25 (1.3.1.3); 1.428.24 (1.4.1.1); 2.108.8–9 (2.2.6.2); 2.109.4; 116.11–12, 19–20 (2.2.6.4); 2.219.25 (2.4.1.4); 2.226.2–3 (2.4.1.5); 2.233.4, 13 (2.4.2.2).
105 On fallacies of diction of this type see Aristotle 1967, II.24.3, pp. 326–7.

include a variety of sources dealing with any kind of mental derangement, considerably dilating the *copia* of his text. Most significantly, though, it allowed him to escape the constriction of medical-scientific discourse and realign his work to the domain of moral philosophy, specifically via the Stoic association of foolishness and madness that, as we have noted, was adopted by 'Democritus Junior' in the preface. He was fully aware of the unscientific nature of this argument ('properly or improperly... truly or metaphorically' [1.25.31–4]), but this did nothing to detract from the seriousness of its ethical import, which related not to *philosophia speculativa* but to *philosophia practica*.

That Burton's elision of melancholy and madness was driven by his prioritisation of moral philosophy was made clear by the frequency with which it occurred in his discussions of emotional disturbance. Immoderate anger was said to cause melancholy by overheating the body (1.268.26 [1.2.3.9]), but although citing Aretaeus (1.268.d), he ignored the neo-Galenic medical explanation whereby adust melancholy was produced by the burning of the humours.[106] Instead, he availed himself of an ethical commonplace, '*Ira furor brevis est*', to show that this passion caused mania (1.268.2; 269.3–21, 270.4–5).[107] Equally evident distortions of the definitional categories of melancholy and mania can be found in his survey of concupiscible passions as causes, where he showed little interest in medical detail. Some of these emotions, when immoderate, led eventually to anxiety, fear, or sorrow, and hence could cause melancholy.[108] But he was more keen to make the association between the bracket of emotions rooted in *amor sui*, based on erroneous 'selfe-conceit' (1.298.32, 293.14 [1.2.3.14]), leading us to '*forget our selves*' (1.294.15–16) and become 'insensibly mad' (1.298.20–1). The neo-Galenic teaching whereby excessive joy over-expanded and overheated the heart, initially producing pleasure and laughter but vitiating the production of vital spirits and eventually causing melancholy, was simply ignored.[109] Instead, he produced an example of 'a Smith of *Millan*' that 'for joy ranne madde' (1.301.11–13), explaining that the excessively joyful were unable to 'tell what they say or doe, they are so ravished on a sudaine; and with vaine conceits transported, there is no rule with them' (1.301.17–20). This was

[106] See, for example, Ferrand 1990, p. 229; cf. Galen 1997, II.6.641–3, pp. 264–5.

[107] On the moral identity of anger and madness see Galen 1997, I.1.3, I.5.22, pp. 100, 109–10.

[108] See 1.281.24–5 (1.2.3.11); 1.284.27 (1.2.3.12); 1.288.7–8, 18, 23–4 (1.2.3.13); 1.293.1–2. Cf. Platter 1602–3, I.3, vol. I, p. 113 (= Platter, Cole, and Culpeper 1662, p. 31).

[109] See Wright 1971, pp. 60–1; Bright 1586, p. 164; and Platter 1602-3, I.3, vol. I, pp. 110–11 (=Platter, Cole, and Culpeper 1662, p. 31).

insensible madness, yielding the symptoms of mania, but certainly not of melancholy. In short, Burton revelled in depicting the victims of concupiscible passions as 'mad, mad, mad' (1.300.7). Rather than handling melancholy and madness 'apart', he did precisely the opposite, 'the one being a degree to the other' (1.132.24–5 [1.1.1.4]).

The overwhelmingly ethical and moral-theological character of Burton's discourse on the emotions was also reflected by his tendency to abandon the mode of medical-scientific argumentation in favour of moralising judgements on human historical *exempla*. Although it was contained within a medical-analytical skeleton, the body of his survey of concupiscible passions was concerned with the description of such passions as vicious and sinful. Ambition, covetousness, self-love, pride, and an excessive love of 'Gaming', wine, and women were all denounced as the route to 'Hell and eternall damnation' (1.293.10 [1.2.3.13]). Moralising extended not just through the survey of the sixth non-natural as a cause, but throughout the first and second Partitions.[110] The approach was encapsulated by a quotation from the pseudo-Hippocratic *Letter to Crateuas*, where the 'Father of Medicine' conceded that moral philosophy was indispensable to the therapeutic art (1.283.19–23 [1.2.3.12]).[111]

The triumph of ethics over medical theory in the *Anatomy* is manifested at length in the literary discourse on love melancholy. Again it is instructive to compare Burton's work with that of Ferrand, as both authors chose to illustrate their ideas humanistically by means of literary quotations, mostly from poetic and mythological sources.[112] To understand the purpose of these, though, we must first note some of the contemporary and traditional features ascribed to love poetry. The first was that poets were increasingly being viewed as experts on love in the way that a patient was an expert on his disease, reflecting the waning popularity of the Neoplatonic ideal of love in humanist literary circles from the late sixteenth century onwards.[113] For Ferrand and Burton, poetry was the written symptom of the pathology of love, and provided material testimony of the symptoms of erotic melancholy. Ferrand wrote of the love of Petrarch, and indeed all 'effeminate' courtly love, as exemplifying

[110] See, for instance, 1.262.16–263.2 (1.2.3.6); 1.268.27–270.16 (1.2.3.9); 1.270.19–279.26 (1.2.3.10); 1.315.26–327.26 (1.2.3.15); 1.331.16–333.2 (1.2.4.2); 1.344.7–355.25 (1.2.4.6); 2.7.14–28 (2.1.2.1); 2.14.30–15.1 (2.1.4.2); 2.56.21–57.19 (2.2.3.1); 2.68.6–26 (2.2.4.1); 2.123.4–124.19 (2.2.6.4); 2.209.2–212.1 (2.4.1.1).

[111] See Hippocrates 1525, p. 710 (= Hippocrates 1990, XVI, p. 71); cf. 1.284.h.

[112] See also the comments in Ferrand 1990, p. 221.

[113] Beecher 1992, pp. 50, 57–8, 61.

love melancholy,[114] and Burton expressed a similar opinion of Petrarch and all poets, whose works were 'but as so many Symptomes of Love' (3.193.13 [3.2.3.1]). The authority of poets on the subject of love (like that of Burton on melancholy) was ambiguous, justified but also compromised by passionate, and therefore in a sense diseased, experience.

The triangular association between medicine, poetry, and love as encapsulated in the figure of Apollo, patron of both arts, offered a solution to the ambiguous authority of the poet on love matters. The employment of the medical metaphor of poetry as the agent of both the disease of love and its cure had its most influential expression in Ovid's *Remedia amoris*, where the poet called upon Apollo to unite his two domains of poetry and medicine in order to assist his battle against the disease.[115] This legitimated the paradoxical activity of turning poetry against love ('Discite sanari, per quem didicistis amare').[116] Lucretius had also exploited the power of poetry to enchant the minds of its audience, but turned it against itself by offering a 'sweet' poetic surface coating a 'bitter' philosophy attacking love, the traditional ally of poetry, as a disease of the soul.[117] This gave the Epicurean poet a means of escaping the charge that his words encouraged inordinate passion, and later provided a justification for the claim that poetic eloquence could be used as a rhetorical tool to remedy love through its power to manipulate the imagination. As both Ovid and Lucretius recognised, the success of this strategy depended upon the authorial control of the emotions generated by poetry, his guiding of the interpretation of the audience so that they came to despise rather than yearn for love, and inculcating a detached attitude towards the emotional subject matter of the discourse. One means of doing this, suggested by Stoic practice, was to provide commentary alongside the poetry.[118]

How did Ferrand and Burton address these concerns? For Ferrand, poetic quotations were primarily means of illustrating ideas provided by orthodox medical tradition:

Love, having first entred at the Eyes, which are the Faithful spies and intelligences of the soule, steales gently through those sluces, and so passing insensibly through the veines to the Liver, it there presently imprinteth an ardent desire of the Object, which is either really lovely, or at least appears

114 Ferrand 1990, pp. 253, 311.
115 Ovid 1979, pp. 182–3, 194–5.
116 Ovid 1979, pp. 180–1. See also ibid., pp. 214–15, 228–9.
117 Lucretius 1976, 1.933–49, pp. 78–9.
118 See Nussbaum 1993, pp. 136–45, esp. 139–40.

to be so. Now this desire, once enflamed, is the beginning and mover of all the sedition.

Hinc illae primae Veneris dulcedinis in Cor
stillavit gutta; & successerit frigida cura.

But distrusting its own strength, and fearing it is not able to overthrow the Reason; it presently layeth siege to the Heart.[119]

Occasionally poetic quotations supplemented Ferrand's medical discussion with additional intellectual substance,[120] but they never dictated either the structure or the content of his discourse, which remained resolutely medical. For Burton, poetry occasionally served to illustrate medical ideas, but very frequently it was given no medical context whatsoever and dominated the discussion, as in this description of physical beauty:

An high browe like unto the bright heavens, *cœli pulcherrima plaga,*

Frons ubi vivit honor, frons uni ludit amor,

white and smooth like the polished alabaster, a paire of cheekes of Vermilian colour, in which love lodgeth, *Amor qui mollibus genis puellæ pernoctas.* A corall lip, *suaviorum delubrum,* in which

Basis mille patent, basis mille latent,

gratiarum sedes gratissima, a sweet smelling flowre, from which Bees may gather hony,

Mellilegæ volucres quid adhuc cana thyma, rosasque &c.
Omnes ad dominæ labra venite meæ.
Illa rosas spirat, &c.

(3.81.23–82.3 [3.2.2.2])

In general, Ferrand subjected the authority of poets on love to that of physicians, but, for Burton, the testimonies of poets on the subject were unrivalled.

Burton also employed the classical strategy of using poetry to undermine the power of love on its audience. His description of the intended effects of his discourse in the 'Preface' to the third Partition was indeed an adaptation of the Lucretian metaphor of medicinal-philosophical poetry: 'these my writings I hope, shall take like guilded pilles, which are so composed as well to tempt the appetite, and deceave the pallat,

119 Ferrand 1640, p. 67 (= Ferrand 1990, p. 252).
120 For example, see Ferrand 1990, pp. 248–9.

as to helpe and medicinally worke upon the whole body, my lines shall not onely recreate, but rectifie the minde' (3.5.29–32 [3.1.1.1]).[121] Chilmead's 1640 translation of Ferrand included a similar metaphor with the following appended verses, composed by Richard West (also of Burton's college):

And least severer Druggs should fright, (as some
Will refuse Health, unlesse it neatly come.)
Poetry candies the Philosophy,
Like *Galen* mixt with *Sidnies* Arcadye.
Which (like two Starres conjoyn'd) are so well laid,
That it will please Stoicke, and Chambermaid.[122]

In Ferrand's book, where poetry was thoroughly subservient to medicine, the Ovidian strategy of using poetry against itself was submerged and unselfconscious, and nowhere did the author demonstrate awareness of the rhetorical power of the poetry he quoted. Burton's employment of poetry, however, showed sensitivity towards its rhetorical affectivity, and this was buttressed by his habit of attaching elaborate English translations, paraphrases, or commentaries to the verses he was quoting:

burning lust is but a flash, a gunpowder passion, and hatred oft followes in the highest degree, dislike, and contempt.

— *Cum se cutis arida laxat,*
Fiunt obscuri dentes —

when they waxe old, and ill favored, they may commonly no longer abide them.

— *Jam gravis es nobis,*

be gone, they grow stale, fulsome, loathsome, odious, thou art a beastly filthy queane,

— *faciem Phœbe cacantis habes,*

thou art *Saturni podex*, withered and dry, *insipida & vetula,*

— *Te quia rugæ turpant, & capitis nives,*

(I say) *be gone, portæ patent, profiscere.* (3.222.16–29 [3.2.5.3])

He was adept at employing poetry as a means of discouraging love, exploiting its rhetorical force to conjure up repulsive images of the beloved in the imagination of his reader so that he could 'never affect

[121] On the commonplace of the sugar-coated pill see Curtius 1953, pp. 417–35, and Olson 1982, pp. 35, 131–2.
[122] Ferrand 1640, fol. c^{r}.

her after' (3.222.6). This occurred repeatedly throughout the analysis of cures, and fulfilled the classical requirement that the emotional effect of poetry be controlled for the purpose of dissipating love from the souls of the audience.

The same end was achieved in Burton's analysis of erotic symptoms, which employed poetic quotations in tandem with mocking prose to encourage readers to detach themselves from the distorted perception and deranged behaviour generated by love. Here he aligned the lover with one of his favourite *topoi*, the ridiculous madman:

> All the bumbast Epethetes, patheticall adjuncts, incomparably faire, curiously neat, divine, sweet, dainty, delicious, &c. pretty diminitives, *corculum, suaviolum, &c.* pleasant names may be invented, bird, mouse, lambe, pus, pigeon, pigsney, kidde, hony, love, dove, chicken, ducke &c. he puts on her.
>
> *Meum mel, mea suavitas, meum cor,*
> *Meum suaviolum, mei lepôres,*
>
> my life, my light, my Jewel, my glory, *Margareta speciosa, Cujus respectu omnia mundi pretiosa sordent,* my sweet *Margaret,* my sole delight and darling.... Every cloath shee weares, every fashion pleaseth him above measure, her hand,
>
> *O quales digitos, quas habet illa manus!*
>
> pretty foote, pretty coronets... her every thing, lovely, sweet, amiable, and pretty, pretty, pretty. (3.168.25–169.12 [3.2.3.1])

So far, Burton had admirably fulfilled his therapeutic role of deterring his audience from the charms of love through his use of poetry, but it was not quite that simple. Although whilst discoursing of symptoms and cures he was concerned with suppressing the amorous passions of his audience, in his treatment of causes he was less responsible in his use of poetry than his ancient predecessors, especially when explaining the power of beauty. In the passage just quoted on the 'pleasing grace... alone sufficient to enamour' of the beautiful body (3.81.23–82.3 [3.2.2.2]), for example, he deserted his supposed duty of discouraging the passionate inclinations of his readership.[123] The same went for this description of the enchanting power of the eyes, which conjured up images quite the opposite of repulsive:

> All parts are attractive, but especially the eyes,
>
> — (*videt igne micantes,*
> *Syderibus similes oculos*) —

[123] Cf. the instruction in Lucretius 1976, IV.1063–4, pp. 358–9.

which are Loves Fowlers, *Aucupium amoris... Scaliger* calls the eyes, *Cupids arrowes*; *the tongue, the lightning of love*; *the pappes, the tents*: *Balthasar Castilio*, the causes, the chariots, the lampes of Love,

— œmula lumina stellis,
Lumina quæ possent sollicitare Deos.

Eyes emulating starres in light,
Entising Gods at the first sight.

Loves Orators, *Petronius*.

O blandos óculos, & ô facetos,
Et quâdam propriâ notâ loquaces,
Illic est Venus, & leves amores,
Atque ipsa in medio sedet voluptas.

O sweet and pretty speaking eyes,
Where *Venus* love and pleasure lies.

Loves Torches, Touch-box, Napthe and Matches, *Tibullus*.

Illius ex oculis quum vult exurere divos,
Accendit geminas lampadas acer amor.

Tart love when he will set the Gods on fire,
Lightens the eyes as Torches do desire.

(3.84.17–85.23)

At times like this, when Burton's page was filled with poetry, it became, in his own words, 'as so many Symptomes of Love' (3.193.13) – a devious rhetorical effect which was paralleled elsewhere in the *Anatomy* by the author's written exhibition of the passionate symptoms of Democritean or Heraclitean melancholy.

Such ludic literary-rhetorical qualities were nowhere to be found in Ferrand's *Traité*, which unlike the *Anatomy*, and despite its humanistic trappings, consistently strove in a scholastic fashion to raise rational and systematic medical-philosophical inquiry above chaotic experience. This contrast was manifested by a different balance between the medical and non-medical traditions in the *Traité* and the discourse on love in the *Anatomy*. Where the former consistently assimilated its literary and non-medical quotations and ideas into an essentially Galenic medical-scientific discourse, the latter took this medical discourse as its point of departure and more often than not assumed its details. It was really only the analytical structure of this part of the *Anatomy* that was conventionally medical. Whereas Ferrand's overarching preoccupation was with the certainty of medical discourse, above all in the curative power of pharmaceuticals, Burton never let his interest in medicine encroach upon his moral and spiritual priorities.

This is clear in both authors' treatment of the subject of idleness as a cause of love melancholy. For Ferrand, idleness was harmful primarily because 'all the Actions of the Minde, as Pensivenesse, and too much Thinking, doe dry up the Blood, and make it Melancholy', though it was also 'the Mother of unchaste Love' and dissolute living.[124] Burton, however, simply stated that 'Idlenesse overthrows all', offered a detailed moral exposition of the ways in which 'love tyrannizeth in an idle person', and noted almost in passing that Bernard of Gordon had called it 'the proper passion of nobility' (3.62.23–63.10 [3.2.2.1]). Both writers combined medical, moral-philosophical, poetic, and literary ideas and authorities, and herein lies their eclectic and encyclopaedic common ground. But their goals differed. Where Ferrand introduced the subject with a concise Galenic explanation, Burton either took it as a given or was simply more interested in achieving rhetorical effect by means of pithy generalisation. Whilst Ferrand contented himself with a moralistic *topos*, for Burton the whole point was a moral one, which the medical and literary quotations were designed to buttress. It is this contrast that leads us to a type of *parodia* in the *Anatomy*, insofar as what looked from the structural 'outside' like a medical treatise turned out to be an adaptation of a medical treatise. The parodic dimensions of the *Anatomy* were constituted here by Burton's use of a formal medical structure to represent the experience of pathological love through poetic discourse, and to explore its ethical and spiritual dimension through moral philosophy and theology.

There are in fact many signs in Burton's discourse that he had little interest in reconciling the medical theory of melancholy with his moral and theological concerns in systematic fashion. This became most conspicuous whenever the author addressed the passionate character of the disease. The emotions had a special status as a point of intersection between moral theology, moral philosophy, and medical psychology: they were simultaneously determinants of sinfulness, virtue or vice, and health or disease; as such, they required different kinds of therapeutic response. In the Galenic perspective, derived from *Timaeus* 86d–87b, because melancholy was caused by the humours it was not a condition

[124] Ferrand 1640, pp. 56–8 (= Ferrand 1990, p. 247).

of moral responsibility, even if it produced apparently vicious symptoms.[125] The patient, according to this view, was to be treated with compassion, and his or her condition pitied or lamented.[126] By contrast, the moral perspective, in which excessive passions were vicious, tended to make the thoughts and actions of the melancholic voluntary, even if dispositionally conditioned, and so subject to praise or blame.[127] Similarly, the Christian view of melancholy tended to condemn the condition as sinful, a consequence of the perverted will, though as with every form of postlapsarian misery it commanded charitable compassion.[128]

A possible solution derived from *Laws* 731d – remediable ills are to be pitied, irremediable ones condemned – but Burton applied no such principle and maintained an ambivalent stance towards the melancholic. In fact, this is the best indicator of the self-conscious imperfection of his synthesis and the ethical limit of his construction of medicine. Frequently he depicted the melancholic as deserving of pity,[129] but he also repeatedly subjected him or her to condemnation and ridicule.[130] Indeed, this equivocation was encapsulated in the oscillation between Heraclitean lamentation and Democritean ridicule that ran throughout the book. We should not regard such inconsistency as a failing. As we have seen, one of Burton's main arguments about melancholy was that it was too complex and infinitely particular to be comprehended by general rules, being full of 'all extreames, contrarieties, and contradictions . . . in infinite varieties' (1.395.29–30 [1.3.1.2]), so the appropriate response was not synthetic but eclectic. He was clear that amongst the myriad cases of the disease '[o]ne is miserable, another ridiculous, a third odious' (1.272.8 [1.2.3.10]), and consequently it was 'to be derided in one, pitied or admired in another' (1.395.19 [1.3.1.2]). There could be no adequate synthesis of the methods of approaching melancholy, because there could be no adequate synthesis of the descriptions of melancholy.

125 See Galen 1997, V.788ff., pp. 160–75.

126 See, for example, Lemnius 1576, fol. 145^r and Du Laurens 1599, p. 81.

127 See Aristotle 1934, III.1–5, pp. 116–53, and VII.14.8, pp. 446–7, where μελαγχολικοὶ are described as 'profligate and vicious'. For analysis see van der Eijk 1990.

128 Erasmus 1970, pp. 70, 83–90, 135–6; Wright 1971, p. 47.

129 See esp. 1.419.27–420.16 (1.3.3.1); 1.434.27–438.27 (1.4.1.1).

130 See 1.238.25 (1.2.2.6); 1.264.22 (1.2.3.7); 2.112.7 (2.2.6.2), and the third Partition, *passim*. On the tension between pity and ridicule in response to melancholy see Schleiner 1991, pp. 145–69.

KNOWLEDGE AND ITS USES

Burton's idiosyncratic presentation of the medical and philosophical materials in the *Anatomy* reflected a moderate, anti-dogmatic scepticism towards the speculative dimension of human learning that had long permeated humanism, but it was also inseparable from his compositional method. To use the *cento* format for the purpose of exploring melancholy encouraged a view of the encyclopaedia as a fragile mass of doctrine with an inherent tendency towards fragmentation and internal contradiction. As the ever-expanding character of the book demonstrated, on every topic there would always be another learned *opinio* available which could be used to supplement, refine, or more likely undermine whatever viewpoint he might have presented through appeal to the *communis opinio doctorum*. Arguably the Hippocratic particularistic experientialism of his medical analysis was also bound up with this method of proceeding, since it enabled attendance to a bewildering mass of contradictory detail without sacrificing intellectual integrity. In this respect, it was no accident that the *Anatomy* shared many of the features of Cardano's *Contradicentia*, a work which discussed *quaestiones* through the textual exposition of authoritative positions but typically eschewed the labour of reconciliation. Whilst Burton clearly adhered to the bulk of conventional orthodox neo-Galenic doctrine, what was 'anatomised' throughout the book was not so much melancholy *per se*, as the multitude of *contradicentia* that characterised the learned discourse on the disease. Little wonder, then, that Burton referred to his book – albeit with pretended humility – as a 'confused lumpe' (1.17.13).

As the *Anatomy* grew across the different editions there were signs that what had begun as only a weakly sceptical enterprise became increasingly doubtful and pessimistic. The impression that this was an appropriate response to an unwieldy and unmanageable intellectual universe can only have been heightened by the contemporary expansion of book publishing, which was increasingly overloading seventeenth-century scholarship across Europe and stimulating amongst encyclopaedists the invention of short-cuts to assist the reading and processing of overabundant printed material.[131] Burton was not unusual in denouncing his 'scribling age' in his preface (1.8.22). But both the lament that followed – 'Who can read them? As already, wee shall have a vast *Chaos* and confusion of Bookes', elaborated in 1624 with the exclamation

[131] See Blair 2003.

'What a Catalogue of new bookes all this year, all this age (I say) have our *Franc-furt* Marts, domesticke [marts] brought out, Twice a yeare?' – and the complaint that 'we are oppressed with them, our eyes ake with reading, our fingers with turning',[132] testified to anxiety and fatigue, and entrenched his view of a proliferation of discourse by which readers were, as he put it darkly, 'rather infected then any way perfected'.[133] This would help explain many of the additions new to the versions issued in 1624 and 1628, which, as we have seen, sharpened his critique of medical and philosophical sectarianism, and indicated a deepening distrust of the integrity of contemporary scholarship.

Yet this did not halt his writing. Here there is an important comparison to be made with Montaigne, whose famously accumulative text, the *allongeails*, expressed sceptical consciousness but also acted as the learned medium for the ongoing philosophical care of the self. We should recall a contrast between the two: for Burton there was no mileage to be gained from direct self-exploration. His purpose was to 'make an Antidote' for his own melancholy (1.7.24), and to 'divert' himself through scholarly investigation of a disease that he considered to be afflicting the world at large. However, as with Montaigne's writing of the *Essais*, his lifelong learned exploration of its possible causes, symptoms, prognostics, and cures was not a disinterested scholarly enterprise, but part of a psychotherapeutic regimen to assist the restoration of healthy, virtuous equilibrium to body and soul.[134] It was not just that knowledge of the causes of melancholy enabled their counteraction, for, as he wrote, understanding the nature of the disease would give 'some satisfaction to melancholy men' (1.418.20 [1.3.3.1]).[135] As well as providing the opportunity to comprehend aspects of his melancholy, the activity of learned investigation – the beneficial Hippocratic exercise of thought as psychic perambulation, or what Montaigne termed the 'exercitation' of reading – offset his pathogenic predisposition to idleness and made him 'busied in toyes' (1.6.29–7.5).[136] Philosophical study, more specifically, was for Burton a 'recreation . . . fit & proper to expell Idlenesse and Melancholy' (2.84.18 [2.2.4.1]), provoking 'hot' emotions like wonder, pleasure,

[132] Burton 1624, pp. 6–7; or 1.10.23–11.3.
[133] Burton 1624, p. 6; or 1.10.3–4.
[134] See also Lemnius 1576, fols. 13v–14r.
[135] See Plato 1926, vol. I, pp. 308–9, vol. II, pp. 212–13 (720d–e, 857c–d), reiterated in Erasmus 1970, p. 68.
[136] Hippocrates 1839–61, VI.5.5., vol. V, p. 316; Montaigne 1603, III.12, p. 619.

and delight (2.86.1–89.6).[137] On the other hand, as he made very clear, excessive intellectual activity fatigued and damaged both body and soul, especially when it was focused on the intricacies of a gloomy subject. Thus he often referred to his work as 'tedious discourse',[138] giving rise to his need for the refreshing 'recreation' of the 'Digression of the Ayre' (2.33.12 [2.2.3.1]). The satirical and ludic literary episodes found scattered throughout the book provided a counterweight to its melancholic content, and some of the subject's more fantastic elements were presented in a way that clearly reflected the author's lighthearted amusement.[139]

The literary poetics of Burton's writing were devised to serve similar purposes in a more complex fashion, and here his self-presentation as a tragicomic 'player' oscillating between the two 'parts' of Democritus and Heraclitus on the 'Stage' of the *theatrum mundi* (3.8.21–3 [3.1.1.1], 3.364.9–365.5 [3.4.1.3]) was essential. As the reference to Samuel Rowlands's *Democritus, or Doctor Merry-Man his Medicines, Against Melancholy Humours* (1607), in the discussion of therapeutic mirth (2.117.2 [2.2.6.4]) indicated, his stylistic figuration of Democritus drew on the late medieval image of the 'laughing philosopher' as 'Doctor Merry-Man'. Here, Democritus served as a comic vehicle for the production of gaiety and counteraction of sorrow in a strictly physiological fashion, by promoting the purgation of noxious black bile and stirring up (or 'lifting') the warm and moist spirits throughout the body.[140] Conversely, 'tearful' Heraclitean tragic lamentations were labelled with the purpose of expressing the central melancholic passions of sorrow and fear – as he wrote, quoting Seneca, '*for the most part all griefe evacuats it selfe by teares*' (2.180.9 [2.3.5.1]).

As Burton's retelling of the pseudo-Hippocratic fable made clear, however, satirical laughter and tragic lamentation were also integral to a consciously cultivated moral-philosophical strategy, as a kind of ethical 'medicine' to 'salve' melancholy (1.111.22–3). 'Democritus Junior'

[137] See Galen 1997, II.5.87–8, p. 141 and VI.687, p. 194; Galen 1978-84, IX.8.22–3, vol. II, pp. 596–7; Bright 1586, p. 123; Montaigne 1603, III.11, p. 614; Wright 1971, pp. 6–7. See the associations of inquiry with wonder at 1.250.6 (1.2.3.2); 2.22.3 (2.2.1.1); 2.27.16 (2.2.1.2); 2.70.25 (2.2.4.1); and 2.93.37.

[138] See for example 1.376.21 (1.2.5.3) and 2.208.4 (2.4.1.1).

[139] See 1.392.22–7 (1.3.1.2); cf. Aristotle 1967, I.11.29, pp. 128–9.

[140] See 1.114.9–10; 1.270.27–279.26 (1.2.3.10); 1.337.11–12 (1.2.4.4); 1.361.13, 25 (1.2.4.7); 2.77.30 (2.2.4.1); 2.108.4–5 (2.2.6.2); and cf. Hippocrates 1990, XVII.4, XVII.10, pp. 81, 93. Burton held a copy of Rowlands's *Democritus* in his library: Kiessling 1988, entry 1366; see also entry 1640. On this aspect of Renaissance literary stylistics see Cunningham 1960, pp. 131–262.

carried the traditional generic association of melancholic discontent with satirical anger. His derisive reaction to the melancholy of the world stemmed not just from the presence of 'so many objects' worthy of ridicule but also, in part, from the 'inward perturbations' of a malcontent temperament (1.113.12–13; cf. 1.5.29). As in the *Letter to Damagetes*, the expression of laughter was also presented as a therapeutic measure for the author – and, by provoking it in his audience, also for his readership – that cemented an ethical distance from the corrupt world as it was reprimanded and corrected. Following the received Aristotelian understanding, its tragic counterpart functioned to the same end, effecting a *katharsis* of cold emotions from the soul and instilling knowledge of self and worldly fortune.[141] Here, then, were the ways in which writing was an 'evacuation' of Burton's melancholy that assisted his pursuit of tranquillity: as physiological purgation of black bile, psychological expulsion of anger and sadness, and moral insulation against vice. The text became the psychological analogue of hellebore.

As well as presenting the fruits of scholarship to its audience, the exploration of the medical theory of melancholy in the *Anatomy* thus served a complex set of philosophical purposes for Burton, providing the vehicle for a practically moralised humanistic vision of medicine, a sceptical view of the speculative tendencies of Renaissance thought, and a therapeutic regimen for his own melancholic condition. But as was appropriate for a true Christian humanist, and as 'Democritus Junior to the Reader' made clear, Burton was far from being either inward-looking or unaffected by the condition of the society to which he belonged. It is to his concern with this that I now turn.

[141] For the extension of the Aristotelian theory beyond pity and fear see Milton 1957, p. 19.

CHAPTER 3

Melancholy and divinity

Burton began the final Section of the *Anatomy* by claiming that religious melancholy was the most widespread and serious form of the disease prevalent in the world, indeed that it 'more besots and infatuates men . . . doth more harme, workes more disquietness to mankinde, and hath crucified the soules of mortall men . . . then warres, plagues, sicknesses, dearth, famine, and all the rest' (3.331.22–8 [3.4.1.1]). The analysis of religious melancholy reveals the depth and scope of the author's commitment to educate and instil in his readership moral and spiritual virtue, and once again this involved an erudite and eclectic exploration of ancient, medieval, and neoteric texts. However, it is here that the character of the book as a consideration of the pressing issues prompted by the intellectual and political climate of Europe as they were manifested in early Stuart England comes into focus. The problem of religious melancholy in the form with which Burton was concerned had been formulated in continental post-Reformation controversy, and his analysis explicitly drew on its origins. For Burton, it was a disease that had long afflicted every society, both Christian and pagan, but it had now come especially to characterise the condition of his own Church and commonwealth. This brought him into probably the most sensitive domain of Jacobean and Caroline politics. As we shall see, this part of the *Anatomy* demonstrates the way in which Burton exploited the flexibility of his humanist conceptual resources, and realised the polemical potential of the medical-scientific theory of melancholy, to create a fully fledged political response to the spiritual pathology that he considered to have taken hold in England.

Although the most extensive treatment of spiritual topics took place in the third Partition, to understand the contemporary religious significance of the argument of the *Anatomy* in full we need to attend to the religious dimension of Burton's position in 'Democritus Junior to the Reader'. Here he claimed that the English body politic had 'the Gospel truly preached, Church discipine established', had enjoyed 'long peace and quietnesse, free from exactions, forraine feares, invasions' and 'domesticall seditions', and was in possession of 'most worthy Senators, a learned Cleargy', and 'an obedient Commonalty' (1.75.24–31). There are good reasons to be suspicious of this passage. It is true that he eschewed religious matters in the rest of his analysis of the domestic body politic, but when he turned to the spiritual madness of the world generally his discussion reflected current English concerns. The first aspect of 'times present' singled out for vituperation was 'our Religious madnesse', which was articulated by reference to a conception of healthy orthodoxy, frequently expressed by Jacobean divines, as a mid-point between the pathological extremes of Roman Catholic 'superstition' and radical puritan 'Schismaticks' (1.39.19–20; 1.41.5; cf. 1.105.28). Atheism, hypocritical zeal, and ignorance completed the catalogue of depravation (1.41.8–22), and although Burton may have been speaking here of all Christendom, his later ironic call for a reforming 'army of *Rosie Crosse* men' for England included their claim to 'amend . . . Religion' alongside 'Policy, manners . . . arts, sciences &c.' (1.84.23–5). Here were indications that he was troubled by the condition of the English Church.

We shall see later that Burton's moral-psychological contention in the preface about the melancholy of humanity, and the vision of moral and political disorder that it grounded, justified some spiritual and ecclesiastical positions which expanded in the last Section of the *Anatomy* into a quasi-medical polemic. It is easy to see how medical concepts of disease and health could be metaphorically mapped on to divinity as heterodoxy and orthodoxy. However, in contrast to other physicians who wrote about religious melancholy, such as Timothy Bright and Felix Platter, Burton eschewed the relative ideological neutrality of medical-scientific discourse in favour of extensive discussion of matters of Church and state.[1] In the Section on religious melancholy, the most important function of the medical analytic framework was in fact to conceal (and so permit) the author's participation in theological and ecclesiological controversy. Here we shall see that the large number of additions made to the second, third, and fourth editions of this part of his book were direct responses to the increasingly fraught political and religious environment of the 1620s and '30s, and so crucial indicators of Burton's polemical intentions.[2]

[1] See Bright 1586, pp. 182–242; Platter 1602–3, 1.3, vol. 1, p. 98 (= Platter, Cole, and Culpeper 1662, p. 27).

[2] For the evolution of particular aspects of Burton's religious position see Renaker 1979 and Faulkner 1998.

With close attention to these modifications and their contextual significance we will be able to assess the shifting complexion of the *Anatomy* in relation to Jacobean and Caroline religious disputes, explore the implications of this analysis for the nature of these controversies themselves, and finally address the relationship between the spiritual and humanist philosophical aspects of the overarching argument of the work.

Despite Burton's close engagement with the religious issues of his environment, his allegiances have been difficult to identify. Mainly this is because he was largely concerned with the identification of heterodox beliefs and practices as forms of religious melancholy and madness (as he had signalled in the preface, the two were elided throughout),[3] which left his views on orthodoxy nebulous. Critical opinions on Burton's religion have diverged considerably; for some he was a Calvinist, for others an Anglican.[4] Both judgements are inadequate. There are Calvinist elements in Burton's position, but these sit uncomfortably with important aspects of his agenda. Labelling him an Anglican is a better reflection of his theological and ecclesiological views, but it is anachronistic. Originating in the Restoration, the term 'Anglicanism' was not in proper use until the nineteenth century, when it was retrospectively applied to Elizabethan moderates to legitimate the status quo. It is now widely agreed that the traditional idea of an opposition between 'Anglicans' and 'puritans' in the English Church captures neither the perceptions of those involved in the disputes of the era, nor the doctrinal divisions motivating those disputes.[5] In what follows, I shall clarify the question of Burton's religion in terms immediately relevant to him and his contemporaries, beginning with a brief outline of the religious disturbances afflicting England and Europe, and progressing with surveys of the theological environment prevailing in the English universities and the Jacobean and Caroline ecclesiastical establishment, before assessing the character of his argument about the religious melancholy of his age.

ENGLAND AND EUROPE

We cannot be certain of precisely when Burton began to write the *Anatomy*, yet we know that the years of its composition broadly coincided

[3] See, for example, at 3.387.40–388.30.

[4] For Burton as an Anglican, see Macaulay 1931, p. 105; Babb 1959, pp. 86–7; Donovan 1967; Heyd 1984; Vicari 1989, pp. 92–4; and Faulkner 1998, p. 29; as a Calvinist see Tyacke 1978, p. 81 and Stachniewski 1991, pp. 219–53.

[5] On such terminology see Collinson 1980, pp. 484, 488, and Lake 1993b; on 'Anglicanism' particularly see Lake 1988, pp. 4–5, Maltby 1998, pp. 9, 236, and Tyacke 2000.

with an extended period of religious turmoil across Europe, which was in turn pressurising the fragile ecclesiastical order that had been established in England in the second half of the sixteenth century. Indeed, it is essential to an understanding of Jacobean and Caroline politics that the conflicts played out in England were part of a long-term disturbance of order in and between European states that had been set in motion and progressively deepened by post-Reformation religious divisions, and that contemporaries viewed the conflicting imperatives of political unity and confessional identity in the context of a continental crisis. From 1618 onwards, violent Habsburg and Spanish anti-Protestant policies in Bohemia and the Palatinate had drawn outraged reactions from Reformed communities across Europe, and the opposition to the Habsburg empire was galvanised in April 1621 with the expiry of the Twelve Years truce between Spain and the Dutch provinces – which then struck an alliance with the recently deposed Frederick V – and the subsequent entry of Sweden and Denmark into the fray. With Germany the main battleground, the forces of Protestantism and Catholicism engaged in a bloody conflict in which perhaps three or four million died, if not from military action then from the accompanying diseases and famines.

England participated only at the margins of the Thirty Years War, periodically giving financial aid to the international Protestant cause and waging a brief war with France (1627–9). But the European confessional conflict threatened the crucial compromise between moderate and radical Protestants established by the Settlement of 1559. The final parliamentary sessions of James's reign in 1621 and 1624 were accordingly dominated by the question of war in the Palatinate. Initially determined to avoid religious war, and the dependence on parliament it would entail, the *Rex pacificus* pursued peace through a marriage treaty with Spain. For many moderate as well as radical Protestants, this compounded the betrayal of the Protestant cause represented by non-intervention in Bohemia, and suspicions of the king's Catholic sympathies were reinforced by his unwillingness to act against recusants. These were deepened in August 1622 by his suspension of the recusancy laws and issuing of the 'Directions concerning Preaching', which forbade clergy to 'meddle with matters of State' and outlawed 'bitter invectives and indecent railing speeches against the persons of either Papists, or Puritanes'.[6]

[6] I am quoting the reproduction of the 'Directions' in Abbot 1622, pp. 2–3.

With the failure of the Spanish match in October 1623 and Imperial gains in Germany, the tide turned. In the parliamentary session of 1624, the case for war with Spain triumphed in parliament, and James sanctioned the recruitment of an English army to recover the Lower Palatinate. But in the early years of Charles's reign the position of the Protestant cause became increasingly precarious. A succession of Habsburg victories in Germany and a French alliance with Spain not only led to war with England in June 1627 but significantly increased the domestic political temperature. Discontent had been simmering in the country at the arbitrary taxation of the Forced Loan, and the deteriorating situation on the continent aggravated radical Protestant discontent at the apparent triumph of crypto-popery at the royal court, where Charles appeared to be sponsoring the spread of Arminian theology and preparing the kingdom for the reintroduction of Roman Catholicism. Meanwhile, opposition to the king's war with France grew, and the humiliating failure of the military campaigns led by the allegedly crypto-Catholic Buckingham, to Cadiz in 1625 and the Isle of Ré in 1627, were taken as signs of divine disfavour at the governance of the English Church and state.

ENGLISH THEOLOGY AND ECCLESIASTICAL POLITICS

It is well known that early seventeenth-century political ferment was inextricable from the chronic disharmony afflicting the Church. Whilst the institutionalised hostility towards Roman Catholicism in Elizabethan and Jacobean Protestantism provided a basis for religious consensus, the Reforming enterprise in England had been dogged by persistent theological and ecclesiological conflict. This was partly the result of a tension in English Protestantism between visions of the Church as a national entity and as an international community of the faithful locked into historical-eschatological struggle against Rome. The fault line was deepened and ramified in the second half of the sixteenth century, as the Lutheran movement in northern Europe became overlaid with, and in many cases supplanted by, forms of Calvinism. The drive to achieve consensus in the English ecclesiastical establishment, reflected in the breadth of the Elizabethan Settlement and the doctrinal moderation of the Thirty-Nine Articles, thus repeatedly conflicted with radical Protestant currents in the course of the late sixteenth and seventeenth centuries – as seen in the emergence, marginalisation, and eventual revival of presbyterianism.

The stakes of doctrinal dispute were raised by the ambiguous identity of the English Church and its position in the state. On the one hand, the Church was a national body over which the monarch had supreme authority. The preamble to the Act for the Restraint of Appeals (1553) stipulated that it was a part of an 'Empire' that was 'divided in Terms, and by Names of Spirituality and Temporality', but united and 'governed by one supreme Head and King'.[7] As the dual threat to monarchical sovereignty posed by papalism and sectarian independence became clear, so did the merits of a Church subordinated to the English ruler in Erastian fashion. Herein lay the appeal of Richard Hooker's influential *Of the Laws of Ecclesiastical Polity* (1593–1600). Hooker justified conformity to the ecclesiastical order as determined by the civil power, and countered the puritan severance of nature from grace and of visible from invisible churches, by grounding the civil laws in the divinely ordained laws of nature and elaborating on the Thomist assertion that *gratia non tollit naturam sed perficit.* Scriptural exegesis was therefore irrelevant to obedience, and controversies in the intrinsically uncertain territory of *adiaphora* were to be resolved institutionally. This permitted the incorporation of a broad range of divergent opinions on matters that were non-essential to salvation.[8]

However, it was essential to the spiritual status of the English Church that it was part of the sacred *corpus Christianorum* with apostolic foundations. Hooker had Christianised the political domain, but emphasising the compatibility of civil and ecclesiastical order also threatened to reduce the latter to an aspect of the former. To sacrifice the apostolically ordained authority of the clergy in matters of spiritual doctrine by adopting pure Erastianism risked desacralising the Church, and evoked a vision of civil religion akin to that of the pagan Romans infamously praised by Machiavelli in the *Discorsi sopra la prima deca di Tito Livio* (1513–19). An alternative solution, implemented in the independent Netherlands, was toleration, which diminished clerical influence and augmented secular authority. There had long been a strand of humanism which favoured toleration, originating in Erasmian scepticism concerning *fundamenta* and influencing a range of writers including Georg Cassander, Sebastian Castellio, Jean Bodin, and Jacobus Acontius, and this informed not just Hooker's thought but much of the discussion of *libertas philosophandi*

[7] Quoted from Davies 1950, p. 60.

[8] See Remer 1996, pp. 137–41.

in religious matters that occurred in the English 'Great Tew Circle'.[9] In the mid-seventeenth century, humanist latitudinarians with links to 'Great Tew', such as William Chillingworth, developed Hooker's position with the argument that, since matters of church government were not prescribed by scripture, the diverse forms of external worship in the Reformed Church were equally permissible. But to most English observers the proliferation of congregational identities that had followed toleration in the Netherlands was an unacceptably high price to pay for political stability.[10]

The Jacobean Church was caught, therefore, on the horns of a dilemma pitting spiritual rectitude against civil order. On a period of intense contentiousness the necessity of reconciling these was clear, and much has been written of the 'Calvinist consensus' in English theology at the turn of the century. But this 'consensus' incorporated doctrinal divergences that would subsequently destabilise both Church and state.[11] At one extreme were radical Calvinist puritans, nonconformists separating nature and grace, regarding themselves as an embattled, zealous community of the godly, and labelled 'precisians' by their opponents. Moderate puritans, vehemently anti-Catholic though less hostile to the national Church, and in doctrinal terms strict 'second-generation' Calvinists influenced by theologians such as Theodore Beza, cultivated a style of piety that centred on the equation of external behaviour with signs of predestined election.[12] Most representative of the middle ground were Calvinist conformists performing a double balancing act, committed to the hierarchy and authority of the national Church whilst identifying with western European Calvinist churches, and critical of the puritan emphasis on predestination but adhering to the doctrinal basis of continental Calvinism.[13] A current of so-called 'avant-garde' conformism emerged in the later years of the sixteenth century, entailing a similar commitment towards the English Church, but distinctively emphasising ceremonialism and sacerdotalism. Although maintaining their opposition to Rome, avant-garde divines such as Hooker, Lancelot Andrewes, and John Buckeridge appealed to a resurgent clericalism in the Jacobean Church. They also assumed an unfavourable stance towards Geneva and

9 See Trevor-Roper 1987, pp. 166–230, esp. 192–9, 207; Remer 1996, pp. 42–136.

10 On the issues summarised in the two paragraphs above see Lake 1988, esp. pp. 2, 240; and Pocock 1999–2003, vol. 1, pp. 13–71.

11 See Lake 1987 and Milton 1995, pp. 529–46.

12 See Lake 1982.

13 Lake 1991; Fincham 1993a, pp. 6, 8–9; Milton 1995, p. 8.

what were perceived to be the rigid forms of Calvinism – manifested particularly in an overemphasis on sermons in piety – threatening the Church from within.[14] By the second decade of the seventeenth century the conflict between the visions of spiritual life articulated by avant-garde conformists and Calvinists had thus become evident in disagreements over the priority of prayer or preaching.[15]

These tensions went to the heart of the political establishment, so it is unsurprising that the relationship between the doctrinal Calvinism of James I and his ecclesiology has been difficult to determine. James publicly opposed Conrad Vorstius, but because of the latter's alleged Socinianism rather than his Arminian ideas about predestination, and claimed to have no view on that doctrine other than the one held in the primitive Church.[16] He relished the sermons of Andrewes, but gave staunch Calvinists such as Joseph Hall opportunity to express themselves at court.[17] But his political aim of a moderately ecumenical Church based on Calvinist teaching is clear. Since the monarch was supreme governor of the Church, for James religious conformity was a matter not of conscience but of submission to royal authority. Rites and ceremonies were *adiaphora* to salvation, so nonconformity in such matters indicated disloyalty rather than spiritual transgression. This was the perspective from which James viewed the central question animating contemporary ecclesiastical-political debate, namely whether the threat of radical puritanism outweighed that of Roman Catholicism. For James the pope was Antichrist, but this was largely because he had hubristically assumed the power to depose princes; the king was manifestly unconcerned by moderate papists who had signed the Oath of Allegiance of 1606. As James's diplomatic strategy towards Spain and his subjects' reaction to his foreign policy testify, the problem of Catholic recusancy was perceived in terms of European politics, representing either – as it increasingly seemed for James as his reign progressed – a problem worth tolerating for the sake of peace, or – as it appeared to many of his radical Calvinist subjects – a fifth column preparing for the re-catholicisation of England by force. On the other hand, at least since the Admonition Controversy of the early 1570s, puritan nonconformists had been

[14] Lake 1988 and 1991; Milton 1995, pp. 8–9, 447, 521 and 2002; and Tyacke 2000.
[15] See, for example, Andrewes 1614, pp. 2–3, and Smith 1614, pp. 510–11.
[16] See James I and VI 1612 and Shriver 1970, esp. p. 459. Burton associated Vorstius with Socinus in his fifth edition: Burton 1638, p. 677; or 3.387.26 (3.4.1.3).
[17] See Lake 1991, pp. 113–33, and McCullough 1998a, pp. 101–67, esp. 147–55 on Andrewes.

associated with anti-hierarchical 'popularity', and it was the 'popular tumult' and 'fantasie' of a 'Democraticke form of governement' allegedly harboured by puritans that most exercised James in the *Basilikon Doron* (first ed., 1599).[18]

In the second and third decades of the seventeenth century, under the pressure generated by continental warfare the consensus of the early years of James's reign gradually disintegrated, and with it went the common ground between conformist and nonconformist. As in the 1590s, the labels of popery and puritanism remained the chief currency of dispute,[19] but, along with the persistence of recusancy, growing awareness of the Arminian movement in the Netherlands bestowed a new potency upon these labels. Indeed, the association between anti-puritanism, espoused by avant-garde conformists questioning the high Calvinism of the later Elizabethan era, and Dutch Arminianism became a polemical commonplace in Jacobean disputes over predestination. Although the connection between the theology of Arminius and English anti-Calvinism in these years is controversial – many supposed 'Arminians' appear not to have been directly familiar with Arminius's teachings until after they had been accused of adhering to them, and few English divines admitted to Arminian beliefs – there is a danger of underestimating the significance of contemporary perceptions. For the opponents of William Laud in particular, English Arminianism was real and betrayed a secret sympathy for Romanism.[20]

Polarisation over predestination was temporarily halted by the official English participation in the Synod of Dort in 1618–19. In the years immediately surrounding Dort, which was seen to define a Reformed doctrine of absolute double predestination as Protestant orthodoxy, the king silenced anti-Calvinist preachers such as Andrewes and Edward Simpson of Trinity College, Cambridge, on the issue.[21] But Dort solved nothing for James. In the early 1620s, ongoing contention about the theology of grace appeared to the king as part of a broader sedition in the realm, also manifested in disquiet about his pacific foreign policy and *de facto* toleration of recusants, and it was this which the 'Directions

[18] James I and VI 1603, pp. 38–44; cf. Heylyn 1668, p. 71. On puritan 'popularity' see Lake 1988, pp. 59–65; Cogswell 2002, p. 214; Cust 2002, pp. 239–42.

[19] See Heylyn 1668, p. 126.

[20] For the range of opinion on this matter see Tyacke 1987a, esp. pp. 199–202, and 1987b; Lake 1987; Bernard 1990; Sharpe 1992, pp. 284–308; Davies 1992, pp. 205–50; White 1992; and Milton 1995, pp. 435–7. Cf. the distinction between English and Dutch Arminianism in Heylyn 1668, p. 127.

[21] Fincham and Lake 1985, pp. 190–1; McCullough 1998a, p. 128.

concerning Preachers' sought to extinguish. Alongside the censorship of divines who might 'meddle with these matters of state', the 'Directions' declared that 'no Preacher of what title soever, under the degree of a Bishop or Deane at the least', should preach on 'the deepe points' of the theology of grace 'in any populous auditorie', but should instead leave such matters to 'the Schooles and Universities'.[22] James feared the spread of doctrinal division over predestination in the country at large, but at this time permitted its discussion in appropriate circles – one of Buckingham's chaplains reportedly preached a sermon 'totally for Arminianism' in 1622.[23] The subsequent about-turn in foreign policy briefly assuaged critics of popery at court, but controversy soon resurfaced. In 1624, Richard Montagu published his polemical *New Gagg for an Old Goose*, which appeared to defend Arminianism, and in the following year the same author's *Apello Caesarem*, licensed by Francis White with the provocative declaration 'that there was nothing contained in it but what was agreeable to the public faith, doctrine, and discipline established in the Church of England', appeared to have made a successful bid for royal support against his growing army of critics in the Commons.[24]

By the time Montagu's *Apello Caesarem* had appeared in May 1625, Charles had ascended the throne, and soon afterwards the balance of theological power shifted decisively. In February 1626 the new king aligned himself with the anti-Calvinist cause by having William Laud, then Bishop of St David's, officiate as Dean of Westminster at his coronation. He then promoted Laud to the bishopric of Bath and Wells and the office of Dean of the Chapel Royal, made vacant in September by the death of Andrewes in September, and promised him the future archepiscopate. The steady rise of Laud, who in the following year became a privy counsellor, was accompanied by another royal campaign to suppress predestinarian controversy. In June 1626, drawing on the precedent of the 'Directions concerning Preachers', Charles issued a Proclamation outlawing discussion of doctrinal dispute in the pulpit and press. When this failed, it was followed in 1628 by the republication of the Thirty-Nine Articles with a prefatory Declaration forbidding any interpretation other than the 'literal and grammatical sense' of the Articles and 'all further curious search' on 'those curious points in which

[22] Abbot 1622, pp. 2–3.
[23] See Cogswell 1989, p. 93.
[24] On the publication of Montagu's works see Lambert 1989.

the present differences lie'.[25] Opponents of Arminianism saw this as muzzling the denunciation of heresy. The parliamentary response was to 'reject the sense of the Jesuits and Arminians' put upon church doctrine, and alarm at the king's support for allegedly crypto-Catholic theology provoked the denunciation of Arminianism as 'a cunning way to bring in Popery' in the Commons' remonstrance of 1628.[26] Immediately after the closing of the session in July, Charles signalled his intentions by promoting Montagu and Francis White to the sees of Chichester and Norwich respectively, and moving Laud to the bishopric of London.

What made the predestinarian disputes dangerous from all points of view were their broad theological and political ramifications. Persistent disagreement on the issue provoked thorny questions about the English Church – about the means by which dogmatic orthodoxy was constituted, and the Church's relations with continental Protestantism – that were fundamental to its fractured identity. Advocates of constitutional or 'mixed' monarchy in the Commons were also unsettled by the evident conjunction between sympathy for Arminianism and belief in *iure divino* kingship and episcopacy. Whereas Calvinists preserved the ultimate authority of clergy over spiritual matters insofar as they preached and expounded the Word of God, this was apparently challenged by Arminianism, which suggested that the actions of believers in the social domain not only could contribute to salvation but also were subject to civil authority.[27] The extension of civil authority into previously clerical territory had attracted James to Remonstrant ecclesiology, which in this respect buttressed the divine-right monarchism that had been foreshadowed in the avant-garde conformism of Andrewes and would characterise Charles's 'Personal Rule'.[28]

These issues were crystallising in the 1620s, but the wider sacramental and ceremonial dimensions of the ecclesiastical policies of Charles and Laud were not fully evident until the latter assumed office at Canterbury in 1633. From being 'things indifferent' under James, rites and ceremonies were gradually promoted to the status of matters of faith, though Laudians also made traditional conformist appeals to *fundamenta* and *adiaphora*.[29] 'Laudianism'[30] emerged in a piecemeal fashion, as a series

25 Hardwick 1851, pp. 201–2.
26 Hardwick 1851, pp. 192, 206; Young 1997, p. 62.
27 See Pocock 1999–2003, vol. I, pp. 50–71, esp. 51, 54.
28 See also Howson 1602, pp. 24–7.
29 See Lake 1992.
30 For the shortcomings of this terminology, which I adopt for convenience, see Collinson 1985, pp. 220–1. The case for the alternative use of 'Carolinism' is argued in Davies 1992.

of policies concerning external observance that revolved around the glorification of the 'beauty of holiness', and were represented in a nationwide programme of church refurbishment, altarwise positioning of communion tables, and elevated celebration of feast-days in the church calendar. Lying behind these measures, and also such anti-puritan activities as the anti-sabbatarian campaign spearheaded by the reissuing of the Jacobean Book of Sports, were a number of significant attitudes and beliefs held by Laud and his supporters (such as the 'Durham House Group'). These included an emphasis on the sacerdotal identity of the priesthood; the grounding of episcopacy in a divinely sanctioned hierarchy of natural order; a rejection of the Foxeian apocalypticism and prophetic discourse that had been central to English Protestantism from its beginnings; and a concomitant questioning of the Pope's identity as Antichrist and acceptance of the Roman Church as part of the true, 'visible' Church – albeit one that needed serious reform.[31]

In tandem, Laud pursued an ideal conception of a harmonious national Church fully integrated to the Commonwealth under the sovereignty of the monarch and undistorted by dependence on lay patronage. To this end he sought to tighten ecclesiastical discipline through the episcopal hierarchy, regulate the distribution of crown patronage, quench disorder in the universities, and control the content of religious publications.[32] In 1633 the Articles of the Church were again reissued, with another royal Declaration forbidding 'all curious search' and 'disputes' of matters that ought to be 'shut up in Gods promises', and singling out 'Our Universities' for especial scrutiny in this regard.[33] Although his opponents later denounced these policies as introducing and censoring godly opposition to crypto-Catholic innovation, they were justified by Laud as correctives to the Calvinist excesses of recent years, 'the reducing of [the Church] unto order, the upholding of the external worship of God in it, and the setting of it to the rules of its first reformation'. These goals tallied with Charles's desire to 'reduce all things to the times of Elizabeth'.[34] Here was a vision of an autonomous Church that was returned to its origins as both national and Reformed, and that was

[31] See Milton 1993 and 1995; Sharpe 1992, pp. 317–45; Lake 1993a; Merritt 1998; Fincham 2000 and 2001; and MacKenzie 2002.

[32] See variously Sharpe 1981 and 1992, pp. 284–92, 363–9; Tyacke 1993, pp. 66–7; Fincham 1993b; McCullough 1998b.

[33] *Articles agreed upon by the arch-bishops and bishops* … 1633, sigs. A4^{v}–B1^{v}.

[34] Laud 1847–60, vol. VI, p. 42.

constituted as an apostolic body with a sacerdotal clergy under episcopal command.

UNIVERSITY THEOLOGICAL DISPUTE

The roots of the doctrinal conflicts that erupted in England in the 1620s can be seen in the university controversies surrounding the theology of grace in previous decades. These first erupted in Cambridge in the 1590s, when Peter Baro and William Barrett became embroiled in a series of disputes on predestination,[35] and in March 1595 Lancelot Andrewes, then Master of Pembroke Hall, entered the fray by challenging the doctrine of the perseverance of the elect in a sermon before the queen at Hampton Court.[36] At Oxford, second-generation Calvinism had been dominant since the 1570s, but persistent opposition from *émigré* theologians such as Francesco Pucci and native anti-puritan moderates suggests that the account of the 'Agitations and Concussions' in the university later described by the Laudian apologist Peter Heylyn is plausible.[37] Not long after Burton came up to Oxford in 1593, strict Calvinists such as Henry Airay were venting their spleen in the university against the 'outworne errors of Pelagianisme . . . Libertie of will, universalitie of grace, salvation of all men, and other like damnable errours' poisoning the Church,[38] and avant-garde divines such as John Howson – a Student at Christ Church since 1577 and the future Bishop of Oxford – were denouncing Calvinist spirituality, particularly its emphasis on preaching to the neglect of Prayer Book offices and communion.[39]

In the second of a series of sermons delivered between 1597 and 1602, a copy of which Burton held in his library,[40] Howson argued that the material decay of English churches had come to reflect a degradation of piety in which congregations were now 'holding the only exercise of the service of God to heare a Sermon'. According to the example of primitive Christianity, churches were to be furnished 'in the most sumptuous manner' appropriate to worship through the sacraments and 'christian mysteries'; and according to apostolic authority, prayer was to take priority over preaching. But now, he lamented, churches were 'little better

35 See Porter 1958, pp. 277–412.
36 Andrewes 1629, pt I, pp. 299–308, esp. pp. 302–5. See Tyacke 1993, p. 63.
37 Dent 1983, pp. 92, 100, 103–25, 126–51; Heylyn 1668, pp. 50–6, 61–2, 68–9, 71–3, 95–7, 126–7. Cf. Wood 1792-6, vol. II, p. 350.
38 Airay 1618, p. 302, cited and discussed in Tyacke 1987a, p. 61.
39 See Tyacke 1997, p. 581.
40 Kiessling 1988, entry 845.

then hogstyes', and '*oratoria* are turned into *auditoria*; oratories into auditories'.[41] Having ascended to the vice-chancellorship in July 1602, Howson defended the observance of the holy 'festival daies' of the Church, and again complained that '*Oratoria*' had been 'turned into *auditoria*' and 'Churches into Schooles'.[42] This provoked an inquiry by the Privy Council.[43] In 1607, the chaplain of Christ Church, Humphrey Leech, went further, preaching a sermon in the college openly attacking Reformed orthodoxy and repudiating the Calvinist doctrine of election. Leech continued to do similarly until he left the university two years later and converted to Rome.[44]

It is appropriate that the colleges of Laud and Burton – the two figures I am principally concerned with in this chapter – were playing important roles in the growing university factionalism. Both had significant associations. St John's was a Roman Catholic foundation dating from the time of Queen Mary, and under Elizabeth a number of its fellows had converted to Rome. Christ Church had a royal founder in Henry VIII, hosted the cathedral of the Oxford diocese, and would be home to the relocated palace of Charles during the Civil War.[45] In 1611 Robert Abbot, brother of the current archbishop, denounced an emerging Arminianism in Oxford at the Act, and in the following years he turned his sights against Laud at St John's and Howson at Christ Church.[46] In the account of Laud's life by Heylyn, the former 'heard himself sufficiently abused for almost an hour altogether' in a sermon delivered by Abbot before the university at St Mary's in 1614, 'and that so palpably and grossly, that hee was pointed to as he sate'. As Heylyn related the incident, Abbot turned directly on Laud from the pulpit, questioning whether he was 'ROMISH *or* ENGLISH? PAPIST *or* PROTESTANT?' According to Heylyn, Laud would have been 'more troubled at this harsh usage', had not others, such as '*Howson* and [Richard] *Corbet*, both of *Christ Church*', been 'handled in as ill manner' by Abbot 'not long before' for casting aspersions upon Calvinist doctrine.[47] By 1615 Howson had become a canon of Christ Church, and in June of that year, in front of the king at Greenwich, he was involved in a heated altercation with

41 Howson 1598, pp. 22–7, 40–1.
42 Howson 1602, p. 6.
43 See Dent 1983, p. 212, and Tyacke 1997, p. 571.
44 Dent 1983, pp. 234–7. See Leech 1609, and the refutation in Price 1610.
45 See the approval of Christ Church in Heylyn 1668, p. 8.
46 Tyacke 1997, p. 578.
47 Heylyn 1668, pp. 67–8.

Archbishop George Abbot about the relative dangers of puritanism and crypto-popery.[48]

The following decade, at least in the eyes of its opponents, saw the full emergence in Oxford of Arminianism, beginning in 1623 with a university sermon preached by Gabriel Bridges against absolute predestination.[49] With Charles on the throne, Montagu reported that '[a]t Oxford they are all on fire' over the doctrine,[50] and in 1629, when a parliamentary attempt to investigate the universities was foiled by Charles's dissolution of the session, a group of Oxford anti-Calvinists raised the question of the confessional basis of the national Church.[51] Before long the national situation was brought to bear upon the university with the election of Laud as Chancellor in 1630, and he promptly ensured the ascent of the Arminian Thomas Jackson to the presidency of Corpus Christi. On the basis of the university's established role as a 'seminary' for future ecclesiastical and political office-holders, his priority – reflected in the personal attention devoted to the new statutes eventually completed in 1636 – was to address the indiscipline that was 'the cause of all our ills in church and state'.[52] Within a year of his election, a group of Oxford Calvinists in breach of the 1628 declaration had been hauled up before Charles at Woodstock, and high Calvinist theology on predestination deleted from the Act.[53] In 1634, *An Apology of English Arminianisme* (authored by 'N. O., heertofore of the University of Oxford') stated that 'there are divers, in the *Universities*, most strong in the sayd doctrines' of Arminius, the 'truth of which' was now 'fully acknowledged'. Such views were now unlikely to be met by Calvinist rebuttal.[54]

The position of Christ Church was now clear. In the first two decades of the century, the influence of those such as Howson had been countered by the Calvinist canon John Prideaux, Laud's arch-enemy and Regius Professor of Divinity, and he was apparently supported by the Deans Thomas Ravis, John King, and William Goodwin. But in 1620 the balance shifted decisively with the accession to the deanship of Richard Corbett. His successor in 1629 was Brian Duppa, who was at the

48 See Cranfield and Fincham 1987, and Fincham and Lake 1985, pp. 191, 193–6.
49 Tyacke 1987a, p. 74.
50 Quoted in Trevor-Roper 1987, p. 65.
51 Hoyle 1986, p. 420; Tyacke 1987a, p. 78.
52 Laud 1847–60, vol. V, p. 101, cited in Sharpe 1981, p. 162.
53 Curtis 1959, pp. 173–4; Tyacke 1997, p. 585, and 1993, p. 69.
54 *An apology for English Arminianisme* 1634, sig. A4^r. The dialogue pitted 'Arminius' against 'Enthusiastus'.

forefront of the campaign to elect Laud as Chancellor in 1630, was granted the see of Chichester, and subsequently oversaw the late archbishop's will. Duppa was followed by Samuel Fell, a royal chaplain with an anti-puritan record, who was also granted Laud's patronage. Under Charles, Burton's former tutor and Laud's 'ancient friend' John Bancroft rose to the bishopric of Oxford, where he became a vigorous enforcer of the Laudian policies regarding the Book of Sports and the positioning of altars. This earned him a warm commendation in 1639 from the Christ Church canon Richard Gardiner.[55]

THE INTELLECTUAL COMPLEXION OF LAUDIANISM

Two characteristics of these developments have induced controversy in modern historiography. The first is the intellectually elusive character of the Laudian enterprise. In contrast to his voluminous output on matters of policy, Laud published little that is indicative of his theological preferences, being happy to leave the enterprise of legitimating his projects to his supporters. This has left the commitments of Laud open to question, and some see English Arminianism as a chimera manufactured by the archbishop's enemies and the agenda of later apologists such as Heylyn.[56] It is true that Laud and his contemporary supporters had no real interest in actively and publicly propagating an alternative teaching on predestination. The sacramental piety that they sought to advance was constructed in opposition to the doctrinal dogmatism of orthodox Calvinism, and one of their strategies was to displace predestination from the centre of Reformed soteriology. Yet the manner in which they dealt with Arminian theology, and the way this gelled with Church reforms of the 1630s, gives partial justification to their opponents' suspicions. Whereas doctrinal Calvinists rarely spurned the opportunity to condemn Arminian theology as erroneous, heretical, and popish, Laud and his followers usually suspended judgement on the issue. From this point of view, adherence to any teaching on the theology of grace, whether Calvinist or Arminian, was unwise. But the contemporary perception that the universalist model of piety implied by the Arminian stance on predestination agreed with the Laudian programme – in both, every

[55] See Fincham 1993b, p. 85; 1997, pp. 199, 205, 208–9; 2000, pp. 79–80, 90; and 2001, 928–9, citing Richard Gardiner, *A sermon concerning the Epiphany preached at the cathedrall church of Christ in Oxford* (Oxford, 1639), sig. A3i.

[56] See, for example, White 1992 and Sharpe 1992, pp. 286–92.

single believer was invited by God actively to pursue their own salvation – was essentially correct.

This is one reason why 'that great bugbear of Arminianism' caused Laud so much discomfort.[57] He claimed at his trial that 'I have nothing to do to defend Arminianism, no man having yet charged me with the abetting any point of it'.[58] It is not just the context of this evasive remark that suggests we should treat it with suspicion, however.[59] His subsequent defence was to assert that he had 'ever Consented' to James's 'Opinion' of 'the Article of the Church of England', and to muddy the waters by recalling that James had insisted on 'a great deal of difference' between the Arminians Vorstius and Pieter Bert (Bertius) (the latter had claimed that the denial of perseverance in his *Hymenaeus desertor, sive de sanctorum apostasia problemata duo* (1601) accorded with the teaching of English Church).[60] Laud's position is summed up by his closing argument, in which concern for Protestant unity and dislike of controversy combined with a pointedly anti-Calvinist approval of Lutheranism:

> . . . for the peace of *Christendom*, and the strengthening of the *Reformed Religion*, I do heartily wish these Differences were not pursued with such Heat and Animosity, in regard that all the *Lutheran Protestants* are of the very same Opinions, or with very little difference from those which are now called *Arminianism*.[61]

The association of Arminianism with Lutheranism proved useful for Laud's supporters, as it permitted them to deal with predestination in a way that undermined the Calvinist orthodoxy whilst maintaining their Reformed credentials. In his *Tischreden* (1566), Luther had described how he had been 'thoroughly plagued and tormented with such cogitations of predestination', but concluded that 'God reserves his secret will to himself'. He had also written elsewhere that 'forever tormenting oneself with the question of election' rather than turning to Christ produced only anxiety and was a sin comparable to murder.[62] Similarly, although Melanchthon expressed views anticipating Arminius – agreeing with Chrysostom that 'God draws, but he draws him who is willing' – in

57 Laud 1847–60, vol. VII, p. 275. See Trevor-Roper 1987, p. 69.
58 Laud 1695, p. 353.
59 As admitted in Sharpe 1992, p. 286.
60 Laud 1695, p. 353; James I and VI 1612, p. 15.
61 Laud 1695, pp. 352–3.
62 Luther 1995, p. 310 (no. 661); Luther 1955, pp. 137–8 (letter to an unknown person, 8 August 1545).

the Augsburg Confession he remained silent on predestination.[63] As there was a good case for seeing the Thirty-Nine Articles of 1563 as embodying the moderate Lutheran suspension of judgement about predestination, appealing to this position in the 1630s could justify the Laudian reforms as a return to the early stages of a Reformation that had since deviated from the example of the primitive church and patristic orthodoxy.[64] Heylyn presented the clearest instance of this viewpoint, associating the 'first *Reformers*' in England with approval of Lutheranism rather the Calvinism as a better approximation of the 'Primitive Patterns',[65] and conflating '*Arminianism*' with 'the *Melanchthonian doctrine of Predestination*' and the 'true original and native' tenet of the English Church 'at her first *Reformation*'.[66] Heylyn bestowed false coherence upon the *ad hoc* policies of the Personal Rule, but the similarity he perceived between Lutheran and Laudian stances on predestination is important. The least ambiguous statement we have from Laud himself on the doctrine, that 'the truth whatsoever it be . . . is not determinable by any human reason in this life', together with his assertion of the essential identity of Arminianism and Lutheranism, suggest that Heylyn's explanation of his patron's viewpoint is plausible.[67]

The question of whether Laud was secretly a doctrinal Arminian cannot be resolved here, but we should attend to the character of Laudian scepticism about areas of Christian dogma, which was directed against second-generation Calvinist scholasticism. This is evident in two sermons preached in 1634 by the royal chaplain and Fellow of All Souls College, Thomas Laurence, the first at Oxford and the second in front of the Archbishop at Salisbury. For Laurence, scholastic Calvinist teachings on predestination were not just hubristic intrusions upon the *arcana Dei*, but acts of spiritual violence upon individual believers. In contrast to the 'curiositie', 'needlesse speculations', and 'frothy agitations' of those 'unquiet heads' who propagate 'Schoole-Divinity' and thereby make 'that yoke heavy' which 'God himselfe made easie and light', he argued that 'the clew of predestination' should 'not be reel'd up at the spindle, nor the decrees of God unravelled at the lome', and that instead Christians should be turned 'to those happy regions' of the life of devotional

63 Melanchthon 1834–60, vol. XVI, cols. 192–3, and vol. XXI, col. 330.
64 Cf. Howson 1598, p. 25.
65 Heylyn 1668, p. 4. See also ibid., p. 126.
66 Heylyn 1668, pp. 30–1, 126–7. See also pp. 79–80 for a similar view of Dutch Arminianism.
67 See Laud 1847–60, vol. VI, pt 1, p. 292, and vol. VII, p. 275.

practice.[68] The sceptical Laudian vision of the ineffability of the divine mystery of predestination could ground an argument about tranquillity of soul with pastoral as well as polemical appeal, and indeed this psychologically therapeutic imperative was partly responsible for Laud's difficulties with the theology of grace. Writing to William Fiennes, Laud recorded his abomination at the idea that 'God from all eternity reprobates by far the greater part of mankind to eternal fire, without an eye at all to their sin', as it made 'the God of all mercies' into 'the most fierce and unreasonable tyrant in the world'.[69] His comment '[f]or that Christ died for all men is the universal and constant doctrine of the catholic church in all ages, and no error of Arminius', shows how the attempt to counteract the notion of God as a tyrant could provoke suspicions.[70] When scepticism about the limits of human comprehension was extended to encompass the totality of heavenly mysteries, it could also command the humility required by the divine presence in the world, and so gel with the forms of ceremonial and sacramental worship appropriate to the Laudian celebration of the 'beauty of holiness'. This structure of belief was rarely explicit, but it can be seen in Laurence, who claimed that his position on the frailty of the intellect did not permit him to 'justify' any particular doctrine, but defended the Lutheran understanding of the eucharist because it 'better preserved the honour of the Altar'.[71]

These were characteristically Laudian concerns, positions, and beliefs, but there is still a danger of reifying the religious ideologies of this period, and herein lies a second source of historiographical difficulty. Neither Calvinism nor Laudianism existed as fully formed, self-contained, or static intellectual systems to which individuals chose to subscribe. In fact, there are strong indications that Calvinism and Laudianism intermingled in many respects.[72] In a period that experienced religious and political instability and change across the continent, and intense controversy at home, the theological climate was uncertain, and individuals not only held beliefs straddling apparently antagonistic categories, but also developed new and abandoned old commitments. Both Thomas

[68] Laurence 1635, pp. 16–17, 22, 25, 27–8. On Laurence see Lake 1993a, pp. 164, 171, 179.
[69] Laud 1847–60, vol. VI, pt 1, p. 133. See Tyacke 1993, p. 66.
[70] Laud 1847–60, vol. III, p. 304.
[71] Laurence 1635, pp. 30–1, 32–4. Cf. Howson 1598, pp. 11–12, 15, 19–21, 37–9, though the scepticism is here attenuated. On this aspect of Laudianism see Pocock 1985, p. 296, and Lake 1993a, p. 184.
[72] See particularly Milton 1995, esp. pp. 533–6, and 2003.

Jackson and Francis White espoused anti-Calvinist views but retained the Protestant apocalyptic explanation of church history.[73] Criticisms of sermon-centred piety originated in the anti-puritan case made by John Whitgift in the 1580s, but were also made by Calvinist conformists such as Richard Bancroft.[74] In his early career, Laud himself defended the doctrine of perseverance against Cardinal Bellarmine.[75] Similarly, Heylyn's *Microcosmos* (first edition, 1621) exhibited many of the features of Jacobean Calvinism, including distress at the recent fortunes of the Palatinate, the Foxeian account of the history of the Church, and the identification of the Pope as Antichrist.[76] But perhaps most significant is the trend set in motion by the demise of the Jacobean 'Calvinist consensus'. As the 1620s progressed doctrinal Calvinists committed to the English Church were presented with a conflict of loyalties. It seems likely that with the transfer of power many conformists re-examined their beliefs and acquiesced in the new direction of the national Church, drifting towards Laudianism in the later 1620s, settling into it in the 1630s, and emerging elsewhere in the 1640s.[77]

RELIGIOUS MELANCHOLY

As Burton wrote the *Anatomy*, then, the religious-political turmoil that afflicted Europe fuelled controversy and confessional instability not just in England but in his immediate university environment. Indeed, the role of Christ Church in the ongoing theological disputes seems to have influenced Burton's treatment of the religious aspects of melancholy. Before proceeding to explore the relationship of the *Anatomy* to this historical environment, however, we should first briefly revisit the way in which the spiritual heritage of his general argument about melancholy, and its structure as established in the preface, enabled him to adapt a discourse on what was ostensibly a medical subject to express his religious concerns. After recapitulating the argumentative framework he employed to analyse spiritual melancholy, I shall continue by addressing its satirical and serious religious-ideological content, which as it evolved across the expanding editions of the *Anatomy* showed Burton to be commenting on the controversies surrounding him, and adapting what began as a case for

[73] See Milton 1993, p. 210.
[74] See McCullough 1998a, p. 164.
[75] See Tyacke 1993, p. 58.
[76] Heylyn 1625, pp. 110, 118.
[77] See Milton 1995, p. 535, and 2003, pp. 183–4.

Calvinist conformism into a distinctively humanist argument in support of Laudian policy.

As we saw in chapter one, theories of melancholy from the classical era onwards had imbued the disease with religious significance, and it subsequently became intertwined with medieval and early modern teachings concerning spiritual despair drawn from the patristic theory of *acedia*. It was the latter development above all that lay behind the heightened significance of the disease in early modern spiritual discourse.[78] Extreme passions of the soul, and the condition of despair in particular, had been given prominent roles in Protestant theology. But as the publication of countless works across Europe portraying the Christian life as a perpetual psychomachy shows, disturbing emotions were also of deep significance in Counter-Reformation spirituality as products of the postlapsarian soul's disordered condition.[79] Crucially, these religious connotations made the theory of melancholy ripe for use in sectarian controversy. In neo-Galenic medical writings, the irrational symptoms of chronic fear, sorrow, and delusions often attributed to diabolical influence were described, in accordance with the principles of classical moral psychology, in unequivocally negative terms: no spiritual or corporeal good could come of them. Religious controversialists could thereby plausibly redescribe passionate spirituality as psychopathology; both Luther and Zwingli, for instance, associated Anabaptism with madness and melancholy, and ridiculed schismastics with the charge that they were suffering from deranged enthusiasm and melancholic delusions. Here was the quasi-medical basis of late Elizabethan and Jacobean criticisms of puritans as misguidedly zealous and deranged. In the *Basilikon Doron*, James I denounced the destabilising influence of puritans by describing them as 'brainsick and headie preachers', who were misled by 'their owne dreames and revelations' into 'breathing nothing but sedition and calumnies, aspyring without measure, rayling without reason, and making their owne imaginations (without any warrant of the word) the square of their conscience'.[80]

The final Section of the *Anatomy* juxtaposed this stock condemnation of Protestant radicalism with a parallel and equally traditional Reformed critique of Roman superstition, and in so doing it constructed the moderate orthodoxy as the *via media* between the erroneous extremes

78 More generally see Schleiner 1991, pp. 74–110, and Heyd 1995, pp. 11–71.

79 See Delumeau 1990, pp. 186–326; cf. MacDonald 1982, pp. 113–15.

80 James I and VI 1603, sig. A5^{r}, p. 42; cf. Howson 1598, p. 12. See also Ormerod 1605, sig. D2^{v}, cited and discussed in Schleiner 1991, pp. 118, 121.

of Rome and Geneva. This was conventional enough. Burton's innovation was to integrate a basically polemical position within a medical-scientific framework – a strategy supported by his continued employment of neo-Galenic topics – and to anchor this perspective in his moral-psychological argument about melancholy, providing his intervention in contemporary religious conflict with a humanist philosophical rationale. Largely eschewing medical details, his approach was initially dictated by the Paracelsian intimation that 'against material diseases material remedies should be applied; against spiritual diseases, spiritual remedies'.[81] But more important to the structure of his account was the conception of love elaborated by the Neoplatonists Leone Ebreo and Marsilio Ficino: religious melancholy was a disease in which the desire properly drawn from human beings towards divine beauty was either defective or perverted (3.332.5–337.7 [3.4.1.1]). This enabled the Augustinian description of the condition as a degeneration of righteous *amor Dei*, and its by-product charity, into sinful and vicious *amor sui*. Burton's analytical framework was completed by the denotation of the 'two extreames of *Excesse* and *Defect*' manifested by 'Superstition' and 'Impiety', or in 'Idolatry and Atheisme' (3.337.24–7). The former category indicated not the theological impossibility of an excessive love of God, but rather being 'zealous without knowledge, and too sollicitous about that which is not necessary' (3.337.27–32).

The contemporary polemical significance of this idea of 'excessive' religious love was immediately apparent, as was the psychological imperative that underwrote it. According to Burton, this category was inhabited both by those who concerned themselves with 'impertinent, needlesse, idle, and vaine ceremonies' and by those who proudly considered that they were 'better Christians, better learned, choice spirits, inspired, know more, have speciall revelation, perceave Gods secrets, and thereupon presume, say, and doe that many times which is not befetting to bee said or done' – in other words, 'all superstitious Idolaters, Ethnickes, Mahometans, Jewes, Heretickes, Enthusiasts, Divinators, Prophets, Sectaries, and Schismatickes' (3.337.32–338.10). This approach subsequently evolved into a denunciation of the parallel excesses of puritanism and Roman Catholicism.[82] Burton was concerned

[81] See 1.173.31–2 (1.2.1.1), 2.3.24–5 (2.1.1.1) and Paracelsus 1996, p. 167. Cf. Platter 1602–3, 1.3, vol. 1, p. 120 (= Platter, Cole, and Culpeper 1662, p. 34).

[82] Burton's usage of the term 'puritan', e.g. at 1.324–13.14 (1.2.3.15) and 3.406.8 (3.4.2.1), suggests that they were the polar opposite of 'papists'.

less with heterodoxy *per se* than with its effects on the soul. '[A]l the world knowes', he wrote, that 'Religion is twofold, True or false'. The former was 'a sole ease, an unspeakable comfort' which 'rears the dejected soule of man, and amidst so many cares, miseries, persecutions, which this world affords' (3.339.6–11); the latter was 'that vaine superstition ... when false gods, or that God is falsely worshipped', 'a miserable plague, a torture of the soule, a mere madnesse ... or *insanus error,* as *Seneca* [calls it], a franticke error, or as *Austin, Insanus animi morbus,* a furious disease of the soul', bringing fear, suspicion, and vexation (3.338.23–339.3).

ORTHODOXY AND CONTROVERSY

The association of 'True Religion' with tranquillity was critical to Burton's spiritual viewpoint. But having established the framework of his theory of religious melancholy his immediate task was to address the nature of the extremes which 'swarve from this true love and worship of God' (3.337.18–19). The survey of superstition expanded over the course of later editions, but its main ingredients were present in the 1621 copy, which expressed the *topoi* of anti-Catholic and anti-puritan polemic whilst lamenting the destructive effects of controversy on the harmony of the *corpus Christianorum.*

The character of the beliefs and practices of 'Pseudocatholicks' was first established through juxtaposition (*similitudo*) with those of pagans and ancient heretics – 'tell me what difference?' (3.344.20–346.28 [3.4.1.2]). This prepared the way for a catalogue of stock Protestant criticisms: of the doctrines of purgatory and transubstantiation as cruel fictions (3.358.5–50; 385.30–6 [3.4.1.3]); of excessive ceremonialism, idolatry and other practices confusing human tradition with divine law (3.367.5–369.6; 383.13–386.15); of the papal usurpation of territorial jurisdiction (3.351.23–7 [3.4.1.2]; 352.4–6; 353.11–13); of 'canonicall and blind obedience' to 'the bull-bellowing Pope' (3.350.2–351.7); and of the priesthood's use of Latin to conceal scriptural truth from the populace (3.357.14–18, 27–30). This critique also drew on the apocalyptic historiography of the Church formulated in John Foxe's *Acts and Monuments* (1563), which was fundamental to all varieties of English Protestantism well into the seventeenth century, in identifying the Pope as Antichrist (3.381.28–9 [3.4.1.3]; 383.15), noting the invisibility and persecution of the 'true Church' in the medieval era (3.383.27–28;

386.20–21), and referring in the fifth edition to the millenarian anticipation of Christ's second coming.[83]

The Reformation sought to restore the 'true Church' to visibility. But just as Bacon perceived the '*Superstition*, in avoiding *Superstition*; when men thinke to doe best if they goe furthest from the *Superstition* formerly received',[84] Burton saw the anti-Catholic agenda to 'demolish all' and 'admit of no ceremonies at all' being pursued by 'a mad giddy company of Precisians, Schismaticks, and some Hereticks even in our owne bosomes' as another dangerous 'extreame' (3.386.30–5). The erroneous rejection of 'such as are things indifferent in themselves' (3.386.34–387.5) was clearest amongst 'those rigid Sabbatarians' who denied the divinely sanctioned use of 'honest sports, games, and pleasant recreations' (3.391.7–392.5 [3.4.1.4]),[85] and opposed 'all humane learning, because they are ignorant themselves and illiterate'.[86] Most troubling, however, was the questioning of the authority of the national Church, which resulted in the substitution of private judgement for institutional determination in matters of scriptural interpretation and doctrine, and ultimately the proliferation of sects. According to Burton this was literally symptomatic of a form of derangement originating in *laesa imaginatio* (3.388.24). Being misled by 'their owne phantasticall spirits', such people were prone to deliver 'prodigious paradoxes', 'turne Prophets, have secret revelations, will be of privy counsell with God himselfe, & knowe all his secrets', and end up 'so far gone with their private Enthusiasmes . . . that they are quitte madde, out of their wits' (3.387.15–16, 39–40). Hence the multiplication across Europe of 'peculiar sects' whose 'Religion' – adapting the argument of 'prophane *Machiavel*' about the enervating effect of Christianity – 'takes away not spirits only, but wit and judgement, and deprives them of their understanding' (3.387.34–9). Although earlier he had used the Foxeian narrative, Burton regarded the attempt to 'interpret Apocalypses . . . and those hidden misteries' (3.387.18–21) as part and parcel of an irrational anti-Romanism which was undermining ecclesiastical and civil authority and fragmenting the *corpus Reformatorum* (3.387.27–9).

It is tempting to see here a simple reflection of a typically Jacobean conception of orthodoxy as the *via media* between Rome and Geneva,

[83] Burton 1638, p. 680; or 3.392.13–14 (3.4.1.5).
[84] Bacon 1985, XVII, p. 55. Burton cited this essay at 3.357.6 (3.4.1.2); cf. 1.395.34–396.1 (1.3.1.2).
[85] Cf. Howson 1602, p. 17.
[86] This was added in the fifth edition: Burton 1638, p. 680; or 3.391.k (3.4.1.4).

but this is only partially satisfactory. In the first place, Burton's articulation of 'True Religion' was vague. It was 'where the true GOD is truly worshipped' (3.339.6–7 [3.4.1.1]), or when 'we ... love God' and 'our neighbour as we should' (3.337.8–9), and the only specifically Reformed requirement was that 'his word' should be 'our rule' (3.339.32–3); those wondering precisely '[w]hat Religion is, and of what parts it doth consist' were sent elsewhere – 'every Catechisme will tell you' (3.365.23–5 [3.4.1.3]). Anchoring theological orthodoxy in the authority of the Church, and referring controversy to institutional resolution pre-empted allegations of contentiousness,[87] but here it also made a disturbing inference from the view that the tenets of faith were to be determined solely by clerical decree. How were Burton's readers to interpret the paradox that 'every' one of the many available catechisms, Reformed or otherwise, expressed orthodoxy, even if they were in disagreement?[88] Was it not that 'True Religion' had itself become lost in the plurality of competing claims to orthodoxy?

This is also suggested by the fact that throughout the denunciation of the extremes of Roman Catholicism and puritanism the truthful mid-point surfaced only as a nebulous ideal absent in the world.[89] According to Burton, the extent of superstition was such that 'all times have beene misaffected, past, present, *there is not one that doth good, no not one, from the Prophet to the Priest*' (3.340.3–6). Asking of 'this present ... [h]ow small a part is truly religious?', his answer was that, to begin, only one 'fift part of the world ... now professeth CHRIST', and 'hardly that,' since this part was 'so inlarded and interlaced with severall superstitions, that there is scarce a sound part to be found, or any agreement amongst them' (3.340.36–341.18). In fact, the history of Christianity was the history of the gradual obscuring of the true Church by schism, controversy and heresy – from the division of Eastern from Western Christendom, and the subdivision of the former into '*Nestorians, Jacobines, Syrians, Armenians, Georgians*' and others who over time 'have added so many superstitions, that they be rather semi-Christians', to the similar plight of the 'Westerne Church with us in *Europe* ... so eclipsed with severall scismes, heresies and superstitions, that one knowes not where to finde it' (3.341.25–342.1). Catholic Europe was shot through with 'Papists'; Scandinavia, despite its Lutheran monarchies, was full of 'Idolaters';

[87] See the similar position of the early Hobbes outlined in Tuck 1993a, pp. 124–7.
[88] For catechisms in Burton's library see Kiessling 1988, entries 769 and 1642.
[89] This also suggested at 1.39.24–5; 1.41.7–10. I am here in partial agreement with Fish 1972, p. 348.

Germany hosted '*Calvinists*' and '*Lutherans*' but also heretical sects and rulers that were 'professed Papists'; parts of France, Ireland, Britain, the Swiss Cantos, and the Netherlands were populated by '*Calvinists*, more defecate then the rest', but these were 'at ods amongst themselves' and 'not free from superstition' (3.342.1–29). Whilst this indicated the orthodoxy of different forms of Protestantism, its language made a different point. English divines commonly described members of the true, Reformed Church as 'Catholic Christians' (i.e., belonging to the universal Protestant Church), but Burton employed the divisive terminology of Lutheranism and Calvinism to implicate Protestant sectarianism in the degradation of Christianity.[90] 'I say nothing of *Anabaptists*, *Socinians*, *Brownists*', he continued, and rounded off the lamentation of the absence of 'True Religion' with the observation of the 'superstition in our prayers, often in our hearing of Sermons, bitter contentions, invectives, persecutions, strange conceipts, besides diversitie of opinions, scismes, factions, &c.' (3.342.35–7).

Although in Burton's portrayal orthodoxy had been eclipsed by superstition and schism, his use of the *via media* strategy communicated more than a moderate commonplace. The middle ground was itself the site of intense controversy.[91] On the one hand, detailed critique of Roman superstitions was unlikely to cause much offence in Elizabethan and Jacobean England. But attacks on 'Precisians' were more contentious, and Burton's insistence on their derangement was provocative. The polemical slant of the argument is also evident in his designation of puritans as the 'enemy within' the English Church (3.386.31 [3.4.1.3]), and his silence on the increasingly evident problem of recusancy. Possibly this was prudential – it was a sensitive topic for James I in the early 1620s, though that did not prevent others from expressing their views.[92] As we shall soon see, his complacency about crypto-popery was significant.

But in this part of the book Burton's polemical position was largely submerged within an anti-dogmatic historical commentary on the splintering of pagan and Christian religion into a succession of sects that proliferated and regenerated endlessly, '[a]s a damme of water stopt in one place breakes out into another', and that sustained the 'diversitie of opinions' which had 'so eclipsed' religious truth 'in all ages' (3.342.37 [3.4.1.1]; 341.34–5; 340.25–6). From this perspective, the conflicting

90 This point is explored in more detail below: see n. 130.
91 See Lake 1995 for a case-study.
92 See Cogswell 1989, pp. 44, 138, 168–70.

claims of '*Papists*', Protestants, and even '*Turkes*' were equally defective, 'there is a generall fault in us all' (3.390.13–16 [3.4.1.4]). Here was an incipient scepticism about the earthbound character of spiritual dogma emerging from humanist historical study. This explains Burton's reluctance to identify or discuss instances of religious orthodoxy, which was such that 'one knowes not where to finde it' (3.341.35–342.1 [3.4.1.1]). But the scepticism proceeding from awareness of the roots of the diversity of belief in human history had a positive counterpart, in the ecumenical impulse to reverse the dogmatic atomisation by refocusing attention on general religious truths discoverable across the ages. Such an attitude could be found by humanists in the writings of both Cicero and Plutarch, who had analysed the religious cults of different societies on the premise that each contained some intrinsic spiritual value, and it was at least implicit in Burton's historical curiosity. Although he did not refer to the ecumenical programme of Hugo Grotius,[93] he shared the latter's readiness to employ ancient examples and texts to elucidate the essentials of a vision of true religion unencumbered by the dogmatic particularities that bred contentiousness. Hence the *Anatomy* used Cicero, Pliny, and Seneca to articulate a classical idea of *religio* purged of *superstitio* (3.338.25–6, 31; 339.4–6),[94] perhaps with the Grotian implication that belief in a single caring, immaterial god who created the world had underpinned 'the true Religion, which has been common to all Ages'.[95]

When Burton discussed the cure of superstition, he demonstrated both an awareness of the sceptical-ecumenical implications of his historical analysis and a reluctance to concede what now appear to be its most obvious consequences. The obstinacy of scismatics, he wrote, 'hath induced many Commonwealths to suffer them to injoy their consciences as they will themselves', the most famous 'common Sanctuaries' in Europe being '*Poland* and *Amsterdam*' (3.392.17–18, 21–2 [3.4.1.5]). This prompted a discussion of the merits of *cuius regio eius religio* in an era of bloodshed and persecution (3.394.15–16), and seemed to draw the author towards 'a generall toleration' through consciousness of the historical diversity and imperfection of dogma (3.393.4–394.6). However, in the final analysis Burton could not stomach the idea of plural orthodoxies. Instead, he advocated a '*medium*' course in dealing with the heterodox that began with '*faire meanes*' of persuasion but,

[93] But cf. the ecumenical sentiment at 3.366.12–16 (3.4.1.3).

[94] See, for example, Cicero 1933, I.42, II.28, pp. 112–13, 192–3.

[95] See Tuck 1993a, pp. 129–30; Pocock 1999–2003, vol. I, pp. 41–2, 51, 63–4, 66; Miller 2000, pp. 105–10, 146–7.

if necessary, proceeded with excommunication, legal injunction, and, in a distinctive touch, the compassionate therapeutic ministration of 'Physicke' rather than 'fire and fagot', to 'reduce them *ad sanam mentem*' (3.394.29–395.18). This was not an argument for sceptical ecumenism, but simply a denunciation of 'our . . . bitter contentions, invectives', and 'persecutions' (3.342.35–6 [3.4.1.1]).

Most of these views were relatively uncontentious, and many seem calculated to offend as few contemporary readers as possible. Few in England would have openly disagreed that the extremes of Roman Catholicism and radical puritanism should be shunned, and the same could be said of Burton's indictment of schism. But this was an intensely political vision. Disavowal of contentiousness was itself a controversial position of sorts, expressing the imperatives of conformity and discipline cherished first by James and then by Charles and Laud.[96] I shall now turn to the elements of Burton's argument about melancholy that were more provocative, and that reveal the gradual evolution of his position in response to the troubling developments of the 1620s.

WAR AND RELIGION

The first signs that Burton was prepared to intervene in controversial religious territory can be seen in 'Democritus Junior to the Reader' – not in the diatribe against 'Religious madnesse' (1.39.21), but in the moral-psychological critique of warfare. Democritus Junior's account of military conflict, which, as with the other forms of human folly denounced in the preface, drew on the Stoic equation of passion and madness, restated the Christian humanist case that had been elaborated by John Colet, Erasmus, More, and Juan Luis Vives in the early decades of the previous century.[97] But it was also designed by its author to comment on Jacobean and Caroline debates about foreign policy in response to the escalation of conflict on the continent in the 1620s. Of particular importance here was the Augustinian doctrine of the just war, which had been revived by sixteenth-century theologians to help counter the threat of the Ottoman empire, and which, particularly when redescribed as the holy or 'godly' war commanded by God to be waged against the enemies of true religion, was especially popular amongst English Protestants (1.46.32–47.8). On these grounds, in the years surrounding 1621 many of Burton's

96 As illustrated in Lake 1995, pp. 59–60, and Milton 1995, pp. 63–4.

97 See Burton's references at 1.42.30–32; 1.43.19–2; 1.45.11–12, 42.m; and 1.45.23–5.

countrymen were agitating for war against Spain and military intervention to support the European Protestant cause in the Palatinate. As we saw, however, they were being frustrated by the *Rex pacificus*, who viewed with abhorrence the prospect of participation in confessional war that had no clear end in sight and who persisted in a divisive diplomatic strategy for peace.

Burton's response to these debates was to expand the section of his preface condemning military conflict (1.41.23–48.14). By 1632 this had become well over three times its original size, with the bulk of his additions appearing in 1624 and 1628. In a distinctively humanist denunciation, he attributed war to the sinful passions of pride, ambition, greed, hatred, anger, and different kinds of lust – notably the *libido dominandi*.[98] Erasmus had influentially expressed a similar argument at length in the *Querela pacis* (1517), which drew support from the Stoic equation of warfare with fratricide to maintain its intrinsic opposition to Christian fellowship.[99] For Burton as for Erasmus, the peaceful harmony of the Christian commonwealth, 'the most excellent of all things', mirrored the state of the virtuous, well-ordered Christian soul in which reason controlled the passions.[100] The predominance of armed conflict was therefore a sign of political-psychological pathology, or '*Mundus furiosus*, a mad world' (1.45.2).[101] As with all forms of melancholic delirium, war was rooted in the fallen condition of man and showed him to be subject to beastly passions (1.42.33–43.1), because it was one of the divine punishments for original sin (1.44.3–4; 47.5–6). Like his humanist predecessors, he was specifically concerned to rebut misguided chivalric ideals (1.45.25–46.1; 46.2–24), and although in the second edition he conceded to the Machiavellian humanist the valuation of what Cicero had termed the '*warlike vertues*' such as courage when employed for defensive purposes (1.45.12–20), he nowhere associated military expertise with civic greatness.[102]

Although Burton was not explicitly dealing with foreign policy, his position in the first edition was generally supportive of '*Iacobus pacificus*' (as he approvingly referred to the king elsewhere),[103] and contributed to the flood of anti-war literature that issued from the presses in support of

[98] See 1.41.26–27; 1.35–6; 1.43.16–17; 1.44.12; 1.46.12–13, 21–3.
[99] Erasmus 1917, pp. 6–10, 51–2; cf. Erasmus 1997, p. 104.
[100] Erasmus 1917, pp. 19–40, 63–5; Erasmus 1970, pp. 59, 64–5, 145.
[101] See also 1.42.27, 29–30; 1.42.33–4; 1.43.32; 1.44.19; cf. Erasmus 1917, pp. 10, 18, 37.
[102] Contrast Bacon 1985, XXIX, pp. 95–9.
[103] Burton 1621, p. 182; or 1.320.27 (1.2.3.15). See also Burton 1977, p. 263.

James's stance in the years 1621–3. The first part of his strategy was to buttress the case against the 'rage' of armed conflict by recalling memories of bloodshed across the continent, in 'the late civill warres in France', 'at our late *Pharsalian* fieldes in the time of *Henry* the sixt, betwixt the houses of *Lancaster* and *York*' (Burton's ancestor William Burton had been killed at the battle of Towton in 1461) as well as 'those *French* Massacres, *Sicilian* Evensongs, the Duke of *Alvas* tyrannies' and 'our Gunpowder machinations'.[104] He also indicated opposition to the idea of a 'holy' war, recalling Erasmus's warning that Christian adherence to such teaching made it 'more likely that we shall turn into Turks'[105] by adding that it was 'yet more to be lamented' when 'they perswade them, that by these bloody warres, as *Turkes* doe their Commons, to incorage them to fight, *If they dye in the field they goe directly to heaven, and shall be canonized for Saints*'.[106]

As we noted above, after the collapse of the plan to marry Charles and the Spanish Infanta in late 1623, in the parliamentary session of the following year James acceded to demands for war with Spain. Printed criticism of warfare disappeared almost entirely in the country at large, and previously fashionable Erasmian meditations on the adage *dulce bellum inexpertis* were suddenly deemed unacceptable in parliament.[107] But in the edition of the *Anatomy* published in 1624, Burton chose not to alter his stance and effectively signalled discontent at the recent turn of events, turning what had been an unexceptional defence of pacifism into an implicit critique of the current vogue for warfare. In the first place he expanded his general lamentation of the horrors of bloodshed considerably.[108] Although, as he had admitted in the first edition, 'all [wars] are not to be condemned', advocates of martial glory were now said to 'mistake most part, *auferre, trucidare, rapere, falsis nominibus virtutem vocant, &c.* ('Twas *Galgacus* observation in *Tacitus*) they term theft, murder, and rapine, vertue, by a wrong name'.[109] He also redoubled his attack on the notion of a holy, 'Christian' war. What was 'more to be

[104] Burton 1621, p. 29; or 1.44.4–26.
[105] Erasmus 1997, pp. 108–9.
[106] Burton 1621, p. 30; or 1.46.31–47.2.
[107] Cogswell 1989, pp. 179, 310.
[108] See Burton 1624, pp. 24–6; or 1.41.26–7; 1.46.33–5 and note l; 1.42.3–5; 1.42.9–12; 1.42.17–18; 1.42.21–30; 1.43.7–14; 1.43.16–19; 1.43.21–2; 1.43.30–1; 1.44.1–3; 1.44.20 and note a; 1.45.1; 1.45.20–23; 1.46.24–31; 1.47.8–11; 1.47.14; 1.47.24; and 1.47.29–48.1.
[109] Burton 1624, p. 26; or 1.45.12–23. For similar views see Erasmus 1970, p. 160, and Montaigne 1603, III.1, III.12, pp. 476–83, 620–4.

lamented' was when men 'put a note of *divinity upon the most cruell and pernicious plague of humane kinde*, adore such men with grand titles, degrees, statues, Images, honour, applaud and highly reward them for their good service', and (again) make Christians comparable to '*Turkes*'.[110] In the third edition, after domestic opposition to war had revived in the wake of Buckingham's campaigns in Cadiz and Ré, Burton became more explicit. On top of a new series of additions amplifying the horrors of war,[111] he further criticised those who had persuaded Christians that 'this hellish course of life is holy' and 'promise heaven to such as venter their lives *bello sacro*', and advocated the suppression of 'brutish Stories' supporting this idea.[112]

Unswerving pacifism carried clear domestic implications. In the eyes of those agitating for war in the early 1620s, it signalled a suspiciously lukewarm attitude towards the fate of continental Protestantism.[113] There is no reason to cast doubt upon what would presumably have been Burton's defence against an allegation of Romanist sympathy – namely that his position was derived from mainstream Christian humanist principles, and indeed was consistent with his argument about the role of perturbations in generating melancholy in the world. However, it is significant that in the early 1620s this part of the *Anatomy* effectively put Burton in the company of Richard Corbett, who as Dean of Christ Church had attracted widespread abuse for his praise of Buckingham's part in the diplomatic mission to Madrid.[114] Burton showed no particular animosity towards the Spanish, and not just, perhaps, because he inclined towards cosmopolitan irony: '*Turkes* deride us, wee them, *Italians*, *Frenchmen*, accounting them light-headed fellowes . . . *Spaniards* laugh at all, and all againe at them' (1.56.26–57.2).

THE ENGLISH CHURCH

Calvinist suspicions of Burton's pacifism throughout the 1620s would not have been allayed by his approach to the condition of the national Church. For a start, as one might expect for an author with Catholic

110 Burton 1624, pp. 26–7; or 1.47.8–11, 29.
111 See Burton 1628, pp. 29–33; or 1.41.24; 1.41.27–8; 1.41.36–7; 1.42.6–9; 1.42.12–16; 1.42.18–19; 1.42.30–43.7; 1.43.14–16; 1.43.24; 1.43.25; 1.43.29–30; 1.44.3–4; 1.44.5–7; 1.44.9–13; 1.45.3–6; 1.45.12–20; 1.45.23–5; 1.46.2–6; 1.46.11–24; 1.46.32–3; 1.47.3–8; 1.47.16–21.
112 Burton 1628, p. 32; or 1.46.32–47.8.
113 See Lake 1995, pp. 64–7.
114 See Cogswell 1989, pp. 46–7.

family connections, he was more exercised by the encroaching claims of papal jurisdiction than by recusancy or institutionalised crypto-popery.[115] Although he wrote of the dangers of superstition in 'our Church', there was never any clear suggestion of an organised sect of Romanists in England analogous to the puritans.[116] Neither Charles nor Laud would have found much to quarrel with here. The fact that these elements of the *Anatomy* were present in the first edition suggests that some of Burton's theological roots lay in avant-garde conformism. His view of puritanism in particular as an internal threat to the unity of the English Church expressed the moderate Protestant hostility to presbyterianism traceable at least as far back as Hooker.

There are other indications that the vision of the Church in the first edition of the *Anatomy* can be described as avant-garde conformist. Criticising the excessive puritan rejection of 'Romish ceremonies and superstition', he implied his own support for a host of characteristically avant-garde preferences, including 'fasting dayes . . . crosse in Baptisme, kneeling at Communion . . . Church musicke', 'Bishops Courts, and Church government', the sacerdotal trappings of 'hoods, habits, cap and surplesse', and a high estimation for the 'comments of Fathers'.[117] What was Hookerian ceremonialism or sacramentalism in 1621, however, by 1638 looked like Laudianism; Burton's decision to retain such views in subsequent versions meant that they could then seem to justify aspects of the Laudian programme. This was especially true of his defence of the baptismal cross, kneeling at communion and church music – all issues that became important for Laudian divines – and of his view of 'that purity of the Primitive church' cherished by the early Reformers as an example for imitation.[118]

Some of the modifications made to subsequent editions suggest that Burton's avant-garde ideas evolved throughout the 1620s in a direction that reflected the growing confidence of the contemporary opposition to Calvinism. In the first two editions he repudiated the 'ordinary sermons' of '[o]ur indiscreet Pastors' who 'thunder out Gods judgments without respect', but in the 1628 copy he added a typical anti-Calvinist reference

[115] See especially 3.351.23–7 (3.4.1.2); 352.4–6; and 353.8–354.1.

[116] There is a possible exception at 3.367.16–18 (3.4.1.3), but note the ecumenical thrust of the discussion.

[117] Burton 1621, pp. 755–6; or 3.386.33–387.13 (3.4.1.3).

[118] See 3.386.20–5 (3.4.1.3); 3.366.16–19; and 3.445.7–9 (added in the fourth edition: Burton 1632, p. 721 (3.4.2.6)). For the avant-garde heritage of Laudianism and English 'Arminianism' see Lake 1988 and 1993, and Milton 1995.

to those 'auditories' (recalling the controversial opposition of *auditoria* and *oratoria*) where the 'scrupulous points' of predestination were discussed to the detriment of the consciences of the listeners.[119] In the same edition he made the existence of 'so many Preachers' part of 'our Religious madnesse' denounced in the prefatory satire.[120] A similar implication may be drawn from the addition to his original denunciation of the 'superstition' contained in 'our hearing of Sermons', which in the 1632 copy became something that he saw occurring 'often'.[121] He was also consistently critical of the puritan rejection of 'Holydayes' and 'honest recreations' from the first edition onwards, professing his support for the Jacobean 'Book of Sports' on the grounds that entertaining 'exercise' could alleviate melancholy (2.82.14–17 [2.2.4.1]), and tying this aspect of 'precise zeale' to the desire to 'tyrannize over our brothers soules' and 'punish our selves without a cause' (1.387.9; 391.26–9 [1.3.1.2]). Across the course of subsequent editions, these criticisms evolved into an explicit polemic against the 'observation of Sabbaoths'[122] by those who were 'too sterne, too riged, too precise, too grossely superstitious'[123] – a group he identified in 1632, in Laudian fashion, as 'those rigid Sabbatarians'.[124]

By the time of the fourth edition, Burton was expressing anti-Calvinist sentiments that ten years previously would have raised suspicions of crypto-Romanism. In the midst of a discourse on idleness in the first Partition, he digressed to reveal his dismay at the iconoclastic extremes of some of the early English Reformers.

Mee thinkes therefore our too zealous innovators were not so well advised, in that generall subversion of Abbies and religious houses, promiscuously to fling downe all, they might have taken away those grosse abuses crept in amongst them, rectified such inconveniences, and not so farre to have raved and raged against those faire buildings, and everlasting monuments of our forefathers

119 Burton 1628, p. 625; or 3.415.21–8 (3.4.2.3). See also 3.416.1–7.
120 Burton 1628, p. 28; or 1.39.23–4.
121 Burton 1632, p. 645; or 3.342.35–6 (3.4.1.1). Cf. the ridicule of sermons at 1.20.34–21.1.
122 Burton 1624, p. 538; or 3.414.32–4 (3.4.2.3).
123 Burton 1628, p. 611; or 3.391.22–3 (3.4.1.4).
124 Burton 1632, p. 681; or 3.392.4–5 (3.4.1.4). For other anti-sabbatarian additions, see Burton 1624, p. 528, or 3.391.29–392.5 (3.4.1.4); Burton 1628, pp. 257, 611, or 2.82.17–19 (2.2.4.1); 3.391.9–12 3.4.1.4); Burton 1632, pp. 273, 680 or 2.83.12–15 (2.2.4.1); 3.391.12–15 (3.4.14); Burton 1638, pp. 668, 680–1, or 3.376.29–31 (3.4.1.3); 3.391.15–22 (3.4.1.4); Burton 1651, p. 276, or 2.82.6, 12–14 (2.2.4.1). Most of these are documented in Faulkner 1998, pp. 25–7.

devotion, consecrated to pious uses: some monasteries and Collegiate Celles might have beene well spared.[125]

His main lament here was for the disappearance of havens for those who wished 'to sequester themselves from the cares and tumults of the world'. But the opposition of frenzied reforming 'innovators' who 'have raved and raged against those faire buildings . . . consecrated to pious uses' was redolent of avant-garde conformist and Laudian criticisms of the Henrician destruction of the Church's patrimony, a positive respect for the pre-Reformation Church, and an attachment to the 'beauty of holiness'.[126] Burton's sacramentalism, suggested by his defence of bells in church, is further supported by Anthony Wood's report that he 'always gave the Sacrament in Wafers' to his parishioners at St Thomas – a practice that was unusual at the time, and had long been seen by puritans as 'popish'.[127]

No less revealing are Burton's views concerning the Church of Rome and continental Protestantism. Although he was relentlessly hostile towards 'papist' superstition, and indeed identified the Pope as Antichrist, he conceded Rome's status as part of the 'true Church' (3.381.25–9 [3.4.1.3]). This set him at odds with mainstream English Calvinism, where the religion of Rome, the Babylon of Protestant apocalypticism, was the antithesis of Protestantism and entirely false, and aligned him with those emphasising the doctrinal corruption but institutional integrity of the Roman Church. It is true that elsewhere he wrote of the 'true Church' before Luther as being 'hid and obscure' (3.386.20–1), but his condemnation of sects who spoke 'as if they alone were the true Church' indicated scepticism about the literal application of Foxeian historiography (3.368.2). Equally, although Burton felt no Laudian discomfort at the idea of the Pope as Antichrist, the force of the apocalyptic opprobrium was mitigated with the suggestion that there had long been 'many' other '*Antichrists*' at work, 'even in the *Apostles* time' (3.381.29–31) – a position later articulated by Richard Montagu.[128] His lengthy anti-Romanist invective was principally directed against the ecclesiastical hierarchy and scholastic theologians for deluding the masses and encouraging the 'blind zeale' of superstition. Their victims deserved pity.[129]

125 Burton 1632, p. 87; or 1.244.11–18 (1.2.2.6).

126 Cf. for example, Howson 1598, pp. 33, 37–9, and see also Burton 1632, p. 56 or 1.80.17–19. On this issue see Milton 1995, pp. 66, 331–4.

127 Wood 1815, vol. II, p. 652. Generally see Milton 1995, p. 499, and Haigh 2003.

128 Milton 1995, pp. 114–16.

129 See, for example, 3.368.5–6 (3.4.1.3) and 385.7–11.

Burton's stance towards the continental Reformed churches had a corresponding ambivalence. He wrote approvingly of European 'Calvinists' and 'Lutherans' as adherents to the Protestant orthodoxy, but his use of such labels was implicitly critical of sectarianism, and communicated a sense of distance between the Reformed Church of England and its continental counterparts. As I noted above, English Calvinists typically preferred to refer to the universal, 'catholic Reformed' Church, the true Church unified across continental and English boundaries, and rejected such divisive terminology as counter-productive in the struggle against the false church of Rome. Isaac Bargrave summed up the sentiment in a sermon delivered to the Commons in February 1623: 'Away with these distracting names of Lutheran, Calvinist, Puritan, &c. Wee are all children of the same father . . . cursed may hee be who endeavours to put them asunder.'[130] By contrast, Burton referred to the English Church as a separate entity, often in doctrinal agreement with the continental Lutherans or Calvinists, but not part of a universal Reformed Church. Like the Laudians, the unity with which he was principally concerned was national (3.438.4–33 [3.4.2.5]).

However, we should not be constrained by descriptive labels devised by historians *ex post facto*, and, as we have already remarked, there is much to suggest the fluidity of the categories of belief in this period. Some of Burton's theological commitments were consistent with Calvinism, and some of his avant-garde attitudes were shared by moderate Calvinist conformists.[131] Although critical of the radical Protestant fringe, he conformed to the central principles of the Jacobean Calvinist consensus, never explicitly departing from the doctrine of salvation *sola gratia* and *sola fide*, or criticising the doctrinal basis of continental Calvinist churches. Yet after the Synod of Dort, which effectively defined moderate Calvinism as the orthodoxy of the English Church, it was hazardous for avant-garde divines to express beliefs that were evidently in tension with continental Protestantism. It is impossible to gauge whether Burton's valuation of Church authority and conformism outweighed his avant-garde or Laudian sacramentalism. In an environment of such theological and ecclesiological eclecticism such an exercise would be misleading as well as trivial. Far more important is the task of understanding what the argument about religious melancholy in the *Anatomy* was intended to

130 Bargrave 1624, pp. 35–6. On this sermon see Cogswell 1989, pp. 169–70. More generally see Milton 1995, p. 378.

131 See Fincham 1993a, p. 6.

accomplish. To see this in full we must address Burton's treatment of the associations between melancholy, despair, and predestination.

PREDESTINATION AND DESPAIR

As the absorption of the patristic theory of *acedia* by early modern conceptions of melancholy suggests, the spiritual, moral, and medical methods used to understand and treat despair in this period often overlapped to the point of becoming practically indistinguishable. From antiquity onwards, physicians had offered treatment for the psychic disturbances that accompanied disease, and the melancholic's chronic emotions of fear and sadness had long been considered both physiologically destructive and amenable to a variety of medical and psychological therapies. But early Christian spirituality, especially that of Augustine, had presented an alternative perspective on such passions, interpreting them as signs of the sinfully depraved postlapsarian will. It is easy to see how in the pervasively Augustinian religious culture of early modern Europe the melancholic emotions of fear and sadness became spiritually loaded, and incorporated within schemes of redemption as well as medical therapy.

In keeping with their Augustinian heritage, the principal strains of Reformed theology gave prominent roles to extreme passions of the soul and the condition of despair. For Luther, the experience of sadness was potentially salutary, insofar as it might lead to the comprehension of human weakness and could prepare the way to salvation *sola fide* by provoking a turning to God for help. But sadness itself was a devilish temptation, and the presumption and inadequate comprehension of divine omnipotence of individuals who chose to struggle with their own means would herald the onset of sinful despair. This was Lutheran *tristitia* or spiritual melancholy.[132] Calvin eschewed such ambivalence and made despair integral to the eschatological process. Self-examination before the mirror of the divine law would lead to anxiety and dejection, but this was instrumental in provoking the turning to God for the reception of saving grace. Properly interpreted, spiritual despair in Calvinism was a sign of providence, a part of the punishment preceding redemption.[133] In seventeenth century England, Calvinist interpretations of sorrow as a divinely sent affliction propaedeutic to godly virtue, and of fear

[132] Luther 1995, pp. 282, 291–2, 300, 301, 302, 304, 305, 307.
[133] Calvin 1936, II.8.3, vol. I, p. 398.

as a useful stimulus to the realisation of spiritual weakness, were applied by physicians and publicly articulated by Calvinist divines on a regular basis.[134]

Others in the Reformed Church perceived such ideas as spiritually and psychologically dangerous. At the end of the century, for example, the presbyterian divine Richard Baxter sounded a caveat born from experience against 'placing Religion too much in fears, and tears'.[135] This was just one expression of a long standing critique of the passionate behaviour associated with radical Protestant piety which originated in the early stages of the continental Reformation, and which from the beginning had focused on the effects on the individual soul of meditation on the predestinarian decree. As we have seen, Luther warned that meditation upon one's future election was sinful, spiritually hazardous, and productive only of anxiety. In Germany from the 1560s onwards, his followers developed this view into a charge against their Calvinist rivals, who were accused of fostering melancholy through overemphasis on predestination.[136] Here were the roots of the sociological association of radical Protestantism with suicide.[137]

The common Calvinist defence against this accusation rested upon a distinction between the despair indicating a naturally caused melancholy and that betokening a divinely afflicted conscience. If the latter was not an incarnation of the former, then allegations that Calvinist piety induced psychological disease were without substance, and it was by such means that the polemical force of the connection between predestination and melancholy was limited by English Calvinist physicians and divines until the end of the sixteenth century. Even if in practice the divide between the disciplines was commonly traversed, at a theoretical level medical and theological perspectives on the disease were kept apart, and the spiritual dimension of melancholy (particularly in its aetiology) was either denied or downplayed. Contrary to the implications of medical-psychological works such as Levinus Lemnius's *De habitu et constitutione corporis* (1561), for instance, the physician and Calvinist divine Timothy Bright insisted in his *Treatise of Melancholie* (1586) that 'the affliction of soule through conscience of sinne is quite another thing then melancholy', and

134 See, for example, Reynolds 1640, pp. 221–3, 226–7, 298–9. For relevant surveys see MacDonald 1982; Lake 1982, pp. 123–5; Harley 1993, esp. pp. 101–6, and 1996, pp. 274–5.

135 Baxter 1696, pt. III, §184, p. 86.

136 Schleiner 1991, pp. 74–5.

137 See Midelfort 1996.

that those who 'match them' are 'unreverent and prophane persons'.[138] The puritan divine William Perkins was also anxious to refute the idea that the afflicted conscience and melancholy were 'all one'.[139] Both Bright and Perkins agreed that although they were often 'mixed together' in one person and could 'be an occasion (though no direct cause)' of each other,[140] the former was caused by 'the severity of Gods judgement, summoning the guilty conscience', and so responded only to assurance, whereas the latter arose from a diseased imagination and so was treatable by medicine.[141] Perkins conceded that the Christian life was characterised by passionate psychomachy, but wrote of the 'sanctified affections' of the elect.[142]

The Lutheran connection of predestination with despair was rarely far from sight in such discussions, and when the disputes revolving around the Calvinist theology of grace had escalated in the 1620s its polemical utility was apparent. As Thomas Fuller later recalled, one of the arguments supporting the Jacobean 'Directions Concerning Preaching' had been that 'many ignorant Preachers' had mishandled the doctrine of predestination so that 'the cordiall was turned into a poyson'.[143] Accordingly, once Burton had dissected the 'excessive' side of religious melancholy in his survey of superstition, when he moved on to its 'defective' counterpart to analyse religious-melancholic despair, it was obvious that he would be dealing with controversial material. We shall now see that in the course of his analysis, the Calvinist defence against the Lutheran charge was undercut, and that the propagation of predestinarian doctrine was implicated in cases of spiritual despair. In the circumstances this was telling. By attending to the additions and modifications Burton made to the editions of 1624, 1628, 1632, and 1638, it will be possible to gauge the nature and extent of his involvement in the controversies about predestination that surrounded him. When this is aligned to his wider religious beliefs and attitudes, a coherent agenda emerges.

Of the two types of 'defective' religious melancholy, atheism and despair, the latter most exercised Burton, and in my view the main reason for the difference in length between the Subsections devoted to these

138 Lemnius 1576, fols. 144^{r}–145^{r}; Bright 1586, pp. 187, 190.
139 Perkins 1606, p. 194.
140 Perkins 1606, pp. 198–9.
141 Bright 1586, pp. 187–9; Perkins 1606, pp. 194–5. See also Bright 1586, pp. 193–8, and Perkins 1591, fols. 20^{r-v}.
142 Perkins 1591, fols. 33^{v}–35^{r}, 41^{r}–47^{v}.
143 Fuller 1655, p. 110.

topics, which became more pronounced in later editions, concerns the controversies of the 1620s and '30s. In his treatment of superstition, an uncontentious invective against the Church of Rome acted as a prelude to a critique of puritanism. In the same way, the discourse about atheism prefaced a controversial attack on those disseminating the doctrine of predestination for inducing despair.

Despair came in 'many kindes', 'holy' and 'unholy', 'finall . . . which befalleth reprobates' and 'temporall . . . which may befall the best of Gods children' (3.408.26–7; 410.16–19 [3.4.2.2]), and Burton was aware of the Calvinist distinction between the despair of the divinely afflicted conscience and that which accompanied melancholy. Indeed, he quoted Bright and Perkins and agreed that 'there is much difference' between the two (3.412.4–10 [3.4.2.3]).[144] But – and herein lay the full polemical force of Burton's innovatory conceptualisation of religious melancholy – by including his discussion of despair under the 'defective' heading, the effect of this distinction had already been negated. In fact, Burton's admission of the 'difference' was an insincere sop to the Calvinist theory, which was ignored in a discourse that wilfully fused melancholy and spiritual despair: 'and yet melancholy alone againe may be sometimes a sufficient cause of this terror of conscience' (3.412.8–10). He then confirmed the connection between predestination and melancholic despair with medical testimony, establishing through a succession of *exempla* that the dejected condition induced by fear of damnation was indeed a form of melancholy (3.412.13ff.; cf. 411.31–3, 330.24–331.1 [3.4.1.1]).[145] Later he could be found freely discoursing about the 'melancholy Symptoms' of despair, and comparing them to the signs found in 'other [forms of] melancholy' (3.420.5–6, 27–30 [3.4.2.4]; cf. 1.385.6–8 [1.3.1.2]). Correspondingly, whereas Perkins had been at pains to emphasise the 'sanctified affections' of the elect, Burton continued to present a humanistic analysis of passions as perturbations – always potentially dangerous psychic phenomena to be moderated.

With this framework in place Burton gave free rein to his polemical instincts, which were unerringly directed against those who encouraged meditation on divine judgement. He noted that the 'terrible meditation of hell fire and eternall punishment much torments a sinfull silly soule' (3.413.32–3 [3.4.2.3]),[146] and that 'the very inconsiderate reading of

144 Most of this passage was added in Burton 1624, p. 537; cf. the weaker formulation in Burton 1621, p. 773.

145 See Platter 1602–3, 1.3, vol. 1, p. 98 (= Platter, Cole, and Culpeper 1662, p. 27).

146 This phrase began a passage new in Burton 1632, p. 697; or 3.401.32–402.15 (3.4.2.1).

Scripture it selfe, and misinterpretation of some places of it', could have the same effect.[147] To this end in the first edition he cited five scriptural *topoi* which 'terrifie the soules of many' by conjuring thoughts of 'predestination' and 'reprobation'.[148] The sentiment, which sided with Luther and the early English Reformers against Calvin and the Reformed tradition from Beza to Perkins, was that the decree was better left shrouded in mystery. Burton's doctrinal preference was explicit: '*They doubt of their Election, how they shall know it, by what signes? And so farre forth saith* Luther, *with such nice points, torture and crucifie themselves, that they are almost mad, and all they get by it is this, they lay open a gappe to the divell by Desperation to carry them to hell.*'[149] This argument was amplified in the second edition with more scriptural quotations, and Burton made it plain that he had in mind the misguided curiosity of scholastic theology, 'wherein they trouble and pussle themselves about those questions of grace, freewill, perseverance, Gods secrets . . . which the Casuists discusse, and Schoolemen broach, which diverse mistake, misconster, misapply to themselves, to their owne undoing, and so fall into this gulfe'.[150] He could have blamed the Devil for such 'inconsiderate readings', as Marlowe had in *Doctor Faustus*.[151] But instead, amongst the theologians denounced were many second generation Calvinists, who had supported theories of absolute and double predestination with references to these places in scripture.[152]

Burton next broadened his attack to encompass preachers whose sermons made the despair theoretically produced by predestinarian speculation a reality for Christians at large. Such 'thundering Ministers' being 'wholly for judgement', they produced 'the greatest harme of all', for 'they can speake of nothing but hell fire, and damnation' (3.415.2–11). In the first edition, Burton was speaking of 'Papists',[153] and had proceeded to elaborate on the activities of '[o]ur indiscreet Pastors' who in their 'ordinary Sermons . . . thunder out Gods judgments . . . and pronounce them damned . . . making every small fault and thing indifferent, an irremissible offence' (3.415.21–30).[154] Here, his condemnation of Roman sermons was balanced with a parallel critique of those being

147 For this anti-puritan charge see Howson 1598, pp. 16–17.
148 Burton 1621, p. 775; or 3.414.18–21 (3.4.2.3).
149 Burton 1621, p. 775; or 3.414.35–415.2 (3.4.2.3).
150 Burton 1624, p. 538; or 3.414. 21–35 (3.4.2.3).
151 Marlowe 1976, V.2.93–8.
152 See Muller 1986, p. 45.
153 Burton 1621, p. 775; or 3.415.13 (3.4.2.3).
154 See also the addition in Burton 1624, p. 160; or 1.385.6–8 (1.3.1.2).

delivered in England, though his anti-puritan attitude was evident in the assertion of the validity of 'sports and recreations' and adiaphorous ceremonies (3.415.27–31). In the second and third editions, he sharpened his censure of puritans by binding it more closely to predestination. In 1624, Burton wrote of '[o]ur indiscreet Pastors' that 'they can speake of nothing but *reprobation*, hell fire'.[155] In 1628, he related how in their 'ordinary sermons' delivered 'intempestively... in all auditories' they 'rent' and 'teare' their listeners' consciences so that they were almost made 'mad':

> ... they speake so much of election, predestination, reprobation *ab æterno*, subtraction of grace, preterition, voluntary permission, &c. by what signes and tokens they shall decerne and try themselves, whether they be Gods true children elect, *an sint reprobi, prædestinati, &c.* with such scrupulous pointes, they still aggravate sinne.[156]

In the fourth edition he added that 'there is no mercy with them', and 'no salvation, no balsome for their diseased soules'. In the 'Consolatory Digression' he also reiterated his Lutheran veneration for God's 'deepe, unsearchable & secret Judgment'.[157]

This analysis of the causes of despair prepared the ground for another argument that pertained to predestination. To understand this we must digress on the concept of the conscience, which as we have seen bridged the domains of medicine and divinity and had a problematic status in melancholy. As Burton explained in his anatomical digression (1.159.11–27 [1.1.2.10]), the operations pertaining to the conscience were located in the rational part of the soul, specifically in the power of understanding. In this account, the conscience was formed by a series of innate rational processes known as the *syllogismus practicus*. The first, forming 'the *major* proposition' in the syllogism, was synteresis: the power of impartial judgement of acts before they were performed, as to whether they were good or evil according to divine and natural law (1.159.11–13). The second, forming the '*minor*' proposition, was the *dictamen rationis*, which 'doth admonish us to doe good or evill' by applying the judgement of the synteresis to our own situation (1.159.15–16, 23–5). The conscience was therefore 'the conclusion of the

[155] The word 'reprobation' here was new in Burton 1624, p. 538; or 3.415.10 (3.4.2.3).
[156] Burton 1628, p. 625; or 3.415.22–31 (3.4.2.3). See also Burton 1628, p. 304; or 2.156.16–17 (2.3.3.1).
[157] Burton 1632, pp. 339, 698; or 2.165.19–20 (2.3.3.1) and 3.415.10–11 (3.4.2.3).

Syllogisme' in the understanding, and was 'that which approves Good or Evill, justifying or condemning our Actions' (1.159.16–18).

This understanding of the conscience was central to Calvinist soteriology, where the internal operation of the *syllogismus practicus* was seen to provide assurance. Perkins developed an account of this nature in his *Treatise of Conscience*, where the conscience was theorised as being 'of a divine nature . . . a thing placed of God in the middest betweene him and man, as an arbitratour to give sentence & to pronounce either with man or against man unto God'. This 'sentence' was the conscience's judgement via the *syllogismus practicus*.[158] Taking his cue from the injunction to seek assurance in 2 Peter 1:10–11,[159] Perkins connected the practical syllogism to the divine decree of predestination, claiming that the conscience conducted an 'experiment' to detect the presence or absence of the signs of election and thereby gained access to the infallible testimony of the Holy Spirit.[160] This 'experimental' approach to the theology of grace was located at the centre of puritan practical piety.[161] Although not universally approved by Calvinist theologians – for some it appeared to be in tension with the principle of *sola gratia*[162] – the practice of searching for signs of election via the practical syllogism was widely advocated by puritans, who sometimes included in their works tabular illustrations depicting the 'lines of salvation and damnation'. These showed the signs of both election and reprobation, and encouraged the location of one's position in the process of salvation (*ordo salutis*) or its terrifying opposite.[163] This experimental piety had been given the official stamp of Protestant orthodoxy by the twelfth article of the Synod of Dort, which referred to the *fructus electionis infallibiles*.[164]

In Burton's account, the conscience mediated the relationship between man and God and was the 'last and greatest cause' of despair. As 'a great ledgier booke, wherein are written all our offences', it acted as a thousand witnesses to accuse us', thereby effecting 'a deepe apprehension' of 'unworthinesse' and 'Gods anger justly deserved' in sinners (3.416.11–417.1 [3.4.2.3]). This was uncontroversial. But the second edition of the *Anatomy* associated 'anguish of conscience' with

158 Perkins 1608–9, vol. 1, pp. 511, 529 and 510–48 generally.
159 Quoted in Perkins 1606, I.6.5, p. 86, and Perkins 1608–9, vol. 1, p. 437.
160 Perkins 1606, 1.6, p. 74.
161 For instance in Perkins 1608–9, vol. 1, p. 361.
162 See, for example, Bullinger's view discussed in Muller 1986, p. 46; see also pp. 26, 46, 85–6, 109–110.
163 See the tables in Perkins 1608–9, vol. 1, sig. ¶2, and p. 909.
164 DeJongh (ed.) 1968, p. 233.

predestination, describing the sentiment of being 'forsaken of God' as the absence of a 'sense or feeling of mercy, or grace', having 'no hope, no faith', and the suicidal fear of being already condemned as 'reprobate'.[165] This foreshadowed what was to come in the rest of the book. If the alterations made by Burton to his analysis of 'defective' religious melancholy showed his increasing concern with predestination, it was in the final Subsection on the 'Cure of Despaire' that this developed into a polemical case against radical Calvinism.

***

In the first edition of 1621, the conclusion of the last Subsection filled just over one quarto page, and probably dissatisfied readers searching remedies for despair. It emphasised the necessity of combining medicine and divinity, recapitulating the cures for non-religious melancholy with the addition of 'hearing, reading of Scriptures, good Divines, good advice and conference'.[166] The Section ended with an instruction to look elsewhere for comfort and an injunction that was simultaneously encouraging and minatory.

> Many excellent exhortations, parænericall discourses are extant to this purpose, for such as are any way troubled in mind *Perkins*, *Greenham*, *Hayward*, *Bright*, *Hemingius*, *&c.* are copious in this subject. Consult with them and such others.
>
> SPERATE MISERI, CAVETE FÆLICES.
>
> *FINIS.*[167]

The first version thus ended with an ambiguity that was counterproductive in terms of the goals of conventional consolatory discourse, and presents the prevailing view that Burton had always intended the *Anatomy* to be wholly curative, comforting, or even benevolent for a melancholic readership with a difficulty.[168] Counterpoising hope with fear was an Augustinian strategy appropriate to a readership needing to avoid the extremes of despair and presumption – and maintain a healthy physiological equilibrium – but not to anyone suffering from despair and the cold and dry imbalance of melancholy.[169]

165 Burton 1624, p. 542; or 3.422.2–8, 20–5 (3.4.2.4). Cf. Burton 1624, p. 539; or 3.417.3–11 (3.4.2.3).
166 Burton 1621, p. 783; or 3.424.27–425.1 (3.4.2.6).
167 Burton 1621, p. 783; or 3.425.15 (3.4.2.6).
168 See Vicari 1987, Miller 1997 and the views of Bamborough and Dodsworth at 6.281.
169 See also the quotations in Burton 1621, p. 784; or 3.468.8–10 (3.4.2.6).

In the second edition Burton made a lengthy addition to the final Subsection, which continued to expand in subsequent versions, adding 'at the request of some friends' a host of 'comfortable speeches' for those in despair.[170] There is no reason to doubt this, and the Subsection was superficially similar to the other spiritual *consolationes* to which it referred, reproducing through quotations or paraphrases many of the same arguments to combat despair (3.425.13–15 [3.4.2.6]).[171] But this discourse was not so simple. Burton made it clear that on their own these arguments were futile. The only readers 'capable' of benefiting from them were those who had already been already 'humbled for their sinnes... confessed... throughly searched and examined', and so were 'capable' of receiving comfort (3.425.24–9). This indicated a sacerdotalist approach to consolation, and also placed a limit on the intended therapeutic effects of the text on its readership. More importantly, there was another external impulse for writing – the escalation of religious controversy in the later 1620s and '30s. The result was a *parodia* of spiritual consolation, which simultaneously communicated arguments to dispel despair and commented on the disputes dividing the Church and the universities.

Burton established the goal of his consolation by quoting the *Antidotum adversus pestem desperationis* (1599) by the Danish theologian Niels Hemmingsen. This was 'good Hope out of Gods word, to be embraced' and 'perverse Security and presumption from the divels treachery, to be rejected' (3.425.30–3),[172] and was a significant choice. Hemmingsen, a well-known Lutheran, had discouraged conjecture about predestination and was popular with English anti-Calvinists.[173] Accordingly, Burton's appropriation of Hemmingsen's rhetorical poles prepared the way for a critique of Calvinist piety. The concluding words in 1621 ('SPERATE MISERI, CAVETE FÆLICES') suggest that hopefulness and the avoidance of complacency were essential to spiritual health, and in subsequent editions it became clear that he considered both to be incompatible with speculation about the decree. From the beginning he associated despair with predestination, noting that those afflicted 'account themselves reprobates... already damned, past all hope of grace'

[170] Burton 1624, p. 544; or 3.425.18–19 (3.4.2.6). As the remainder of the Subsection (3.425.16–446.6) appeared after 1621, all citations of this part of the work refer to the edition of 1624 unless otherwise indicated.

[171] Cf. Bright 1586, pp. 207–42, and see Bamborough 1983, pp. 442–5, for Burton's other sources.

[172] The word 'presumption' was added in Burton 1628, p. 632.

[173] White 1992, pp. 89–90; Tyacke 1987b, p. 206.

(3.426.18–20). In the following dialogic encounter, the authorial voice offered comfort to a despairing interlocutor preoccupied with predestination and its related pietistic practices. It thereby both demonstrated the destructive effects of 'needlesse speculation' about the theology of grace and commented on the problems this was raising in his own environment.

In the first place, the sufferer articulated the position of being cast down by experimental Calvinist piety, and a comforting voice lamented that those in despair 'have cauterized consciences, they are in a reprobate sense... they cannot hope for grace' (3.429.25–6). Although the 'experiment' was revealing no 'good conscience... no fruit, no feeling', and 'no likelihood of it in thy self', the downcast figure was urged against the testimony of the conscience to 'despaire not, or thinke thou art a reprobate, [Christ] came to call sinners to repentance' (3.430.11–13). The argument here offered to mitigate the effects of the failed search for the fruits of election was taken straight out of Perkins's *Cases of Conscience*: 'A true desire of mercy in the want of mercy is mercy it selfe, a desire of grace in the want of grace is grace it selfe' (3.431.9–10).[174] In Burton's hands, however, Perkins's response proved inadequate, provoking atheism and blasphemy in the sufferer, who before long was accounting 'the Scriptures false... Heaven, hell, resurrection, meere toies and fables... Religion, policie, and humane invention' (3.432.3–6). The role of predestination in this response was suggested by the allegation that God was 'author of sinne' (3.432.9–10), one of the well-known Roman criticisms of the predestinarian doctrine expounded by Calvin and Beza. In the 1632 edition, this association was strengthened with the added accusation of 'a cruel, destructive God' who had chosen 'to create our soules, and destinate them to eternall damnation'.[175]

Having given over the best part of a folio page to atheistic blasphemy, Burton excused himself by labelling it 'horrible and execrable', and (with some irony) 'not fit to be uttered' (3.432.27). The comforter then claimed that 'no man living is free from such thoughts in part, or at some times', and argued that they were the product of the Devil's manipulation of the imagination (3.433.1–26).[176] But the downcast voice would not be diverted from predestination. Answering the injunction to 'meditate withall on Gods word' (3.434.22), Burton's suggestion was that this

174 Perkins 1606, I.7, p. 98.

175 Burton 1632, p. 711; or 3.432.10–11 (3.4.2.6).

176 Contrast the reaction predicted in Perkins 1591, fol. 46^{v}.

would make matters worse, since 'the more' those in despair 'search and reade Scriptures, or divine Treatises . . . the more they are intangled and precipitated into this preposterous gulfe'. Relating *topoi* such as '*Many are called, few are chosen*' to 'Gods eternall decree of predestination' leads them to 'doubt presently whether they be of this number or no', and 'This grinds their Soules, how shall they discerne they are not reprobates?' (3.433.27–435.1). This recapitulated the Lutheran argument against scholastic casuistry, but it also denounced the 'fatall tables' of experimental Calvinism.[177] In the third edition, puritan sermons were surreptitiously included in the condemnation, as the sufferers' condition was said to be worsened by their 'misconceaving all they read *or heare*'.[178] And the consolatory response to the question 'how shall they discerne they are not reprobates?' implied that the 'experiment' originated in the diabolically corrupted imagination: 'how shall they discerne they are? From the divell can be no certainety' (3.435.1–2).

Counterpoising the false testimony of reprobation with its opposite, the misleading security of 'presumption', Burton used the next response of the despairing voice to criticise another aspect of experimental predestinarianism – the idea of the temporary faith of the reprobate. According to Perkins in *A Treatise tending unto a declaration whether a man be in the estate of damnation or in the estate of grace* (1589), the non-elect could excel in the 'certaine fruites' of the elect by means of an 'ineffectual' calling, which could be so powerful that the reprobate seemed to ascend the *ordo salutis* itself.[179] This compromised the *syllogismus practicus*, as what appeared to be the assurance of the elect could be the 'security' or 'presumption' of the reprobate; there would be cases where 'none but Christ' would be able to 'discerne the sheep from the goates'.[180] Referring to this situation, Burton had his sufferer express fear that his or her faith was the temporary, 'weake and faint' kind of the damned without the 'signes, and fruits of sanctification', and question 'how shall I believe or discerne my security from carnall presumption?' (3.436.6–9). The consolatory response pointed to the necessary absence of the signs of election before conversion. But it was also without an argument to overcome the problem produced by the Calvinist scholastics,

177 See the same criticism in Corbett 1955, p. 58.

178 Burton 1628, p. 638; or 3.434.28 (3.4.2.6), my italics.

179 Perkins 1591, fols. 1^{r}–13^{r}, esp. 2^{r-v}, 6^{v}–7^{r}, 9^{v}–11^{v}, 16^{r}–17^{r}, 29^{v}. This doctrine derives from Calvin 1936, III.2.11, vol. I, pp. 608–9.

180 Perkins 1591, fol. 12^{v}.

who had neglected to provide means of distinguishing true from temporary faith: 'if not yet called, pray thou maist be' (3.436.13–17).[181]

Burton proceeded to abandon his consolatory task to construct his commentary on the doctrinal controversy surrounding predestination. He began with an ironic reference to two theologians who were responsible for some of the severer formulations of the Calvinist doctrine, and so themselves guilty of the activities subsequently denounced.

Notwithstanding all this which might bee said to this effect, to ease their afflicted mindes, what comfort our best Divines can afford in this case, *Zanchius*, *Beza*, *&c.* This furious curiosity, needlesse speculation, fruitlesse meditation about Election, reprobation, free-will, grace, such places of Scripture preposterously conceaved, torment still, and crucifie the soules of too many and set all the world together by the eares. To avoid which inconveniences, and to settle their distressed mindes, to mitigate those divine Aphorismes (though in another extreame) our late *Arminians* have revived that plausible doctrine of universall grace, which many Fathers, our late *Lutherans* and moderne Papists doe still maintaine, that we have free-will of our selves, and that Grace is common to all that will beleeve. (3.436.19–29)

Here was the first explicit reference to Arminianism in the *Anatomy*, and it is important to treat it with care. Burton was not supporting 'our late *Arminians*', and he was possibly suggesting that they were in error 'in another extreame' from Zanchi and Beza (this would imply a parallel criticism of radical Calvinism). However, the point that Arminianism had been designed 'to mitigate those divine Aphorismes' suggested its utility in dealing with the despair induced by predestinarian speculation, and the remarkable admission that the notion of 'universall grace' was 'plausible' indicates guarded approbation. It appears distinctly less cautious when aligned with his previously expressed scepticism about the limits of human knowledge about the divine will.[182] Although important, the error implied through the association of Arminianism with 'moderne Papists' was counterbalanced by the authoritative support of 'many Fathers' as well as 'our late *Lutherans*'.

Burton gave his readers more reason to suspect that he viewed Arminian ideas with sympathy when he followed up his discussion of universal grace with an observation that was startling in the environment of the mid-1620s. 'Some againe', he wrote, 'though *lesse* orthodoxall, will have a farre greater part saved, then shall be damned' (3.436.29–31; my italics). Not only the Church of Rome, then, but also the Arminians had

[181] See, for example, the analysis of Beza in Bray 1975, p. 110.
[182] See Burton 1624, p. 538; or 3.414.27–30 (3.4.2.6).

a valid claim to 'orthodoxy'. Initially retreating from this contentious issue, he embarked on a discussion of the unquestionable heresy of the Piedmontese humanist latitudinarian Celio Secondo Curione, who 'will have those saved that never heard of, or beleeved in Christ, *ex puris naturalibus*', and believed only those 'that refuse Christs mercy and grace' to be 'in the state of damnation' (3.436.29–437.32). As Burton pointed out, Curione had drawn on Origen to support his contention that virtuous pagans might be saved (3.437.19–21). This had also prompted Erasmus to elevate the position of Origen over and against Augustine, as an authority whose teachings were better suited towards the *philosophia Christi*.[183]

Burton saw much to cherish in the ideal of a simple, non-theological piety, and elsewhere in the *Anatomy* it is possible to detect in his habit of describing pagan virtue as if it were spiritually authentic a tendency to gravitate towards this formally heterodox soteriological position.[184] Elaborating on Curione, he turned to the question of whether virtuous non-Christians could be saved, an opinion that had been held 'by the *Valentinian* and *Basilidean* hereticks', and had been 'revived of late in *Turkie*... defended by *Galeottus Martius*, and favored by *Erasmus*'.[185] In the editions of 1624 and 1628 this was straightforward enough. However, in the 1632 version Burton muddied the distinction between Reformed orthodoxy and non-Reformed heterodoxy. Now, he pointed out, this view had also been maintained by 'some ancient Fathers' and '*Zuinglius*... whose Tenet *Bullinger* vindicates, and *Gualter* approves', and that there were 'many Jesuites that follow these Calvinists in this behalfe', but that '*Hofmannus*, a Lutheran professor of *Helmstad* and many of his followers, with most of our Church, and Papists are stiffe against it' (3.437.32–438.12). This was an unmistakable provocation to those staunch Calvinists who continued to identify with their continental counterparts, and who had spent so much energy refuting the 'crypto-popery' of Arminianism throughout the 1620s. Not only were the revered figures of the Swiss Reformation – Zwingli, Bullinger, and Rudolph Walther ('*Gualter*') – shown to share common ground with heretical sects and Jesuits; they were also aligned against 'most of our [English] Church', as well as their bitter rivals the Lutherans and the 'Papists'.

183 Levi 2002, pp. 11, 26, 101, 254.
184 See, for example, at 2.145.4–11 (2.3.3.1), or 2.169.4–5 (2.3.3.1).
185 Burton 1632, p.716; or 3.437.32–438.2 (3.4.2.6).

Suddenly the guillotine of orthodoxy was dropped on these controversies, and Burton appeared to retreat from his anti-Calvinist position. 'But these absurd paradoxes are exploded by our Church, we teach otherwise',

> That this vocation, predestination, election, was from the beginning, before the foundation of the world was laid, we holde *perseverantia sanctorum*, we must be certaine of our salvation, we may fall but not eternally, which our *Arminians* will not admit. According to his immutable, eternall, just decree and counsel of saving men and Angels, God calls all, and would have all to be saved according to the efficacy of his vocation: all are invited, but only the elect apprehended, the rest that are unbeleeving, impenitent, whom God in his just judgement leaves to be punished for their sinnes, are in a reprobate sense.[186]

This was how the second edition of 1624 defined the English Church's teaching on predestination. At first glance it accords with supralapsarian Calvinist teaching – the decree was conceptually prior to the Fall of man – and includes the doctrine of perseverance. But it was not double. The reprobate were simply 'left' by God to be 'punished for their sinnes' and be 'in a reprobate sense', rather than being actively willed by Him to be so.[187]

This divergence from the Articles of the Synod of Dort, which stipulated absolute and double predestination, was the first sign of Burton's enterprise to put an optimistic gloss on the doctrine. Perseverance was justified not theologically, but as a psychological necessity, and it is interesting that his apparent opposition to Arminianism here was based on the fact that, as Laud had pointed out, it seemed less merciful on this point. (Moreover, the sense of the text is that the 'absurd paradoxes . . . exploded by our Church' were not those of 'our *Arminians*', but rather of the comfortably heretical Curione.[188]) In order to stress the universal nature of God's invitation to salvation, but being constrained by the necessary existence of the reprobate, he had recourse to the scholastic distinction – made by Calvin, Ursinus, Zanchi, and Perkins – between the absolute 'sufficiency' and partial 'efficiency' of God's 'invitation' to salvation.[189] However, Burton had little appetite for doctrinal precision,

186 Burton 1624, p. 553; or 4.438.26–439.1 (3.4.2.6).

187 On the similar reticence of Calvin and Bullinger see Muller 1986, p. 44.

188 This is clearest in the second edition. In the third, Burton distinguished between Curione and moderate 'Calvinists' by indicating that he was now 'return[ing] to my author' (Burton 1632, p. 716; or 3.438.15 [3.4.2.6]). After the passage on 'our late *Socinians*' had been added to the fifth edition, this became less obvious (Burton 1638, p. 716; or 3.438.18–22).

189 See the precedent in Howson 1602, p. 5.

as his confused usage of the term 'efficacy' indicates.[190] The discussion closed with the moderate commonplace that 'we must not determine' who were reprobates, a restatement of God's 'universall invitation', and a reminder of the inadequacy of human judgement in the matter that recalled earlier strictures about the limitations of theological speculation (3.439.1–4).

Burton's position on predestination in 1624 represented moderation purchased at the expense of clarity. In the next edition, he elaborated the confusion. 'We', in the English Church, 'teach otherwise',

> That this vocation, predestination, election, reprobation *non ex corruptâ massâ, prævisa fide*, as our *Arminians*, or *ex prævisis operibus*, as our Papists, *non ex præteritione*, but Gods absolute decree, *ante mundum creatum*, (as most of our Church holde) was from the beginning, before the foundation of the world was laid, (or from *Adams* fall, as others will, *homo lapsus objectum est reprobationis*) with *perseverantia sanctorum*, we must be certaine of our salvation, we may fall but not finally, which our *Arminians* will not admit. (3.438.26–33)

The addition of the word 'reprobation' seemed to make double predestination the orthodoxy, but the author's refusal to detail the causes of reprobation left this in doubt, and the text retained the formula stipulating that God 'leaves' them to their condition. Similarly, although this distinguished between Arminianism and Romanism on the basis of the divine foreknowledge of the faith or works of the elect, the question of human ability to contribute actively towards salvation, on which the controversy of the period turned, was not addressed directly.[191] Instead, he exposed more disagreement. 'Gods absolute decree' was apparently '*ante mundum creatum*' (in accordance with the creabilitarianism of Beza), but this was the opinion not of all 'our Church' but only of 'most'. This discrepancy within 'our Church' – recall his insistence on the continued presence of error *within* the Church of England as well as outside it – was developed with the admission that 'others' believed the decree to be subsequent to the Fall. In Burton's portrayal, then, the 'orthodoxy' of 'our Church' suffered from confusion, not only over the question of whether predestination was single or double, but also over the question of whether it was creabilitarian, supralapsarian or infralapsarian.[192]

[190] Cf. 3.428.27; 3.429.24 (3.4.2.6).

[191] That Burton may have been espousing Molinism, as suggested by Bamborough and Dodsworth at 6.290, seems unlikely. Cf. the position of Hooker analysed in Lake 1988, pp. 184–6. On English Molinism at this time see Hughes 1998, pp. 239–40.

[192] Cf. the exposition in Vaughan 1626, pp. 141–2, 144–6.

This was an accurate diagnosis of a situation that persisted in the major texts of the Reformed tradition.

In the 1638 version, the text became an even more sensitive barometer of the theological uncertainty of Burton's environment. Registering the perceived rise of Arminianism in England and Oxford with the further reduction of supralapsarianism's dominance, the belief of what was formerly 'most of our Church' was now that of 'many of our Church'.[193] In another deceptive 'clarification' serving to underline the controversy and heighten the syntactical ambiguity that was its mirror, he inserted 'or *homo conditus*,' before '(or from *Adams* fall . . .)', and ended this wilfully confusing discussion with one of his most ironic additions.

I might have said more of this subject, but forasmuch as it is a forbidden question, and in the Preface or Declaration to the Articles of the Church, printed 1633, to avoid factions & altercations, we that are Universitie Divines especially, are prohibited *all curious search, to print or preach, or draw the Article aside by our owne sence and Comments, upon paine of Ecclesiasticall censure.* I will surcease, and conclude with *Erasmus* of such controversies; *Pugnet qui volet, ego censeo leges majorum reverenter suscipiendas, & religiose observandas, velut a Deo profectas, nec esse tutum, nec esse pium, de potestate publica sinistram concipere aut serere suspitionem. Et siquid est tyrannidis, quod tamen non cogat ad impietatem, satius est ferre, quam seditiose reluctari.*[194]

Here, perhaps, were echoes of the Erasmian discussions of *libertas philosophandi* conducted in the 'Great Tew' circle. None of the royal proclamations made in 1626, 1628, and 1633 forbidding contentious discussion of disputed doctrine had prevented Burton from doing precisely that in the pages which immediately preceded this reference, and his emphasis on the fact that the restriction had been placed specifically on 'we that are Universitie Divines' underscored the irony. Whilst the concluding quotation from Erasmus buttressed his opposition to contentiousness, and advocated reverence to the public authorities, it also surreptitiously labelled them as potential tyrants ('*Et siquid est tyrannidis*') and called the careful reader's attention to the possibility that this part of the text was criminal. The fact that Burton was not brought before Laud's Commission for contravention of the ban on discussion of predestination was probably because the *Anatomy* did not openly support any position. Or perhaps he benefited from double standards. According to Anthony Wood, Calvinists breaching the order were forced

193 Burton 1638, p. 716; or 3.438.29 (3.4.2.6).
194 Burton 1638, p. 717; or 3.439.4–13 (3.4.2.6).

to recant in public and on 'bended knees in the Convocation House', whereas 'Arminians' guilty of the same crime were required only to make their recantations privately to the vice-chancellor.[195]

Burton never supported an Arminian interpretation of predestination, preferring to distance himself from dogmatic commitment. His refusal to choose between the different interpretations of the finer points being disputed, as with the satirical juxtaposition of conflicting opinions throughout the book, underlined the gulf of uncertainty dividing what Thomas Browne called the 'fallible discourses of man upon the word of God' from the infallible, unfallen discourse of 'true' religion, the orthodoxy contained in scripture.[196] A profession of Arminianism not only would have been risky in the circumstances, but would have undercut the force of his critiques of sectarianism and 'needlesse speculation' about the doctrine as causes of religious melancholy. On the other hand, the alterations made in the 1624, 1628, 1632, and 1638 editions indicate *both* growing interest in the divisive and increasingly hair-splitting controversies surrounding predestination, *and* his increasing hostility towards certain forms of radical Calvinism – or, perhaps, increasing willingness to make this hostility overt. There are hints elsewhere that Burton was drawn towards a moderate anti-Calvinist understanding of grace. He consistently emphasised the mercy of God and the universality of the call to repentance, rather than the undeserving nature of those chosen by God to receive the miracle of grace.[197] He voiced disapproval of the notion of divine cruelty implicit in the most severe versions of predestination (3.436.4–5). He wrote of repentance – albeit metaphorically – as if it had an automatic, quasi-sacramental, efficacy in attracting divine grace, almost to the point of rendering the power of Christ's sacrifice dependent on this act (3.429.15–16; 428.30–429.3). And unlike the opponents of the Laudians in the 1620s and '30s, he did not label Arminianism as either crypto-papist or quasi-Pelagian heresy.

Perhaps most telling of all was that by the end of Burton's spiritual consolation it was far from clear that the comforting voice had dispelled the despair of the sufferer. Having concluded his discussion of predestinarian controversy, he acknowledged that he had strayed from his consolatory duty (3.439.14). Resuming this, he reproduced the Calvinist teaching according to which affliction of the godly was

[195] Wood 1792–6, vol. II, pp. 381–2.

[196] Browne 1977, I.23, p. 91.

[197] See, for example, 3.426.27 and ff.; 3.429.31; 3.435.30–436.4 (3.4.2.6); cf. Bright 1586, pp. 201–2.

a providential trial, designed to prepare the soul for the reception of grace by assisting comprehension of human helplessness and sinfulness and prompting repentance (3.439.26–442.36). But the final response from the suffering voice showed no sign of benefiting from this doctrine ('I cannot hope, pray, repent, &c.' [3.441.32–33]), and despite his merciful efforts to downplay the implications of predestination, the comforter's arguments were still framed in terms of grace, election, damnation, and reprobation.[198] In the final passages of the encounter, Burton seemed to lose patience with combating the psychological consequences of the decree, and switched to a highly questionable mode of consolatory discourse. Now he offered a catalogue of therapies that began with occult-medical remedies to drive out evil spirits (3.443.21–5), continued with remedies whose theological spuriousness was signalled by their popularity with 'Gentiles, present Mahometans, and Papists' (3.444.8–23), and rejected these as 'fopperies and fictions' in favour of remedies directly from Christ (3.444.26–9). The consolatory discourse closed with a brief survey of practical diversionary tactics, adapting those appropriate to non-religious melancholy to the condition of despair, and all tending towards one famously pithy aphorism – '*Be not solitary, be not idle*' (3.445.36).

Despite Burton's announced intention to offer his readers 'comfortable speeches' in the expanded final Subsection, the tone of this spiritual *consolatio* was ultimately one of unsettling ambiguity. The concluding words of the Subsection found in the 1621 copy remained in all the subsequent editions. Why did he not end with a simple optimistic exhortation? In the light of what we have suggested about his theological concerns about predestination, the answer is clear. The two responses to the decree excluded by the warning 'SPERATE MISERI, CAVETE FÆLICES', were atheistic despair and the 'full assurance' that puritans like Perkins had held up as the goal towards which all believers should strive.[199] (It is no surprise that, unlike its typical Calvinist counterparts, Burton's lacked the testator's assertion of the belief that he was elect, or any lamentation of his sinfulness.[200]) If, as he had been urging, speculation about one's election or reprobation was to be avoided, it was above all because it would lead to one or other of these equally dangerous conditions. This was the real controversial force of his appropriation of

[198] See 3.439.18; 3.440.11; and 3.442.11–13, 29–31 (3.4.2.6).
[199] See, for instance, Perkins 1591, fol. 24^{v}.
[200] See Kiessling 1990, pp. 97–101. On Calvinist wills see Tyacke 1993, pp. 61–2.

Hemmingsen's consolatory aims in the *Antidotum adversus pestem desperationis*: it provided a psychological argument that could be turned against radical Calvinist piety, that would at the same time clear a space to be filled by an emergent spiritual alternative. The final quotation from Augustine, which Burton had underlined in his copy of the *Antidotum* – where it also ended the consolation – hinted at what this might look like: '*Vis à dubio liberari, vis quod incertum est evadere? Age pænitentiam dum sanus es, sic agens, dico tibi quod securus es, quod pænitentiam egisti eo tempore quo peccare potuisti*' (3.446.3–5).[201] Although it would be imprudent to extrapolate a doctrinal commitment from this piece of ventriloquism, it is here that the text came closest to departing from Reformed orthodoxy by attributing sacramental efficacy to repentance with respect to salvation. Taken literally, it suggested that acts of penitence freely undertaken 'at a time when you could have sinned' guaranteed the soul's safety. For all his concessions to Calvinism, Burton's deeper desire was to combat the psychological effects of its conception of human helplessness. His final gesture in the *Anatomy* was towards the freedom of the will, and the potential of the individual to contribute to his or her salvation or damnation.[202]

HUMANISM AND THE EARLY STUART CHURCH

One way of making sense of Burton's arguments about the different forms of religious melancholy is to see them as contributing to a broadly anti-Calvinist ideological agenda that gradually crystallised in response to the religious developments of the 1620s and '30s, so that by the time the fifth edition of the *Anatomy* was published in 1638 – remnants of his earlier Calvinism notwithstanding – it could justifiably be taken as a largely unequivocal declaration of support for the ecclesiastical policies of Charles and Laud. Whereas the first edition of the book mingled avant-garde and moderate Calvinist conformism, the later editions tell a different story. As we have seen, in the editions of 1624, 1628, 1632, and 1638 Burton substantially modified the complexion of his text – amplifying his critique of Calvinist scholasticism, experimental predestinarianism, and various aspects of puritan piety – in ways that surely reflect the increasingly overt anti-Calvinism of Oxford (and Christ

201 Kiessling 1988, entry 776.

202 See also 3.437.24–5 and 3.438.15–16 (3.4.2.6), both of which passages could be read as denials of perseverance.

Church in particular) in the 1620s, and the Laudian dominance of the university after 1630. His treatment of predestination, whereby discussion of the doctrine was portrayed as harmful to the disciplinary unity of the English Church, could be seen as a Laudian silencing tactic – despite the manifest irony of his citation of the royal decree of 1633 – that cleared the space required for a reconstitution of orthodox worship in sacramental and ceremonial terms.

There are several plausible explanations for this development. Possibly in the changed circumstances Burton felt safer to express his true beliefs, which he had held all along. Or following the 'conformist drift' of these years he may have changed his views, in which case he could have been coerced or persuaded by those in the ascendancy. If the latter, then this aspect of the *Anatomy* could be taken as a sign that the Laudian strategy of securing the allegiance of Calvinist conformists was working. Perhaps all of these processes were at work in some way. However, we should not overlook Burton's general consistency. Unlike many of his contemporaries, he never expressed radical Calvinist beliefs that he would subsequently abandon, and in this respect it is telling that nearly all of his significant modifications to this part of the book were additions and amplifications rather than subtractions. In an unstable religious environment, the message projected by Burton's adherence to sacramentalism and ceremonialism gradually mutated from avant-garde conformism to Laudianism, and this was as much a reflection of the fact that the ground around the author was shifting as it was the product of his evolving ideological position. The *Anatomy* exemplifies Bourdieu's dictum: 'Quand le livre reste et que le monde tout autour change, le livre change.'[203]

There is nevertheless something unsatisfying about describing the *Anatomy* as a Laudian text, and the same must be said of judgements of Burton as a doctrinal Calvinist *manqué*, avant-garde conformist, Lutheran, or whatever label seems best to fit his apparent theological and ecclesiological preferences. This is not just because he is a perfect illustration of the truism that seventeenth-century individuals did not cleanly inhabit the classificatory categories that historians have devised for them. Even if it is granted that Burton's work in its later incarnations came to be generally supportive of the Laudian programme, it was not primarily devised as such. The central aim of the Section devoted to religious melancholy was to understand the nature of the spiritual

[203] Bourdieu and Chartier 1985, p. 236.

disorders perceived by the author in the world surrounding him, and where possible to alleviate them, and here his concerns stemmed not from any desire to legitimate an existing set of religious policies but from his humanist moral-psychological preoccupation with melancholy. What requires explanation, then, is the nature of the concurrence between Laudianism and Burton's humanism, and the circumstances by which it was facilitated. Here there is little assistance in the recent historiography of the early Stuart Church, which has all but erased humanism as a significant aspect of religiosity except as a component of the intellectual ancestry of puritanism.

Arguably Burton's work came to support Laud more by accident than by design. This is borne out when we measure Burton's humanist ideals and methods against his often implicit religious-political stance. Such seems to be the case for the coincidence of his Christian humanist ideal of the peaceful and harmonious commonwealth with the Jacobean and later Caroline agendas in foreign and domestic religious policy. In foreign affairs, Charles and Laud followed James (and the Dutch Remonstrants) in their opposition to Protestant military interventionism, and this was integral to their vision of the well-ordered commonwealth undisturbed by either continental violence or religious divisions at home. Yet Burton did not articulate his pacifism in deliberative terms as diplomatic strategy, and he was silent about the fate of the Palatinate. His primary purpose was to counteract the militaristic aspect of the destructive, sinful, and psychologically disturbing madness of humanity, and even if its contemporary implications were clear the conjunction with royal policy here seems partly the product of chance.

But we should not be puzzling over how and why the religious agenda of a humanist scholar resembled that of the Jacobean or Caroline establishment. Even if few of his countrymen could demonstrate the diverse fruits of an education in the *studia humanitatis* as impressively as the author of the *Anatomy*, his intellectual commitments and habits were hardly exceptional amongst the university-trained political elite of the period, whether in England or in Europe generally.[204] Another significant example here was Burton's brother, the famous antiquarian William, also a humanist with Laudian sympathies, and who resented the destructive iconoclasm of the early English reformers.[205] 'Laudianism' may have been forged out of specific theological and ecclesiological materials, but

[204] See the emphatic judgement in Grafton 1996, p. 220.
[205] See Cust 2004–5.

it also drew upon a universe of intellectual discourse and intersected with a number of political concerns that were distinctively humanistic. As we shall see in the next chapter, the humanist model of political order that was constituted through the moral-psychological analogy between the peaceful commonwealth and the tranquil soul retained its relevance in Jacobean and Caroline England. Two dramatic productions which drew upon this model, William Strode's *Floating Island* and William Cartwright's *Royall Slave*, had been commissioned by Laud before they were performed in Christ Church in 1636. The first play earned the approval of the king, if no-one else, and the author was made a canon of the College. The second was widely acknowledged a great success, and Cartwright was subsequently requested by Laud to supervise the new Oxford press.[206]

The Christian humanist vision of the well-ordered commonwealth, free from foreign or domestic antagonism, was readily translatable into the Laudian vision of the harmonious and disciplined national Church integrated to the requirements of the civil authority. Aspects of Burton's analysis of religious discord suggest that, although the politics which lay behind the ecclesiastical policies of the early Stuart monarchs arose from an increasingly pervasive divine-right absolutism that had displaced the republicanism and moderate constitutionalism of the Elizabethan era, they were also bound up with a longstanding humanistic tradition of theorising about the relations between Church and state. Although not necessarily Erastian, the terms of this discussion could suggest the equality, if not priority, of the political in relation to the spiritual benefits of religious harmony. In this respect, the precedent had been set most famously by Machiavelli, who in his commentary on the Roman republic had underlined the importance of the ruling power's adherence to religious principles to the maintenance of civil concord, and identified neglect of worship as a sure sign of the decline of a commonwealth.[207] This perspective, which had also been approvingly detected in classical Roman authors by Lipsius in the *Politica*,[208] can be detected in a number of seventeenth-century English writers, where it gradually evolved into a fully fledged doctrine of 'civil religion'. When extolling the 'infinite blessings' of the 'fruits of unity', for instance, Francis Bacon began by describing 'Religion' as 'the chief band of human society'. For Bacon,

[206] Sharpe 1981, pp. 151–2.
[207] Machiavelli 1970, I.12, pp. 142–3. See also Pontano 1997, p. 70.
[208] Lipsius 1594, IV.2, pp. 61–3.

as for Machiavelli, this was illustrated by the historical truth that 'Quarrels, and Divisions about *Religion*, were Evils unknown to the Heathen', and led him to interrogate the manner and circumstances in which the 'temporal sword' should act to enforce unity.[209] When pursued to its conclusion, this approach would ground the complete subordination of religious to civil authority later theorised by Thomas Hobbes in the third and fourth parts of *Leviathan* (1651), and by James Harrington in *The Commonwealth of Oceana* (1656).

What we see in the *Anatomy* is the point where the humanist tendency to discourse of a classically modelled 'civil religion' intersected with Laudian (or proto-'Anglican') views of the necessary inextricability of ecclesiastical and political order. The influence of the former on Burton was substantial, though the manner in which it was handled suggests nervousness. In 'Democritus Junior to the Reader', the flourishing and harmonious commonwealth was said to be bound together by 'charity... alliance, affinitie, consanguinitie', and 'Christianitie' (1.51.5–6), whereas the 'most frequent maladies' of the body politic were reportedly found 'when Religion and Gods Service is neglected', and a deficient fear of God was associated with disobedience to the prince and declining prosperity (1.67.29–31).[210] Such specific though unacknowledged accordance with Machiavelli is revealing. As we shall see in his critique of 'reason of state', Burton rejected the purely instrumental conception of religion as 'policy, invented alone to keepe men in awe' (3.346.f [3.4.1.2]) and castigated 'Captaine *Machiavel*' for his advice that the prince should 'counterfeit religion... to keepe the people in obedience' (3.347.12–17). Yet like many humanists he granted the Florentine's classical premise, namely that 'Religion' was one of the 'chiefe props and supporters of a well-govern'd commonwealth' (3.347.23–4). That Burton was torn between disapproval of the atheistic tendency implicit in this approach, and admiration for its political wisdom, is suggested by his discourse on the efficiency of classical and pagan rulers in preserving civil order through such 'superstitious' means (3.347.29–349.28), and by the fact that the *exemplum* of China – a body politic praised extensively in 'Democritus Junior to the Reader' – was said to be maintained by 'such tricks and impostures' on the part of its 'Polititians' (3.349.27–8).

[209] Bacon 1985, III, pp. 11, 14–16.
[210] Cf. Machiavelli 1970, p. 141. The words 'innovated or altered' were added in Burton 1632, p. 47. See also Burton 1624, p. 53; or 1.92.4–17.

Burton was anxious to dispel the whiff of impiety that accompanied the humanist discourse of civil religion, but such denunciations also concealed the fact that he had drawn a considerable quantity from its source. There was, he wrote, 'no greater concord, no greater discord, then that which proceeds from Religion', and his illustration of the point in the third edition with the remark that '[i]t is incredible to relate, did not our dayly experience evince it, what factions *quam teterrimæ factione*... have beene of late for matters of Religion in *France*, and what hurlie burlies all over *Europe*, for these many yeares' (3.366.6–12 [3.4.1.3]; cf. 3.396.10–15 [3.4.2.1]) was redolent of Bacon's argument in 'Of Unity in Religion'.[211] Even more suggestive was his agreement with Bacon that the 'bloody battels, rackes and wheeles, seditions, factions, oppositions... Invectives and contentions' that currently existed 'all over Europe' bore out the view of the atheist Lucretius that '*Tantum religio potuit suadere malorum*' (3.367.23–8 [3.4.1.3]).[212]

Such passages would have raised many contemporary eyebrows, but when we turn to the vision of religious order constructed as an antidote to the spiritual discord of the body politic, we can see that there was very little that would have troubled the Church authorities in the 1620s and '30s. Indeed, his model of the harmonious Church and state nestled in comfortably with Laudian and Caroline aspirations. He made a point of stipulating that in his utopia 'Ecclesiastical Discipline' would be established '*penes Episcopos*' and ultimately 'subordinate' to the king (1.90.29–30),[213] later offered apparently Erastian criticism of 'our Priests' who 'domineere over Princes and Statesmen themselves' (3.349.29–31 [3.4.1.2]), and, as we have seen, was particularly severe in his criticism of 'Scismaticks' who questioned the legitimate powers of 'Princes, civill magistrates, & their authorities' (3.387.27–8 [3.4.1.3]). Irrespective of its largely submerged intellectual implications, the practical outcome of his discourse on the civil dimension of religion was supportive of the Stuart establishment.

Another coincidence between humanism and Laudianism can be discerned in Burton's theological commitments, and their direct relationship to his attitude towards 'the Queene of Professions' (1.20.30). The key here is again to be found in the Christian humanism of 'Democritus Junior to the Reader'. Burton's satirical critique of the foolish madness of

[211] Bacon 1985, III, pp. 14–15.
[212] The quotation from Lucretius was new to Burton 1624, p. 515; cf. Bacon 1985, III, p. 14.
[213] See also 1.89.16–23, and cf. Vaughan 1626, pp. 133–7.

humanity fused classical moral-philosophical views of the passions with a patristic *contemptum mundi*, and this closely followed Erasmus in the *Moriae encomium*. Like Erasmus's Folly, Burton's Democritus Junior singled out pagan philosophers for ridicule, citing Lactantius's view that despite their reputed wisdom they were 'Dizards, Asses, mad-men' and 'full of absurd and ridiculous tenents and braine-sicke positions' (1.28.30–29.1). In the second edition, he associated futile speculative-intellectual activity – 'Bookes and elaborate Treatises . . . full of dotage' – with the inability to 'understand . . . the state of their owne Soules' and 'knowe . . . what is right in this life'.[214] This was in line with the traditional humanist critique of scholastic reasoning in divinity, as became evident in the first edition later in the preface, where he returned to the madness of 'Philosophers and Schollers' and cited a series of sixteenth-century humanists who had censured scholastic theology: '*Bale*, *Erasmus*, *Hospinian*, *Vives*, explode as a vast Ocean of *Obs* and *Sols*, Schoole divinity, a labyrinth of intricable questions, unprofitable contentions.'[215] In later editions, this censure of scholastic impracticality was gradually incorporated to the earlier account of 'our Religious madnesse', with an indictment first of 'so much talke of Religion, so much knowledge, so little practise',[216] and then of 'so much Science, so little Conscience'.[217] In the Latin diatribe at the end of the 'Digression of the Misery of Schollers', Burton directed his critical gaze closer to home, decrying the prevalence in the universities of 'idiotic wanderers beyond the pale', who had learned scholastic procedures ('one or two definitions or distinctions') and 'spent the customary number of years in chopping logic [*in dialecticâ*]', as a cause of the corruption of 'the sacred precincts of Theology' and so also of the English Church and commonwealth (1.324.32–8; 325.16–326.3 [1.2.3.15]).[218]

It was, however, in the 1624 version of the *Anatomy* that Burton showed the theological implications of his humanist distaste for scholastic divinity. In the midst of a lengthy Subsection devoted to a heterogeneous 'Heape' of 'Accidents causing melancholy', he turned to curiosity, 'that irksome care . . . an itching humor or a kinde of longing to see that which

214 Burton 1624, p. 17; or 1.29.22, 30–30.1. See also ibid., p. 59; or 1.103.11–20.
215 Burton 1621, p. 64; or 1.101.8–10.
216 Burton 1624, p. 23; or 1.39.22–24.
217 Burton 1628, p. 28; or 1.39.23–4.
218 I am here following the translation by Bamborough and Dodsworth (4.346–9), which I consider justified by the satirical context. See also 2.56.22 (2.2.3.1); 2.99.6–9 (2.2.5.1); and 3.414.33–5 (3.4.2.3).

is not to bee seene'.[219] The psychological point was that the curious 'molest & tire' themselves 'about things unfit and unnecessary', earning 'needlesse trouble' and 'torment', and in the light of what we have seen to be Burton's religious concerns in this period what followed is hardly surprising: 'For what els is schoole Divinity, how many doth it pussle? what fruitlesse questions about the Trinity, Resurrection, Election, Predestination, hell fire, &c. how many shall be saved, damned?'[220] The emphasis on the damaging effect of curiosity about the theology of grace, which was typically amplified in the 1628 copy with the insertion of the topic of 'Reprobation',[221] indicated that he had Calvinist scholasticism particularly in mind; his vituperation against Catholic scholastics made no mention of predestination (3.385.30–386.15 [3.4.1.3]).

Rather than doctrinal Arminianism, it was this traditional humanist critique of scholasticism that lay at the heart of Burton's argument about predestination, and it is tempting to suggest that herein lies one of the reasons for the elusive nature of English 'Arminianism'. If divines who disapproved of radical Calvinist expositions of the theology of grace rarely appealed to the teachings of Arminius or his followers on this issue, this was because the non-dogmatic humanism permeating the intellectual culture of the English universities had made this unnecessary, except in cases – which, given the anti-speculative nature of the argument, were by definition rare – where systematic theological discussion was considered appropriate. Of course, humanistic commitments did not foreclose strong Calvinist allegiance. Joseph Hall considered 'the infinite subdivisions' of scholastic theology unsuitable for consumption by ordinary Christians, and argued that the full comprehension of the divine decree was indifferent to salvation. But although he drew the distinction between 'theological conclusions' and essential 'principles of religion', he maintained that the former were 'fit for the discourse of a divine'. In the face of the growing domestic threat of Arminianism, Hall responded to the imperative to re-articulate the doctrine of predestination which had been agreed at Dort.[222]

Similarly, Burton's humanist contemporary William Vaughan supported Dort's castigation of Arminianism and supported absolute and double predestination in his *Golden Fleece* (1626), yet also suggested that the subject of the 'curious inquisitions' of Arminius was beyond the

219 Burton 1624, p. 147; or 1.363.33–364.3 (1.2.4.7).
220 Burton 1624, pp. 147–8; or 1.364.5–8 (1.2.4.7).
221 Burton 1628, p. 159; or 1.364.8 (1.2.4.7).
222 See the analysis of Hall's position in Lake 1995, pp. 58–61, 64–75.

reach of 'humane capacities' and should be avoided by those with 'tender constitutions'.[223] This was an awkward stance; humanist anti-scholasticism was more readily compatible with the anti-Calvinist agenda, and may have prepared the ground for curiosity about Arminianism. This seems to be the case for Burton, who bought Arminius's *Opera theologica* in 1630. It was coincidental, perhaps, that this was in the year that Laud was elected as Chancellor of Oxford, as his argument about predestination was already fully formed. Rather than being influenced by Arminian teaching, it is likely that he was interested in its potential conjunction with his own humanistically inspired views, and more generally in its important role in contemporary disputes. The lack of annotation in his copy of the *Opera* supports this interpretation.[224]

The roots of Burton's spirituality were in the Erasmian *philosophia Christi* popular in English humanist circles of the previous century. Erasmian scepticism concerning the human capacity to grasp speculative theological questions had permitted the burden of resolving unavoidable doctrinal disputes to be transferred from the individual to the Church authorities, and found its correlative in a preference for a simple, practical piety. Both resonated throughout the *Anatomy*. But there was also a substantial, more up-to-date anti-Calvinist dimension to the humanistic approach to theology Burton implemented in his argument about despair. His conception of the psychological damage effected by predestinarian speculation was expressed primarily in terms of an anti-scholastic critique, but it also drew support from Lutheran theology, and the contents of his library suggest an unusual degree of interest in later Lutheran authors besides Hemmingsen, such as Aegidius Hunnius and David Chytraeus.[225] More substantially, the humanistic spirituality of the *Anatomy*, which privileged moral over systematic theology, balanced the claims of reason against those of faith, and eschewed the construction of a doctrine of God (3.369.12–32 [3.4.1.3]), echoes the ethical preoccupations, aversion to controversy, and moderate Lutheranism of Melanchthon. We should recall Burton's extensive use of Melanchthon's *De anima* throughout the book, and its importance to the account of the soul in the first Partition. In the Subsection devoted to the will, Burton used Melanchthon to temper the radical Calvinist conception of human

[223] Vaughan 1626, pp. 141–6.

[224] Kiessling 1988, entry 56. His interest in the ongoing controversies is attested by many other titles: see entries 391, 469, 557, 558, 559, 753, 844, 845, 846, 1704, 1145, 1293.

[225] See Kiessling 1988, entries 776–8, 856–8, 349–52. On the significance of this kind of interest see Milton 1995, p. 442.

unfreedom, balancing an account that saw the postlapsarian will as 'depraved . . . in spirituall things' with one that preserved it as 'free in his Essence', and ultimately theorising it as constrained 'in respect of Gods determinate counsell' yet 'free in respect of us, and things contingent' (1.160.2–35 [1.1.2.11]). This was within the confines of Calvinist orthodoxy, but his interest in preserving a theoretical space for the possibility (indeed the spiritual necessity) of human self-correction is suggestive (1.160.23–8).[226]

Burton's work underlines the polemical usefulness of a Lutheran stance to the case against the Calvinist theology of grace, and it also points to the depth of the humanistic resources that could be deployed in support of the Laudian vision of the Church. We have already noted that scepticism towards the Calvinist pursuit of certainty in unknowable matters manifested itself in the Laudian veneration of the 'beauty of holiness'. The *Anatomy* illustrates in detail the manner in which these two perspectives could coincide through humanistic engagement with patristic spirituality, which had influenced Erasmus and Luther as well as Laud and his supporters. For it is not just that Burton's views on the ignorance of postlapsarian man undergirded his humanist critique of Calvinist-scholastic speculation about 'those hidden misteries' (3.387.21 [3.4.1.3]; cf. 3.414.28–32 [3.4.2.3]). At the beginning of his analysis of religious melancholy, he made it clear that the human *amor Dei* manifested itself in its spiritually healthy form as the appropriately adoring response to divine beauty. Here, then, was a humanist's eclectic conception of human worship, constructed from Platonic, Neoplatonic, Augustinian and scriptural sources, which commanded a ceremonialist vision of the Church tallying with the Laudian exaltation of the 'beauty of holiness':

Amongst all those divine attributes that God doth vindicate to himselfe, Eternity, omnipotency, immutability, wisdome, majesty, justice, mercy, &c. his beauty is not the least . . . *I am amazed, saith Austin, when I look up to heaven and behold the beauty of the starres, the beauty of Angels, principalities, powers, who can expresse it?* . . . *If we so labour and be so much affected with the comelinesse of creatures, how should we bee ravished with that admirable lustre of God himselfe?* . . . This beauty and *splendor of the divine Majesty*, is it that drawes all creatures to it, to seeke it, love, admire, and adore it . . . He sets out his Sonne and his Church, in that *Epithalamium* or mysticall song of *Solomon*, to enamour us the more, comparing his head *to fine gold, his locks curled and blacke as a Raven, Can.* 4.5. *cap. his eyes like doves, on rivers of waters, washed with milke, his lippes as lillies, dropping downe pure juyce, his hands as rings of gold set with chrysolite: and his Church to*

[226] Cf. the denunciation of the 'Arminian' doctrine of free will in Vaughan 1626, p. 140.

a vineyard, a garden inclosed, a fountaine of living waters, an orchard of Pomegranates, with sweet sents of saffron, spike, calamus and cynamon, and all the trees of incense, as the chiefe spices, the fairest amongst women, no spot in her, his sister, his spowse, undefiled, the onely daughter of her mother, deare unto her, faire as the Moone, pure as the Sunne, looking out as the morning. That by these figures, that glasse, these spirituall eyes of contemplation we might perceave some resemblance of his beauty, the love betwixt his Church and him. And so in the 45. Psalm this beauty of his Church, is compared to a *Queene in a vesture of gold, of Ophir, embrodered rayment of needleworke, that the king might take pleasure in her beauty*... this vision of his, this lustre of his divine majesty cannot otherwise be expressed to our apprehensions, *no tongue can tell, no heart can conceave it*, as *Paule* saith. (3.332.10–334.1 [3.4.1.1])[227]

The ideal of a Church that mirrored the beauty of the God for whose worship it was established, and was constituted spiritually on the basis of well-ordered *amor Dei*, returns us finally to what is perhaps the most important aspect of Burton's spiritual psychology.[228] Religious melancholy was a condition in which the human love of God naturally inspired by His beauty had become corrupted. Like other forms of the disease, it manifested itself in a variety of disturbing passions: inordinate fear of divine punishment, anxiety over the decree, and so on. Accordingly, Burton's most pressing task was to diagnose the causes of such perturbations and seek the means to alleviate them. In effect, this was a reworking for contemporary England of the classical philosophical enterprise to destroy the unnecessary fear generated by superstition.[229] It was a task resumed by Hobbes, who proposed a version of Christianity that relieved rather than inculcated fear in the believer.[230] As a spiritual expression of the moral-psychological concern that dominates the *Anatomy*, the final Subsection was above all an argument about spiritual tranquillity, its loss and potential restoration. It is here that we must locate the source of Burton's profound hostility to puritanism, and at the same time the deepest concurrence between his aims and those of the Laudian project. In his eyes, radical Calvinism, and the vision of the hostile and capricious deity built into it, exploited mankind's natural propensity to melancholy and threatened to plunge the individual into despair. What the religious-melancholic soul needed, therefore, was

[227] The non-scriptural authors quoted in this passage include Augustine and Plato; the Neoplatonists Plotinus (3.336.15–17), Leone Ebreo (3.334.23–4), and Marsilio Ficino (3.336.1–3, 15) were also used in this Subsection to describe divine beauty.

[228] See the Augustinian account of charity at 3.31.26–32 (3.1.3.1).

[229] See Cicero 1971, II.72, pp. 536–9.

[230] Tuck 1993a, pp. 131–2.

displacement of anxious speculation about its future by tranquil adoration of the sublime beauty of God.

SPIRITUAL POLITICS IN THE *ANATOMY*

In his analysis of religious melancholy, Burton attempted to construct a position which would not sacrifice Reformed orthodoxy to the host of divisive pressures that had come to bear upon Church and state in post-Reformation England. Insofar as the *Anatomy* articulated a detailed response to these pressures, it demonstrates that it was not necessary to abandon traditional humanistic commitments, nor was it absolutely necessary – as we shall see – to adhere to an absolutist conception of divine-right monarchy, in order to support Caroline as well as Jacobean ecclesiastical policies. Whilst many did fuse humanism and puritanism, this was simply one available option.[231] As Burton's case shows, there was nothing fundamentally incompatible between a strong commitment to humanist philosophy, indeed humanist political principles, and the Laudian programme of the 1620s and '30s. It also suggests that the currently problematic historiography of the early Stuart Church, particularly with regard to the vexed questions posed by English 'Arminianism' and the intellectual character of Laudianism, would benefit from closer and more sensitive attention to the dynamics of the humanistic university environment which had produced its principal figures. Thomas Jackson, for instance, has been regularly cited as a prominent Laudian Arminian, but it has been forgotten in recent years that his works were deeply imbued with humanist Neoplatonism. In a manner very similar to Burton, Jackson ridiculed the 'perplexed labyrinths' of scholastic theology, partially conceded the authenticity of pagan virtue, and extolled the perfect beauty of the divinity as a source of spiritual ecstasy.[232] Bearing out Burton's perception of the puritan antipathy towards 'humane authors, arts, and sciences, Poets, histories, &c.', Jackson's humanistic 'proficiency in civill conversation and learning' was later used by William Prynne to buttress the case against Laud, since it 'made his errours and preferment' by the Archbishop

[231] For the links between humanism and puritanism see Norbrook 1984 and Todd 1987. Sensible caveats are sounded in Norbrook 1984, p. 23, and Peltonen 1995, p. 14; and see Pocock 1999–2003, vol. I, pp. 18, 41–2, 52–3, 63–4, for an account that resists the prevailing tendency.

[232] See Hutton 1978, pp. 641–4.

'more dangerous, more pernicious'.[233] There were surely more cases where humanist philosophy interacted closely with contemporary religious politics to similar effect.

Yet, whilst Burton's intellectual resources provided him with a vocabulary for articulating a vision of integrated political and religious order that was not only relevant to the Jacobean and Caroline polity but gelled with the concerns of Laudian polemicists, they were also threatening to push this vision into territory which he was not prepared to enter. It was not only the humanistic tendency to discourse of 'civil religion' and appraise pagan antiquity in morally positive terms that was driving his argument for religious-political order towards an unacceptable position. As his suggestively nervous discussion of toleration as a potential 'cure' for superstition indicates, his consciousness of the irreducibility of religious diversity was pressuring him to concede the ecclesiological fragmentation inevitably attendant on freedom of conscience. In articulating a quasi-medical view of heterodoxy as a 'disease' to be 'treated' in the commonwealth, the classically derived analytical structure of his argument was carrying him in the same general direction, towards a viewpoint in which the problems to be solved concerned the broad social and political effects of religious belief rather than its theological rectitude, or even its relationship to the destiny of the individual soul rather than social harmony. The same can be said of his repeated usage of the concept of *adiaphora*, which effectively turned out, as it had for Hooker and James I, to legitimate a quasi-Erastian call for the political regulation of religious practice by characterising it as non-essential to salvation – though in this case the result was not religious freedom but constraint. Burton's Christian humanism, in other words, was coming apart at the seams. Such was the price to be paid for harnessing the polemical potential created by a fusion of humanist politics and philosophy with medicine in order to heal the religious divisions of the era. But the inescapable reality was that the Erasmianism of the early English Reformation, where unambiguously Protestant evangelism, religious pacifism, and moderate classical humanist politics could be credibly advanced together, could no longer be applied where it mattered. As we shall now see, this was not the only cause of Burton's concern with melancholy whose origins are to be traced to the problems of his contemporary environment.

[233] Prynne 1646, p. 532, cited in Hutton 1978, p. 638.

CHAPTER 4

The melancholy body politic

The *Anatomy* was presented as a serious scholarly work for posterity, but its account of religious melancholy demonstrates the extent to which Burton tailored its contents to fit contemporary concerns. The final Section responded to the religious problems of the early Stuart polity in ways that, as we have seen, were largely supportive, in places perhaps coincidentally, of the Jacobean and Caroline regimes. Yet much of the rest of the *Anatomy* communicated anxiety and resentment, not just through the intellectually pessimistic atmosphere created by periodic bouts of scepticism, but directly through passages expressing discontentment with prominent aspects of the author's environment. When we turn from Burton's analysis of pathological spirituality to his discussion of pathological politics, we discover a vision that was unequivocally negative with respect to the role of contemporary governance in determining the condition of his commonwealth. My final two chapters are accordingly concerned with the political dimension of Burton's *philosophia practica*, as it was expressed in his critique of seventeenth-century England.

Humanist perceptions of English political affairs in the later decades of the sixteenth century and the early decades of the seventeenth were rooted in longstanding concerns about the virtue of the monarch and the court, the necessity of counsel to good governance, and the maintenance of a stable constitution. However, they were also becoming increasingly coloured by the recognition of new pressures coming to bear on rulers and subjects in an era of escalating religious and political uncertainty. The majority of late Elizabethan and Jacobean humanists were supporters of monarchy, but intertwined political and intellectual developments at home and abroad were undermining contemporary confidence in good governance and lending credence, in certain learned circles at least, to a diagnosis of dysfunction in the polity. Burton's political critique belonged to this growing literature of discontent.

Following the argument of Democritus in the *Letter to Damagetes*, the form of the madness addressed by 'Democritus Junior' was concerned with human irrationality, vice, and passions. As such, the preface drew upon a cluster of moral-psychological themes which were fundamental to contemporary humanist discussions in England and Europe of the order of the commonwealth, and used these as the basis for a critical appraisal of the ethical and functional health of the political community. I shall begin here with a brief outline of these themes, before turning to their articulation in Jacobean England, their relationship to absolutist and 'reason of state' theory, and the extent to which they structured contemporary perceptions of crisis by providing the conceptual vocabulary for diagnosing dysfunction at the centre of power. We will then be in a position to grasp the historically specific meanings of Burton's concern with the melancholy afflicting the body politic.

Before proceeding I should issue a caveat. I shall not be discussing some areas of political discourse that have been associated with pre-Civil War England – such as concerned the details of Roman or common law and the ancient constitution – and the issues of arbitrary taxation and the exercise of the royal prerogative will feature only in passing. Burton was almost totally silent on such questions. This was perhaps due to his distance from the institutional centres of power, most notably from parliament, and unwillingness to involve himself in open discussion of specific, day-to-day political issues. It also underlines the thoroughly non-parochial, European character of his writing, which consistently eschewed a narrow domestic focus, and drew upon concerns that could be found articulated across the continent. This is not to say, however, that the political concerns of the *Anatomy* were not fundamentally shaped by its author's observations of the condition of the English polity.

PSYCHOLOGY AND POLITICS

For Renaissance humanists, as is well known, what united ethics and politics – which together with 'oeconomics' formed the three parts of moral philosophy – was their central concern with moral virtue. In classical fashion, humanist ethics were concerned with the virtue of the individual as the essential ingredient of happiness, and politics in turn were conventionally predicated upon the assumption that the well-being of the state depended upon the virtue and happiness of its members. The ethical basis of political theory was thereby manifested in a number of themes that were discussed throughout the fifteenth and sixteenth centuries, and well into the seventeenth century. The first of these, the doctrine gleaned from ancient Roman moralists that virtue is true 'nobility' (*virtus vera nobilitas est*), had been widely propagated by humanists in Italy and northern Europe, and issued as a challenge to those supporting the Aristotelian contention that worldly riches were a necessary component of virtue. Good governance of a commonwealth was typically depicted as rule by those who possessed moral virtue, constituted particularly by the classical cardinal virtues of justice, temperance, fortitude, and prudence. These were held to conduce to actions strictly in accord with Christian morality, and provided the framework through which humanists would discuss – and conventionally endorse, at least until the mid-sixteenth century – the crucial Stoic equation of the honourable (*dignum* or *honestum*) and the useful (*utile*) as a guide to political action.[1]

A second theme integrating humanist ethics and politics concerned the disputed question of what form of living was best suited to the fulfilment of human nature *vis-à-vis* its capacity for virtue and happiness. The terms of this debate were again explicitly derived from classical sources. On one side, a variety of Italian and northern European humanists turned particularly to the works of Plato and the tenth book of Aristotle's *Nicomachean Ethics* to stipulate the life of leisure (*otium*) or contemplation (the *vita contemplativa*) as the surest means of attaining happiness and the unencumbered pursuit of the higher moral and intellectual purposes intended for man by God. This position often entailed the eschewal of the activities associated with corrupt and demeaning public duty, and so could be used to sanction monarchy, in which the citizen-body was not explicitly required to play an active role. On the other side of this debate, humanists turned particularly to Aristotle's *Politics* and the works of Cicero to esteem the life of civic activity (*vita activa*) and political participation (*negotium*) as best suited to realise the potential of human nature and produce true happiness. This argument was favoured by admirers of republican city-states, but could justify participatory ideals in monarchical contexts. It was an important component of the humanist praise of 'civil' life, which gradually evolved in the seventeenth century into an ideal that mediated the traditionally

1 See, for example, Palmieri 1997, pp. 151–3; More 1989, esp. pp. xxii–xxiii, 21. On these aspects of humanist moral and political philosophy see Skinner 1978, vol. I, pp. 228–36, and 2002, vol. II, pp. 224–36; and Lines 1996.

conflicting imperatives of action and contemplation through emphasis on the value of friendship, conversation, and beneficence.[2]

Considerations of *vera nobilitas* and the type of life best suited to its achievement were also integral to the larger project of the search for the best form of commonwealth (*optimus status reipublicae*). Although historically not the exclusive preserve of humanists, this enterprise fully manifested their conception of the direct relationship between philosophy and politics as it provided the discursive vehicle for the performance of their cherished role as counsellors to those wielding power. It typically resulted in the production of idealised images of monarchy in 'mirror of princes' texts, and in prescriptive constitutional works such as More's *Utopia* and its generic successors. In elaborating and analysing the dynamics of constitutional forms, humanists drew upon a range of classical sources. Some turned primarily to Roman authors – to Cicero for a conception of the fully thriving *res publica* tailored above all to the attainment of collective glory through the honourable accomplishments of its citizen-body; or to Seneca for a model of virtuous, rational monarchy as the linchpin of the harmonious commonwealth. Others combined reflection on these texts with close engagement with Plato and Aristotle, who supplied an explicitly eudaimonist political vision in which the arrangements of the commonwealth enabled its inhabitants to achieve happiness in the manner best according with their nature.[3] Whatever their preferences, humanists were generally in agreement with the classical axioms that the ideal state was that in which the laws upheld and protected the common good of its citizens, and that the commonwealth should be designed for the maximal flourishing of virtue in its members.

The centrality afforded by classical humanist ethics and politics to virtue entailed a dependence in both fields upon principles of moral psychology. Political theory drew upon the universally acknowledged direct association of virtue with the control of the rational parts of the soul – in the terms of early modern faculty psychology, the understanding and the will – over its irrational parts, particularly the sensitive appetites responsible for the emotions or passions. In both

[2] Generally see Baron 1966, pp. 121–9; Miller 2000, pp. 68–77, 49–55, 100–1; Skinner 1988, pp. 428–9, and 2002, vol. II, pp. 215–17; Viroli 1992, pp. 105–7. For the English case see Peltonen 1995, pp. 10, 20, 27–31, 39–44, 134–5, 141–3, 148–9, 169, 175, 210–11, 239–40, 247, 273, 283, 296; and 2002, pp. 93–4, 96, 101.

[3] See Nelson 2004, pp. 1–86.

ethical and political contexts, rational motivation and activity were said to be in accordance with virtue, and thereby productive of a corresponding psychological and political order in the individual and the state. Conversely, thoughts or actions stemming from passions – insofar as the latter conflicted with reason – were held to be vicious, and the cause of simultaneous disorder in the psychological and political domains. The classical opposition between virtuous rationality and vicious passion accordingly undergirded conventional humanist discussions of *virtus vera nobilitas* and the respective merits of the *vita activa* and *vita contemplativa*, and it informed the search for the *optimus status reipublicae*.

For the first of these, it was fundamental that cardinal virtues were deemed to be dispositions of the soul in accordance with reason. This point was made explicit by the Florentine humanist Matteo Palmieri in his *Vita civile* (1435–40), which offered an account of the civil virtues that was deeply indebted to Platonic and Stoic ethics. Prudence, according to Palmieri, was 'the true ability to examine and discern by reason what is good or bad for human beings'; fortitude 'calls for mental firmness which is unbending and unshaken in defending duty and reason', and its human manifestation 'makes reason the empress and mistress of our desires and courageously masters itself, keeping our sensual impulses subordinated and obedient to our true understanding'; temperance or moderation was 'the stable and ordered rule of reason, which commands the obedience of any shameful desires while maintaining its own dignity'; and finally justice, the 'queen and mistress' of the other virtues, as Cicero had described it, 'subsumes all of them'.[4] The argument about *vera nobilitas* was frequently justified in a similar fashion, as in Bartolomeo Sacchi's *De principe* (1471), which made reference to both Platonic and Stoic teachings on virtue.[5]

The same holds true for humanist measurements of the merits of the active and contemplative lives, where the role of reason in the good life acted as the central criterion. For those advocating the primacy of the *vita contemplativa*, human nature was conceived Platonically as having its highest good constituted by the unhindered 'godlike' pursuit of truth through the exercise of the rational intellect. Public political life was the domain of deception and vicious passion, unstable and unreliable, and political activity was therefore thought to be precisely opposite

[4] Palmieri 1997, pp. 152–60. [5] Sacchi 1997, pp. 90–2, 95, 97–8, 99.

to the rational, truly happy and fulfilled life of the leisured philosopher. This perspective, often encapsulated by portrayals of corrupt courtly life, tallied with Ficino's exaltation of 'genial' melancholy, which required solitude. On the other side, those who defended the active life and *negotium* as the sphere of the fulfilment of human nature could draw on either Stoic or Aristotelian moral psychology. According to the former, the life of contemplation could not be fully rational or virtuous since it entailed a neglect of our natural duty to others, which flowed from the instinct of οἰκείωσις rooted in the soul. Instead, humans were required to live in a political community.[6] This viewpoint had been elaborated for a republican context by Cicero in the *De officiis*,[7] which provided a template for moral conduct in the public domain, and from which generations of humanists derived a scale of civic values in support of the *vita activa*.[8] When the humanist Stefano Guazzo advocated virtuous sociability in *La civil conversazione* (1574), he drew explicitly upon the Stoic tenet that human associations were natural and so 'necessary to the perfection of man'.[9] Justification for political participation could also be grounded in the Aristotelian conception of activity in political society as a fulfilment of the soul's moral capacities.[10] For Italian and northern European humanists, the essence of the *vita activa* was encapsulated in the offering of counsel and proposals for the reform of the commonwealth, and, together with the argument that *virtus vera nobilitas est*, this provided the basis for what became the typically humanistic critique of the leisured idleness and ignorance of the nobility.[11] From this point of view, which directly conflicted with the Neoplatonic valuation of solitude as the domain of inspiration, melancholy was the vicious and debilitating result of a failure of civic responsibility.[12]

Classical understanding of the opposition of reason and passion also structured the conventional humanist vision of the well-ordered and just state, in which the common good was to be upheld by *ratio* through the application of law. Commonly this had been elaborated with reference

[6] See Cicero 1931, III.20–2, III.62–8, pp. 284–97 and 312–35; Cicero 1913, I.6.19, pp. 20–1.
[7] Cicero 1913, I.6.19, I.7.22, pp. 20–1, 22–4.
[8] See, for example, Palmieri 1997, p. 151. For the influence of Roman Stoicism on humanist political theory see Skinner 1978, vol. I, pp. xiv, 38–9, 42–3, 87–8, 186, 230, and 2002, vol. II, pp. 217–20; Wood 1968; and Viroli 1992, p. 85.
[9] Guazzo 1581, pp. 12–13.
[10] Viroli 1992, p. 235; cf. Aristotle 1923, I.2, VII.2, pp. 45–7, 335–9.
[11] More 1989, pp. 16–17, 19, 51–4, 60–1, 107–8; Guazzo 1581, pp. 2–3.
[12] Italian debates on this issue are charted in Brann 2002, pp. 16–17, 38–45, 48–72, 215–32, 336–9.

to the longstanding Aristotelian conception of the just law, as a rational surrogate preserving the state from self-interested, emotional, or ignorant judgements. By upholding the common good in this way, civil law provided the conditions in which citizens were able to attain happiness.[13] A similar psychological understanding of law was developed by humanists through reference to the authority of the Stoic paradox, recorded by Cicero, that only the wise man is free.[14] In the Stoic moral understanding, freedom was an internal disposition of the soul enabling the individual to live virtuously, namely according to *recta ratio* rather than the vicious false judgements that were emotions.[15] Obedience to the law – whether the rational law of nature that governed the cosmos or, in the variant elaborated by Cicero, the civil laws that were part of the *ius naturae* and framed in accordance with reason – thus guaranteed freedom from the passions. As Bartolomeo Scala described in his *De legibus et judiciis dialogus* (1483), obedience in this fashion enabled the citizen to live a rational life of virtuous happiness.[16] Thomas More incorporated this principle in his *Utopia*, where the outlawing of private property removed a structural stimulus to greed and pride and thereby safeguarded the rational freedom of the citizen-body.[17] As James I later alluded to the principle underlying these doctrines in the *Basilikon Doron* (1599), '*Nam ratio est anima legis*'.[18]

It was fundamental to this political psychology that law tempered the passions, not only of the citizen-body as a whole, binding them into a pattern of free, rationally virtuous action, but also of the ruling power: in humanist discourses on monarchy, the good prince was to abide by the principles of rationality and moral virtue dictated by the law of nature. In a negative sense, the virtue of the good monarch was typically constituted by his being subject to the law as the rational standard protecting the common good – a principle that supported the regularly articulated distinction between the just monarch and the tyrant.[19] The just ruler was a rational, virtuous and law-abiding agent whose

[13] For example see Marsilius of Padua 1979, I.11, pp. 37–9. Cf. Aristotle 1923, V.9, pp. 434–47, and 1934, X.9, pp. 629–31.

[14] Cicero 1942, V.34, pp. 284–5.

[15] See Seneca 1932, XV.7, pp. 140–1, quoted in Lipsius 1595, I.14, p. 33; ibid., I.6, pp. 13–14; du Vair 1598, pp. 75–6; Charron 1620, II.58, p. 220; Hall 1628, II.7, pp. 304–5.

[16] Scala 1997, pp. 184, 186–7, 189–90. See also Viroli 1992, pp. 244–5, and Peltonen 1995, pp. 66–7.

[17] More 1989, pp. 56–7.

[18] James I and VI 1603a, p. 86.

[19] See particularly Aristotle 1923, III.5.1–4, IV.8.3, pp. 204–7, 324–7.

highest priority was the benefit of the whole political community. His tyrannical counterpart was an irrational agent subject to the slavery of passions, whose vicious actions, motivated by selfish desire, were unregulated by law and destructive of the freedom of his subjects and the common good.[20]

Positively, the ruler's regard for the common good was constituted by his cultivation of the classical cardinal and princely virtues, along with the Christian virtue of *fides*. This was conventionally described as a moral-psychological endeavour of rational self-mastery aiming at freedom from destructive passions, and princely authority was frequently expressed through analogies with God's dominion over the universe and the rule in the soul of reason over the sensible appetites.[21] Drawing on Seneca's praise of Scipio in his *De principe* (1468), Giovanni Pontano described the greatest challenge of the ruler as psychological self-conquest, since 'someone who governs others ought to be entirely free from the passions' such as anger, hate, love, lust, anguish, or envy.[22] The opposite pole of the same classical scheme informed descriptions of tyranny. According to Erasmus in the *Institutio principis Christiani* (1516), the tyrannical ruler was dispositionally led by 'emotional impulse' to be a cruel, stupid, and despotic 'slave to his desires'.[23] Bartolomeo Scala had described tyranny in similar terms in his *De legibus*, as the lawless and tempestuous outcome when 'immoderate desires dominate those who rule and hold the reigns of power'.[24]

JACOBEAN THEORIES OF MONARCHY

The civic ideology of classical humanism which had originated in Italy and subsequently spread to northern Europe was applied by many English writers to the Elizabethan and Jacobean commonwealth,[25] which was viewed by contemporaries not only as a *dominium politicum et regale* but also in humanistic terms as a 'monarchical republic' or a monarchy with a mixed constitution.[26] For the majority of English humanist

[20] See, for example, Sacchi 1997, p. 90; Erasmus 1997, pp. 25–6; Machiavelli 1970, I.58, pp. 252–7.
[21] See, for example, Erasmus 1997, pp. 23–4, 37, 53.
[22] Pontano 1997, pp. 69–70.
[23] Erasmus 1997, pp. 35–6; see also ibid., pp. 9, 25–44, 62–3, 69–70.
[24] Scala 1997, pp. 190–1. See also ibid., pp. 89–90; Guicciardini 1994, pp. 33–4; Lipsius 1594, II.14, p. 166.
[25] As been demonstrated in Peltonen 1995, *passim*.
[26] See Collinson 1987 and 2002; Peltonen 1995, pp. 47–52, 178–89.

writers of this era, the linchpin of the harmonious commonwealth remained the soul of the ruler, who was conventionally described as the 'head' of the body politic with a duty to infuse the whole with his or her moral and spiritual virtue. But in accordance with this organic conception of order, the proper functioning of the polity was also routinely constituted by factors external to the king, the most important of which related to the qualities of the advice he received and the moral character of the court. It is true that monarchical subjects were primarily constructed as 'reverent' and 'obedient' in relation to their ruler,[27] and so were distinct from the thoroughly active citizens found in the republican writings of the fourteenth- and fifteenth-century Italian city-states. However, English monarchical theory in this period emphasised not just the magnitude and concentration of power in the person of the ruler but also the severity of the moral and spiritual responsibilities accompanying the offices of king and courtier, and the indispensability of upright and undeceptive counsel to the unity and health of the body politic. In emphasising the duty of the ruler to recognise the supremacy of the common good in this way, it was broadly consonant with so-called 'constitutionalist' theory.

If we turn, for example, to the chapter on politics in *Salomons Divine Arts* (1609), by the Calvinist divine Joseph Hall, we find this humanistic model of monarchy recast and sanctioned through scriptural quotations. Here the good king was constrained by the duty to be virtuous, forbidden from being 'lascivious . . . riotous . . . dissembling' or 'oppressing', enjoined to be 'Just, Mercifull, slow to anger; Bountifull' to others, and required to be 'Temperate, Wise' and 'Valiant' in himself. Although Hall's advice that the ruler should be 'Secret' in his determinations legitimated the *arcana imperii*, this was immediately balanced by the reminder that the king's heart was known by and so accountable to God, and the strict requirement that his actions and disposition be '*universally holy*'.[28] A similar conception of monarchy, with distinctively Calvinistic emphasis on the role of the conscience in the realisation of princely virtue, was exemplified by James I in his *Basilikon Doron*. James's purpose, he announced in the dedicatory epistle, was to advise his son Prince Henry that there was a 'just symmetrie and proportion' between the divine duties and rights of kingship, so that 'ye are rather born

[27] As in Hall 1609, p. 132. [28] Hall 1609, pp. 110–16.

to *onus*, then *honos*; not excelling all your people so farre in ranke and honour, as in daily care and hazardous paines'.[29] Good governance was underwritten by the ruler's 'vertuous life', constituted by his rational mastery of passions and appetites, and in the wise and just 'person of his Court, and companie'.[30]

James insisted that the actions of both king and courtier should directly reflect their inner psychological dispositions, not least because they presented exemplary patterns that would be imitated by monarchical subjects.[31] Courtiers were required to be 'men of knowne wisdome, honestie, and good conscience', so that they could be counsellors who spoke in the 'plainest' manner and 'do not disguise the truth', being 'free of all factions and partialities . . . especially that filthie vice of Flatterie, the pest of al Princes, and wracke of Republickes'.[32] Hall agreed. The well-governed commonwealth depended both on the moral character of the court, ideally populated by courtiers who were 'Discreet, Religious, Humble', and 'Charitable, Diligent, Faithfull',[33] and also on the wisdom and justice of the 'Counsailor', without whom 'all our thoughts (*even of policy and state*) come to naught'.[34] The necessity of good, 'plain' counsel which was freely delivered – on which humanists writing on monarchy from Erasmus to Francis Bacon were in agreement – formed an important component of the *vita activa*; it also lay behind the responsibility of the virtuous prince to maintain an impartial '*eare*' and not listen to 'lyes', a tendency which was said to breed wickedness in his company and pervert his rule.[35]

Late Elizabethan and Jacobean theories of monarchy differed from their predecessors in important respects, partly as a result of the rise of alternative models of politics that had been stimulated by the deepening crisis on the continent. Traditional humanist political theorists were struggling to present a solution to the problem of the role of the Church in the state that was attractive to those in power, and from the later decades of the sixteenth century onwards the republicanism of early Elizabethan humanist political theory, exemplified by the writings of

[29] James I and VI 1603a, Epistle Dedicatory (unpaginated). See also James I and VI 1598, sigs. B3^r–B5^r.
[30] James I and VI 1603a, pp. 1, 84–8, 95–100. Cf. ibid., pp. 24–5, 29–30.
[31] James I and VI 1603a, pp. 60–2, 70, 83–4, 103–4, 149, 150.
[32] James I and VI 1603a, pp. 68–9, 72, 132–3.
[33] Hall 1609, pp. 129–34.
[34] Hall 1609, pp. 116–28.
[35] Hall 1609, p. 117; James I and VI 1603a, p. 46. See Colclough 2005, pp. 62–76.

those such as Sir Thomas Smith, was being gradually reconstituted around the notion of the divine right of kings. For many, the divergence from the traditional conception of monarchy found in the absolutism exemplified by Bodin's *Six livres de la république* (1576) was deeply troubling and would attain immense political significance. But the Italian and northern European humanist heritage of this emergent absolutism is evident in some of its central features. Undivided monarchical sovereignty was invested with authority superior to civil law, yet absolutists typically conceded that divinely appointed kings were obliged to obey the laws of God and nature, and rule strictly in accordance with the common good in a fashion that was encapsulated by their metaphorical identities as 'head' of the body politic or *pater patriae*.[36] Theories of divine right kingship could incorporate longstanding humanist notions, even if the resulting synthesis remained murky on the nature of the monarch's obligation to take into account his subjects' views.[37]

In the reign of James's notoriously lofty successor, the traditional humanist conception of the moral constituents of the healthy body politic, 'head' included, in conjunction with a conception of *iure divino* kingship, retained its relevance. This is well testified by the two plays performed at Oxford by the Students of Christ Church for the royal visitation of August 1636.[38] In William Strode's *Floating Island*, the order of the commonwealth was secured against the chaos threatened by a variety of passions – represented by the characters 'Irato', 'Audax', 'Melancholico', 'Desperato', and 'Sir Timorous Feareall' – by the eventual triumph of reason, enacted in the rule of the king 'Prudentius' and aided by his counsellor 'Intellectus Agens'.[39] *The Royall Slave*, William Cartwright's rather more elegant portrayal of the value to the state of erudition and psychological self-mastery, concluded with the distinctively Senecan message that to be ruled by one who is learned and virtuous is 'freedome'.[40]

***

[36] For example, in James I and VI 1598, sigs. $B4^{v-r}$, $D3^{r-v}$; note the limitation of the subject's obedience at sig. $C5^{v}$. See Sommerville 1996, pp. 180–90 and Burgess 1992, p. 849.

[37] See James I and VI 1598, sigs. $C7^{v}$–$C8^{v}$.

[38] For the political context of these two plays see Sharpe 1981, pp. 151–2.

[39] Strode 1655.

[40] Cartwright 1639, sig. $H4^{v}$.

More challenging to the traditional humanist paradigm in England was the increasing popularity of 'reason of state' literature, associated with continental neo-Stoicism and the emerging Tacitist movement, and bound up with the increasingly bloody realities of European post-Reformation politics. The key figure bridging these developments was Justus Lipsius, who in the *De constantia* (1584) proposed a controversial disjunction between the ethical interior of the human being and his or her external behaviour. If, as Lipsius seemed to suggest, happiness, virtue, and liberty were purely internal psychological qualities, then the idea – dear to proponents of the *vita activa* – that the well-functioning commonwealth was constituted by the virtuous actions of its inhabitants no longer held. Moreover, as Lipsius showed in the *Politicorum libri sex* (1589), prising apart inner moral virtue and political action could also justify immoral acts by rulers. Whereas the *De constantia* used Stoicism to present the forms of virtue appropriate to a climate of political chaos for the individual subject or citizen, the *Politica* used Tacitus to show (in a manner that echoed Machiavelli) that such conditions necessitated reassessment of the ethical standards applicable to governing. In a political environment afflicted by turmoil, it was necessary for the restoration of order and stability that some actions conventionally understood as moral vices should be thought of as political virtues.[41] Of particular usefulness to the Prince was the 'vice' of dissimulation, which Lipsius redescribed as a 'mixed' type of political prudence.[42] A similar viewpoint was expressed with regret by Montaigne, for whom dissimulation and bloodthirstiness had now become a lamentable political imperative in his homeland. 'The Common-wealth requireth', as Florio translated Montaigne's essay, 'some to betray, some to lie, and some to massaker'.[43]

Lipsian political psychology tallied with the questioning of the conventional status of the virtues being manifested in the increasingly popular theories of 'reason of state'.[44] Although still operating within an intellectual universe in which classical philosophy served as a useful source of precepts and examples, and exhibiting an essentially humanistic preoccupation with the proper role of virtue in the administration of the commonwealth,[45] the proponents of reason of state challenged the

[41] Lipsius, 1594, IV.13, pp. 112–13.
[42] Lipsius 1594, IV.13–14, pp. 112–23.
[43] Montaigne 1603, III.1, p. 476.
[44] See Tuck 1993b, pp. 40–64.
[45] On the continuities between conventional humanism and Tacitean neostoicism see Peltonen 1995, pp. 134–5, and Clavero 1991, pp. 16, 28.

axiomatic equation of virtuous and effective governance upheld by previous generations of theorists. For Giovanni Botero in his *Della ragion di stato* (1589), and a host of writers in the Italian vernacular, the preservation of the political community would occasionally demand measures that transgressed traditional ethical codes and the law. Government was no longer the art of continuously practising moral virtue, but of knowing when one could be virtuous, and indeed when it would serve the legitimate political goals of the commonwealth instead to be vicious.

Botero was also instrumental in reconfiguring the humanist concern with civic greatness, producing comparative analyses of existing states in the extremely successful *Delle cause della grandezza delle città* (1588) and the *Relazioni Universali*, the first part of which was published in 1591 and appeared in complete form in 1596. Here he integrated the increasingly evident necessities of traditional military virtue and strong princely rule with the benefits of economic and commercial industriousness, providing an up-to-date, technically amoral political geography to match his self-consciously realist attitude to the workings of existing governments.[46] Botero's works were immensely popular in England. The translation of the *Relazioni* by the ardent colonialist and member of the Virginia Company Robert Johnson, first published in 1601, was reissued in progressively enlarged form in 1603, 1608, 1611, 1616, and 1630. The *Delle cause della grandezza delle città* also appeared in two vernacular translations in 1606 and 1635, by Robert Peterson and the recusant poet Sir Thomas Hawkins respectively.

These authors were attempting to loosen the ethical straitjacket put upon the ruling power by conventional humanist politics, and it is clear that both reason-of-state theory, and the broader disenchantment with the traditional vision of the virtuous political community expressed by writers like Lipsius and Montaigne, were bound up with an acceptance of the increasingly absolutist tendencies of seventeenth-century continental monarchies.[47] Admittedly, we should not underestimate the potential flexibility of arguments commonly associated with reason-of-state politics, since concepts such as *arcana imperii, necessitas*, and the notion of the unchallengeable supremacy of the preservation of the state (along with its accompanying Roman legal formula *salus populi suprema lex esto*)

[46] Botero 1606, pp. 1, 4–9, 11–13, 48–53; and Botero 1608, sigs. B1^r–B3^v.
[47] See, for example, Lipsius 1594, IV.9, pp. 78–92.

could be incorporated to anti-monarchical argument.[48] But the close relationship between reason of state and absolutism was reflected in the way both located the power and responsibility of the Prince in an ethical sphere that was distinct from that of his subjects. This was reflected in justifications not only of *arcana imperii* but also of prerogative powers. Although extraordinary and theoretically bound by the monarch's duty to rule for the sake of the common good, necessity could legitimise the Prince's violation of civil law.[49]

However, the complex Tacitean narratives of treachery and political corruption under absolute rule prominent in many neo-Stoic and reason-of-state texts had a political doubleness. As Lipsius noted in his 1581 commentary on the *Annales*, Tacitus depicted lawless rulers as well as rebellious subjects, 'ill-fated attempts to recover lost liberty' as well as the disorders and 'evils of liberty restored'.[50] Whilst for Lipsius these accounts of political disorder and immorality yielded negative lessons indispensable for the cultivation of princely prudence, for critics of reason of state the corrupt *exempla* presented by Tacitus were unsuitable reading that encouraged the spread of vice throughout the body politic. As Trajano Boccalini recorded both sides of the case being made against the Roman historian in his *Ragguagli di Paranasso* (1612–13) (in the English translation issued in 1626 as *The new-found politicke*), 'he perverteth lawfull Princes into cruell Tyrants, he transformeth natural Subjects ... into most pernicious Foxes'.[51] Some critics in England read Tacitus as a republican sympathiser who had effectively preached sedition – hardly surprising when Sir Henry Savile, an associate of the rebel Earl of Essex, had publicly gleaned from the historian such lessons as 'that a good Prince governed by evill ministers is as dangerous as if he were evill himselfe'.[52]

Equally disturbing for its critics was that the neo-Stoic coupling of external obedience with internal freedom could translate into disobedience masquerading as conformity, breeding what Boccalini termed a 'false doubleness' enjoining subjects as well as princes hypocritically 'to doe that which a man saies not, and to say that

[48] Baldwin 2004.
[49] See generally Weber 1995, pp. 902–13; Sommerville 1996, pp. 180–6. For the English case see Mendle 1993. Cf., for example, James I and VI 1598, sigs. D1^{r-v}.
[50] Cited and translated in Morford 1993, p. 138.
[51] Boccalini 1626, p. 17.
[52] Tacitus 1591, sigs. ¶3^{r-v}.

which one meaneth not'.[53] I shall return to this issue in the next chapter, but for now we should note that, along with Tacitism,[54] it was this neo-Stoic 'doubleness' that James I rejected in the *Basilikon Doron*: first in his insistence that the 'outward' actions of the monarch should directly 'testifie the inward uprightnes' of his heart,[55] and more fiercely in his criticism in the 1599 edition of the 'Stoick insensible stupiditie that proud inconstant LIPSIUS perswadeth in his Constantia'.[56] That the king was becoming increasingly worried by the political implications of the domestic spread of what Hall was simultaneously identifying as the type of the religious 'Unconstant' is perhaps testified to by his subsequent emendation of this passage in later editions, which now targeted the 'manie in our dayes' who 'preassing to win honor, in imitating that auncient sect', exhibited 'inconstant behaviour in their owne lives'.[57]

COURT AND COUNSEL

As we have seen, according to the predominant humanist view it was the proper conduct of the monarch that guaranteed the proper functioning of the commonwealth, but this in turn was partially constituted by the ruler's receptivity to good counsel. In England this was principally manifested in two institutional locations. The first was parliament, where members had the opportunity to offer guidance and advice, and the second was the royal court, where courtiers competed not only for favour and patronage but also to deliver their views to the king's person. The ideal situation was one in which both forums of counsel functioned effectively to enable subjects to participate actively in government. But it was becoming increasingly clear to Jacobean observers that the reality was often different. James's position in relation to parliament revealed the tension between his humanistic conception of monarchical rule and belief in the *arcana imperii* and divine rights of office. After the failure of the Great Contract in 1610, he punitively dissolved parliament in January 1611, and the same fate befell both the disastrous 'Addled' parliament of 1614 and the session of 1621, after members had enraged the king with their criticisms of the proposed marriage

53 Boccalini 1626, pp. 18–19. See also ibid., pp. 29–32.
54 Salmon 1989, pp. 224–5.
55 James I and VI 1603a, p. 150.
56 James I and VI 1599, p. 117.
57 James I and VI 1603a, p. 98.

between Charles and the Spanish Infanta. It is not surprising that, as James's reign progressed, the Commons were becoming increasingly preoccupied with their freedom of speech,[58] that some feared that the English commonwealth was becoming less representative and distinctly continental, and that criticisms of James's hostility towards parliament were being voiced in the Privy Council and the country at large. In this sense, the 'personal rule' of Charles I reprised a significant part of his father's reign.[59] Elizabeth's rule had hardly been a model of harmonious co-operation. But as the domestic and international political environment deteriorated in the 1620s, it increasingly seemed – especially to Protestant radicals – that her successors were failing to live up to the example of Gloriana.

The ideal of the court as the location of good counsel was faring no better. According to the lament of Sir William Cornwallis the Younger in his *Essayes* (1600), 'our Age is so obstinate as not to be capable of Advise', and 'nothing more decay the fairest braunches of our Commonwealth, then this neglect'.[60] Here the commonly perceived problem was not that the monarch was unreceptive to counsel *per se*. Rather, it was that the channel of counsel was distorted, either through royal favouritism or through the general immorality of the court environment. Contemporary concerns about favouritism had been aired in the last two decades of Elizabeth's reign, coinciding with heightened factionalism and a dramatic deterioration in the image of the court,[61] and they continued unabated through the reigns of James and Charles. Whilst protestations about the corrupt influence of royal favourites such as George Villiers, the Duke of Buckingham, were expressed in parliament, they were also frequently voiced by rival courtiers discontented at their monopoly of royal favour, who chose to give literary expression to their sentiments in humanist vein through the depiction of a king being misled by flattery and evil counsel. Contemporary anxieties about the power of figures such as Henry Howard, Earl of Northampton, Robert Carr, Earl of Somerset, Sir Thomas Lake, and Buckingham over James and subsequently Charles therefore focused, not narrowly on their control of royal patronage, but on their morally and politically detrimental effects upon monarchical rule and the court environment. Since, as James himself had asserted, the court was to be taken as an exemplary image that would be

58 See Colclough 2005.
59 Thrush 2002, esp. pp. 99–102.
60 Cornwallis 1600, sigs. $C2^r$, $C3^r$.
61 See Smuts 1987, pp. 73–84.

imitated throughout the commonwealth, the influence of favourites was deemed to be a serious problem with implications for the whole body politic.

Critics of favouritism and corruption at court were usually careful to avoid the direct imputation of blame to the ruler, but certain dimensions of the growing *corpus* of anti-court literature lent themselves to dangerous interpretations. This was particularly true of the Tacitist poetry composed by the so-called Jacobean 'Spenserians', which associated the dominance of evil counsellors at court with tyranny, and was often delivered from the standpoint of an idealised 'country'. Such was the vision articulated in William Browne's *Shepheards Pipe* (1614), Christopher Brooke's *Ghost of Richard the third* (1614), and George Wither's *Satyre: Dedicated to his most excellent majestie* (1615).[62] The problem with favourites partly concerned freedom of speech, in that their flattery and power to censor rivals foreclosed the opportunity for others to express themselves with the frankness necessary to good counsel. Having been imprisoned for his popular denunciation of the multifarious corruption of the English commonwealth in *Abuses stript, and whipt* (1613), Wither acknowledged in the *Satyre* that 'the *Court* will not my lines approve', but protested that he should be permitted the liberty traditionally afforded to all practitioners of the literary art of castigating vice.[63]

More fundamentally, the activity of royal favourites upset the moral-psychological health of the whole body politic. William Vaughan, who had published a Latin encomium of Essex in 1598, reminded his dedicatee King Charles in *The Golden Fleece* (1626) that the 'example' of abuse, 'like a Leprosie, is transferred from Court to Citie, from the Citie to the Countrey'.[64] Favourites like Essex and Buckingham were demagogic subversives, who by courting popularity threatened to unleash the destabilising passions of the mob through their influence on the king. They also compromised the monarch's dutiful quest for rational self-mastery and encouraged passionate rule. This conception of the corrupting effect of bad counsel had been implied by James himself, who had paralleled the ruler's psychological struggle against his 'owne outward flatterer φῖλαυτια with the task of avoiding the 'counterfeit

62 See Norbook 1984, pp. 41–8, 195–234; Peltonen 1995, pp. 165–7, 276–8, 287; and O'Callaghan 2000.

63 Wither 1614, sigs. $E1^{r-v}$, $F2^{r}$.

64 Vaughan 1626, sig. $A4^{v}$. For the encomium of Essex see Vaughan 1598, sigs. $B1^{r}$–$C3^{v}$.

wares' of flatterers at court.[65] As the Oxford divine and royal chaplain Daniel Price explained in a sermon, delivered in 1614 and dedicated to the young Prince Charles, it had been his virtuous dead brother's great achievement to remain impervious to the '*Cankers* or *vipers* of a Courtly life, *Lust, Pride, Ambition, Irreligion*', as well as 'the *wormes* or *moaths* of *greatnesse*, sloath . . . *flatterie* [and] *vanitie*', which were 'as *visible* as *indivisible* from such Courtly places'.[66]

Price's loyalty was unquestionable, but like many of his Calvinist countrymen he was suspicious of James's attitude towards Catholics, and praise of Prince Henry, whose household had in his lifetime become the focus for Tacitists and militant Protestants frustrated by the king's pacifism and suspicious of foreign Catholic influence at court, could have a politically critical edge.[67] This might seem distinctly sharper when set against the contemporary discontent with Jacobean and Caroline favourites in the 1620s, as in the portrayal of Henry's participation in 'mature debate and consultation (which are the true foiles that give cleernesse and assurednesse to counsells)' in the *Discourse of the most illustrious Prince, Henry late Prince of Wales written Anno* 1626 (1641), by his former treasurer Sir Charles Cornwallis.[68] Such exemplary openness to good counsel contrasted markedly with the behaviour of both James and Charles, whose subscription to the notion of the *arcana imperii* typically outweighed their moderating humanistic influences. Against the rising tide of popular dissatisfaction with his foreign policy and pursuit of a Spanish match, James issued two proclamations in December and August 1620 against 'excess of lavish and licentious speech in matter of State'; the notorious 'Directions concerning Preaching' of August 1622 censored output from the pulpit; and he afterwards invited his subjects to 'Come councell me when I shall call' but darkly threatened more action against unsolicited advice.[69] In such moments, which suggested that James was more comfortable ruling subjects than citizens, he was closer than he might have wished to Lipsius – for whom, quoting Livy, kings were '*leaders and not followers of counsell*'. Counsel should not be

[65] James I and VI 1603a, pp. 68–9. See also Forset 1606, pp. 15–16.
[66] Price 1614, pp. 11–12; see also pp. 4–5. For Price's career see McCullough 1998a, pp. 189–96.
[67] See the strategy in Price 1614, pp. 10–11.
[68] Cornwallis 1641, p. 8.
[69] Larkin and Hughes (eds.) 1973, vol. 1, pp. 495–6, 519–21; James I and VI 1958, pp. 182–91, both cited and discussed in Cogswell 1989, pp. 20–35.

treated with contempt, Lipsius admitted; but, he added, 'Doest thou yeeld anything herein? then thou loosest all.'[70]

The same could of course be said of James's son, whose resort to arbitrary, extra-parliamentary taxation in the shape of the Forced Loan indicated a conception of monarchical rule in which prerogative powers had significantly increased prominence. Although the assassination of Buckingham in August 1628 raised hopes that Charles would subsequently receive better counsel, and inaugurated a period in which favourites no longer seemed to dominate the monarch, what followed was, notoriously, a period of rule in which parliament was simply not summoned to counsel the king. Moreover, the Caroline court of the 1630s was largely composed of what many contemporaries saw as a monopolistic, crypto-Catholic 'Spanish faction' that did not consider the sound advice that could be given by others in the commonwealth, particularly those supporters of the international Protestant cause who had in previous decades expressed their views to the king at court or in parliament.

Critical commentary on this state of affairs manifested itself in a variety of literary forms. At its most extreme, in the writings of Spenserian poets, Tacitist criticisms of courtly corruption expressed disgust at the failure of counsel and implied that the commonwealth had descended into tyranny. In many cases such a grave and dangerous diagnosis was not without a significant personal material dimension, insofar as its exponents perceived themselves to be marginalised from power and deprived of patronage – an issue I shall explore in detail in the next chapter. However, as with the overtly pessimistic neo-Stoic advocacy of retirement, this type of political critique also conveyed nostalgia for a traditionally conceived healthy body politic composed of virtuous citizens. And it is, broadly speaking, this type of political vision which was articulated in characteristically idealistic and trenchant terms by Burton in the *Anatomy*.

DISSECTING THE BODY POLITIC

To grasp the character of Burton's political vision, we need first to remind ourselves of his case concerning the melancholy afflicting the world in 'Democritus Junior to the Reader'. Here he diagnosed universal melancholy in the world by conflating the condition in Stoic fashion

[70] Lipsius 1594, IV.9, p. 81.

with a madness which manifested itself predominantly in the spiritual and moral-psychological symptoms of vice, sinfulness, and foolish susceptibility to destructive passions. But it did not stop there. In a manner that was conventional in contemporary humanist political philosophy, as well as forming the core of a substantial ethical and spiritual argument, Burton's moral psychology grounded an ideal conception of human social and political order in virtuous *ratio*. This in turn provided the framework for a wide-ranging dissection of the effects of melancholy on society at large. As he explained, the macrocosmic sign of an epidemic of 'diseases of the mind' and vicious passions (1.56.11) was social turmoil and moral confusion, the pandemonium of 'the world turned upside downward' (1.52.27–55.3).[71] Such chaos and conflict were the products of immoderate affections, 'opinion without judgement' (1.53.10–11), and were defects of the spiritual virtues and passions that bound society together, namely 'charity, love, friendship, feare of God, alliance, affinitie, consanguinities', and 'Christianitie' generally (1.51.5–6; cf. 3.29.6–38.20 [3.1.3.1]).

'Democritus Junior to the Reader' was structured, then, by the classical connection between individual psychological disorder and social or political unrest, and this enabled Burton to range in his diatribe across the three principal territories of moral philosophy – ethics, politics, and oeconomics.[72] A world populated by melancholic individuals whose actions were determined by passions rather than by reason, by vice and sinfulness rather than by moral and godly virtue, was one of unruliness and confusion, and so the appropriate object of political as well as moral-spiritual censure. Within this argumentative framework Burton proceeded to play out such typical humanist themes as *virtus vera nobilitas*, in his Christian-Stoic censure of mankind's selfish love of 'Queene mony' and false valuation of 'money, greatnesse, office, honour, authority. . .men admired out of opinion, not as they are, but as they seeme to be' (1.51.20–9), and in his criticism of the contemporary folly of warfare. His disapproval of the disjunction between seeming and being, manifested in a denunciation of spiritual hypocrisy reminiscent of Joseph Hall and James I, also signalled his opposition to Lipsian political psychology. Externally conforming to the corrupt world, according to Burton, constituted a mismatch between inner and outer

[71] On this moralistic *topos* see Delumeau 1990, pp. 128–36.

[72] See, broadly, 1.24.17–33.4; 1.37.22–41.22; 1.48.15–66.28; 1.99.20–109.11 (ethics); 1.41.23–48.14, 66.29–97.12 (politics); and 1.97.13–99.19 (oeconomics).

being that was necessarily offensive to God, involving sinful activities such as 'shifting, lying, cogging, plotting', and 'counterplotting', and resulting in a proliferation of '*Hypocrites, ambodexters*, out-sides', and 'Stage-players' prepared to be 'of all religions, humours, inclinations' for their own selfish goals (I.51.29–52.21).

Burton proceeded to extend the range of his analysis to non-human bodies in the macrocosm, which was commonly considered to include not just the natural world but the forms of political and social organisation found within it. His claim was that melancholic madness was afflicting not only 'all Creatures, Vegetall, Sensible, and Rationall', but also 'Kingdomes and Provinces... Cities and Families' (I.24.24–25.2), and as he continued it became clear which type of body he was particularly interested in:

Kingdomes, Provinces, and Politicke Bodies are likewise sensible and subject to this disease, as *Boterus* in his Politicks hath proved at large. *As in humane bodies* (saith he) *there be divers alterations proceeding from humours, so there be many diseases in a Commonwealth, which doe as diversly happen from severall distempers*, as you may easily perceave by their particular Symptomes. (I.66.29–33)

The organic metaphor of the body politic was of course a classical commonplace that could be used for a range of effects, but to understand its function in this part of the text we need first to recall its prominence in both Platonic and Stoic political theory, as a device that simultaneously illustrated the necessity of harmonious order to the 'healthy' and happy commonwealth, and delineated the contours of the authority and moral obligations of the monarch. Initially employing it for the former purpose, Burton described disunity or any form of political disorder as a 'disease' requiring treatment.[73] At this stage, his analysis closely resembles that of Edward Forset, whose classical vision of the state in *A Comparative Discourse of the Bodies Natural and Politique* (1606) hinged upon the construction of the lawful power of the ruler as the equivalent of reason in the soul – reflected in the divinely appointed offices of both to care for the welfare of the whole[74] – but which also asserted a series of parallels between such political and

[73] For similar approaches see Lipsius 1594, IV.3, pp. 64–5 and 1595, I.16, I.22, II.17, II.18, pp. 39, 56–7, 101, 103, 105; James I and VI 1958, sigs. D3^{v}–D4^{r}; Lemnius 1576, fols. 11^{r}–12^{r}; Forset 1606, p. 93.

[74] Forset 1606, pp. 4–8.

psychological necessities as subduing 'seditous disorders' and taming 'perturbations of the mind'.[75] Just as the 'flourishing and felicitie' of the well-ordered commonwealth was analogous to the health of the well-balanced body,[76] so the diseases of the body politic were comparable to those arising 'in the body naturall' from perturbations and 'distemper of humours'. The origin of political diseases, from 'Atheisme, Popery, and disloyaltie' to 'the fierce and smart contentions of the learned', and generally the vice or sinfulness of the populace or ruler, was to be found in a moral 'disorder of manners'.[77]

Burton's similar contention was that the disruption of the unity of a peaceful and rationally ordered commonwealth, or any factor hindering the healthy flourishing of that commonwealth, could be described as a political disease. His argument thereby corresponded to the Galenic theory according to which a disease was an impairment of the natural activities of an organ or organism.[78] Both authors premised their analyses upon occult correspondence, but were unwilling to supply details (I.66.14–18) and preferred to give medically informed exercises in rhetorical comparison between the two kinds of bodies.[79] More importantly, although Burton initially paid some attention to potential geographical factors, drawing on Botero (I.67.16–17), as with Forset the main thrust of his discussion was upon internal causes of discord (I.67.28–9). The first of the 'maladies' of the body politic was spiritual, when 'Religion and Gods Service is neglected, innovated or altered, where they doe not feare God, obey their Prince, where Atheisme, Epicurisme, Sacriledge, Simony, &c. And all such impieties are freely committed' (I.67.29–32). As we saw in the last chapter, this wholly accorded with the classical view of the spiritually pure *res publica*,[80] and his proceeding analysis of political dysfunction was likewise rooted in the classical moral-psychological argument associating passion, vice, and melancholic madness.

This was clearly the case for the discontent Burton voiced against specific elements in the body politic. Lawyers attracted particularly severe vituperation. Instead of being 'Oracles, and Pilots of a well govern'd Commonwealth' (I.71.17–18), they were motivated by the vicious passion of greed to prefer their own to the common good (I.50.11–20; 72.4–14),

[75] Forset 1606, pp. 17–18. [76] Forset 1606, p. 4. [77] Forset 1606, pp. 71–5.
[78] See Galen 1991, I.5.4, II.1.1–5, pp. 22, 40–1.
[79] See Forset 1606, sigs. ¶iij^r–Aij^r, pp. 1–2. [80] See also Cicero 1933, I.2, pp. 6–7.

and together with judges abused the law to foment controversy, confusion, and social discord (1.49.4–50.11; 71.1–74.8). This critique was premised on the conception of law as the surrogate of reason, providing the harmonious order that guaranteed freedom and happiness to the inhabitants of the state. As the Platonic version of this theme was expressed here, the existence of 'many laws, many law suits, many Lawyers' in a body politic was 'a manifest signe of a distempered Melancholy state' racked by conflict and misery (1.71.1–4).[81] Although lawyers were frequently the objects of this type of criticism, the length and severity of the diatribe suggested personal animus. This impression is reinforced by the presence of the same sentiments in the speech put in the mouth of 'Democritus Junior' by Burton's fellow humanist William Vaughan in *The Golden Fleece*.[82] It might even be detected in his will, which noted at the outset that 'there be so many Casualities to wch our life is subject, besides quarrelling and Contention, wch happen to our successors after our deathe by reason of unsetteled estates'.[83]

Burton was also concerned to pursue the second feature of the Stoic metaphor, namely the question of the responsibilities and qualities of the 'head' of the body politic. This was indicated, not just by his attribution of political melancholy to misguided or inadequate religious policy (1.67.29–30), but more explicitly by his subsequent singling out from the myriad of 'common grievances . . . generally noxious to a body politic' of '*Impotentia gubernandi*, *ataxia*, confusion, ill government' proceeding from vicious or incompetent rulers (1.68.8–19). This argument retained a humanist commitment to government by rulers of true *virtus* and godliness as the only means of securing harmonious unity in a body politic. Indeed, the absence of such qualities in princes and magistrates was for Burton the root of the contemporary destruction of peace in the commonwealths and cities of his day, as 'when they are fooles, idiots, children, proud, wilful . . . oppressors, giddy heads, tyrants . . . the whole body grones under such heads, and all the members must needs be misaffected' (1.68.13–17).[84] This was evinced *in extremis* by the 'slavery' currently imposed on Egypt by the tyrannical archetype, the 'imperious

[81] Burton was twisting his sources: Plato wrote of a state suffering not from melancholy but one that was 'full of sickness' [νόσων πληθυουσῶν] and 'intemperance' [ἀκολασίας] (Plato 1930–5, pp. 268–9 [405a]). See the Platonic criticisms of legal institutions in More 1989, pp. 38, 84–5, and Forset 1606, pp. 75–7, 91.

[82] Vaughan 1626, pt I, p. 25; cf. ibid., pt II, pp. 34–40.

[83] See Kiessling 1990, p. 97.

[84] Cf. the view of magistracy in Forset 1606, pp. 72–8.

Turke' (I.68.24–31), which afforded the opportunity to reinforce the correlation between human and political melancholy. Under a tyrant, he claimed, the non-ruling 'members' of the body politic were necessarily 'misaffected' and 'discontent' (I.68.16–17), and became directly analogous to '*a sicke body*' suffering from melancholy after being weakened by repeated purging (I.69.4–9).[85]

The lesson that Burton wished to drive home was that an ungodly ruler who could not control his vicious passions spelled disaster for the commonwealth.

Whereas the Princes and Potentates are immoderate in lust, Hypocrites, Epicures, of no religion, but in shew: *Quid hypocrisi fragilius?* what so brittle and unsure, what sooner subverts their estates then wandring and raging lusts, on their subjects wives, daughters, to say no worse? They that should *facem præferre*, lead the way to all vertuous actions, are the ring-leaders oftentimes of all mischiefe and dissolute courses, and by that meanes their Countries are plagued, *and they themselves often ruined, banished or murdered by conspiracie of their subjects* ...[86] (I.69.10–17)

Underpinning this critique of princely vices, to which he added malice, envy, factiousness, and selfish greed (I.69.20–8), was the assertion of a direct correspondence between the soul of the ruler and the health of the body politic. For this he turned to Cicero's argument in the *De legibus* that it was the exemplary effect of vice in the *princeps* that most harmed the commonwealth, stating that 'as the Princes are, so are the people, *Qualis Rex talis grex*... their examples are soonest followed, vices entertained' (I.70.7–16).[87] To clarify the warning sent to rulers by this doctrine, and continuing the Roman perspective with reference to Sallust, Burton pointed out that immoral princes bred a 'Commons' that would be 'upon all occasions ready to mutine and rebell'. The threatening conclusion was a comparison of 'the deboshed rogues' of Catiline with the domestic rebels '*Jack Cade*, *Tom Straw*, *Kette*, & his companions' (I.70.23–8).

The conception of the moral duties of the prince built into this argument was conventional to the humanist discourse that had prevailed in learned circles in England since the previous century. Nevertheless,

[85] Quoting Robert Dallington, *A survey of the great dukes state of Tuscany In the yeare of our Lord* 1596 (London, 1605), p. 66.

[86] Quoting Botero, *De illustrium statu et politia* (Ursel, 1602), I.4.

[87] Cicero 1928, III.14.31–2, pp. 494–7, quoted by Burton at I.70.y. Cf. Seneca 1928–35, II.2.1, pp. 432–3.

Burton was both critical and specific about the objects causing him discontent. The negative manner in which he expressed concerns about the moral-psychological rectitude of the ruler, and the severity of the constraints imposed by the imperatives of religious orthodoxy, justice, and the supremacy of the common good suggested censure. He did not risk direct criticism of the existing rule of James or Charles, but constructing the figure of the princely 'head' of the commonwealth organically established its responsibility for the health of the rest of the political body in a fashion that brought uncomfortable implications for the ruling power. The first of these concerned the status of contemporary 'Polititians', whose immorality was being manifested both in the vogue for Machiavellianism and Tacitism and in the generalised degeneracy of the court.

We have already seen that Burton's commitment to a traditional Christian humanist morality placed him in opposition to the contemporary neo-Stoic ethic that separated the inner and outer being. He was also antagonistic to the associated politics of reason of state. This seems to be implied in the first edition, where Democritus Junior's censure of rulers who were 'of no religion, but in shew' (1.69.11) was perhaps intended as a rebuttal of the emphasis placed in reason-of-state writings on the political instrumentality of religion.[88] His condemnation of hypocrisy similarly opposed the cultivation of the appearance of virtue as a goal in itself.[89] In the main treatise, he revisited the issue when dissecting the activities of 'Polititians' as causes of superstition. Here he took the opportunity to dismiss the cultivation of religion for political ends, which, as he informed his readers, was a pagan tactic recently discussed by authors like Machiavelli and Botero, but also the lesser-known German Tacitists Arnold Clapmar and Henning Arnisaeus, and the Polish historian Marcin Kromer (Cromerus):

... it hath ever beene a principall axiome with them, to maintaine religion, or superstition, they make Religion policy, *nihil æquè valet ad regendos vulgi animos ac superstitio*, as *Tacitus* and *Tully* hold. 'Tis that *Aristotle* and *Plato* inculcate in their Politicks, and all our late Polititians ingeminate. *Cromerus lib. 2. pol. hist. Boterus lib. 3. De incrementis urbium, Clapmarius lib. 2. cap. 9. de Arcanis rerump. Arniseus cap. 4. lib. 2. polit.* Captaine *Machiavel* will have a Prince, by all meanes to counterfeit religion, to be superstitious in shew at least, as *Numa, Licurgus,*

[88] Cf. Bacon 1985, III, p. 11; Botero 1606, pp. 36–41. See also Burton's remarks at 3.346.32–347.3 (3.4.1.2).

[89] See Machiavelli 1970, I.11, pp. 140–1.

and such law-makers were, *non ut his fidem habeant, sed ut subditos religionis metu facilius in officio contineant,* to keepe the people in obedience.[90]

Against the 'hypocrisie' of these '*Machiavellians*', who abused the knowledge that '*magnum ejus in animos imperium*' (a quotation from Lipsius's *Politica*),[91] he sided with the Huguenot Innocent Gentillet, who had implicated the 'tyrannicall science' of Machiavelli in the massacre of St Bartholomew's Day in his *Discours sur les moyens de bien gouverner* (1576), and whom he noted 'hath copiously confuted' the infamous Florentine (3.347.18–19 [3.4.1.2]).[92] This placed a strict limit on the tentative support we have seen him exhibit elsewhere for the humanistic approach to 'civil religion'.

Burton's hostility to reason-of-state politics was more overt in later editions of the *Anatomy*, where his additions to the text registered awareness of the increased English interest in Tacitism in the 1620s. In the 1624 edition, the Ciceronian criticism of princely faults in 'Democritus Junior to the Reader' was supplemented with a telling quotation from Aristotle concerning the necessity of a combination of virtue and political competence grounded in theoretical knowledge. The defective individuals with whom he was concerned were first described unspecifically as 'Emperickes in pollicy, *ubi deest facultas, virtus* (*Aristot. Pol.* 6. *cap.* 8) *&* *scientia*'.[93] But the attached note made it clear that the 'Emperickes' in question were those around him who had abandoned the traditional humanist political commitment to the Stoic equation of the *honestum* and the *utile.* His point was that Tacitists and aficionados of 'reason of state' were not pursuing the true goals of politics, properly conceived in the moral terms of the good of the whole commonwealth.

For most part we mistake the name of Polititians, accounting such as read *Machiavel* and *Tacitus,* great statesmen that can supplant and overthrowe their adversaries, enrich themselves, get honours, dissemble, but what is this to the *benè esse,* or preservation of a Common-wealth? (1.69–70.v)

At the same time, he added to the criticisms of Machiavelli in his discourse on the causes of superstition, charging that he advised princes to 'seeme to be devout, frequent holy exercises, honour divines, love the Church' and 'affect Priests' (3.347.14–15 [3.4.1.2]). To drive the point

90 Burton 1621, p. 723; or 1.346.33–347.17 (3.4.1.2).

91 Lipsius 1594, 1.3, p. 4. For Burton's attitude towards Lipsius see 1.108.12–21 and 2.188.20–4 (2.3.6.1). There may be an echo of James I's criticism of Lipsius at 1.58.7–8.

92 See Gentillet 1602, sig. Aij^r.

93 The reference seems to be to *Politics* V.9 (1309a).

home, the third edition of 1628 harnessed the authority of Augustine, who had censured Scaevola's opinion '*expedire civitates religione falli*, that it was a fit thing citties should bee deceaved by religion ... if the world will be gulled, let it be gulled, 'tis good howsoever to keepe it in subjection' (3.347.4–8).[94] Burton also had Democritus Junior associate these immoral political pretenders with quasi-scholastic impracticality, adding their eagerness to 'dispute of politicall precepts' to the list of vices (1.69–70.v).

This condemnation, and the thoroughly moral conception of practical politics it implied, was hardly controversial, Tacitism having received the official seal of disapproval from the reigning monarch. But it was just one aspect of a broader critique developing in the *Anatomy* in the editions of 1624 and 1628. Its development suggests Burton's growing discontent at a progressive deterioration in the condition of the political environment, perhaps reflecting the expanding critique of reason-of-state politics across the continent at this time.[95] Whilst his additions to the second and third editions testify to concern at the rise of a dangerous new strain of politics, they also suggest that he was becoming increasingly preoccupied with the court – the morality of which contemporary Tacitism and Machiavellianism was threatening to corrupt. Although in 1624 no-one could credibly portray the king as a Tacitist, it was perfectly possible to view those surrounding him, either in court or in parliament, as failing in their duty to advise him wisely and virtuously in a number of ways. Expressing anxiety about the influence of immoral 'Polititians' was Burton's way of voicing concern about the health of the body politic, implicitly about its ruling 'head' and those surrounding it.

In the first edition, towards the end of his rant Democritus Junior included a standard indictment of the servility of courtiers, who 'ebbe and flowe with their Princes favours ... torment one another with mutuall factions, emulations', and referred the reader to Lucian, Aeneas Sylvius, Agrippa, 'and others' on the subject of 'these mens discontents, anxieties'.[96] In the 1624 version, these 'others' became 'many others',[97] minutely raising the tenor of the criticism and indicating, perhaps, that Burton had been reading more of this subject, or that its importance had increased. This is supported by other additions

94 Augustine 1984, IV.27, pp. 168–70; Burton's reference was erroneous.
95 See Tuck 1993b, pp. 131–6.
96 Burton 1621, pp. 63–4; or 1.100.6–15.
97 Burton 1624, p. 57; or 1.100.15.

to the work. In 1621, whilst analysing pride as a cause of melancholy in the first Partition, Burton took the opportunity to show its effects at court: 'Commend an ambitious man, some prowd Prince or Potentate', he wrote with reference to Erasmus's *Moriae encomium*, and 'he sets up his crest & will be no longer a man, but a God', the effect being 'many foolish Princes, brought into a fooles Paradise by their Parasites'.[98] In 1624, he reflected further on the 'false *Encomions*' that 'many Princes' attracted.[99] In 1628 and 1632 new Juvenalian scorn for the deluded prince, and denigrating comparisons of this figure to Domitian, 'the *Persian* Kings',[100] and 'our modern Turkes, that wil be Gods on earth',[101] implied antipathy towards *iure divino* kingship.

Similarly, when Democritus Junior developed his indictment of hypocrisy, he delivered a relatively unremarkable criticism of flattery in the first edition by lamenting to 'see a man protest friendship, kisse his hand, smile with an intent to doe mischiefe, or cosen him whom he salutes, magnify his friend unworthy with hyperbolicall elogiums' (1.52.22–4). But in 1624, the rhetorical effect of the indictment was heightened with a series of topsy-turvy parallels, and then directed at servility in princely courts, where one could see 'men buy smoke for wares, castles built with fooles heads, men like apes follow the fashions . . . if the king laugh, all laugh', and so on.[102] Towards the end of the 'Consolatory Digression', he added more criticism of courtly morality to the second edition, quoting Aeneas Sylvius's observation that preferment followed '*meanes*' rather than '*vertues*', so that '[a]n illiterate foole sits in a wise mans seat, and the common people hold him learned, grave, and wise'.[103] The third edition amplified Democritus Junior's ridicule of emulation at court with more Juvenalian derision,[104] before he turned to the vice of ambition. The denunciation of this vice in 1621 – 'To see a man role himselfe up like a snowe-ball from base beggery, to right worshipfull and right honourable titles, injustly to screw himselfe into honors and offices'[105] – was again redirected

98 Burton 1621, pp. 165–6; or 1.300.8–301.2 (1.2.3.14).
99 Burton 1624, p. 107; or 1.294.6–13 (1.2.3.14).
100 Burton 1628, p. 117; or 1.300.12–13, 15–17 (1.2.3.14).
101 Burton 1632, p. 125; or 1.300.23–5 (1.2.3.14).
102 Burton 1624, pp. 29–30; or 1.53.2–9.
103 Burton 1624, p. 286; or 2.190.24–191.6 (2.3.7.1).
104 Burton 1628, p. 36; or 1.53.5–6.
105 Burton 1621, p. 34; or 1.53.19–21.

in 1624 towards courtly morality, but this time targeted the jealousy and slavishness bred by favouritism.

To see the κακοζηλίαν of our times, a man bend all his forces, meanes, time, fortunes to be a favorites, favorites, favourite, &c. a parasites, parasites, parasite, that may scorne the servile World, as having enough already.[106]

Here the author was careful on three counts: accusing not the favourite himself but his cronies; not suggesting malign influence over the king, though this was implied by the indictment of flattery; and, maintaining the traditional satirist's defence against libel (Horace, *Satura* 1.4), not naming names. Many of his readers would have been more than ready to supply the name of Buckingham and the charge of evil counsel, in 1624 as well as 1628.[107] Few would have dared to mention the responsibility of the monarch for the morality of the court, though this implication was difficult to avoid. The same holds true for his subsequent lament, 'To see wise men degraded, fooles preferred' (1.54.27), which pointed to a connection between courtly political vice and scholarly alienation, via a dysfunctional system of patronage, which we shall see Burton articulate in the next chapter.

***

There was another, less traditional aspect to Burton's vision of the commonwealth. Although the account of causes and symptoms in this theory of political pathology was predominantly moralistic, it was not exclusively so, and Burton drew freely upon works of historical and political geography to demonstrate that the melancholic body politic was defective not only in happiness but also in prosperity and greatness. The 'sicke' political body that had 'need to bee reformed' was typically full of 'complaints, poverty, barbarisme, beggary... Idlenesse, Riot, Epicurisme, the land lye untilled, waste, full of bogges, Fennes, Desarts, &c. Cities decayed, base and poore townes, villages depopulated, the people squalid, ugly, uncivill' (1.67.8–12). Conversely, political bodies 'free from Melancholy' had 'people civill, obedient to God and Princes, judicious, peaceable and quiet, rich, fortunate, and flourish, to live in peace, in unity and concord, a Country well tilled, many faire built and populous Cities' (1.66.34–67.6).

[106] Burton 1624, p. 30; or 1.53.24–6.

[107] See also Burton 1624, p. 58 and 1632, p. 71; or 1.101.28–102.3, and Burton 1628, p. 73; or 1.106.21–3.

The subsequent analysis owed a great deal to Botero,[108] and provided an impressively detailed comparative dissection of the merits and faults of commonwealths that ranged across and beyond Europe. But the author's attention was primarily fixed on the condition of his own body politic. It is telling that this part of the preface routinely employed deliberative rhetoric, and so was technically presented as an enterprise of counsel. This is indicated by his direct addresses to those with power ('Tell me Polititians', 'That Prince therefore . . . that will have a rich Country' [1.77.21; 78.23]), and by policy advice, particularly on matters of trade, offered as remedies for the commercial decay of England (1.79.26–80.7; 83.21–84.11). Here Burton contributed to contemporary debates about civic greatness that had been sparked by the projected union of England and Scotland at the beginning of the century and were reignited in the crisis years of the 1620s.[109] But his survey is most striking for its combination of the Roman humanist discourse of civic greatness with the newly emerging imperatives of profit, trade, and industrious arts. Healthy bodies politic were depicted as industrious, prosperous, civilised, and populous, and were accorded honour and glory; their sick, inglorious, and dishonourable counterparts were said to be beset by idleness, poverty, decay, and barbarism.

Yet for all its evident 'modernism' – manifest in Burton's admiration for the commercial ingenuity of those 'most industrious Artificers', the Dutch (1.74.27–75.1) – in this vision the healthy and flourishing body politic remained dependent upon the classically virtuous ruler. As he wrote, 'to shut up all in briefe, where good government is, prudent and wise Princes, there all things thrive and prosper, peace and happinesse is in that Land', but 'where it is otherwise, all things are ugly to behold, incult, barbarous, uncivill, a Paradise turned into a wildernesse' (1.74.10–13). The second edition emphasised that the conjunction of virtue and material prosperity for all was sanctioned by the authority of Aristotle and the elder Cato.[110] This was typical of the humanist vision of the preceding century, in which the harmonious prosperity of the state was to be fuelled by discipline and industriousness as well as by the traditional moral virtues.[111] Although he admitted the value of

108 See, for example, Botero 1635, I.8–10, pp. 23–51.
109 See also Burton 1621, p. 52; or 1.75.27–8, and Peltonen 1995, p. 219.
110 Burton 1624, p. 37; or 1.67.2–5.
111 Todd 1987, pp. 123–30. See also Burton 1624, p. 39; or 1.70.19–20, and the new references to Cicero, *De legibus* III.3.8, and Plato, *Republic* IV, in Burton 1628, p. 45; or 1.67.b.

courage and the necessity of arms for defensive purposes (1.45.12–21), unsurprisingly in the light of his withering critique of warfare he nowhere connected military expertise with civic greatness, nor did he articulate the Aristotelian ideal of the armed citizen so admired by his contemporary Francis Bacon. His preference, following Botero, was rather for a peaceful and commercially productive commonwealth (1.95.6).[112]

It was in this part of the preface that Burton voiced his most direct and extensive criticisms of the condition of the English body politic, and so – having clearly established the responsibility of the 'head' for the health of the 'body' – also where he was at his most cagey and self-protective. When compared with 'those rich united Provinces of *Holland*, *Zeland*, *&c.*', with 'so much land recovered from the Sea, and so painefully preserved by those Artificiall inventions', England looked distinctly melancholic:

> . . . so many thousand acres of our Fens lye drowned, our Cities thin, and those vile, poore, and ugly to behold in respect of theirs, our trades decayed, our still running rivers stopped, and that beneficiall use of transportation, wholly neglected, so many Havens void of Ships and Townes, so many Parkes and Forrests for pleasure, barren Heaths, so many Villages depopulated, &c. (1.74.28–75.5)

Immediately, however, he appeared to retract his implied diagnosis, admitting that 'I may not deny but that this Nation of ours . . . is a most noble, a most flourishing kingdome, by common consent of all Geographers, Historians, and hath many such honourable Elogiums' (1.75.7–14), and praising the benefits of 'expert Seamen, our laborious discoveries, art of navigation' and 'true Merchants' as superior to 'even the *Portugals* and *Hollanders* themselves' (1.75.7–21). He now moved to offset any more serious accusations of political discontent with an apparently comprehensive pronunciation of the healthiness of the entire domestic body politic, and more importantly, the ruler responsible:

> Wee have besides many particular blessings, which our neighbours want, the Gospel truly preached, Church discipline established, long peace and quietnesse, free from exactions, forraine feares, invasions, domesticall seditions, well manured, fortified by Art and Nature, and now most happy in that fortunate union of *England* and *Scotland*, which our fore-fathers have

[112] Cf. Bacon 1985, XXIX, pp. 95–9, though see Burton's concession at 1.240.15–16 (1.2.2.6).

laboured to effect, and desired to see: But in which wee excell all others, a wise, learned, religious King, another *Numa*, a second *Augustus*, a true *Josiah*, most worthy Senators, a learned Cleargy, an obedient Commonalty, &c. (1.75.23–31)

There are good reasons to doubt the sincerity of this passage. Some of his claims would have been credible in 1621 – most obviously, to have 'the Gospel truly preached' – but the widely perceived threat to European Protestantism from Spain and the Habsburgs, along with his countrymen's vivid memories of the failed invasion of 1588 and the Gunpowder Plot, both of which had become central to a burgeoning providential nationalism, would have made a mockery of the idea of such perfect and uninterrupted domestic serenity. We have already seen Burton's serious concerns about not only English 'Church discipline' but also recent domestic and continental bloodshed and 'our gunpowder machinations'. It would be going too far to draw a serious parallel between the author's previous remarks about the prevalence of the hypocrite's praise for 'unworthy' men with 'hyperbolicall elogiums' and 'smile with an intent to doe mischiefe' (1.52.23–5) with his description here of James. But the passage remained unchanged under Charles, and seems to have been an all-purpose defensive shield that required no alteration prompted by authentic admiration. Excepting the reigning monarch from a generally targeted political or religious criticism was a well-recognised self-protective strategy employed by preachers at the Jacobean court, which if omitted could easily result in imprisonment.[113]

What effectively undermines a literal reading of this important passage of text, however, is the extensive undercutting effect performed by the catalogue of complaints that were immediately reeled off in its aftermath. 'Yet amongst many Roses, some Thistles grow', he continued, 'some bad weedes and enormities, which much disturbe the peace of this body politicke, Eclipse the honour and glory of it, fit to bee rooted out, and with all speede to be reformed' (1.75.31–4). What was a moment ago labelled 'a most flourishing kingdome' was now said to be beset by 'Idlenesse', which was 'the *malus Genius* of our Nation' and the cause of 'many swarmes of rogues and beggers, theeves, drunkards, and discontented persons, many poore people in all our Townes . . . base built citties, inglorious, poore, small, rare in sight, ruinous, and thin of inhabitants' (1.76.1–10).

[113] See McCullough 1998a, pp. 144–6.

Burton had classical sources for his denunciation of idleness and mendicancy, notably *Republic* 564b–c and *Laws* 936b–c (1.81.8–12). These had also supported Erasmus's conception of idleness as the root of evil in the commonwealth, and More's castigation of the nobility in the first book of *Utopia*, which was cited at several points in the discussion.[114] However, his approach was again more directly indebted to Botero, who 'justly argues, fertility of a Country is not enough, except Art and Industry be joined unto it' (1.76.10–11). In this respect, the previously favourable comparison with the United Provinces (and, after 1624, with Germany and Portugal as well)[115] became unfavourable, as English idleness was shown to stifle commercial productivity and prosperity. 'The Low-countries generally have three cities at least for one of ours, and those far more populous and rich, and what is the cause, but their industry and excellency in all manner of trades?' (1.76.17–33). By comparison, he pointed out, 'our Island of Great *Britaine*' had been in historical decline – 'See that *Domesday*-Booke, and shew those thousands of Parishes, which are now decaied, Citties ruined, Villages depopulated, &c.' (1.78.11–16) – so that 'there is only *London* that bears the face of a Citty . . . . The rest (some few excepted) are in meane estate, poore and full of beggers, by reason of their decaied Trades, idlenesse of their Inhabitants, riot, which had rather begge or loyter, and be ready to starve, then work' (the third edition added that these places were 'ruinous most part' due to 'neglected or bad policy')[116] (1.80.9–15). Such was his estimation of the virtues of 'industry, good policie, and commerce' that China, about which he had gleaned information from Jesuit missionary literature, became the paragon of the flourishing, populous commonwealth where there was 'not a begger, or an idle person to be seene' (1.77.15–16; 79.4–6).[117]

This was a bitter indictment of the inglorious condition of the author's own body politic, and although he stopped short of a technical diagnosis of melancholy, the terms of his analysis made this conclusion inescapable. As the criteria set out at the beginning of the discussion of political bodies had made clear, the depopulation, poverty, and idleness of England all meant that it 'must needs be discontent, melancholy, hath a sicke body, and had need to bee reformed'. Only in '*Italy* in the

114 See Erasmus 1997, p. 83; More 1989, pp. 16–19.
115 Burton 1642, p. 43; or 1.76.17–31.
116 Burton 1628, p. 55; or 1.80.13–14.
117 See Vicari 1989, pp. 50–5, 197–206, and Chapple 1993.

time of *Augustus*, now in *China*, now in many other flourishing kingdoms of *Europe*' (here unspecified) could this type of melancholy be said to be absent (1.66.34–67.13). His account focused on material decay, but his moral and spiritual concerns resurfaced when he rounded off his analysis with a call for general reform which pointedly did not except England. 'We have good Lawes, I deny not, to rectify such enormities, and so in all other Countries, but it seemes not alwaies to good purpose.'[118] So, '[w]e had need of some generall visiter in our age, that should reforme what is amis; a just army of *Rosie* Crosse men, for they will amend all matters, (they say) Religion, Policy, manners, with arts, sciences, &c.' (1.84.21–6)

The desire for reform was what ostensibly provoked Democritus Junior to construct a 'poeticall commonwealth', where Burton revealed his positive political preferences more directly than in the largely negative critique which had gone before. Most importantly, being guided by an overarching concern for the 'publike good' over private interests (1.89.15; 90.29; 91.21–3), it was assembled in accordance with the principles of humanist political theory which we have seen him apply to dysfunctional commonwealths. Although his choice was for a 'Monarchicall' form (1.90.2–3), the ideal of government was clearly a constitutionalist one explicitly incorporating both aristocracy – the cities were to be governed by 'Noblemen and Gentlemen' (1.88.5) – and a popular element. He was cautious about the latter, permitting the existing social hierarchy of 'severall orders, degrees of nobilitie', and its corollary of hereditary inheritance, to persist (1.89.20). He was nevertheless prepared to draw republican political implications about office-holding from his fundamental moral commitments. Judges and 'all inferiour Magistrates' would be chosen by election, 'as the *Literati* in *China*, or by those exact suffrages of the *Venetians*', on the basis of their 'learning, manners, and that by the strict approbation of deputed examiners' (1.91.26–92.1).

In the second edition, Burton developed the republican and popular dimensions of his utopia through a rigorous application of the principle *virtus vera nobilitas*: 'I say with *Hannibal* in *Ennius*, *Hostem qui feriet erit mihi Carthaginensis*, let him be of what condition he will, in all Offices, Actions, hee that deserves best shall have best' (1.92.23–93.2).

[118] After the first edition the disapproval was strengthened: Burton 1621, p. 55, had 'good Lawes . . . but it seemes to small purpose many times' (Burton 1621, p. 55; cf. Burton 1624, p. 48).

Elsewhere in this version his commitment to elective office was attenuated by his admission of the distribution of 'dignities' according to heredity and by patronage (1.89–26–32), but at the same time he appointed republican officers '*like Solons Areopagites*, or those *Roman* Censors' to monitor others appointed to positions of authority in order to control dishonesty, 'for men are partiall and passionate, covetous, corrupt, subject to love, hate, feare, favor, &c.' (1.91.26–92.8). He was also less cautious about the social inclusivity governing appointments to civic honours, and indicated antagonism towards the aristocratic governments of contemporary republics. Although only just having rejected pure democratic 'parity' as a 'kinde of government' (perhaps an anti-puritan sentiment) (1.89.16), when he explained his position further he was keen to show his readers not just that he was far from being a divine-right monarchical absolutist but also that he detested continental aristocratic republicans:

For I hate these severe, unnaturall, harsh, *Germane*, *French*, and *Venetian* Decrees, which exclude Plebeians from honours, be they never so wise, rich, virtuous, valiant, and well qualified; they must not be Patritians, but keepe their owne rancke, this is *naturæ bellum inferre*, odious to God & men, I abhorre it. (1.89.32–90.2; cf. 2.136.19–24)

Without further specifications as to the powers involved, it is difficult to interpret such comments as advocacy of a 'mixed' or 'tempered' constitution, though it is worth recalling that elsewhere he referred to the conclusion of 'many polititians' (including Aristotle, Machiavelli, and Sir Thomas Smith) that 'their pure Formes of Commonwealths, Monarchies, Aristocraties, Democraties, are most famous in contemplation, but in practise they are temperate and usually mixt'.[119] If he was evasive on this issue, it was clear that his commitment to monarchy was wholeheartedly constitutionalist, as his approving quotation from Claude de Seyssel's analysis of France as '*a diapason and sweet harmony of Kings, Princes, Nobles and Plebeians, so mutually tide and involved in love*', indicates (1.92.14–17).[120] It also did not foreclose the attractiveness of republican and even democratic elements for his vision of utopian

[119] Burton 1628, p. 36; or 1.170.31–171.1 (1.1.3.4). Cf. also 1.64.1–5.

[120] Seyssel's *De republica Galliae et regum officiis* in the translation by Johann Sleidan (Hanau, 1608) was quoted in Burton 1624, pp. 40, 55, 56, 126; or 96.d, 98.11–19, 20–1, 327.22–3 (1.2.3.15). Burton's copy was extensively annotated: Kiessling 1988, entry 1493.

government, which might best be classified as an instance of the constitutional hybrid based on virtue that he elsewhere labelled 'Democraticall Monarchies (if I may so call them)' (2.139.20).

Given that many contemporaries saw England as a 'monarchical republic' or a monarchy with a 'mixed' constitution, it is perfectly plausible to view these aspects of Burton's utopia as embodying his views of how the political arrangements of his nation should function in their proper, 'healthy' state, or even, perhaps, be improved. The latter is certainly the case for other features of his imaginary commonwealth, which in many ways formed the mirror image of his depiction of the melancholic English body politic. It was composed principally of commercially vibrant, prosperous, and well-maintained cities (1.86.26–87.5), and land that had been enclosed to maximise productivity (1.88.10–18). Following and citing More's *Utopia*,[121] it was composed of active labourers and so was free of 'Beggers, Rogues, Vagabonds, or idle persons' (1.93.3–22; cf. 2.82.35–83.4 [2.2.4.1]). It provided close regulation for the legal system to stamp out abuses (1.91.7–26), but at the same time adhered to the commonplace Platonic requirement restated in *Utopia* that there be 'few lawes, but those severely kept' (1.90.6).[122] To similar ends, it also outlawed monopolies (1.96.7), registering the widespread concern with an issue which had been galvanising oppositional politics in parliament and the localities since the second half of the reign of Elizabeth.[123] Finally, as we noted in chapter three, two passages of text new to the second and third editions reinforced his criticisms of the contemporary thirst for warfare, making it clear that Burton's utopians would avoid bloodshed when possible (1.96.13–16, 97.7–8; 96.21–3).[124]

THE POLITICS OF MELANCHOLY

As one would expect in a work that grounded its political theory in the classical moral psychology of the pseudo-Hippocratic *Letter to Damagetes*, the terms of Burton's discussion of the melancholic commonwealth appeared to privilege the eudaimonist concerns found in Greek political

[121] On Burton's use of *Utopia* see McCutcheon 1998.
[122] See Erasmus 1997, p. 80; More 1989, pp. 84–5; James I and VI 1603a, p. 28; Forset 1606, p. 73.
[123] See Neale 1953, vol. II, pp. 376–93, and Archer 1988, esp. pp. 32–4, 41–3.
[124] Cf. More 1989, pp. 87–8.

philosophy over the goals of *fama* and *gloria* more typically found in their Roman counterparts. Hence the evidently deep indebtedness of his analysis to both More's *Utopia* and Plato's *Laws*. However, as we have seen, he also drew extensively upon the writings of Cicero and Seneca, drawing an association between the happiness of the 'healthy' body politic and not only its glory but also its peaceful tranquillity. Similarly, although his explicit emphasis was on the benefits of inner, psychological freedom from the domination of unruly passions, in practice this condition was extrapolated to a view of the political community whose members would possess valuable freedoms of action, including participation in government. This bridging was not a difficult task, since both these Roman authors had expressed Hellenistic ethical-therapeutic concerns in their political writings that had also reverberated throughout the *Letter to Damagetes*.[125] As such, the moral psychology of the *Letter* provided Burton with the conceptual apparatus to fashion a model of the virtuous and healthy commonwealth, alongside its vicious, dysfunctional opposite, to express a typically humanistic reforming impulse. Or, to sum up the dual polarity of his message in classical terms, his criticism of the court indicated a Platonic estimation of the *vita contemplativa* as best suited to a degenerate monarchical polity, yet the positive appraisal of republican activism and utopianism pointed to his cherishing of the ideal of the *vita activa*.

Apart from Burton's humanistic political psychology, what is most interesting about his discussion is its use of a fusion of an implicitly Galenic medical-analytical approach – the functional view of the 'body politic' said to be healthy when all its 'parts' are performing correctly and harmoniously – with the vision of the materially prosperous commonwealth articulated by Botero. This is one of the reasons why the most serious problem of the melancholic commonwealth was idleness. It was not only a vice, but symptomatic of economic stagnation and a pathological breakdown of natural political-physiological function. This helps to explain why activity – civic-participatory as well as commercial – was taken to be the sign of the healthy, happy, tranquil, non-melancholic body politic. Insofar as this pertained to England, Burton was offering a novel version of the classical humanist vision of the polity as a monarchical *res publica* that expanded, albeit in peculiarly

[125] Though conflicts between Greek and Roman political philosophy were ignored; see Nelson 2003.

scientistic fashion, into the functional-economic sphere. This further testifies to the flexibility permitted by his intellectual eclecticism. He adhered to the conventional moral basis of politics, and could incorporate the distinctively modern concerns of Botero without being compelled to subscribe to the politics with which they were frequently associated. If there is one characteristic that can sum up Burton's method it is this ability to pick and choose for his own purposes – in this case, appropriating Botero's insistence on the centrality of peace to commercial prosperity, and jettisoning his reason-of-state politics as a means of updating the Christian-pacifist and humanist vision of the commonwealth.

The prominence of Botero's political geography in 'Democritus Junior to the Reader' also indicated that this was a discussion that was not only up to date, but international in scope and constructed out of materials that were currently circulating across the continent. Burton was concerned with the problems of the early Stuart polity, but it was a distinctive feature of his discussion of these problems that it drew extensively upon contemporary European intellectual discourse. Insofar as the *Anatomy* applied this discourse to a domestic target, for the consumption of a domestic readership, it is worth mentioning Burton's rumoured participation in the translation and adaptation of Trajano Boccalini's *Ragguagli di Parnasso* (1612–13). The *Ragguagli*, an ironically witty and detached commentary on European politics, appeared in an English version – *The new-found politicke, Disclosing the secret natures and dispositions as well of private persons as of statesmen and courtiers* (1626). Its dedicatory epistle to Charles I divulged the identities of the translators of the first and third parts as William Vaughan and John Florio, but recorded only of the second translator that he was 'one, unto whom the common-wealth cannot as yet be beholding for his name',[126] and there has been speculation that this was Burton.[127] Vaughan himself appeared to imply this in his *Golden Fleece*, also published in 1626. In its first part, he depicted Charles's resolve to reform his realm in accordance with the prescriptions of the Boccalini translation, and then described how three figures were admitted into the palace of Apollo as 'the first messengers which blazed and reported these joyfull tidings': these were himself, Florio, and 'one *Democritus Junior*, which published *the*

[126] Boccalini 1626, sig. ¶2.
[127] Yates 1934, pp 308–9; Kiessling 1988, entry 172.

Anatomie of Melancholie'.[128] Boccalini was referred to on two occasions by Burton in his third edition (1.85.23–4; 337.14 [1.2.4.4]), and his library held a copy of the English version with annotations in his hand, several of which marked the chapter reporting the case against and then for Lipsius, and his use of Tacitus – a subject that we have seen to be one of his preoccupations in the *Anatomy*.[129]

Burton's direct involvement is unlikely. Boccalini had indirectly criticised Spanish imperialism,[130] and *The new-found politicke* adapted his message for its domestic market by emphasising to its dedicatee the perils of concluding a peace treaty with the Catholic power. The book contained, according to its new subtitle, 'Many excellent Caveats and Rules fit to be observed by those Princes and States of Christendome, both Protestants and Papists, which have reason to distrust the designes of the King of *Spaine*',[131] and its second, anonymously translated part was devoted to undermining Spanish expansionism. This agenda sat uncomfortably alongside the political and religious thrust of the *Anatomy*, which, as we have seen, not only was pacifist, cosmopolitan, and devoid of obvious anti-Spanish sentiment, but more importantly became increasingly lukewarm towards the radical Protestant cause as the 1620s wore on. Moreover, there is little sign in the *Anatomy* that Burton was interested in the polemical activity of commenting directly on immediate but ephemeral issues of foreign policy. His labours rather tended towards the production of a message which would be of long-term relevance – even if this message was itself the product of contemporary concerns. The anonymous third translator of *The new-found politicke* was almost certainly the humanist pamphleteer Thomas Scott, who was vehemently anti-Catholic, and by contrast with Burton was strongly in favour of war with Spain. The second part of the work in fact partially reprinted Scott's own *Newes from Pernassus* (1622), which had translated and adapted Boccalini's more overtly anti-Spanish later work, the *Pietra del paragone politico* (1615). Scott's viewpoint thereby tallied with that of Vaughan, who was unequivocally hostile towards Arminianism.[132]

As well as a lifelong interest in medicine, what Burton did share with Vaughan was deep discontent with the condition of the English

[128] Vaughan 1626, pt 1, pp. 22–3.
[129] Kiessling 1988, entry 172. Burton's annotations were to Boccalini 1626, pp. 3, 4, 7, 9, 14, 16, 21.
[130] See Tuck 1993b, pp. 102–3.
[131] See also Boccalini 1626, sig. ¶2.
[132] Vaughan 1626, pt 1, chs. 1, 17–18, pp. 22, 133–46.

commonwealth, and it was perhaps partially in an act of sympathetic homage to this aspect of the former's work that the latter had assumed the pseudonym 'Orpheus Junior'. For both, England was a 'diseased country' on account of the decay of its trade.[133] For Vaughan, the most effective 'physic' for this was colonial expansion – Burton referred approvingly to this aspect of the *Golden Fleece* in the 1628 edition of the *Anatomy*[134] – and he too made wittily ironic use of Rosicrucianism to articulate a desire for wholesale domestic political reform.[135] Their most significant common ground, though, was to be found in their denunciation of political corruption, their consciously submerged attribution of responsibility to the 'head' of the body politic for this, and their accompanying complaints at being undeservedly deprived of patronage. In *The Golden Fleece*, the conversation that ensued between Florio, 'Orpheus Junior', and 'Democritus Junior' after they had been admitted to the court of Apollo expressed Vaughan's bitterness through complaint at material deprivation and dissatisfaction with the professions of divinity, law and medicine, and this prompted him to advocate political withdrawal:

> ... when *Orpheus Junior* had attended awhile, and observed the small pittance he was like to bee fed withal... meeting one day with his friends *Democritus*, a new comer as himselfe, and with *John Florio* aforenamed, sometimes servant to the virtuous Queene *Anne*, hee brake forth into these speeches. How long shall wee suffer our selves to be dallied with hopes of preferment in this Learned Court?... we are like as I see, after a few Summers spent in tedious and toylesome expectation, to starve with cold in the first hard winter... If we had studied Divinity, we might have had some fat benefice. If wee had spared but two houres or three in a weeke from our more serious imployments, in the *Lawes* which they terme *Common*, though sometimes wrested according to privat fancies, by this time wee have heaped together whole pyles of treasure by the ruines of such Clients as runne headlong, like tame Woodcocks, into knowne nets. If wee had practised *Physicke*, by the death of some few Patients, wee might have scraped together a better estate, then thus to consume our fruitlesse labours in awaiting for Offices, which no sooner become vacant, but others doe step before us... For my part, except I find my worth better respected and requited, Ile retire my selfe from *Court*, and bend my fortunes to the *Newfoundland*.[136]

[133] Vaughan 1626, II.1, pp. 1–6.

[134] Burton 1628, p. 533; or 3.260.24–7 (3.2.5.5). See also Burton 1628, p. 235; or 2.43.2–9 (2.2.3.1).

[135] Vaughan 1626, II.16, pp. 85–7; III.12, pp. 81–92.

[136] Vaughan 1626, I.1, pp. 23–4.

Whereas the response of 'Orpheus Junior' was to retreat to the colonial fantasy of the 'new Cambrioll', in Vaughan's portrayal the reaction of 'Democritus Junior' was to lament the corruption of learning and direct the vituperation directly at the immorality of the pursuit for patronage at court.

To this *Democritus Junior* answered: *My noble friend*, I must confesse, that true and solid Learning is almost downe the wind in this decrepit age of the world, by reason of the multitude of sc[r]ambling Schollers and riotous Writers, who like emptie barrels yeeld a hollow sound without substantiall fruit. Your many swarmes of over-swaying *Lawyers* lend their greedie hands to pull downe this famous fabrick:

Since hired double Tongues grew in request,
Nor Armes nor Arts could take their wonted Rest.

In regard of the many emulous concurrents for places here in *Court*, which importunately presse upon his *Majestie* for promotion, it is difficult and in a manner impossible for such modest persons, as wee are, who out of our magnanimitie of spirit scorne to fawne like spaniels, to climbe into any high vocation. There bee two kinds of Factions heere, the *Papists* and the *Lawyers*, who although their number be but few in this *vertuous Court*, yet powerfull enough to suppresse and supplant a greater man then you, if they joyne together and bandie against you.[137]

Here was a reworking of the *Anatomy*'s non-confessional discontent with the condition of scholarship, the greed of lawyers, and the corruption of the court to accord with his own anti-Catholic vision. That this was Vaughan arrogating Burton's support for his enterprise in a none-too-subtle fashion became clear, as he went on to have Democritus Junior advertise Orpheus Junior's critiques of Catholics and lawyers in *The Golden-Grove* (1600) and *The spirit of detraction conjured and convicted in seven circles* (1611), and then warn of the 'revengefull threat' posed to him in return by the Jesuit Robert Parsons.[138] But, as we shall now see, Vaughan's recasting of Democritus Junior to express the plight of the alienated scholar – denied substantial preferment, frustrated at failed reform, and withdrawn from politics – was faithful to Burton's purpose.

[137] Vaughan 1626, I.I, p. 25. [138] Vaughan 1626, I.I, pp. 25–6. See also ibid., II.12, p. 68.

CHAPTER 5

Utopia, consolation, and withdrawal

Although the vibrant eclecticism of the *Anatomy* is a sign of the continued productivity of humanist philosophy in Jacobean England, the work is also an eloquent testament to the deepening anxiety felt by many of its practitioners in the face of political reality. Humanists continued to cherish their traditional role as servants and moral reformers of the commonwealth, but the necessities engendered by an era of widespread religious conflict were beginning to place their values in question and erode their political influence. Many Jacobean humanists could be considered well prepared for this problem, as their Elizabethan predecessors had gone to great lengths to address themselves to the practical and court-centred nature of a great proportion of political endeavour. Yet their dependence on the court environment, and the patronage it provided, created serious intellectual and material difficulties. In this chapter, I shall be addressing Burton's portrayal of the predicament of the early Stuart scholar, as manifested in his interweaving of political and personal concerns throughout his work. As we shall see, this constituted a characteristically melancholic commentary on the status of the learned culture to which he had devoted his life.

From the later decades of the sixteenth century onwards, humanists' prospects of acting as counsellors to the powerful in Church and state had steadily worsened. The court of Henry VIII had provided prominent positions for such scholars as Thomas Lupset, Richard Pace, Sir Thomas Elyot, Sir Thomas More, and John Clerk. Richard Cox, Sir John Cheke, and Sir Anthony Cooke had acted as tutors to the young Edward VI. Cox had also been recruited to a team of humanist notables charged with justifying the king's divorce that included Sir Thomas Starkey, William Marshall, Thomas Berthelet, and Thomas Paynell. Sir Thomas Smith had been the Principal Secretary to Edward VI and Elizabeth, and Miles Coverdale, Sir John Cheke, and Roger Ascham all contributed substantially to the ecclesiastical and educational reforms of their era.

Elizabeth was well disposed towards the universities and their Latinate intellectual culture,[1] but as her reign progressed the dynamics of the patronage networks that had been sustaining the linkage between humanism in the universities and political power began to change. Most significantly, the concentration of power at the royal court heightened the importance of royal patronage to the detriment of aristocratic patronage, with the consequence that locations other than the court – the Inns of Court, universities, and commercial and professional circles in London and elsewhere in the realm – became ever more dependent on the favour of the Crown and its officers.[2] In this situation, the dominance at court of such figures as Essex and Cecil, and subsequently Northampton, Somerset, and Buckingham, meant that those in search of preferment were compelled to concentrate their efforts upon perceptibly narrower patronage channels. This situation was exacerbated by the financial problems afflicting the Crown from the 1590s onwards, and the concomitant depletion of patronage resources in government offices, whilst the number of educated gentry seeking employment was multiplying.[3]

Of course, the scale of this problem can be exaggerated. It did not prevent James allocating important governmental offices and tasks to scholarly figures like Sir Francis Bacon and Sir Robert Cotton, and, as we have seen, under Charles and Laud many bishoprics and other substantial benefices were bestowed upon university men. Yet many contemporaries saw their prospects as bleak. As well as facing increased competition in a system where demand exceeded supply, Jacobean scholars looked on as offices, titles, privileges, and monopolies were often dispensed in an apparently corrupt manner on the basis of payment – itself part of the Crown's drive to augment its finances in a period when other sources of revenue, such as parliamentary subsidies, were proving insufficient.[4] These developments undoubtedly contributed to the quantity and extremity of the hostility expressed towards the royal favourites monopolising patronage in the Jacobean and Caroline eras, and so also to the rising tide of literature produced by excluded individuals complaining about court corruption. This was clearly the case for the Spenserian poets Brooke, Stafford, and Wither, whose critiques of courtly vice coincided with the death of their patron, Prince Henry.

[1] See Binns 1990b. [2] See MacCaffrey 1961, pp. 124–5.
[3] Peck 1981, pp. 41–6. [4] Smuts 1981 and Peck 1990, esp. pp. 3–5.

As the patronage system connecting the royal court and the country at large became more dysfunctional under James, the credibility of the claim of humanist pedagogy to be providing preparation for ecclesiastical and political power and influence was manifestly diminishing from its Tudor apogee. Whilst the universities continued to be productive centres of scholarship, they were becoming victimised by their own success. By producing more and more graduates for fewer employment positions they were overloading their capacity to perform the role of training educated servants for the state, and seemingly producing groups of dangerously disaffected intellectuals.[5] 'I think that we have more need of better livings for learned men than of more learned men for these livings,' concluded Thomas Egerton, Lord Chancellor Ellesmere, at a conference before the privy council in May 1611, 'for learning without living doth but breed traitors, as common experience too well sheweth.'[6] Admittedly, responsibility for this threatening situation was not always shouldered by the royal court. Lay patrons had long been charged with neglecting to promote students to vacant benefices, and established clergy were accused (in many cases rightly) of rapacious practices such as simony that excluded young aspirants.[7] Whoever or whatever was to blame, the implementation of the ideal of universities as the anchor of the state and the foundation of its spiritual rectitude, as articulated in the mid-1590s by John Case in his *Apologia academiarium* – or as later expressed by Charles I in a letter to the Oxford Convocation, 'seminaries of virtue and learning' preparing 'the better part of our subjects . . . to do service in church and commonwealth' – had run into serious difficulty.[8]

This concern with the marginalisation of the intellectual elite was bound up with a disenchantment that was deepening amongst many humanists across Europe, where the relationship between the university educated scholar and political life was increasingly exemplified by the figure of the isolated virtuous philosopher – excluded from office in the autocratic state, but participating in a *respublica literaria* that positioned itself over and above the depravity and bloodthirstiness of aristocratic elites and court-centred politics.[9] Experienced in acute form and diagnosed with clarity in learned circles in France and the Low Countries, this problem formed the backdrop for the reformulation of the conventional

[5] See Curtis 1962.
[6] Folger Lib., MS. v.a 121, fol. 124, cited in Curtis 1962, p. 28.
[7] Lytle 1981, pp. 76–9.
[8] On Case's *Apologia* see Binns 1990a, pp. 251–2. Charles I is quoted in Sharpe 1981, p. 152.
[9] Comparato 1996; Miller 2000.

humanistic relation between the philosopher and the state found in the widely read late sixteenth- and early seventeenth-century works of Lipsius, Montaigne, and Pierre Charron. Preoccupied with the moral-psychological imperative of the therapy of the passions, these writers deployed Hellenistic ethics to advocate a turn towards individualistic privacy, and away from political participation as traditionally conceived. In Jacobean England, aspects of this vision did not go unchallenged, and in some senses Burton was one of its critics. But at the very least the pressures operating on the bond between counsel and its moral-philosophical underpinnings prompted anxious meditation upon the credibility of the existing humanist political self-image.

This was the historical predicament that lay at the heart of Burton's conception of the melancholy afflicting contemporary English scholars. It was a diagnosis that resurfaced periodically and prominently throughout the *Anatomy*, explicitly in the extensive vituperation of the 'Digression on the Misery of Schollers', and with more subtlety in his reworking of the two philosophical genres of the utopia and the *consolatio*. The first of these is familiar, though hardly straightforward. For our purposes here, we should recall that Thomas More had presented utopianism as arising from the deadlock faced by humanist political philosophy in an environment of corruption; and it is in *Utopia* that we see the first symptoms of the syndrome that would produce the alienated humanist intellectual of the seventeenth century: the exuberant fantasy of the impossibly perfect commonwealth is, paradoxically, the product of despair at the failure of Ciceronian political commitment, and more particularly at the futility of offering counsel to a prince surrounded by an irredeemably degenerate court. It is also worth noting that Bacon wrote the *New Atlantis* in his final years, after the spectacular and humiliating destruction of his once glittering political career in 1621. As Burton suggested, what gave birth to the utopian imagination was a political form of melancholy.

The perturbations of melancholy also prompted Burton to write the 'Consolatory Digression'.[10] In contrast to utopianism, the character of consolatory writing is now less well known, but was of equal significance for his conception of the crisis afflicting scholarship, and as a vehicle for the expression and alleviation of discontent. In its classical form, the *consolatio* was the literary embodiment of philosophy's claim to remove perturbations from the suffering soul through the persuasive application of reason, through either argument or didactic *exempla*, and its most

[10] For a study of Burton's *consolatio* see Lievsay 1951.

influential exponents were Cicero, Seneca, and (pseudo-)Plutarch. In Christianised form, it figured prominently in the patristic and medieval *cura animarum*, and of course received its greatest expression in Boethius's *De consolatione philosophiae*. However, the early modern flowering of consolation in a variety of forms – from epistles and funeral orations to full-length treatises and dialogues – can be traced to the psychological and spiritual preoccupations of such famously productive authors as Petrarch and Coluccio Salutati.[11]

These Italian humanists accentuated three characteristics of the *consolatio*, all of which can be seen in their later northern European counterparts.[12] In the first place, as it was concerned with forms of persuasion that worked with or against passions, the success or failure of the enterprise came to be seen as depending as much on effective rhetorical technique as it did on philosophical-spiritual rectitude.[13] It was therefore fitting that the different kinds of argument appropriate to consolation were frequently discussed in sixteenth-century treatises on rhetoric, most importantly in Erasmus's *De conscribendis epistolis* (1521).[14] Another feature of Italian humanist *consolationes*, which had been integral to their classical forebears, was their sensitivity towards the requirements of moral and spiritual rectitude. The *consolatio* became a place for investigating the relationship between classical and Christian teachings about death, the immortality of the soul, and the role of passions in the healthy life.[15]

Whilst the consolatory discourse was typically aimed at alleviating the distress of a friend, writing it also came to be conceived as self-therapeutic. There were two main humanistic models here, both deriving their prestige from the rhetorical *topos* that the most effective consolation would be delivered by someone also experiencing anguish. The first was the work of Boethius, and the second that of Cicero, the *Consolatio seu de luctu minuendo*. Only fragments of the latter remained, but its significance was indicated by the controversy surrounding the publication of a forgery in Venice in 1583,[16] and by the opening of Girolamo Cardano's

[11] See McClure 1986 and 1991.
[12] I am unaware of any comprehensive study of northern European *consolationes* in this period, but see Cunningham 1974 for a case-study; for England see Boyce 1949, Miles 1965–6, Beaty 1970, and Pigman 1985, pp. 11–39.
[13] McClure 1986, pp. 458–61.
[14] Erasmus 1985, XLIX, pp. 148–71. See also Wilson 1553, fols. 36^v–47^v; Day 1586, pp. 201–3; Peacham 1593, pp. 100–1.
[15] McClure 1986, pp. 446–50, 452–6, 462–3.
[16] See Sage 1918; Burton alluded to its spuriousness at 1.7.32–8.2.

own *De consolatione* (1542), which lamented the loss of '*Marcus Tullius* bokes of comforte, wrytten at the deathe of his daughter' – particularly as it proceeded 'from his owne naturall affection and extreme perturbation of mynde'.[17] The humanist *consolatio* was therefore often designed to provide comfort for author and reader – as for Petrarch after the loss of his grandson in *Seniles* X.4 (1361–73), Giovanni da Ravenna in his *De consolatione de obitu filii* (1401), and Francisco Filefo in his *Oratio consolatoria ad Iacobum Antonium Marcellum de obitu Valerii filii* (1461); for Thomas More in his *Dialogue of Comfort against Tribulation* (1533–4), written in the Tower of London whilst its author awaited execution; and indeed for Cardano, for whom the *De consolatione* was assembled not 'to drive away the cares & anxiety of mind in others' but instead 'not a little [to] content my selfe'.[18]

Another feature of the *consolatio* that became significant with the progress of Reformation and Counter-Reformation was its developing spiritualisation, and in some cases confessionalisation. As we saw in chapter three, Protestant theology exhibited deep concern with the nature of despair and the proper response to it, and the burgeoning literature of spiritual comfort was, generally speaking, a 'purified' adaptation of the *consolatio*, which had incorporated Christian elements from the Church Fathers onwards.[19] In the *Dialogue of Comfort*, More conceded that classical philosophers had 'some good drugs . . . in their shops', but underlined that these were inadequate to ease psychological suffering on their own unless they coincided with the 'bills made by the great physician God'.[20] Similarly, Henny Peacham cautioned that the consolation 'be not weake by reason of the foundations consisting only in Philosophy and humane wisedome which do many times rather increase sorrow then diminish it'.[21] In England, the final decades of the sixteenth century marked the beginning of an extended period in which sermons, treatises, and epistles offering spiritual comfort, commonly composed by divines and expounding scriptural *topoi*, issued from the presses in remarkable numbers. These took their place alongside vernacular translations of contemporary continental equivalents and

[17] Cardano 1576, fol. 1^r.
[18] Cardano 1576, fol. 1^v.
[19] See McClure 1986, pp. 444–8, and 1991, pp. 1–17; Pigman 1985, pp. 27–8; and Mennecke-Haustein 1989.
[20] More 1951, pp. 7–8.
[21] Peacham 1593, p. 101.

classical *consolationes*.[22] Such writing sometimes acquired confessional identity through circulation in different print communities. On the one side, the numerous works providing solace to afflicted consciences typically indicated doctrinal Calvinist allegiance in authorship and intended audience. On the other, to take a famous example, after circulating in manuscript form More's *Dialogue of Comfort* was first published under Mary in 1553, and reissued in Antwerp in 1573 by the recusant printer John Fowler.[23]

A final characteristic of some late humanist *consolationes* can be seen in Montaigne's *Essais*, where scepticism about the self-sufficiency of rational argument in alleviating destructive passions led to the recommendation of the purely rhetorical technique of 'diversion'. Deflecting the imagination of the sufferer elsewhere was incompatible with conventional Stoic consolation, as it did not uproot the problem at source (according to the 'argument from excess' all passions tended to become ungovernable: since all were products of the same kinds of false judgement, to permit the presence of one passion was potentially to admit them all). Diversion had therefore usually been excluded from the category of truly efficacious remedies by classical writers.[24] In his essay 'Of diversion', Montaigne explored this technique and made clear its opposition to philosophy, indeed to the ancient *consolatio* itself. 'I was once employed in comforting of a trulie-afflicted Ladie', he reported, and soon discovered his inability to make conventional methods perform their task. So, 'I attempted not to cure it by strong & livelie reasons' or by 'the severall fashions of comfort prescribed by Philosophie', but 'faire and softlie declining our discourses, and by degrees bending them unto subiects more neare; then a little more remote . . . I unperceavablie removed those dolefull humours from hir'. This was effective 'diversion'.[25] Later in the essay, having drawn the parallel with the medical diversion of humours,[26] Montaigne elaborated

[22] See, for example, Robert Linaker, *A comfortable treatise for the reliefe of such as are afflicted in conscience* (London, 1590; repr. 1601, 1610, 1625); Robert Southwell, *The triumphs over death* (London, 1595; repr. 1596, 1600); William Gilbert, *Architectonice consolationis* (London, 1640). For vernacular translations see Juan Pérez de Pineda, *An excelent comfort to all Christians, against all kinde of calamities*, trans. John Daniel (1576); Caspar Huberinus, *A riche storehouse*, trans. Thomas Godfrie (London, 1578); *Seneca the philosopher, his book of consolation to Marcia*, trans. Sir Ralph Freeman (London, 1635); Hugo Grotius, *The Mourner comforted*, trans. Clement Barksdale (London, 1652). For further examples see Gowland 2006, p. 10.

[23] More 1573.

[24] See Cicero 1927, IV.27.58–28.84, pp. 392–423, and Plutarch 1928, pp. 118–19 (103f). Cf. however, Cicero 1927, III.31.75–6, pp. 314–15.

[25] Montaigne 1603, III.4, pp. 499–500.

[26] Montaigne 1603, III.4, p. 500.

on the difficulty of attaining the philosophical ideal of control of the passions.[27] In his own case, he found it to be 'a shorter course to alter and divert, then to tame and vanquishe' his perturbations, and thereby 'I save my self amid the throng of other studies and ammusements, where it looseth my track, and so I slip away'. Instead of meeting the disturbance head-on, through diversion the soul was restored to health by a movement away from itself.[28]

Burton's concern with melancholy prompted him to formulate both utopian and consolatory discourses, and, whilst both were justifiable in terms of their contribution to the common good, they were also presented as part of his project to express his discontented vision of the world and alleviate the melancholic anxiety that accompanied it. In what follows, I shall explore this dynamic in the *Anatomy*, first addressing the late humanist political and moral-psychological context that shaped Burton's figuration of himself as an alienated scholar. As we shall see, this gave rise to an almost overwhelmingly pessimistic denunciation of the system of patronage on which humanism had always been compelled to depend. However, it also expressed the author's unswerving commitment to the ideal of intellectual autonomy as essential to the commonwealth, and as such manifested the enduring potential of humanism to provide vocabulary for political critique.

THE PHILOSOPHER AND THE COMMONWEALTH

As I recalled in the last chapter, some of the most significant developments in humanist ethics and politics in the later sixteenth century were rooted in a close re-engagement with Roman Stoicism, whose increased appeal in France and the Low Countries was bound up with the contemporary escalation of religious violence. The intellectual ambition of neo-Stoic writers such as Lipsius and Guillaume du Vair was evident in their extensive attempts at reconciling the moral philosophy of Seneca and Epictetus with Christian teaching, but this enterprise also brought their attention to the moral psychology underlying the central themes of humanist politics. In particular, the longstanding debate about the respective merits of the active and contemplative lives assumed a new urgency in view of the evidently widespread turmoil in political society. In the *Philosophie morale des Stoïques* (1594), du Vair presented Stoic

[27] Montaigne 1603, III.4, p. 502. [28] Montaigne 1603, III.4, p. 502.

sapientia – characterised as the control of the passions by the rationally guided will – as a source both of inner strength and of moral duty to assist the commonwealth in the midst of civil war.[29] Especially important, according to du Vair, were the political responsibilities of the philosopher, who having depended on his homeland for his physical existence and upbringing, was required to assist its passage towards health by performing his 'dutie to make his fellow citizens modest and obedient'.[30]

For others engaging with Hellenistic philosophy in this era, the pressure of bloody turmoil in the external world prompted a prising apart of the public and private ethical domains. This was what occurred in Lipsius's *De constantia* – a *consolatio* of sorts, being subtitled in Sir John Stradling's translation as *A comfortable conference, in common calamities* [that] *will serve for a singular consolation to all that are privately distressed, or afflicted, either in body or mind* – where Stoic moral psychology grounded a radical reinterpretation of the conventional humanistic relationship between the individual and the commonwealth.[31] Taking as his starting-point the Stoic tenet that the only true good is the soul's virtue, and the only true evil its vice, Lipsius portrayed himself in *De constantia* as being urged by his mentor Langius to disregard false external goods and evils, and to ignore opinion as the deceptive product of the senses.[32] Instead, Langius argued, he should cultivate in his soul the quality of constancy, the guarantor of a state of psychological liberty, and defined in the English translation of 1595 as '*a right and immoveable strength of the minde, neither lifted up, nor pressed downe with externall or casuall accidents*', in accordance with '*Right Reason*'.[33] Measuring mankind's natural cosmopolitanism against conventional political citizenship,[34] the bonds between the individual and the state were, according to Lipsius, 'but externall and accidentall', the product of 'custom', not nature.[35] His readers were therefore urged to perform civic duties and be 'good commonwealths-men' only insofar as this did not affect the fundamental duty to keep the soul free of vicious passions and cultivate rational self-mastery.[36]

[29] Du Vair 1598, pp. 6–7, 15–19, 22–3, 27, 29–34, 44–6, 49–50, 81, 115–16, 154–5, 166–8.
[30] Du Vair 1598, pp. 71–2, 167–8.
[31] On Lipsius's moral psychology see Levi 1964, pp. 67–73, and Tuck 1993b, pp. 45–64.
[32] Lipsius 1595, I.5, I.7, pp. 12, 15.
[33] Lipsius 1595, I.4, p. 9.
[34] Lipsius 1595, I.9, p. 20. Cf. Seneca 1932, IV.I, pp. 186–9.
[35] Lipsius 1595, I.II, pp. 24–7. See also ibid., p. 28.
[36] Lipsius 1595, I.II, pp. 27–8.

This was a call for psychological rather than physical withdrawal from political affairs,[37] but Lipsius was clear that philosophical *sapientia* was best attained and exercised in a version of the *vita contemplativa*. In Langius's encomium of 'the industrious care of gardens', philosophical withdrawal into their 'contayned' space of tranquillity was contrasted with the toilsome domain of 'cities and troublesome assemblies of people'.[38] Here the benefits of physical withdrawal from the domain of public life were stated so strongly that the godlike Langius appeared almost Epicurean, withdrawn 'from the cares and troubles of this world', free from passions, contemptuous of 'the great vanitie of humane affaires', untroubled by such issues as 'who possesse the sceptre of *Belgica*, or who be deprived of it', and striving only to subject his mind to 'RIGHT REASON and GOD' in order to 'subdue all humaine and earthly things to my MIND'.[39]

The ethical problems faced by the individual in an era of religious violence were discussed in similar terms by Montaigne and Pierre Charron, both of whom drew freely upon Hellenistic doctrines. In his essay 'Of Solitude', Montaigne criticised the *vita activa* as a cover for ambition and greed,[40] and recommended withdrawal from the crowd.[41] But the true goal was psychological: 'a man must severe himselfe from the popular conditions, that are in us . . . sequester and recover himselfe from himselfe'.[42] Montaigne here drew on Seneca, but was also indebted to the Epicurean goal of self-sufficiency within the limits of natural necessity, and constituted by the enjoyment of 'true' pleasures.[43] The Platonic intellectualism of the *vita contemplativa* was potentially hazardous, since 'occupation of bookes, is as painefull as any other, and as great an enemie unto health, which ought principally to be considered'.[44] Instead, the route to tranquillity of body and soul (ἀτăραξία) was self-mastery in withdrawal.[45]

For Montaigne, the degradation of civil life necessitated a separation of the private and public domains, permitting the coexistence of an internal liberty of soul, grounded in wisdom and nature, with an outward

37 Lipsius 1595, I.22, p. 56.
38 Lipsius 1595, II.2–3, pp. 61–7.
39 Lipsius 1595, II.3, p. 66.
40 Montaigne 1603, I.38, pp. 118–19.
41 Montaigne 1603, I.38, p. 119.
42 Montaigne 1603, I.38, p. 119.
43 Montaigne 1603, I.38, pp. 123–4.
44 Montaigne 1603, I.38, p. 122.
45 Montaigne 1603, I.38, pp. 123–4. See Screech 1983, pp. 67–70, 92–4, and Starobinski 1985, pp. 1–30.

conformity to political authority and social norms grounded in custom.[46] As with Lipsius, the *vita contemplativa* was a wholly psychological state of detachment from political affairs. The performance of public duties was part of the happy and well-regulated life,[47] but was constituted as a self-consciously superficial engagement with the world,[48] a 'loan' of the external self to the commonwealth.[49] Similarly, for Charron in *De la sagesse* (1601), wisdom consisted of '[r]emaining in the world, without being of the world',[50] participating in the 'publike and common' domain on the level of 'apparent things', but retaining an inner freedom of judgement and will – for 'what hath it to doe with our inside, our thoughts, and judgements?'[51] Charron's wise man would 'play one part before the world, and another in his minde', conforming 'for publike reverence' in accordance with law and custom, but 'inwardly' judging 'of the truth as it is, according to the universall reason', and retaining a 'deferring of a settled resolution' (Sceptical ἐ ποχῆ) in the face of the inevitable proliferation of inconstant 'opinion'.[52] We must, he wrote, 'lend ourselves to others', and 'give our selves to none but to our selves', 'take businesse upon us, but not incorporate them into us'.[53]

These elegant reformulations of the traditional problem thereby employed Hellenistic moral psychology to reconcile the imperatives of activity and contemplation. Charron's wise man 'must be officious and charitable' and 'contribute to publike society',[54] since 'to practise the counsel of the Epicures (Hide thy self)' in a solitary retirement would be simultaneously 'to flie a good life' and to invite a new set of 'inward and spirituall affaires and difficulties'.[55] On the other hand, because our 'soveraigne good' was 'tranquillitie of the spirit', we were duty bound to insulate our inner selves against 'the generall corruption of the world'.[56] The godlike sage would perform only duties that were 'just and necessary', without the passionate 'ardencie' which would corrupt his soul.[57] Just as '[t]he Maior of *Bourdeaux*, and *Michell* Lord of *Montaigne*,

46 Montaigne 1603, I.22, III.10, pp. 46–55, 600–12.
47 Montaigne 1603, III.10, p. 602.
48 Montaigne 1603, III.10, p. 601.
49 Montaigne 1603, III.10, p. 604.
50 Charron 1620, II.1, p. 239.
51 Charron 1620, II.2, p. 246.
52 Charron 1620, II.2, pp. 246, 249–50.
53 Charron 1620, II.2, p. 246.
54 Charron 1620, II.2, p. 264.
55 Charron 1620, I.59, pp. 214, 215.
56 Charron 1620, II.1, II.2, II.12, pp. 236, 264, 365.
57 Charron 1620, II.2, p. 264.

have ever been two, by an evident separation',[58] Charron's wise man played 'two parts, two persons; the one strange and apparant, the other proper and essential', remembering he had to 'keepe and carrie himself apart' from the world.[59] Also emerging here was a new understanding of 'civil' life, conceived no longer in terms of service to the commonwealth, but in terms of membership of literary-philosophical communities providing conversation and friendship.[60] Stefano Guazzo portrayed himself as oppressed by 'great melancholie', but the solution was neither contemplative solitude nor public participation in courtly life; rather, it was the 'companie' and 'conversation of other men' who cultivated the inner qualities of constancy and beneficence.[61] The domain in which virtue and happiness were attainable was no longer the commonwealth, stained with corruption and bloodshed, but the company of like-minded individuals.

***

Although these works were influential in learned circles, and were translated into English in the later decades of the sixteenth century and early decades of the seventeenth,[62] their restructuring of the traditional humanist conception of the relationship between the philosopher and the commonwealth did not meet an entirely positive reception in Jacobean England. The writings of Joseph Hall, famously described by Thomas Fuller as 'our English Seneca' but also author of seven volumes of scriptural *Contemplations*, show that absorption of Stoic moral philosophy in this period could sit alongside conventional humanist political psychology as well as Reformed orthodoxy.[63] In *Heaven on Earth* (1606), Hall advocated an ethic of inner self-mastery, identifying 'steadiness of the minde' and spiritual fortitude as the path to tranquillity in a manner that was deeply and self-consciously indebted to the Stoic ideal of *sapientia* but still carefully Christianised.[64] In the *Characters of Virtues and Vices* (1608), this ethic was tied to the author's preference for the *vita*

[58] Montaigne 1603, III.10, p. 605.
[59] Charron 1620, II.2, pp. 264–5.
[60] See Miller 2000, pp. 11, 68–73, 146–9, 158–9.
[61] Guazzo 1581, pp. 2–4.
[62] Guazzo's *La civil conversazione*, trans. George Pettie (1581); Lipsius's *De constantia*, trans. Sir John Stradling (1594); Du Vair's *Philosophie morale du stoïques*, trans. Thomas James (1598); Montaigne's *Essais*, trans. John Florio (1603); Charron's *De la sagesse*, trans. Samson Lennard (1606).
[63] Fuller 1662, p. 130; Hall 1628, pp. 829ff.
[64] Hall 1628, pp. 73–4, 93–8.

contemplativa, where the wise man was depicted as being fully aware of 'the falsenesse of the world', seeking 'quietnesse in secrecie', hiding himself 'in retirednesse', and keeping 'his tongue in himselfe'.[65] The '*Happy man*' similarly 'knowes the world, and cares not for it', and 'lives quietly at home, out of the noise of the world.'[66]

Hall presented extensive arguments in favour of contemplation in the *Epistles* of 1608.[67] In a letter to Sir Edmund Bacon, he described the 'happiness, not to be a witnesse to the mischiefe of the times', in terms that unified the Christian monastic and classical humanist values of retreat. The 'philosophicall Cell' was not only a place for the 'honest and manly pleasure' of knowledge, but 'a safe shelter from tumults, from vices, from discontentments', untroubled by such disturbing contemporary political speculations as '[w]hether the Spaniard gaine or save by his peace', or '[w]ho is envied, and who pitied at Court'. All who 'live publike' and 'in the open world' had to be pitied for suffering 'such cares' and 'abundance of vexations'.[68] Writing to Matthew Milward 'of the pleasure of study and contemplation', Hall adumbrated his pessimistic vision of worldly living with the classical argument that contemplation permits man to become as godlike as possible. Since the *vita contemplativa* was entirely devoted to the exercise of 'that honourable and divine part' of us, the mind, it was 'fittest to bee imployed of those which would reach to the highest perfection'.[69]

As with Lipsius, Hall's neo-Stoicism was directed against the false valuation of an external world stained by deception, corruption, and bloodshed. But Hall was sceptical of the compatibility of pure Stoicism and Christianity, presenting classical precepts as useful but defective 'natural wisdome' and insufficient for spiritual 'tranquillitie'.[70] His vision of the good life and emphasis on the benefits of contemplation drew upon classical *sapientia*, but originated in Christian *contemptus mundi* and spiritual valuation of humility. What most attracted the Calvinist Hall to the contemplative life was not the active exercise of our reasoning capacities or sage-like indifference to external 'goods' or 'evils', but the thorough devaluation of human existence in this world. It was necessary 'to distinguish wisely, betwixt a Stoicall dulnesse, and a Christian

65 Hall 1628, p. 173.
66 Hall 1628, pp. 181–2.
67 See Peltonen 1995, pp. 131–2.
68 Hall 1628, II.2, pp. 296–7.
69 Hall 1628, IV.3, p. 342.
70 Hall 1628, pp. 74–5.

contempt' in favour of the latter,[71] and the ultimate destination of the inner journey enabled by withdrawal was not the purification and possession of the self but attendance to the voice of God and submission to his judgement.[72] 'Not *Athens* must teach this lesson', he wrote in an axiomatic allusion to Tertullian, 'but *Jerusalem*'.[73]

Hall was also opposed to Lipsius's ethical separation of internal and external domains.[74] In advocating retirement he emphasised that 'it is hard to see' the evils of the world 'and be guiltlesse'.[75] But his fundamental objection to the kind of moral psychological dualism espoused by Lipsius, Montaigne, and Charron stemmed from the teaching based on Matthew 7:16 ('Ye shall know them by their fruits'), according to which a mismatch between the inner and outer man was sinful hypocrisy.[76] From this perspective, Lipsian moral *constantia* indicated religious *inconstantia*, a perverse condition of spiritual self-alienation. This was made clear in Hall's depiction in the *Characters* of the 'Unconstant' as one who swayed from one confessional identity to another (as did Lipsius himself), who 'of late . . . is leapt from *Rome* to *Munster* . . . what he will be next, yet he knoweth not'. The inner fortitude, self-mastery, and freedom of the *De constantia* were in fact their opposites: 'he is servile in imitation, waxey to perswasions, wittie to wrong himselfe, a guest in his owne house, an Ape of others, and in a word, any thing rather than himselfe'.[77]

Although Hall made it clear that the *vita activa* fulfilled earthly goals that were spiritually inferior to their contemplative Christian counterparts, as appropriate for a dispenser of epistolary advice to the nobility and recipient of King James's patronage he was careful to preserve a space for the valuation of 'free' service to the commonwealth, in war and peace, as the badge of the 'truly noble' and the route to 'sincere glory'.[78] He also made his own contribution to political theory in the second book of *Salomons Divine Arts* (1609), which laid out a rigorously Christianised version of the humanist model of princely government.[79] In the final analysis, his position was not dissimilar to that of other English humanists who had engaged with Stoic practical ethics in the later sixteenth

71 Hall 1628, I.2, pp. 276–7. Cf. Lipsius 1595, I.17, pp. 41–3.
72 Hall 1628, pp. 175–6.
73 Hall 1628, p. 73, alluding to Tertullian, *De praescriptione haereticorum* VII.
74 See McCrea 1997, pp. 175–84.
75 Hall 1628, II.2, p. 296.
76 See Erasmus 1970, p. 119.
77 Hall 1628, p. 191. Cf. Cicero 1933, I.2, pp. 6–7.
78 Hall 1628, pp. 179–80.
79 Hall 1609, pp. 107–42.

century. Roger Baynes had employed Stoic doctrine in *The Praise of Solitarinesse* (1577), which concluded that despite the benefits of contemplation the philosopher should always be prepared to perform his natural duty and swap *otium* for *negotium*.[80] In *Vertues Common-wealth* (1603), Henry Crosse expounded Stoic arguments against false estimations of 'riches, parentage, office, place, dignity', and criticised hypocrites who 'drawe the curtaine of pollicie in the portraiture of pietie'. Crosse presented an ethic of political activism in his definition of the 'just man' as one who 'neglecteth his owne for the good of the Common-wealth', and his description of fortitude as being prepared 'to dye honourably like a Martyr and a souldier of Christ' rather than living 'to see the ruine and desolation' of one's 'whole Countrey'.[81] He also drew his readers' attention to the distinction between the 'morrall wise man' and the 'good Christian', denigrating classical ethics (and peculiarly inverting Lipsius) as being designed only 'to fashion the outward man to civill obedience, making that the end which are but motives to the end'.[82]

As we have seen, however, we can discern an altogether less contented strain of Jacobean humanism that engaged with continental neo-Stoic ethics, and also their Tacitist political adjunct. In the poetry of the Spenserians, the critique of courtly vice, the portrayal of a breakdown of the appropriate lines of communication between ruler and subjects represented by the ideal of a king receptive to 'plain' counsel, and the aggressive assertion of the right to satirical freedom of speech that followed from these, all implied a conception of the healthy common-wealth that was moralised in traditional terms. It was also frequently bound up with bitterness at being excluded from the patronage networks that were the lifeblood of the *vita activa*, and in this respect it is significant that several neo-Stoic writers had been deprived of a patron by the death of Prince Henry. Whilst the praise of the benefits of withdrawal into privacy may often have been accompanied by a jaded view of contemporary politics, it was a nevertheless a gesture enacted publicly and in print, and so calculated to achieve a particular effect.[83] In the sustained vituperation of *Staffords Niobe: or his age of teares* (1611), Anthony Stafford assumed an authorial position that amalgamated Senecan retirement with contemplative privacy, Tacitist denunciation of courtly

80 Baynes 1577, p. 86. See Peltonen 1995, pp. 27–31.
81 Crosse 1603, sigs. B3r, B4v, D1r, H1v. See Baldwin 2001, pp. 354–5.
82 Crosse 1603, sigs. Bv–B1r.
83 See Shiflett 1998, pp. 2–5.

life, and general moral-spiritual disgust, and cited his alienation from the vicious society of 'these accursed times' as evidence of his virtuous worthiness for patronage, appealing as an unknown stranger to the Earl of Salisbury.[84] Although William Browne and George Wither expressed contempt for the corrupt slavishness bred by the court, and cultivated a quasi-autonomous print community (*Abuses stript, and whipt* was dedicated to 'him-self, *G. W.*'),[85] this could itself be seen as a strategy of virtuous self-presentation that invited the patronage on which they continued to depend.

For these writers, the denunciation of contemporary politics was itself a form of political action that could serve personal and ideological ends.[86] Wither was careful to justify his heated satirical prose in classical humanist fashion as an instrument to aid the commonwealth through the punishment of vice, and although his argument for satirical freedom of speech was self-protective, there is no reason to doubt his sincerity.[87] In this respect, he was in agreement with the mainstream Jacobean humanist opinion that the health of the body politic depended on the active participation of its virtuous members.

MELANCHOLY AND UTOPIA

As we saw in the last chapter, as 'Democritus Junior' Burton delivered a stinging critique of the decayed and unhealthy condition of the English body politic. It is worth quoting at length his call for general reform, as it shows his penchant for employing seriocomic irony as a strategy to avoid attracting hostile attention without compromising his argument. 'We have good Lawes, I deny not, to rectify such enormities, and so in all other Countries', he began, 'but it seemes not alwaies to good purpose', so,

> We had need of some generall visiter in our age, that should reforme what is amis; a just army of *Rosie* Crosse men, for they will amend all matters, (they say) Religion, Policy, manners, with arts, sciences, &c. Another *Attila*, *Tamberlane*, *Hercules*, to strive with *Achelous*, *Augeæ stabulum purgare*, to subdue tyrants, as he did *Diomedes* and *Busiris*: to expell theeves as he did *Cacus* and *Lacinius*; to vindicate poor captives, as he did *Hesione*: to passe the Torrid Zone, the deserts

[84] Stafford 1611, sigs. ¶3^{r}–¶4^{v}, 'To the Reader' (unpaginated), pp. 4–5, 19–24, 104–8, 111–2, 196–7. See Peltonen 1995, pp. 128–31.
[85] Wither 1613, sigs. A4^{r}–A8^{r}.
[86] Wither 1614, sigs. B8^{v}–C1^{v}.
[87] Wither 1614, sigs. C2^{v}, D7^{r}, E1^{r}, E7^{v}, F3^{r}, F4^{v}.

of *Lybia*, and purge the World of monsters and *Centaures*: Or another Theban *Crates* to reforme our manners . . . *As* Hercules *purged the World of Monsters, & subdued them, so did he fight against Envy, lust, anger, avarice, &c. and all those ferall vices & monsters of the mind.* It were to be wished we had some such visitor, or if wishing would serve, one had such a ring or rings, as *Timolaus* desired in *Lucian*, by vertue of which he should bee as strong as 10000 men, or an army of Gyants, goe invisible, open gates & castle doores . . . alter affections, cure all manner of diseases, that he might range over the world, & reforme all distressed states & persons, as he would himselfe . . . Cure us of our Epidemicall diseases, *Scorbutum, Plica, morbus Neapolitanus, &c.* End all our idle controversies, cut off our tumultuous desires, indordinate lusts, roote out Atheism, impiety, heresy, schisme and superstition, which now so crucifie the World. (1.84.21–85.15)

On one level this was serious; it reiterated the message of the contemporary world's sinful passions and disorders that had been delivered throughout the preface. On another, it was entertainingly flippant, in its ironic call for Rosicrucian reformers – the parenthetical 'they say', as usual with Burton, indicated scepticism – and pagan mythological aid for 'distressed states & persons' that were, or ought to have been, Christian.[88]

Here, facetiousness also expressed a deeper despair at the futility of the reform required, thereby manifesting the humanist frustration with politics that lay at the heart of 'Democritus Junior to the Reader'. This was first made clear when Burton proceeded to associate resignation at the impossibility of reform with utopianism. On the one hand, he admitted that he had been expressing 'vaine absurd, and ridiculous wishes not to be hoped: all must be as it is' – in 1628 interpolating a reference to Boccalini's *Ragguagli* – 'there is no remedy, it may not be redressed'.[89] On the other, this deadlock prompted him to free himself from the constraints of real political activity, and indulge in the construction of a fanciful utopia. 'Because therefore' reform was 'impossible', he wrote, 'let them be rude, stupid', and 'wallow as so many swine in their own dung', 'I will yet to satisfie & please my selfe, make an *Utopia* of mine owne, a new *Atlantis*,[90] a poeticall commonwealth of mine owne, in which I will freely domineere, build Citties, make Lawes, Statutes, as I list my selfe. And why may I not?' (1.85.28–38).

What is crucial for understanding the role of the utopian episode in the argument of 'Democritus Junior to the Reader' is that in the process of its

88 The reference to Rosicrucian reform was added in Burton 1628, p. 58.

89 Burton 1628, p. 59; or 1.85.22–5.

90 The reference to the *New Atlantis* was new in Burton 1628, p. 59, possibly influencing the proposal for 'Colledges' in Burton 1628, p. 60; or 1.87.24–31.

composition Burton interweaved amongst its solidly Christian humanist ideological features two personal and pessimistic themes tailored towards his contemporary English environment. The first of these concerned the futility of radical political reform, which not only prompted the construction of this imaginary commonwealth, but was also built into its nature. Perhaps the most striking feature of Burton's utopia is, paradoxically enough, its realism – following the down-to-earth Platonic reforms of the *Laws* rather than the idealism of the *Republic* – and manifested in self-consciously pragmatic compromises made on account of the corruption of the world.

The first sign that this '*Utopia* of mine owne' was tainted by worldly imperfection was that its inhabitants were far from being homogeneously virtuous – hence there were 'prisons for offenders' in every city (1.87.5–8) – or even sane – hence the presence of hospitals for 'madmen' (1.87.12–13). Even more telling was the manner in which he dealt with '[b]rokers, takers of pawnes' and 'biting usurers', which admittedly ought to have been outlawed, but were 'necessarily' tolerated because 'wee converse here with men, not with Gods ... it must be winked at by Politicians' (1.95.9–16). Such pragmatic political 'winking', here indicating the conscious repression of a desire for radical reform that would inevitably be frustrated by a corrupt environment, resurfaced in Burton's seeming dismissal of '*Utopian* parity' as 'a kinde of government, to be wished for, rather then effected'.[91] Not only did this reiterate the final, despairing sentiment of More's *Utopia*,[92] and lament that his predecessor was advocating a radical structural measure – i.e., '*Platoes* community in many things' – that was 'impious, absurd and ridiculous'; from the third edition onwards it prepared the way for a mockery of the futility of all utopian enterprises, as he added the plans of Johann Valentin Andreae's '*Respub. Christianopolitana*', 'that new *Atlantis*' of Francis Bacon, and (after 1638) '*Campanella's* city of the Sun' to the list of 'witty fictions, but meere *Chimera's*' that had no hope of becoming reality.[93]

This distinctly un-utopian acceptance of the world 'as it is' became more pronounced in the second edition, where it is indicative of a deepened pessimism on the part of the author about the possibility of reform. As we have seen, it was in the 1624 copy that he felt the need to

[91] Cf. the rejection of 'paritie' in Forset 1606, p. 45.

[92] More 1518, p. 162: 'confiteor permulta esse in Utopiensium republica, quæ in nostris civitatibus optarim verius, quàm sperarim'. See the allusions at 1.85.35–6; 1.86.20; 1.89.16; and 1.24.34.

[93] Burton 1628, p. 61, or 1.89.17–18; and Burton 1638, p. 63, or 1.89.17.

create republican-style censors to monitor others in authority who were predicted to be corrupt and self-interested. It was also here that he expressed disgust at the quality of the raw human material out of which he was attempting to fashion his commonwealth.

If it were possible I would have such Priests as should imitate *Christ*, charitable Lawyers should love their neighbours as themselves, temperate and modest Physitians, Politicians contemne the world, Philosophers should knowe themselves, Noblemen live honestly, Tradesmen leave lying and cosening, Magistrates corruption &c. but this is unpossible, I must get such as I may.[94]

Burton's utopia, compromised by the corrupt environment in which it was imagined, represented not a hopeful incarnation of More's *eu*-topia – it was never unambiguously labelled *optimus status reipublicae* – but rather the melancholic despair that ensued from recognising the vanity of *ou*-topia. Challenging the reforming optimism that characterised the Christian humanistic movement to which he was so deeply indebted, it was a programme constantly struggling against, but never radically uprooting, transforming, or overcoming the vicious sinfulness of its inhabitants.[95] Here was a world-weariness tending towards Seneca's sentiment in the *De otio* (and also present in More's work) that the futility of reform left withdrawal as the only available option: 'if that state which we dream of can nowhere be found, leisure begins to be a necessity for all of us, because the one thing that might have been preferred to leisure nowhere exists'.[96]

The second pessimistic theme that Burton worked into his utopia was also presented as a cause of the lamentable state of affairs in the real world, namely the failure of the state to bestow roles of political influence upon its philosophically learned inhabitants. Again, this developed a theme found in the *De otio* (Burton wrote in private leisure [I.7.3–5]), where the moral corruption of the *res publica* to such an extent that reform was impossible, or in such a way that the wise man was not accorded appropriate power or influence, was used to justify the withdrawal into privacy to cultivate knowledge and virtue.[97] Burton's dissatisfaction with the iniquities of the existing system of ecclesiastical and political patronage in England was suggested in the first place by the utopian arrangements for the distribution and administration of offices

94 Burton 1624, p. 52; or I.91.2–7.
95 Cf. More 1989, p. 110.
96 Seneca 1928–32, VIII.4, vol. II, pp. 200–1. See Parrish 1997.
97 Seneca 1928–32, III.2, vol. II, pp. 186–7.

and honours. He disapproved of the hypocritical gifts bestowed on commonwealths by private patrons, 'gowty benefactors' who 'by fraud and rapine... have extorted all their lives' (1.87.14–18). He stated that he would stamp out corruption in the administration of church livings, and also that 'those Rectors of Benefices [are] to be chosen out of the Universities, examined and approved as the *literati* in China' (1.90.30–91.1). Again, pagan China (like More's Utopia) held a significant advantage over its Christian European counterparts, the nature of which was clarified with the provision that anyone who 'invents any thing for publike good in any Art or Science, writes a Treatise, or performes any noble exploit, at home or abroad, shall be accordingly enriched, honoured, and preferred' (1.91.21–3). In an attached note referring to the observations of Matteo Ricci, Burton recorded that China had become a quasi-Platonic state in which moral virtue and knowledge were the sole criteria that qualified for political office (1.91.p; cf. 1.66.z, 2.139.23–8 [2.3.2.1]). As we have seen, the elective magistracy of this utopia imitated Chinese practices, which attracted him because they rewarded 'learning' as well as 'manners'. In fact, he insisted that in his system 'first Schollers' would 'take place, then Souldiers'.[98]

This aspect of Burton's utopia reinforced his opposition to the strain of humanistic political writing that associated greatness with military strength, and that it was constructed in opposition to the author's perception of the prevailing circumstances in his own environment was made clear elsewhere. Ending his denunciation of the false valuation of martial prowess, Burton lamented how bloodthirstiness was 'recompenced with turgent titles', so that '[o]ne is crowned for that which another is tormented' (1.48.1–2). This led him directly to the enslavement of virtuous philosophers to the favour of a degenerate aristocracy, and it was again through More's *Utopia* that he communicated his vitriol. 'How would our *Democritus* have bin affected', he asked,

> to see a wicked caitiffe, or *foole, a very idiot, a funge, a golden asse, a monster of men, to have many good men, wise men, learned men to attend upon him with all submission, as an appendix to his riches for that respect alone, because he hath more wealth and mony, and to honour him with divine titles, and bumbast Epithets,* to smother him with fumes and eulogies,[99] whom they know to be a dizard, a foole, a covetous wretch, a beast, &c. because he is rich. (1.48.15–21)

[98] See Burton 1628, p. 63; or 1.92.1–4.

[99] The words 'to smother him with fumes and eulogies' were added to Burton 1624, p. 27.

ON MISERY AND CONSOLATION

Burton developed the themes of the marginalisation of the learned and of vicious aristocratic ignorance in the famous 'Digression on the Misery of Schollers', and also in the 'Consolatory Digression'. The former, placed towards the end of the first Partition, was as its title indicated formally a lamentation 'De miseria', but it was also where he resumed the satirical vituperation and political criticism of 'Democritus Junior to the Reader'. The latter constituted his reworking of the classical genre of the *consolatio*, and whilst it was clearly designed to serve several purposes – by no means the least of which was to provide the *Anatomy*'s readership with a host of classical and Christian arguments to alleviate melancholy in accordance with the sixth, passionate 'non-natural' therapeutic category (2.125.5–22 [2.3.1.1]) – it also provided the author with the opportunity to reflect on the nature of such arguments, and their utility in relation to his own position as a self-consciously melancholic scholar. Equally importantly, both digressions shared the practical Christian-Stoic moral purpose delivered in the preface, namely the cultivation of self-mastery and psychological rectitude. In the first case, this was articulated through contemptuous satirical laughter that enforced distance from the corrupt and sinful world; in the second, it was manifested by the application of philosophical or spiritual argument to uproot despair from the soul as the product of the erroneous valuation of worldly *fortuna*.

What is striking about Burton's *consolatio* in comparison with many of its generic predecessors is its incorporation of social and political themes raised elsewhere in the work, in such an openly satirical manner and at such length, that substantial parts of it read as a discourse intended less to provide comfort than to give the author the opportunity to vent his personal discontent. In fact, the 'Digression of the Misery of Schollers' and the 'Consolatory Digression' were both preoccupied with the corrupt aristocracy. Burton had first discussed this problem in the medical context of the aetiological role of idleness in melancholy. In a passage that is a composite of additions made to the second and third editions, he took the opportunity to turn this pathological account of idleness into an attack on the English nobility. Idle persons, he wrote, are 'never well in body and minde', and so are especially susceptible to melancholy, and this was 'the true cause that so many great men, ladies and Gentlewomen, labour of this disease . . . for idlenesse is an appendix to nobility . . . to worke, I say, they may not abide'.[100] The same went for the gentry, of which idleness was 'the badge', and who were allegedly excessively fond of gaming and immoderate drinking (1.222.24–8 [1.2.2.2]; 238.23 [1.2.2.6]; 289.8–292.9 [1.2.3.13]). Later in the 'Consolatory Digression', he mocked the vicious stupidity of those who 'brag of Gentility ... as if they were demi-gods', and proceeded to vituperate against an imaginary 'Nobleman', as 'an *Atheist, an oppressor, an Epicure, a gull, a disard, an illiterate idiot, an outside, a gloworme, a proude foole, an arrant asse* ... a slave to his lust and belly ... Now goe and bragge of thy gentility' (2.136.27–9, 138.30–139.15 [2.3.2.1]).

The higher social orders were thus unsuitable to be patrons of learning. This claim was elaborated in the 'Digression on the Misery of Schollers', where the 'hazards and inconveniences' of a life of learning, in particular the melancholy that was likely to accompany it, were shown to be worsened by the treatment scholars received from those who ought to have supported them. '[T]hese griping Patrons', he wrote, were 'so farre now adaies, from respecting the *Muses*, and giving that honour to Schollers, or reward which they deserve, & are allowed by those indulgent priviledges of many noble Princes', that anyone fortunate enough to 'wade through' all the troubles of a university career 'shall in the end be rejected, contemned ... exposed to want, poverty, and beggary' (1.306.29–307.11, 314.23–5 [1.2.3.15]). Patrons, generally 'rotten at core', were particularly greedy and ignorant (1.316.26). Both were common complaints (as was the self-protective admission that some were 'well deserving' [1.321.26–33]),[101] but from a humanist standpoint ignorance had more serious implications. Noble patrons who were 'barbarous, idiots, dull, illiterate, and proud' were 'unfit to doe their country service, to performe or undertake an action or imployment, which may tend to the good of a Commonwealth, except it be to fight, or doe country Justice, with common sense, which every Yeoman can likewise doe' (1.317.16–28). Likewise the gentry, whose 'sole discourse is dogs, hawkes, horses, and what newes?' (1.321.15–16).

Aristocratic contempt of learning was thereby implicated in the contemporary decline of the *vita activa*. 'How much better is it', he asked in the 'Consolatory Digression', 'to bee borne of meane parentage, and to excel in worth, to be morally noble, which is preferred before that naturall nobility, by Divines, Philosophers, and Politicians, to be learned, honest ... fit for any manner of imployment, in Country and

[100] Burton 1628, p. 78, and Burton 1632, p. 84; or 1.240.24.32 (1.2.2.6).
[101] See Lytle 1981 pp. 74–5, 102–3.

Commonwealth ... then to be *Degeneres Neoptolemi*, as many brave Nobles are, only wise, because rich, otherwise idiots, illiterate, unfit for any manner of service?' (2.141.10–16 [2.3.2.1]; cf. 1.104.5–105.1). This was also a symptom of a broader disintegration of the relationship between politics and philosophy, reflected in the marginalisation of scholarship. 'In former times', Burton recalled, 'Kings, Princes, and Emperours' such as '*Julius Cæsar ... Antoninus, Adrian, Nero, Severus, Julian, &c.*' were 'the only Schollers, excellent in all faculties ... *Plato's* kings all.' But 'those heroicall times are past; the *Muses* are now banished in this bastard age, *ad sordida tuguriola*, to meaner persons and confined alone almost to *Universities*'. Here was melancholic nostalgia for an idealised antiquity when 'Schollers were highly beloved, honoured, esteemed', rewarded as 'Princes companions' and 'admitted to their tables' (1.318.19–319.9 [1.2.3.15]), that also restated the humanist case for the political worth of the scholar-philosopher.

Burton next wandered into the dangerous territory of royal patronage. 'How beloved of old, and how much respected was *Plato* to *Dionysius*?', he asked. 'How deare to *Alexander* was *Aristotle*, *Demeratus* to *Philip* ... *Seneca* to *Nero*? *Simonides* to *Hieron*? how honoured? ... those daies are gone' (1.320.16–23). Having implied a decline in princely standards, he moved to insulate himself against the charge of *lèse-majesté* with a quotation from Juvenal that established the monarch as the last remaining incarnation of a classical ideal. '*Et spes, & ratio studiorum in Cæsare tantùm*', he wrote in typically erudite fashion,

> as he said of old, we may truely say now, he is our *Amulet*, our Sunne, our sole comfort and refuge, our *Ptolomy*, our common *Mæcenas, Jacobus munificus, Jacobus pacificus, mysta Musarum, Rex Platonicus: Grande decus, columenque nostrum:* A famous Scholler himselfe, and the sole Patron, Pillar, and sustainer of Learning. (1.320.24–9)

After James's death Burton added a coda for his successor in the third edition, which continued to provide security, albeit in a noticeably flat tone. 'But hee is now gone, the Sunne of ours set, and yet no night followes ... We have such an other in his roome ... and long may he raigne & flourish amongst us.'[102]

Burton was understandably reluctant to criticise the administration of royal preferment, but he left no doubt about his opinion of the disasters wrought by aristocratic patrons. They were to blame not only for the decline of humanist activism in politics but also for a general decay

102 Burton 1628, pp. 129–30; or 1.320.32–321.3 (1.2.3.15).

of learning. Now, the scholar's prospects of preferment were as distant after 'twentie yeares' of study as they were 'at the first day of his coming to the *University*' (1.308.13–14), and as a result the *studia humanitatis* such as 'History, Philosophy, Philology' – in contrast with 'those three commodious professions of Law, Physicke, and Divinity' – were deemed superfluous and 'fitting only table talke' (1.311.16–22). This meant impoverishment, and, of the many injuries listed in the 'Digression', it was the consequent slavishness of the learned population that prompted Burton's most angry response. In contrast to his classical counterparts, who 'needed not to beg so basely' or 'crouch to a rich chuffe for a meales meat', the scholar was now unfree, compelled to go 'serving-man like' to find 'a new master' (1.308.21; 319.13–15), and to compromise his virtue with flattery. 'To say truth,' he intoned bitterly, philosophers had lost their freedom; ''tis the common fortune of most Schollers, to be servile and poore', and 'in those dedicatory Epistles, for hope of gaine, to lye, flatter, and with hyperbolicall elogiums and commendations, to magnifie and extol an illiterate unworthy idiot' (1.309.7–9, 27–9). The lament was summed up in a laconic marginal note, '*Servile nomen Scholaris jam*' (1.319.r). Small wonder that Burton considered that 'the conceipt alone' of the hardships afflicting scholars 'were enough to make them all melancholy' (1.307.20).

This digression ended on a sour note with a tirade, composed in Latin for a learned audience, against the intellectual and moral decay engendered in the university community by its slavish dependence on corrupt patronage. The greed and venality that permeated the academy had led to a degeneration of the qualities of those admitted to degrees: 'Id solum in votis habent annui plerumque magistratus, ut ab incipientum numero pecunias emungant, nec multùm interest qui sint, literatores an literati, modò pingues, nitidi, ad aspectum speciosi, & quòd verbo dicam, pecuniosi sint' (1.325.12). As a consequence, a mass of 'viles scurræ . . . Idiotæ . . . larvæ pastorum, circumforanei, vagi, bardi, fungi, crassi, asini, merum pecus, in sacrosanctos Theologiæ aditus, illotis pedibus irrumpant', with dire consequences for the English Church and commonwealth – 'hi sunt qui pulpita complent, in ædes nobilium irrepunt, & quum reliquis vitæ destituantur subsidiis, ob corporis & animi egestatem, aliarum in Repub' (1.325.16–25). Although he was careful to insert his usual self-protective qualification, excepting bishops and the many good and learned men belonging to 'Ecclesia Anglicana' and issuing 'à florentissimis Academiis' (1.325.27–32; 326.18), he was adamant that the love of profit had turned a formerly learned clergy into ambitious parasites who would do anything for public honour, office, or favour from their noble patrons (1.326.4–27). In this 'squalor Academicus', he added in the second edition, only a madman would have thought that promotion was made on the basis of erudition and virtue, 'quod olim revera fuit, hodiè promittitur'.[103] The result was not just that scholars and divines had been sucked into a quagmire of courtly flattery (1.327.4), but that the university had come to embody the vicious inversion of its ideal, now being a seminary of impiety, wickedness, and disorder in the state. 'Quot tot Respub. alis afficiatur, à nobis seminarium, ultrò malum hoc accersimus, & quâvis contumeliâ, quâvis interìm miseriâ digni' (1.324.32–4). Such was the unabated pessimism of this invective that one wonders quite what Laud, Chancellor of Oxford after 1630, and the driving force behind the new statutes of 1636 designed to turn the university into the perfect model for the commonwealth, would have made of this when it appeared unchanged in the editions of 1632 and 1638.

The case against patrons in the 'Digression of the Misery of Schollers' thus implicated the English aristocracy in the melancholic pathology of the national body politic. But whilst this was a strong restatement of traditional humanist ideals for an era in which they seemed to be under threat, Burton made no attempt to conceal the fact that his own material interests were at stake. He constantly emphasised the personal nature of his antagonism, underlining his own exclusion from the patronage system as a symptom of his unwillingness to give up his independence and trade virtue for preferment. 'For my part', he confessed in the midst of the digression, 'if it be not as I would, or as it should, I doe ascribe the cause . . . to mine owne infelicity' rather than to the 'naughtinesse' of patrons (1.314.27–30). This was openly disingenuous. He continued by recalling that 'I have beene baffled in my time by some of them, & have as just cause to complaine as another', and the attached marginal note made clear that he considered that the true nature of his 'infelicity' was to be virtuous: 'I had no money, I wanted impudence, I could not scramble, temporize, dissemble: *non pranderet olus, &c.*'. In the second edition, he added that '*vis dicam, ad palpandum & adulandum penitus insulsus, recudi non possum, jam senior ut sim talis, & fingi nolo, utcunque male cedat in rem meam & obscurus inde delitescam*'.[104] A passage new to the fourth edition explained that his 'negligence' stemmed from a combination of

[103] Burton 1624, p. 126; or 1.326.30–2 (1.2.3.15).
[104] Burton 1624, p. 119, n. †; or 1.314.q (1.2.3.15).

reluctance to ask for favour from the wealthy and powerful ('I have had some such noble friends acquaintance and Schollers, but most part, (common courtesies and ordinary respects excepted) they and I parted as wee met; they gave me as much as I requested, and that was ———'), the fact that he was not 'ambitious', and that he felt he had been given 'enough, and more peradventure then I deserved'.[105]

***

Whilst serving the conventional purposes of the humanist *consolatio*, the 'Consolatory Digression' revisited the problem of the alienated scholar in the light of moral philosophy. It opened in typical fashion with Burton's acknowledgement of his ancient and neoteric predecessors from Plato to Cardano (2.125.12–15 [2.3.1.1]), and in the process of providing his audience with comforting arguments from these and other sources, like his Italian humanist predecessors he took the opportunity to address the problematic relationship between Christian and classical moral psychology. In Burton's exposition, there was much to approve of in the therapeutic arguments of the Stoics, but his fundamental commitment was to the Augustinian doctrine that we should 'balance our hearts with love, charity, meekenesse, patience, and counterpoise those irregular motions of envy, livor, spleene, hatred, with their opposite virtues, as we bend a crooked staffe another way' (2.187.8–10 [2.3.6.1]). In accordance with this position, he made it clear in the third edition that he regarded Stoic ἀπάθεια as unacceptably harsh, and that Platonic or Aristotelian μετριοπάθεια (as had been advocated by Plutarch) was a more appropriate goal for the sufferer.[106] As More had required in the *Dialogue of Comfort*, the classical arguments Burton mobilised against dejection were placed within a Christianised ethical framework. Much of his spiritual comfort was delivered as Pauline παράκλησις, admonitory consolation leading to contentation.[107]

Burton also made it clear that his *consolatio* was to be seen as geared primarily towards himself. 'If I make nothing', he wrote at the end of a miniature *exordium* that had placed the utility of the following discourse for others in doubt (1.125.22–126.20),

[105] Burton 1632, pp. 134–5; or 1.314.31–315.18 (1.2.3.15). See also Burton 1632, p. 138, n. †; or 1.319.w.

[106] Burton 1628, pp. 315, 317; or 2.177.3–4, 180.13–24 (2.3.5.1). See also 2.188.18–23 and 2.125.27, but cf. Burton 1628, p. 320; or 2.185.22–6.

[107] Hebrews 6.18–19; 12:5–11; 13.22. See Lievsay 1951, p. 336, and Burton's strategy at 2.160.4–30.

as *Montaigne* said in like case, I will marre nothing, 'tis not my doctrine but my study, I hope I shall doe no body wrong to speake what I thinke, and deserve not blame in imparting my minde. If it be not for thy ease, it may for mine owne, so *Tully, Cardan*, and *Boëthius* wrote *de consol.* as well to helpe themselves, as others. (2.126.22–7 [2.3.1.1]; cf. 1.7.30–2.2)

The reference to Montaigne's essay 'Of practice', in which a meditation on death led to the revelation of writing as self-portraiture and self-dissection, is significant here.[108] Florio had translated the relevant passage thus:

Now as *Plinie* saith, every man is a good discipline unto himselfe, alwayes provided he be able to prie into himselfe. This is not my doctrine, it is but my studie; And not another mans lesson, but mine owne. Yet ought no man to blame me if I impart the same. What serves my turne, may happily serve another mans; otherwise I marre nothing, what I make use of, is mine owne.[109]

Whereas Montaigne was 'impart[ing]' his 'lesson', Burton was also 'im-parting' – distributing, dissecting, anatomising – the contents of his 'minde'.[110] Whilst preserving the stress on the uncertainty of his consolation's effectiveness, he signalled his intention to appropriate Montaigne's self-expressive project: 'be it as it may, I will essay' (2.126.27 [2.3.1.1]).

What was particularly on Burton's mind here was the problem of how to cope with the corruption of contemporary politics and its effect on his fortune. Hence he used the 'Consolatory Digression' to articulate his earlier claim that his exclusion from the patronage system reflected personal virtue, registering his discontent at his lack of preferment – and with the political environment more generally – which we have seen to be increasing in the editions issued after 1621. The world of political activity he had rejected was not only vicious and slavish, but precarious and ultimately miserable. Those who rise to power at court, he wrote in a passage first found in the second edition, 'fat themselves like so many hogges, as *Æneas Sylvius* observes, that when they are full fed, they may be devoured by their Princes . . . honor is a tempest, the higher they are elevated, the more grievously depressed'.[111] In a section of text that again grew throughout the 1620s, the corollary of this was depicted as a situation in which 'he that is most worthy wants imployment . . . and he

108 See Montaigne 1603, II.6, p. 220.
109 Montaigne 1603, II.6, p. 219.
110 Burton's adaptation derived from Florio's translation; Montaigne's original has simply 'si je la communique' (Montaigne 1974, vol. II, p. 69).
111 Burton 1624, p. 265; or 2.147.17–22 (2.3.3.1).

that could governe a Commonwealth . . . wants meanes to exercise his worth, hath not a poore office to manage . . . But who can helpe it? It is an ordinary thing in these daies to see a base, impudent asse . . . preferred before his betters.' In short, '[i]t is not honesty, worth, wisdome, that preferres men . . . but as the wise man said, *Chance*, and sometimes a ridiculous chance'.[112]

Here Burton drew on a Stoic ethic of inner fortitude and self-mastery, extracted particularly from the writings of Seneca and Epictetus, to articulate his quest for personal tranquillity over and against the instability and vicious passions of the world of political honour. Here is a typical passage from the first edition:

I am inglorious and poore, *compositâ paupertate*, but I live secure and quiet: they are dignified, have great means, pompe and state, they are glorious, but what have they with it? *Envy, trouble, anxiety, as much labour to maintaine their place with credit, as to get it at first.* I am contented with my fortunes, *spectator è longinquo* . . . Let them run, ride, strive as so many fishes for a crum, scrape, climbe, catch, snatch, cosen, collogue, temporize and fleire, take all amongst them, wealth, honour, and get what they can, it offends me not . . . I am well pleased with my fortunes . . . Come what can come, I am prepared . . . I am the same. (2.188.33–189.12 [2.3.6.1])

But there were signs that he had fallen short of the ideal. He confessed that 'I was once so mad to bussell abroad, and seeke about for preferment, tyre my selfe and trouble all my friends and had my projects, hopes, and designes, amongst the rest', but – in an ambivalent image of resignation communicating residual despair – 'now as a mired horse that struggles at first with all his might and meane to get out, but when he sees no remedy, that all his beating will not serve, lies still, I have laboured in vaine, and rest satisfied . . . Mine haven's found, fortune and hope adue.'[113] In the second edition, he inserted a passage in Latin (and so intended for his fellow scholars) which was altogether less tranquil, and in which the frustration and loathing came to light:

sed nihil labor tantus profecit, nam dum alios amicorum mors avocat, aliis ignotus sum, his invisus, allii largè promittunt, intercedunt illi mecum solliciti, hic vanâ spe lactant, dum alios ambio, hos capto, illis innotesco, ætas perit, anii defluunt, amici fatigantus, ego deferor, & jam mundi tæsus, humanæ satur infidelitatis acquiesco.[114]

[112] Burton 1621, p. 421; Burton 1624, p. 286; Burton 1628, p. 324; Burton 1632, pp. 355–6; Burton 1651, pp. 350–1; or 2.191.5–192.2 (2.3.7.1). See also 2.137.5–7 (2.3.2.1).

[113] Burton 1621, p. 421 (2.3.6.1).

[114] Burton 1624, p. 285; or 2.189.17–22 (2.3.6.1).

'And so I say still', he insisted in the 1628 copy. Though he went on to acknowledge the favours of 'some bountifull patrons, and noble benefactors' (specified in a marginal note as '[t]he right honourable Lady *Francis* Countesse Dowager of *Exeter*', whose son he might have tutored, and '[t]he Lord *Berkley*', another possible tutee of his who also owned the manor in Lindley on which Burton's family lived), immediately the tone of grudging and dissatisfaction was reinstated. These were 'more peradventure then I deserve, though not to my desire, more of them then I did expect, yet not of others to my desert'.[115]

Given the deepening discontent voiced by Burton throughout the different editions of the *Anatomy*, it should be no surprise that his authorial *persona* in the 'Consolatory Digression' was a far cry from sage-like ἀπάθεια. What attracted him to Senecan Stoicism was not so much the goal of psychological freedom from passions, which he considered unattainable (and perhaps undesirable) in its strict form, but the virtue and independence secured by withdrawal from the corrupt and disturbing domain of politics to the seclusion of privacy.[116] What was crucial here was the indifference exhibited by the virtuous man to the external goods of *fortuna*, which lay behind the idea expressed by Seneca in *Epistulae morales* LXXII that worldly affairs and the cares brought by *negotium* should be 'shut out' from the tranquil life of the philosopher.[117] Constructing a Christian-Stoic consolation against poverty and obscurity, Burton associated the virtuous contempt of riches bestowed by inconstant fortune with godliness (2.152.8–12 [2.3.3.1]; cf. 2.154.17–22). This in turn provided the platform for another denunciation, which typically grew across the second to fifth editions, of those who had achieved preferment:

> Thou art an Epicure, I am a good Christian: Thou art many parasanges before me in meanes, favour, wealth, honour . . . a favorite, a golden slave, thou Coverest thy floors with marble, thy roofes with gold. . . what of all this? *Calcas opes, &c.* whats all this to true happiness? I live and breath under that glorious heaven, that August Capitol of nature, enjoy the brightness of stars . . . I am free, and which *Seneca* said of *Rome, culmen liberos texit, sub marmore et auro postea servitus habitavit.*[118]

[115] Burton 1628, p. 323; or 2.189.22–7, p (2.3.6.1).

[116] Cf. the treatment of ἀπάθεια in Lipsius 1644, III.7, pp. 277–95, and the position implied in Blok 1976, p. 53.

[117] Seneca 1917–25, LXXII.7–11, vol. II, pp. 100–3.

[118] Burton 1624, p. 268; Burton 1628, p. 302; Burton 1632, pp. 533–4; Burton 1651, p. 325; or 2.152.14–24 (2.3.3.1). The quotation is from Seneca 1917–25, XC.10, vol. II, pp. 402–3.

The Stoic truth articulated here, subsequently aligned to Christian *contemptus mundi* (2.155.27–156.17), was that riches and advancement in public life were no substitute for tranquillity and freedom from anxiety. The wealthy and powerful nobleman thereby formed the enslaved counterpart of the '[h]appy' man, who was 'freed from the tumults of the world . . . seekes no honours, gapes after no preferment, flatters not, envies not, temporizeth not, but lives privately, and well contented with his estate' (2.153.5–12).

This was not a straightforward encomium of poverty and advocacy of retirement. In a manner reminiscent of Hall's description of the benefits of the 'philosophicall cell', Burton saw withdrawal as a means of liberation from disturbing speculations about the external world, and depicted an inner virtue that was inherently antagonistic to the political domain:

> He is not troubled with state matters, whether kingdomes thrive better by succession or election; whether Monarchies should be mixt, temperate, or absolute; the house of *Ottomons* and *Austria* is all one to him . . . he enquires not after Colonies or new discoveries; whether *Peter* were at *Rome*, or *Constantines* donation be of force . . . He is not touched with feare of invasions, factions or emulations.[119]

Advocacy of the *vita contemplativa* was a moral-psychological response to the corruption of a public domain populated by those incapable of serving their commonwealth virtuously. By the time of the 1638 edition, we can speculate that Burton's disenchantment with public service was virtually complete, as he was agreeing 'with *Libanius Sophista* that rather chose (when honours and offices by the Emperour were offered unto him) to be *talis Sophista, quam talis Magistratus*, I had as lief be still *Democritus Junior*, and *privus privatus, si mihi jam daretur optio, quam talis fortasse Doctor, talis Dominus*'.[120]

SATIRE AND PHILOSOPHY

In places such as this Burton was unquestionably quietist, but his politics were far from deracinated, and it is important to see that his position can be restated in positive terms. Enshrining virtuous independence from a corrupt system of offices, honours, and material rewards, the neo-Stoic model of the scholar-philosopher in effect embodied the value of

[119] Burton 1638, p. 321, and Burton 1651, pp. 325–6; or 2.153.15–21 (2.3.3.1).
[120] Burton 1638, p. 136; or 1.315.19–22 (1.2.3.15).

philosophical liberty and scholarly freedom of speech. This was implicit in Burton's criticisms of the slavish flattery and deceit bred by the dependence of the scholar on patronage we have been exploring above, but he made both sides of the polarity explicit in this argument consoling poverty in the second edition, which juxtaposed the poor man's freedom with the constraints of public office.

A poore man is able to write, to speake his minde, to doe his owne businesse himselfe, *locuples mittis parasitum*, saith *Philostratus*, a rich man imployes a parasite, and as the Maior of a Citty speaks by the Towne-clarke, or by Mr *Recorder* when hee cannot expresse himselfe. *Nonius* the Senatour hath a purple coat as stiffe with jewels, as his mind is full of vices, rings on his fingers worth 20000 sestercies, and as *Perox* the *Persian* King, an union in his eare worth 100^{l} waight of gold . . . but to what end? (2.150.10–18 [2.3.3.1])

Freedom of speech was located in private rather than public 'businesse', but, through its association with the activity of delivering 'plain' counsel to the head of the body politic elsewhere in the *Anatomy*, it constituted a critical commentary on the contemporary conditions bearing on humanists attempting to reform the commonwealth. More specifically, it drew on a valuation of liberty as a form of independence guaranteed by one's condition of living – in the case above, virtuous poverty.

As we have already seen, the details of the utopia in 'Democritus Junior to the Reader' showed that Burton had not abandoned the traditional humanist ethic of political participation, but was instead decrying the limited scope for its contemporary realisation. His utopia was born of frustration at reforms that were 'not to be hoped' (1.85.22), and was presented as a counterfactual textual space in which the author could 'freely domineere . . . as I list my selfe' for self-satisfaction (1.85.35–8) – i.e., able to act according to his own will. The utopian discourse was accordingly the clearest instance of Burton's ongoing meditation throughout the preface on the value of free speech and the dangers by which it was accompanied. Having asserted his intention to 'make an *Utopia* of mine owne', he countered an anticipated censor with arguments justifying the right he had taken to speak freely.

And why may I not?

———————*Pictoribus atque Poëtis, &c.*

You know what liberty Poets have ever had, and besides, my Predecessor *Democritus* was a Politician, a Recorder of *Abdera*, a Law-maker as some say, and why may not I presume so much as he did? Howsoever I will adventure. (1.85.38–86.4)

When he concluded his utopian fantasy, there was also a hint of unwelcome external constraint: 'I could have here willingly ranged, but these straights wherein I am included, will not permit' (1.97.11–12). Given his copious expansion of the work throughout his lifetime it seems unlikely that by this he meant simply a lack of space. He was surely referring to the restrictive conditions under which the satirist was compelled to labour.

This dynamic, in which the author showed himself exercising a potentially transgressive liberty of speech whilst countering the resistance of an imaginary hostile readership, was present from the start of the preface. Anticipating the hostility of the 'Gentle reader' questioning who was 'arrogating another mans name', his response was to claim satirical freedom of speech by quoting the opening of Seneca's *Apocolocyntosis*, in which the Stoic philosopher had ridiculed the dead emperor Claudius (possibly exploiting the carnivalesque licence afforded by the festivities of the Saturnalia). Burton continued: 'as [Seneca] said, *Primum si noluero, non respondebo, quis coacturus est?* I am a free man borne, and may chuse whether I will tell, who can compell me?' (1.1.3–7). The creative gloss is important, as it drew on the fundamental Roman legal status-distinction between the *liber*, subject to no domination, and the *servus*. It is partly – I would suggest largely – to exercise this particular right as a 'free man' that he hid 'in an unknowne habite'. It allowed him 'to assume a little more liberty and freedome of speech' (1.5.32–3), and to write in a 'loose, plaine', and 'free' style ('*stylus hic nullus præter parrhesiam*') (1.17.22–3, b; cf. 1.19.17–20)[121] that was calculated to speak the truth rather than flatter ('I seeke not applause') (1.15.25; cf. 1.27.9–11).

This preoccupation gave rise to a literary game played out through the preface, where the author was by turns aggressive, evasive, and submissive towards an imaginary reader,[122] and which culminated in a series of defensive retractions and reassertions. Having ended his diatribe in the first edition, Burton summed up the case for his defence in the face of anticipated criticisms by presuming 'to answere with *Erasmus*, in like case, 'tis not I, but *Democritus, Democritus dixit:* you must consider what liberty those old Satyrists have had, 'tis a *Cento* collected from others, not I, but they that say it'.[123] This was evasion, and it was not long before he was again on the attack, asking, 'why should any man bee offended,

[121] Cf. Wither 1614, sig. E6^r. [122] See Fish 1972.
[123] Burton 1621, p. 70; or 1.110.20–8.

or take exceptions at it?' When he cited the traditional defence of the satirist's right '[t]o speake of vice, but let the name go free' (which implied that there were names being withheld), it was in order to turn the tables on his implied critic: 'If he be not guilty, it concernes him not; it is not my freenesse of speech, but a guilty conscience, a gauled back of his owne that makes him winch' (I.III.13). He next abandoned the pretence of disowning his former words, quoting the Horatian satirical dictum '*Quamvis ridentem dicere verum quid vetat?* One may speake in jest, and yet speake truth', and protested indifference to the reception of his discourse: 'Object then and cavill what thou wilt, I ward all with *Democritus* buckler, his medicine shall salve it, strike where thou wilt and when: *Democritus dixit, Democritus* will answere it' (I.110.32–111.24). It was, he claimed,

> written by an idle fellow, at idle times, about our *Saturnalian* or *Dionysian* feasts, when as hee said *nullum libertati periculum est*, servants in old *Rome* had liberty to say and doe what them list . . . The time, place, persons, and all circumstances apologize for me, and why may I not then be idle with others? speake my minde freely, if you deny me this liberty, upon these presumptions I will take it: I say againe, I will take it.[124]

Subsequent additions to 'Democritus Junior to the Reader' were calculated to make his readers wonder whether his first edition had attracted the criticism he had anticipated. The lengthy justification of his style at the beginning of the preface (I.II.9–20.4), largely a composite of passages new to the second and third editions, was both defensive and resigned,[125] mentioned having been 'honoured by some worthy men, so have I beene vilifed by others, and shall be', and recorded how earlier versions of the *Anatomy* had been 'egerly read, and . . . not so much approved by some, as scornefully rejected by others'.[126] He also reinforced his closing self-vindication in the 1624 copy by inserting the instruction, 'Take heed you mistake me not',[127] and re-established his rejection of the slavish discourse of flattery associated with literary patronage whilst expanding the haughty dismissal of his enemies: 'If any man take exceptions, let him turne the buckle of his girdle, I care not. I owe thee nothing, I looke for no favour at thy hands, I am independent, I feare not.'[128] In the third edition the defensive role of the satirical

[124] Burton 1621, p. 71; or I.III.24–II2.4.
[125] Burton 1628, p. 8; or I.II.10 and Burton 1624, p. 7; or I.13.3.
[126] Burton 1628, p. 10; or I.14.30–15.5.
[127] Burton 1624, p. 62; or I.110.31.
[128] Burton 1624, p. 63; or I.112.7–9.

persona was underlined again, with more attention drawn both to 'what it is to speake in ones owne or anothers person, an assumed habit and name; a difference betwixt him that affects or acts a Princes, a Philosophers, a Magistrates, a Fooles part, and him that is so indeed',[129] and to the commonplace protection against accusations of libel, 'I hate their vices, not their persons.'[130]

The preface famously closed with a complete about-turn which suggested (in my view insincerely) that the preceding satire had been produced by a melancholic delusion suffered by the author. In 1621 it began thus:

No, I recant, I will not, I confesse my fault, acknowledge a great offence, I have overshot my selfe, I have spoken foolishly, rashly, unadvisedly, absurdly, I have anatomized mine own folly. And now me thinkes upon a sudden I am awaked as it were out of a dreame, I have had a raving fit, ranged up and down, in and out, I have insulted over most kinde of men, abused some, offended others, wronged my selfe, and now being recovered, and perceiving mine errour, cry with *Orlando*, *Solvite me*, pardon that which is past, and I will make you amends in that which is to come; I promise you a more sober discourse in my following Treatise.

If through weaknesse, folly, passion, discontent, ignorance, I have said amisse, let it be forgotten and forgiven.[131]

In the second edition, Burton fortified his defences, acknowledging that 'I may justly suspect the worst', 'I care, I feare', and expressing the hope that 'I have wronged no man, yet in *Medeas* words I will crave pardon . . . And in my last words this I doe desire, / That what in passions I have said, or ire, / May be forgotten, and a better minde / Be had of us, hereafter as you finde.'[132] But for all his apparent submissiveness, Burton's protestation of earnestness in the 1624 copy rang hollow, as his final words – which remained from the first edition – indicated that he would be going back on his former promise to drop his satirical 'knife' and deliver 'a more sober discourse' in the main treatise.

And if hereafter in Anatomising this sirlie humour, my hand slip, as an unskilfull prentise, I launce too deepe, and cut through skinne and all at unawares; or make it smart, or cut awry, pardon a rude hand, an unskilfull knife, 'tis a most difficult thing to keepe an even tone, a perpetuall tenor, and not sometimes to lash

[129] Burton 1628, p. 75; or I.110.24–7.
[130] Burton 1628, p. 76; or I.111.6. See also Burton 1628, p. 71; or I.104.16–17.
[131] Burton 1621, p. 71; or I.112.10–22.
[132] Burton 1624, p. 63; or I.112.10; I.112.25–113.2.

out; *difficile est Satyrum non scribere*, there be so many objects to divert, inward perturbations to molest . . . it is impossible not in so much to overshoot . . . I hope there will no such cause of offence be given; if there be, I presume of thy good favour and gratious acceptance, and out of an assured hope and confidence, thereof, I will beginne.[133]

The disingenuousness of the closing apologia became progressively apparent in the versions issued after 1621. In 1624, he announced that '*Nemo aliquid recognoscat, nos mentimur omnia.* Ile deny all (my last refuge) recant al, renounce all I have said.'[134] In the following edition, he counterbalanced a pretended humility – 'If thou knewest my modesty and simplicity, thou wouldest easily pardon and forgive what is here amisse' – with a shifting of blame – 'or by thee misconceived', and pointed out that he could 'with as much facility excuse' as his detractors could 'accuse'.[135] In a final, ironically submissive gesture, he added the description 'gentle reader' to an audience for whose 'good favour and gratious acceptance' he had only just shown open contempt.[136]

Aside from their amusing effect, these literary manoeuvres were crucial to Burton's construction of his *persona* as a discontented melancholic philosopher struggling against hostile forces to assert his status as a 'free man'. The conflict between independence and censorship was never fully resolved in the text, yet the act of portraying it was a gesture of defiance of sorts; the seeming recantations of the final pages of the preface were ironically critical as well as self-protective. To draw upon the defence of the 'freenesse of speech' traditionally afforded to satire itself suggested that there was something, or someone, to defend against. But the most telling representation of Burton's position was to be found in an extraordinary comment, inserted in the last edition of the book in the midst of his dissection of the political ills of England.

For as *Lucian* said of an Historian, I say of a Politician. He that will freely speak and write, must be for ever no subject, under no prince or law, but lay out the matter truly as it is, not caring what any can, will, like or dislike.[137]

In this uncompromising statement of the necessity of freely delivered counsel to the health of the commonwealth,[138] we see a commitment to

[133] Burton 1621, p. 72; or 1.113.8–22.
[134] Burton 1624, p. 64; or 1.113.18–19.
[135] Burton 1628, p. 77; or 1.113.6–8, 19–20.
[136] Burton 1628, p. 77; or 1.113.19–21.
[137] Burton 1651, p. 59; or 1.84.17–20.
[138] Cf. Machiavelli 1970, 1.18, p. 162.

the political liberty of the scholar, conceived as a status and an accompanying condition of life. It has been characterised by freedom not only from the domination of the prince or even the law, but also the threat of such domination.[139] Little wonder that this, which from the perspective of any divine-right monarchist would have been tantamount to a licence for sedition, appeared for the first time in the edition issued posthumously.

***

The freedom of the philosopher also faced assault from within. The comment appended to the Juvenalian rationale for satire, '*difficile est Satyram non scribere*' (which had also been employed by Wither),[140] is instructive here, as it was not just the conventional corruption of the times that created the moral necessity of vituperation, but also the author's own melancholic passions: 'there be so many objects to divert, inward perturbations to molest' (I.113.12–13). That this was more than a reference to another literary convention, namely the satirical malcontent, is demonstrated by the seriousness of Burton's engagement with Stoic moral psychology and its centrality to the features he attributed to himself as Democritus Junior. It was the consistent message of the preface that the Stoic wisdom consisting of freedom from the passions was entirely absent in the world. His argument was that 'liberty is a power to live according to his owne Lawes', not according to vicious passions or the arbitrary will of another but 'as we will our selves', and, since no living exemplar of this ideal could be found, 'then *è diametro*, wee all are slaves' (I.63.21–32). From this perspective, the Saturnalian freedom permitted to the inhabitant of Burton's utopia to 'doe whatsoever he shall please' was likely to be psychological slavery – as had been quietly suggested by the series of severe punishments for drunkenness, 'riot', and other offences that were listed immediately afterwards in the text of the second edition.[141]

When Burton asked himself towards the end of the diatribe, 'Whom shall I then except?' from the diagnosis of melancholic madness, his playful answer was first that '*Nicholas nemo*, or Mounsieur *no-body* shall go free' (I.107.6–10). This was followed by a derisively ironic list of those

139 These are features of the 'neo-Roman' theory of liberty identified in Skinner 1998. See also Colclough 2003, p. 56, and 2005, pp. 157–95.

140 Wither 1614, sig. A6v.

141 Burton 1624, p. 54; or I.94.2–9.

who could claim to be excepted, comprised by 'such as are silent', 'Senators, Magistrates' and 'great men' of whom it was said to be inappropriate to 'thinke amisse', and '[w]hom next?'

Stoicks? *Sapiens Stoicus*, and hee alone is subject to no perturbations, as *Plutarch* scoffes at him *he is not vexed with torments, or burnt with fire... he is most beautifull, and like a God, a King in conceit, though not worth a groat. Hee never dotes, never mad, never sad, drunke, because vertue cannot be taken away, as Zeno holds, by reason of strong apprehension*, but he was mad to say so... *Chrysippus* himselfe liberally grants them to be fooles as well as others, at certaine times upon some occasions, *Amitti virtutem ait per ebrietatem, aut atribilarium morbum*, it may be lost by drunkennesse or melancholy, hee may bee sometimes crased as well as the rest: *ad summum sapiens nisi quum pituita molesta.* (I.107.17–30)[142]

This set him at odds with Lipsius, who had defended the Stoic tenet 'Sapientem non insanire' against the implications of Chrysippus's admission in his *Manuductio ad Stoicam philosophiam* (1604).[143] For good measure in the fifth edition of 1638, Burton added 'some Cynicks, *Menippus, Diogenes*, that *Theban* Crates' to the group of philosophers whose claims to sanity were to be mocked.[144]

What Burton had asserted was that precisely those philosophers whose psychological goal was ἀπάθεια (or in the case of the Cynics, ἀταραξία) were themselves subject to melancholic perturbations. This had important implications for the author's self-presentation in the preface. As we have noted, Burton's choice of a Democritean *persona* was in large part motivated by the Stoic and Cynic aspects of the 'laughing philosopher'. When he began to describe himself, it was as a philosopher who had withdrawn to the *vita contemplativa*, having 'liv'd a silent, sedentary, private life... penned up most part in my study' (I.3.13–16), and whose 'Treasure is in *Minerva*'s Towre' (I.3.13–16; I.4.15). In the first edition, he chose the Cynic model to express his political isolation and frustrated experience in the patronage system:

Preferment I could never get, although my friendes providence care, alacritie and bounty was never wanting to doe me good, yet either through mine owne default, infelicity, want or neglect of opportunity, iniquitie of times, preposterous proceeding, mine hopes were still frustrate, and I left behind, as a Dolphin on shore, confined to my Colledge, as *Diogenes* to his tubbe.[145]

142 The quotation from Plutarch was inserted in Burton 1624, pp. 60–1.
143 Lipsius 1644, III.18, pp. 346–7.
144 Burton 1638, p. 75; or I.107.30–108.1.
145 Burton 1621, p. 4. William Burton had also compared himself to Diogenes: Burton 1597, sigs. A3^{r-v}.

In the second edition it was added that his exclusion from preferment had provided the benefit that he was 'not in debt for it', and the resemblance of his confinement to that of '*Democritus* to his garden' was also noted (on the illustrated frontispiece Democritus is situated in a garden; recall Lipsius's figuration of the site of tranquillity).[146] It was in fact only in the version posthumously issued in 1651, where he also acknowledged with relief the patronage he did eventually receive, that he made his identification with Stoicism explicit:

Greater preferment as I could never get, so am I not in debt for it, I have a competency (*Laus Deo*) from my noble and munificent Patrons, though I live still a Collegiat Student, as *Democritus* in his Garden, and lead a monastique life, *ipse mihi theatrum*, sequestred from those tumults and troubles of the world, *Et tanquam in speculâ positus* (as [Heinsius] said), in some high place above you all, like *Stoicus Sapiens, omnia sæcula, præterita presentiaque videns, uno velut intuitu*, I hear and see what is done abroad, how others run, ride, turmoil, & macerate themselves in court and countrey.[147]

The tranquillity of the scholarly life was comparable to the psychological satisfaction accompanying Stoic *sapientia*. He was a 'meere spectator' of the anxieties of others in both 'court and countrey', to which he was apparently indifferent, and was left instead to contemplate the 'theatre' of his own self – perhaps echoing Montaigne's approval of the advice of Seneca and Epicurus in 'Of Solitude'.[148] Like Montaigne and Lipsius, Burton used the ancient trope of the *theatrum mundi* to reinforce the distance he had created between himself as a philosopher in pursuit of wisdom and the madness of the external world: '*totus mundus histrionem agit*, the whole world plaies the Foole, we have a new Theater, a new Sceane, a new Commedy of Errors, a new company of personate Actors' (1.37.26–31), presenting a mixture of 'now Comicall, then Tragicall matters' (1.5.11), which proved the melancholy of the world.[149]

Yet the relationship between philosopher and external world delineated here was not the strict separation usually posited in humanist endorsements of the *vita contemplativa*. Burton claimed that the original Democritus was 'very melancholy by nature' and studied black bile 'to the intent he might better cure it in himselfe' (1.2.12; 1.6.6–7).

146 Burton 1624, p. 3; 1.4.16–18. On Burton's frontispiece see Mueller 1949 and Corbett and Lightbown 1979.

147 Burton 1651, p. 3; or 1.4.15–23.

148 Montaigne 1603, I.38, pp. 123–4.

149 Cf. Montaigne 1603, I.42, pp. 140–1, II.36, p. 432; Lipsius 1595, I.8, I.13, II.13, II.26, pp. 18–19, 34, 91–2, 125.

This was a questionable interpretation of the classical sources on his part, and it was clearly designed to refashion the laughing philosopher in his self-image as one who was 'not a little offended with this maladie' (1.7.20–1).[150] Democritus Junior was only partially disengaged from public affairs, taking 'daily' note of 'both private, and publike newes, amidst the gallantry and misery of the world', and more importantly, was some distance from the attainment of tranquillity, 'left to a solitary life, and mine owne domesticke discontents' (1.5.11–21).

That the psychological dimension of Burton's withdrawal was less complete than its physical aspect, and that consequently (again, as for Montaigne) solitude brought with it consciousness of his soul's movements and inner 'discontents', was confirmed by the complexity of his reaction to the world's foolishness. Whereas the pseudo-Hippocratic Democritus cemented his alienation from the rest of humanity through relentless mockery, the contempt expressed by the laughter of Democritus Junior was tempered by a range of other emotions signifying an erosion of his indifference. He admitted that 'sometimes, *ne quid mentiar*', 'I did for my recreation now and then walke abroad, looke into the world', and, unlike the intention of Diogenes and Democritus, this was not 'to scoffe or laugh at all, but with a mixt passion'

> *Bilem sæpè, jocum vestri movêre tumultus.*

> I did sometime laugh and scoffe with *Lucian*, and Satyrically taxe with *Menippus*, lament with *Heraclitus*, sometimes againe I was *petulanti splene cachinno*, and then again, *urere bilis jecur*, I was much moved to see that abuse which I could not amend. (1.5.21–31)

Contemptuous laughter mixed with satirical anger, and also, as befitted a divine, compassionate grief and pity – these indicated a distinctly un-sagelike state of psychological turmoil. As he later made clear, they were also the symptoms of his melancholy. When comparing Democritus and Heraclitus, Montaigne had fully endorsed the Stoic viewpoint by preferring to follow the former, since '[b]ewailing and commiseration, are commixed with some estimation of the thing moaned and wailed', but '[t]hings scorned and contemned, are thought to be of no worth'.[151] What Burton signalled by mingling Heraclitean tears with Democritean laughter was a disjunction between his own *persona* and the Democritus of the classical fable. His physical withdrawal established

[150] This was perhaps deduced from Diogenes Laertius 1925, IX.38, vol. II, pp. 448–9.
[151] Montaigne 1603, I.50, p. 165.

a critical-philosophical 'view from above', but the price to be paid for retaining compassion of any depth was to suffer other perturbations. His appropriation of a classical philosophical stance and its associated moral psychology was thereby limited by his spiritual commitment to feel love, and grief, for his neighbour. In the final analysis, it was this compassion, and the melancholy of which it was a sign, that motivated him to continue, against all moral, spiritual, and political odds, to pursue his desire for the reform of humanity.

***

Once we have perceived Burton's acceptance of melancholy as an inevitable condition of perturbation, it is unsurprising that, in marked contrast to the conventional *consolationes* on which he drew throughout the 'Consolatory Digression', his own version ended on a gloomy note.[152] To explain fully why this was so, we need to consider Burton's stance in this part of the work. The collection of occasionally contradictory therapeutic arguments and positions in the digression – seen most clearly in his ambivalent use of Stoic ideals – was predictable enough, since the author's attitude here, as elsewhere in the book, was that of the detached, sceptical pragmatist. This position was also underlined by the prominent role of diversion 'by some contrary passion, or premeditation' in his recommendations (2.187.14–15 [2.3.16]). Diversion was deemed especially useful for melancholics such as himself (recall his proclaimed desire at the outset to 'write of Melancholy, by being busie to avoid melancholy'), as it could counteract the destructive tendency to meditate on the self, or 'melancholise', in solitude.[153] Diversion would be valuable for melancholy, since if the cause of disquiet was 'just' rather than 'fained', philosophical reason would not provide effective therapy (2.187.12–15 [2.3.6.1]). Earlier in the main treatise, however, it had been established that, since the fall of Adam, reason in man had habitually been 'over borne by *Passion*', and that the ultimate cause of our melancholy perturbations in this respect was to be found in God's 'just and deserved punishment of our sinnes' (1.128.28–9 [1.1.1.1]; 1.161.5–7 [1.1.2.11]).

The problem faced by Burton according to his own conception of the melancholy that afflicted him, therefore, was how he might effectively and legitimately achieve diversion away from this definitive feature of the

152 Cf., for example, Cardano 1576, fol. 102^v.
153 Burton 1628, p. 272; or 2.107.2–7 (2.2.6.2).

postlapsarian condition. This suggests that the self-therapeutic function of his writing about melancholy was at its most effective when its concern was with love melancholy. As 'a bacheler my selfe' and having led 'a Monasticke life in a College' (1.417.11–12 [1.3.2.4]), he claimed that his knowledge of this subject was largely that of 'a Contemplator only', so 'what I say, is merely reading' and 'inexpert' (3.195.24–196.4 [3.2.3.1]).[154] Rather than occupying the traditional poetic role of the physician of lovesickness unable to heal himself,[155] then, this was the part of the *Anatomy* in which the author could divert himself furthest away from his own melancholy and 'recreate himself', or freely 'expatiate in this delightsome field' (3.4.10–13 [3.1.1.1]). This is surely the real reason for the light-hearted character of this part of the work, the prominence of tragicomic literary-rhetorical devices devised to assist the 'evacuation' of melancholy humours,[156] and also for the lengthy *copia* of the Section. In the 1651 edition, it occupied two-and-a-half times more folio pages than the discourse on the religious subspecies, which was far more serious and harmful (3.331.22–8 [3.4.1.1]).[157]

Insofar as lovesickness shared many of the symptomatic features of all melancholy, and also derived from the domination of reason by passion, however, writing about it could only be a partial diversion. The end of the 'Consolatory Digression', entitled 'Against Melancholy It Selfe', showed that the only substantial response Burton could formulate was a form of internal psychological 'diversion', manifested in a turning of the self away from its own worldly existence. In a sense this was surrender. Whereas throughout the *Anatomy* the symptoms of melancholy were equated with vice, sinfulness, and sickness, in this Subsection he initially attempted a positive redescription of the disease as a desirable condition. It was accompanied, he claimed, by such 'comforts' as aptitude to contemplation and prudential wariness (2.207.2–6 [2.3.8.1]). Not only was optimism purchased at the price of self-contradiction; it masked the introduction of a pessimistic devaluation of human life through a truly melancholic desire for the oblivion of insensible madness. 'Dotage is a state which many much magnifie and commend', he wrote in the first

[154] The sense of this claim varied in different editions: see Burton 1624, p. 425; Burton 1628, p. 495; and Burton 1632, p. 545.

[155] See Ovid 1979, pp. 178–9, 198–9. Cf. Burton's remarks at 3.136.26 and 3.196.10–197.4 (3.2.4.1).

[156] See, for instance, 3.128.26 (3.2.2.4); 3.152.4–14 (3.2.3.1); 3.232.31–233.1 (3.2.5.3); 3.250.20–1 (3.2.5.5); 3.299.32 (3.3.2.1); 3.304.24–305.1 (3.3.3.1).

[157] See Burton 1651, pp. 406–632, on love melancholy, and pp. 632–732, on religious melancholy.

edition, and '[s]ome thinke fooles and disards live the merriest lives, they are not macerated with cares, tormented with feares, and anxietie, as other wise men are'. 'In a word', he concluded, dropping the unconvincing pretence, 'as they are distressed so are they pittied, which some hold better then to be envied, better to be sad then merry, better to be miserable then happy: of two extremes it is the best.'[158] In 1628 this uncomfortable ending to the *consolatio* was adumbrated with more melancholic meditations. 'These curious arts and laborious sciences, *Galens, Tullies, Aristotles, Justinians*', to which Burton had devoted his life, 'doe but trouble the world some thinke, we might live better with that illiterate *Virginian* simplicity, and grosse ignorance, entire Ideots doe best.' 'Wearisomnesse of life', he further added, 'makes them they are not so besotted, on the transitory vaine pleasures of the world'.[159] The only consolation to be found here was from acceptance of the self's worldly misery as an inescapable necessity for its future salvation: 'Heaven and earth are much unlike' (2.128.10 [2.3.1.1]).

DEMOCRITUS JUNIOR

Burton's complaints about poverty and marginalisation, and his disenchantment with the corruption of the world that surrounded him, were essential ingredients of his image as melancholic philosopher-divine. But what lay behind his grievance at lack of preferment, and the somewhat ungracious acknowledgement of the patronage he did receive? There was substance to his claim that the *studia humanitatis* risked falling into neglect because 'those three commodious professions of Law, Physicke, and Divinity' were more profitable (1.311.16–22 [1.2.3.15]). However, it was not entirely fair to lay the blame at the door of noble patrons, since the real powers of distribution had largely shifted to the royal court. It was also a well-established humanistic tradition to voice such discontent whilst simultaneously playing the patronage game, and whilst generous appointments for university scholars were increasingly hard to come by, he had certainly not been deprived of opportunities to seek them. As I noted in my introduction, his first opportunity to gain favour had been the performance in Christ Church of his Latin comedy *Alba* in 1605, which seems not to have gone down well with its royal audience. As far as substantial ecclesiastical preferment was concerned,

158 Burton 1621, p. 430; or 2.207.28–31 (2.3.8.1).
159 Burton 1628, p. 334; or 2.207.9–10 (2.3.8.1).

the dominance of particular strains of divinity under James gave him reasonable grounds for dismay, and he had no reason to expect anything from Buckingham, who eventually became the dominant force in the distribution of Jacobean patronage. More promisingly from Burton's point of view, however, Archbishop Laud had bewailed the 'mean' condition of the clergy and devoted himself to redressing what he saw as the impoverishment of the Church, and central to this strategy were his energetic and highly successful interventions in the patronage system.[160]

At first glance, it seems peculiar that Burton was overlooked by Laud. As we saw in chapter three, much of the *Anatomy* clearly supported the ecclesiastical reforms being carried out by Laud and his followers from the later years of the 1620s onwards. Burton's criticisms of lay patrons could even have been seen to coincide with Laud's vision of a wealthier national Church independent of the laity. Several of his Christ Church colleagues with similar religious views had received substantial preferment as a direct result of the archbishop's support. John Bancroft, Laud's 'ancient friend' who had also been Burton's tutor, had been given the bishopric of Oxford, and Brian Duppa, Dean of the College after 1629, had been granted the see of Chichester as well as the vice-chancellorship of the university in 1632. Indeed, one did not need to be an outright Arminian, sacerdotalist, or ceremonialist 'Laudian' to be in receipt of the archbishop's favours. The Calvinist Samuel Fell, who along with his wife and son were remembered by Burton in his will,[161] qualified apparently on the basis of his anti-puritan record. As William Strode's description in *The Floating Island* of the suggestively named character of 'Melancholico' as a 'Male-content turn'd Puritan' and 'unprefer'd . . . because precise' suggested, only staunch doctrinal Calvinists like John Prideaux were clearly excluded on religious-ideological grounds.[162] This did not fit well with Burton's gripe that 'wee that are University men . . . are never used' (1.323.25–7 [1.2.3.15]), and the thanks Laud received in Oxford in 1636 from Secretary Sir John Coke, for 'those preferments which the able men of the university dayly received by his power at court', was not unjustified.[163] Perhaps the career trajectory of Peter Heylyn – a poet and satirist whose proficiency in humanistic scholarship was also attested by his popular and respected historical geography, *Microcosmos* (1621), and

[160] See Tyacke 1993, pp. 58–9, and Fincham 2000.
[161] See Kiessling 1990, pp. 100–1.
[162] Strode 1655, sigs. A4^v, B3^r; Fincham 2000, pp. 78–9, 90–1.
[163] Quoted in Fincham 2000, p. 79.

who as a notorious Laudian polemicist benefited from numerous royal appointments – should have given Burton pause for thought.

There was possibly some truth, not only in Burton's ascription of his relative failure to achieve preferment to a lack of ambition to match his desire, but also in his mention of chance. He seems likely to have been soured by the experience of being compelled in 1631 by the Countess of Exeter to resign the rectorship of Walesby – itself hardly a source of great income or prestige – so that it could be freed up for use by her associate Cranfield in his own patronage network.[164] It was paradoxical that it was Laud's Calvinist predecessor (and enemy), George Abbot, who purchased the copy of the *Anatomy* still held in Lambeth Palace library, where Laud could have consulted it.[165] It was also unfortunate, given that Abbot achieved little success in an ongoing struggle to influence the distribution of patronage.[166] In fact, the only direct connection between Laud and Burton we now have is the uninteresting letter written to Laud on the occasion of Burton's death in 1640 by the Oxford vice-chancellor, Accepted Frewen, to notify him of the deceased scholar's benefactions to the university library and Frewen's consequent attendance at the funeral.[167]

There is no reason not to believe Burton's explanation that the most significant factor here was his distaste for (and perhaps incompetence in) the ambitious politicking and compromise that were generally required for advancement. This is supported by his decision not to temper his pessimistic evaluation of the corrupt condition of Oxford and the English body politic more generally, and also by the disparaging remarks made in the *Anatomy*'s preface about the behaviour of his fellow divines. According to his own description, he was 'by my profession a Divine, and by mine inclination a Physitian' (I.23.2–6). This was a telling distinction, insofar as it suggested a measure of discomfort with the former role, and he was suggestively frank about the reason for his decision to turn his back on his 'profession', in favour of his 'inclination' and more broadly the *studia humanitatis*. In defending himself against what he called the 'greatest exception' that could be mounted against his book – 'that I being a Divine, have medled with Physicke' (I.20.5–6), neglecting his spiritual duties – his response was to explain his choice of subject, and the manner in which he approached it, as a product of disenchantment

164 See Simon 1964, pp. 36–7.
165 Lambeth Palace Library, SR2223.(B8) [**]. See Cox-Johnson 1955.
166 Fincham 2000, p. 92.
167 See Nichols 1795–1811, vol. IV, p. 491.

with the unedifying contemporary scene of the scramble for ecclesiastical patronage. 'Heare me speake', he went on,

There be many other subjects, I doe easily grant, both in humanity and Divinity, fit to be treated of, of which had I written *ad ostentionem* only, to shew my selfe, I should have rather chosen, and in which I have beene more conversant, I could have more willingly luxuriated, and better satisfied my selfe and others. (1.20.21–5)

It was not just that he had been 'fatally driven upon this Rocke of Melancholy' and diverted from 'the Queene of Professions'; 'in Divinity' he 'saw no such great neede' for more writing, as 'there be so many Bookes in that kinde, so many Commentators, Treatises, Pamphlets, Expositions, Sermons, that whole teemes of Oxen cannot draw them' (1.20.29–34). This proliferation of writing on divinity was, he alleged, fuelled by worldly motives, from which he was anxious to dissociate himself:

had I beene as forward and ambitious as some others, I might have haply printed a Sermon at Pauls-Crosse, a Sermon in St Maries Oxon. A Sermon in Christ-Church, or a Sermon before the right Honorable, right Reverend, a Sermon before the right Worshipfull, a Sermon in Latine, in English, a Sermon with a name, a Sermon without, a Sermon, a Sermon, a Sermon, &c. But I have beene as desirous to suppresse my laboures in this kinde, as others have beene to presse and publishe theirs. (1.20.34–21.1)

The point, conveyed with bitter sarcasm, was that he had been unwilling to abase himself slavishly before any 'right Worshipfull' patron. Elsewhere, he portrayed the dilemma faced by the scholar as a choice between the corrupt instrumentalisation of divinity as 'the highway to preferment' and the virtuous poverty of a career in the *studia humanitatis* (1.311.16–312.9 [1.2.3.15]). He went on to castigate 'those Clarkes which serve the turn' to obtain 'Church livings', and an environment in which '[i]f the Patron be precise, so must his Chaplaine be; if he be papisticall, his Clark must be so too, or else be turned out' (1.323.21–4).

Contemporary readers, some of whom would have been potential sources of support, would not have had difficulty in understanding the message. As the vision of the political environment expressed in the *Anatomy* became more pessimistic, it simultaneously revealed, and perhaps fortified, the author's commitment to a humanistic conception of philosophical and literary-satirical freedom. The defiant manner in which this stance was struck, and the classical and Christian sources from which it derived its substance, openly depended upon the denigration of the vice of ambition and worldly activity, and also, therefore, the activity of seeking preferment. The more Burton revealed his discontent at the diseased condition of the body politic, the more he was prompted to give vent to his utopian and reforming impulses. The more his resentment at the slavishness bred in contemporary scholarship by its dependence on corrupt aristocratic patronage grew, so did his estimation of the indispensability of a classically derived conception of independent moral and political critique to the commonwealth. As these trends became more pronounced with the appearance of each edition of the book, then, its author came less and less to resemble someone who valued the hierarchical social protocols and *politique* behaviour required by a patronage system that in the final analysis – as the *Anatomy* made clear – was opposed to the classical humanist devotion to *virtus vera nobilitas*. It was no coincidence that, in comparison to the florid and fulsome equivalents prefacing the works of very many of his contemporaries, Burton's dedication to George Berkeley – a highly litigious nobleman, no doubt to his client's distaste – was brief and uneffusive. This attitude was nicely captured by the anecdote recorded by Thomas Hearne of an encounter with a member of the nobility, where the scholar notably declined to abase himself in the expected manner:

The Earl of Southampton went into a Shop, and inquired of the Bookseller for Burton's Anatomy of Melancholly. Mr. Burton sate in a Corner of the Shop at that time. Says the bookseller, My Lord, if you please I can shew you the Author. He did so. *Mr. Burton*, says the earl, *your servant. Mr. Southampton*, says Mr. Burton, *your servant, and away he went.*[168]

It was also no accident that his utopia was a civil association that would provide its scholars with freedom of inquiry by counteracting the prevailing vices that he considered to be responsible for its contemporary extinction. Here, 'all arts and sciences' would be based in state 'Colledges' where they 'may sooner be perfected and better learned' (I.87.24–7), and the learned individuals these produced would be preferred by strict arrangements designed in accordance with the unavoidable fact that 'men are partiall and passionate, mercilesse, covetous, corrupt, subject to love, hate, feare, favor, &c.' His melancholic fantasy was that all honours and offices would 'bee given to the worthies and best deserving' (I.89.29–30; I.91.26–93.2).

***

[168] Hearne 1885–1921, vol. IV, p. 220 (2 August 1713), cited in Nochimson 1974, p. 105. See also Burton's poem in *Death repeal'd* 1638, pp. 2–3.

Although Burton chose to describe himself as 'Democritus Junior', by oscillating between satirical vituperation and tragic lamentation throughout the *Anatomy* his discourse imitated both Democritus and Heraclitus. These were not superficial stylistic devices, but the product of the author's erudite engagement with the Hellenistic moral psychology that preoccupied many of his European and English humanist contemporaries. It was also indicative of a typical concern to measure the compatibility of Stoic and Epicurean ethics with Christian spirituality with regard to the pressing question of the manner in which the philosopher should concern himself with the world. As Montaigne had made clear, identification with the contemptuously derisive figure of Democritus was a rigorously classical gesture that cordoned off the philosopher's soul from the corruption of the external environment. As such it was preferable to sympathetic association with Heraclitus, who from this perspective appeared to exemplify a wisdom compromised by the experience of psychological pain. Montaigne had passed over in suggestive silence the obvious Augustinian objection that Heraclitean tears were a more appropriate response to the fallen world.

In the *Anatomy*, however, Burton's decision to adopt the figure of Heraclitus as well as that of Democritus expressed what is perhaps the deepest intellectual problem posed throughout the book in a number of forms: that of the relationship between classical philosophy and Christianity. When the author described his response to the world it was as a complex passionate mixture of contempt, anger, distress, and compassion. It is here that the unresolved tensions in his self-image as melancholic philosopher-divine are most evident. The natural response to the degenerate suffering of the melancholic world for a divine who instinctively subordinated classical philosophy to Christian spirituality would have been Heraclitean. As Hall wrote, 'to laugh at & esteeme lightly of others misdemeanours' was only one of many 'slight and impotent' classical remedies for 'unquietnesse'.[169] So why was the *Anatomy* not written by 'Heraclitus Junior'? The awareness that the assumption of the mask of 'Democritus Junior' represented at best an ambiguous commitment to the Christian ethic of charity is surely what lay behind his anxious acknowledgement to an imaginary reader that the work might 'savour too much of humanity' and his 'promise' – with hindsight, obviously insincere – 'that I will hereafter make thee

[169] Hall 1628, I.3, pp. 75–6.

amends in some Treatise of Divinitie' (1.23.17–19). The same can be said of his self-conscious indecision as to whether the melancholic world was more appropriately depicted as tragedy or comedy, 'more to be pittied or derided' (3.331.33–332.1 [3.4.1.1]). This was not *per se* indicative of a lukewarm attitude towards Christianity, but it underlined the author's realisation that his lifelong humanistic intellectual enterprise was spiritually precarious. Classical moral philosophy, no less than medicine, articulated sophisticated and persuasive explanatory models for the experience of melancholy, and presented therapeutic psychological strategies to match. Burton's overriding humanistic impulse to identify with this aspect of ancient philosophy – to the point where his own name was displaced by that of 'Democritus Junior' on his tombstone – derived from his clear perception of what it could offer to the melancholic sufferer.

If the position of melancholic philosopher assumed by Burton in the *Anatomy* was intellectually problematic, it was also productive of an eloquent vision of personal discontent at the debased contemporary relationship between scholarship and politics. The literary activities of constructing a utopia, lamenting and denouncing the marginalisation of scholars, exploring the psychology of withdrawal, and attempting to find consolation all employed classical strategies to produce a critical commentary on the predicament of humanism in early seventeenth-century England. Being excluded from the political commonwealth, he took refuge in the private, leisurely service to the cosmopolitan *respublica literaria*, and it is tempting to see in his idealisation of college life a version of the emergent 'civil' community where sociability, virtue, and conversation provided a haven of tranquillity in a degraded public domain.[170] But Burton had good reason to be melancholy. The conjunction between the image of the Protestant nation and the humanist ideology of the previous century was becoming increasingly hard to sustain in an environment where the long-term political effects of the Reformation were prompting a renegotiation of the traditional parameters of authority and allegiance, and where concomitant religious disputes were fracturing university environments. As the *Anatomy* testified, one result was the dislocation of the position of the humanist, what Burton saw as the encroachment upon scholarship by the

[170] See Seneca 1928-32, IV.1–3, vol. II, pp. 186–9; and the description of Burton's conversational sociability in Wood 1815, vol. II, p. 652.

melancholy of the world. Yet if the deepening pessimism of the book in this respect was powerful, it was also bound up with nostalgic idealism. Burton's writing harked back to an Erasmian past where spiritual commitments could be reconciled to classical moral and political imperatives, a past modelled on an image of antiquity where political activity did not corrupt the philosopher, where scholarship was estimated as an accomplishment worthy of the highest rewards, and where utopianism was real reform. But what prompted him to express these ideals in such melancholic fashion was powerless frustration: 'I was much moved to see that abuse which I could not amend' (1.5.30–1).

Conclusion: Robert Burton's melancholy

Burton's great accomplishments in the *Anatomy* were not his critical appraisal of or additions to the endogenous scholarly theory of melancholy. As we have seen, the latter in particular were few and far between. Rather, they derived from the expansive and flexible manner in which he applied that theory to his surroundings: his exploitation of the medical-pathological category of religious melancholy to give scientific substance to a polemical analysis of contemporary spiritual politics; his employment of the moral-psychological dimension of melancholy to ground a wide-ranging critique of the condition of the domestic body politic; his exploration of the physiological and psychological intricacies revealed by writings on melancholy as a means of delivering a satirical and sceptical humanistic commentary on the limitations of speculative knowledge; and his use of the conceptual resources carried by the theory of melancholy generally to express adherence to the intellectual culture of Christian humanism and lament its contemporary degradation.

It was undeniably a complex and multifaceted polymathic enterprise undertaken by an author with a 'roving humor' (1.4.3), and this was reflected in the diversity of its seventeenth-century reception in England. For many, the *Anatomy* served its purpose as an encyclopaedic source of knowledge that presented the fruits of European medical-scientific learning about melancholy in a clear and accessible form. The astrological physician Richard Napier, for instance, appears to have used the book as a straightforward medical textbook and treated his patients in accordance with its recommendations.[1] The playwright John Ford used Burton's account of erotic melancholy to provide *The Lovers Melancholy* (1629) with medical content, and may also have used it for the characterology of other productions.[2] In 1657 the Bishop of Chichester, Henry King, who had matriculated from Christ Church in 1609, published a collection

[1] See Macdonald 1981, p. 281. [2] See Ewing 1940.

of poems preoccupied with his own and others' melancholic passions, one of which was addressed to an anonymous lady '*upon Mr* Burtons *Melancholy*' and indicated a slightly different view of the book. This recognised the therapeutic potential of the *Anatomy*, but went on to imply that its contents were not to be taken entirely seriously.

If in this Glass of Humours you do find
The Passions or diseases of your mind,
Here without pain, you safely may endure,
Though not to suffer, yet to read you cure.
But if you nothing meet you can apply,
Then ere you need, you have a remedy.

And I do wish you never may have cause
To be adjudg'd by these fantastick Laws;
But that this books example may be known,
By others Melancholy, not your own.[3]

Others saw the *Anatomy* as a useful humanistic digest of the encyclopaedia, a short-cut to the acquisition of a semblance of 'general learning'. Richard Holdsworth, the moderate Calvinist Master of Emmanuel College, Cambridge, included Burton alongside a number of classical and contemporary authors – including Ovid, Ausonius, Erasmus, More, Heinsius, Bacon, Browne, Overbury, and Herbert – in his 'Directions for students in the university'. Here the *Anatomy* fell into the category of works able to provide 'such learning as may serve for delight and ornament and such as the want whereof would speak a defect in breeding rather than scholarship' – that is to say, for the education of young gentlemen, as opposed to those in pursuit of a serious philosophical career.[4] It was undoubtedly out of admiration for this aspect of the book that the late seventeenth-century historian and bookseller Nathaniel Crouch adopted the pseudonym 'Robert Burton', thereby advertising his own enterprise of making classical knowledge available to a domestic readership in easily accessible form.[5]

As Anthony Wood suggested, it was also this that prompted plagiarism of its contents. The *Anatomy* was 'a Book so full of variety of reading', Wood noted, that

Gentlemen who have lost their time and are put to a push for invention, may furnish themselves with matter for common or scholastical discourse and writing. Several Authors have unmercifully stolen matter from the said Book without any acknowledgment, particularly one *Will. Greenwood*, in his Book entit.

[3] King 1657, p. 4. [4] See Curtis 1959, pp. 131–4. [5] On Crouch see Mayer 1993–4.

A description of the passion of Love, &c. *Lond.* 1657. oct. Who, as others of the like humour do, sometimes takes his quotations without the least mention of *Democritus Junior.*[6]

Some borrowed moral-satirical content from the *Anatomy*, such as the anonymous author of *Vulgar errours in practice censured* (1659).[7] Perhaps the most shameless and extensive plagiarist was the physician and satirist Richard Whitlock, who used large portions of Burton's book without acknowledgement in his encyclopaedic 'Morall Anatomy', *Zootomia, or, Observations on the Present Manners of the English* (1654).[8] As George Steevens, editor of Shakespeare and friend of Samuel Johnson (himself a great admirer of Burton), noted in his own copy of the fourth edition of the *Anatomy*, it was 'a book once the favourite of the learned and witty, and a source of surreptitious learning' for those in search of 'what both antients and moderns had advanced on the subject of human passions'.[9]

Whitlock's plagiarism is suggestive, because he clearly shared many of the concerns articulated in the *Anatomy*, particularly with regard to the necessity of anti-dogmatic philosophising, but also to the decay of learning – *Zootomia* reworked Burton's 'Digression of the Misery of Schollers' in order to defend the universities against the puritan assaults of the 1650s.[10] In fact, many of Burton's learned contemporaries latched on to this aspect of his work, and connected it with his general call for moral and political reform. We have already seen how in the *Golden Fleece* William Vaughan adapted Burton's political critique of court patronage to serve his own anti-Catholic ends. In his *Geography delineated forth* (1625), the philosopher and Calvinist divine Nathanael Carpenter, of Exeter College, had also clearly been inspired by Burton to express his personal concerns. 'Scarce had I shut up this tedious discourse', Carpenter wrote, having cited Oxford as a counter-argument to those who would cast aspersions on his 'native Country', than he was 'surprized with a deepe melancholy', and 'entred into a serious consideration of what I had too rashly spoken'. Carpenter then broke into verse, imagining his mother's 'reproofe' of his discourse, his own impassioned response in 'teares', and ended with an explicit imitation of and reference to his esteemed Christ Church contemporary.

6 Wood 1815, vol. I, p. 628.
7 See Curry 1901. See also the comments in Herring 1777, pp. 148–9; July 8, 1754.
8 See Bentley 1969.
9 See Nichols 1797-1815, vol. III, pp. 558–9.
10 Bentley 1969, pp. 89, 92.

All this time as in a fit of phrensy I have spoke, I scarce know what my selfe: I feare me too much, to, or of, my *Country* and *University*, and too little for the present purpose. Now as one suddainly awaked out of sleep, no otherwise then in a dreame I remember the *occasion*: We have all a *semel Insanavimus*, and as a learned man of this University seemes to maintaine, no man hath ever had the happiness to be exempted from this imputation: And therefore I hope my Reader will pardon me this once, if in such a generall concurse and conspiracy of mad men, I sometimes shew my selfe mad for company.[11]

As Carpenter's humanistic attack on contemporary scholasticism and sceptical advocacy of suspended judgement in the *Philosophia libera* (1621) suggest, he must have found much to agree with in the *Anatomy*.[12]

Burton's most historically significant legacy, however, lies in the influence of his formal designation of the religious subspecies of melancholy, and his expansive exploitation of the spiritual-polemical potential of the idea of the disease in general. Sermons and treatises dealing with 'religious melancholy' became commonplace in England after the publication of the *Anatomy*, from Edmund Gregory's *Historical Anatomy of Christian Melancholy* (1658) through to Richard Baxter's *Signs and Causes of Melancholy* (1706).[13] More particularly, whilst the credibility of the book's neo-Galenic medical teachings was gradually declining in the later seventeenth century, its consolidated analysis of puritan 'enthusiasm' as a form of melancholic madness continued to be influential in philosophical circles,[14] where the question of the manifestation of the Spirit in matter came to be crucial in determining the nature of the relationship between divine and human authority, and formed the backdrop to what would become a central theme of the English Enlightenment.[15] Meric Casaubon, a Student at Christ Church and undoubtedly familiar with the *Anatomy*, wrestled with the distinction between authentic and illegitimate inspiration in his *Treatise concerning enthusiasme, as it is an effect of nature, but is mistaken by many for either divine inspiration, or diabolical possession* (1654; 2nd edn, 1656); and the Cambridge Platonist and latitudinarian Henry More drew on and referred to the writings of '*Democritus Junior*, as he is pleased to style himselfe', on the nature of melancholy in his *Enthusiasmus Triumphatus*,

11 Carpenter 1625, II.15, pp. 266–73. Amongst the numerous studies of Burton's literary-stylistic influence see further Grace 1955 (on John Milton); and Jefferson 1952, Jackson 1975, and Selig 1996, pp. 128–54 (on Sterne). Cf. Frye 1957, pp. 309–11.

12 Carpenter 1622. The first edition was published in Frankfurt in 1621.

13 Other works of this nature are listed in Gowland 2006, p. 115.

14 See Williamson 1933, Sena 1973, and Heyd 1995, pp. 44–108.

15 See Pocock 1999–2003, vol. I, pp. 13–49, esp. 23–5.

or, a Brief Discourse of The Nature, Causes, Kinds, and Cure of Enthusiasm (1656).[16] Burton's critique was also put to devastating satirical use by Swift in his *Tale of a Tub* (1704).[17] The terms of the *Anatomy*'s psychological denunciation of 'melancholic' Calvinist spirituality remained relevant to the English religious and political climate in the final decades of the seventeenth century, as the title of a sermon commending mirth heard by Ralph Thoresby in 1681, and recorded in his diary, well testifies: 'Spiritus Calvinisticus est spiritus melancholicus.'[18] Perhaps most strikingly, Burton's bifurcated description of religious-political pathology persisted in both Shaftesbury's *Characteristicks of Men, Manners, Opinions, Times* (1711) and David Hume's withering dissection of the 'pernicious' effects of the 'two species of false religion', superstition and enthusiasm, in his famous essay of 1742.[19]

I would like to end on a paradoxical note: the question of the author's own 'reception' of his text. How are we to assess the outcome of Burton's lifelong enterprise of writing to 'comfort one sorrow with another, idleness with idleness . . . make an Antidote out of that which was the prime cause of my disease' (1.7.23–5)? The format of the *cento* was perfectly suited to this task, permitting him to make of his book a limitless repository of scholarly inquiry and self-expression. By increasing the *copia* of the text – with accounts of new controversies, new opinions gleaned from his reading, new responses to changing circumstances in the world – it became a continuously diverting source of intellectual pleasure, and give him an ever-expanding literary stage on which to play the parts of Democritus and Heraclitus. Continual modifications and additions to his book were surely essential to his therapeutic endeavour against melancholy, a way of keeping his book, and through it, himself, 'alive' (here is surely the most important parallel between Burton and Montaigne). However, writing about the disease was only to 'scratch where it itcheth' (1.7.20), a means of alleviating a perpetual condition only temporarily.[20] It could never have been its permanent cure. In the 'Conclusion' of the first edition, he appeared to concede this in defending himself against imaginary critics of the utility of his work by arguing that 'they that cure others, cannot well prescribe Physicke to themselves'

16 More 1662, XII, pp. 11–13.
17 See Harth 1961, pp. 105–8, 113–16, and Canavan 1973.
18 Thoresby 1830, vol. I, p. 76; entry 9 January 1681.
19 Cooper 1999, esp. vol. I, pp. 12–27, vol. II, pp. 160–3; Hume 1994, pp. 46–50. On the role of melancholy in Hume's thought see Livingston 1998.
20 Cf, Aristotle 1934, VII.14.6, pp. 446–7, on the active and irritable appetites of μελαγχολικοι.

(3.472.25–6). More tellingly, perhaps, his famously pithy closing recommendation, '*Be not solitary, be not idle*' (3.445.36–7 [3.4.2.6]), may well have described a therapeutically sound regimen for someone not already suffering from melancholy; for anyone who was, it constituted an injunction not to indulge its symptoms and make the disease worse. But, for Burton, who in his own account had indeed 'liv'd a silent, sedentary, solitary private life, *mihi & musis*', in Christ Church (1.3.14–16), it amounted to an admission that his unending intellectual and literary enterprise was in fact an experiential immersion in melancholy that could never have been a means of completely counteracting it: 'Experto crede R O B E R T O. Something I can speake out of experience' (1.8.4–5).

How, then, did the growth of the *Anatomy* across Burton's lifetime relate to what seems to be an intrinsically self-defeating activity? It is no accident that, as the book grew in size, his scepticism with regard to human intellectual capacities appears to have deepened, and his view of the contemporary world become more jaded – even if this was accompanied by a strengthening of his commitments to humanistic moral and political principles. One is tempted to say that Burton's investigation of the melancholy of the world as a means of seeking the therapy of his own melancholy contained a dynamic tension from the start, feeding his writing and his disease at one and the same time. The more melancholy that was found in the world, the more melancholic he would become. This is surely the point of Bishop White Kennett's anecdote about Burton, recorded in his *Register and Chronicle Ecclesiastical and Civil* (1728).

> The Author is said to have labour'd long in the Writing of this Book to suppress his own Melancholy, and yet did but improve it: And that some Readers have found the same Effect. In an interval of Vapours he would be extreamly pleasant, and raise Laughter in any company. Yet I have heard that nothing at last could make him laugh, but going down to the Bridge-foot in *Oxford*, and hearing the Barge-men scold and storm and swear at one another, at which he would set his Hands to his Sides, and laugh most profusely: Yet in his College and Chamber so mute and mopish that he was suspected to be *Felo de se*.[21]

The rumour of Burton's suicide was first recorded by Anthony Wood in the *Athenae Oxonienses* (1691–2), where it was said to have sprung out of his suspiciously exact astrological prediction of the date of his death in 1640.[22] The intrigue is deepened by Burton's monument in Christ

[21] Kennett 1728, pp. 320–1.

[22] Wood 1815, vol. II, p. 653. See also Aubrey 1898, vol. I, p. 130. On Burton's astrological notebooks see Bamborough 1981.

Church Cathedral, which by stating that 'melancholy gave him life and death' ('PAUCIS NOTUS, PAUCIORIBUS IGNOTUS, HIC IACET DEMOCRITUS JUNIOR CUI VITAM DEDIT ET MORTEM MELANCHOLIA') clearly implies suicide.[23] The case against this has mainly rested on the fact that he lies buried in sacred ground.[24] But it is by no means certain in such a notoriously close-knit College that his colleagues would not have extended to their famous and popular fellow the charity that he himself advocated in this matter. It would have been ironically appropriate if Burton, who had struggled to avoid the conflicts between his spiritual and humanistic commitments throughout his life, had ended it with a classical act that was silently accommodated to Christian dogma. After his death the Christ Church physician and Laudian poet Martin Lleuelyn noted that his '*white yeares*' were marked by '*Antient* virtues'.[25]

In the *Anatomy* itself, Burton had discussed melancholic suicides at length. He gave a sympathetic account of the pagan arguments that could be used to excuse them, before writing that 'those hard censures of such as offer violence to their own persons . . . are to be mitigated, as in such as are mad, beside themselves for the time, or founde to have beene long melancholy', and attaching a note to explain the type of 'hard' censure he had in mind: 'As to be buried out of Christian burial with a stake' (1.438.7–11, z [1.4.1.1]). Finally he advocated charity towards their distressed souls. It is now perhaps the most poignant passage in the book:

> Thus of their goods and bodies, we can dispose, but what shall become of their soules, God alone can tell, his mercy may come *inter pontem & fontem, inter gladium & jugulum*, betwixt the bridge and the brooke, the knife and the throte. *Quod cuiquam contigit, cuivis potest:* Who knowes how he may be tempted? It is his case, it may be thine? *Quæ sua sors hodie est, cras forè vestra potest;* wee ought not to bee so rash and rigorous in our censures, as some are, charity will judge and hope the best; God be mercifull unto us all. (1.438.21–7)

Elsewhere, more chillingly, he had referred several times to astrological foreknowledge of death as the source of despair and self-fulfilling prophecy.[26] It remains no more than a melancholy rumour, but it is one that lives on in the book.

23 *Contra* Dewey 1971, p. 293.
24 Nochimson 1974, p. 108; Bamborough 1989, p. xxxvi.
25 Lleuelyn 1646, p. 124.
26 See 1.260.24–5 (1.2.3.5); 1.362.24–363.32 (1.2.4.7); and the new reference to suicide in Burton 1628, p. 175; or 1.389.15–16 (1.3.1.2).

Bibliographies

PRINTED PRIMARY SOURCES

Abbot, George (1622). *The coppie of a letter sent from my lords grace of Canterburie shewing the reasons which induced the kings majestie to prescribe directions for preachers*, Oxford.

Aëtius of Amida (1567). *Tetrabiblos, hoc est quaternio, id est libri universales quatuor*, in Henricus, Stephanus (ed.), *Medicae artis principes, Post Hippocratem & Galenum, Graeci Latinate donati*, Paris.

Agrippa, Heinrich Cornelius (1533). *De occulta philosophia libri tres*, Cologne.

(1575). *Of the Vanitie and Uncertaintie of Arts and Sciences*, trans. James Sanford, London.

Airay, Henry (1618). *Lectures upon whole the Epistle of St Paul to the Philippians, delivered in St. Peters Church in Oxford*, London.

Alexander of Tralles (1567). *De arte medica libri duodecim*, in Henricus, Stephanus (ed.), Medicae artis principes, Paris.

(1933–6). *Oeuvres médicales*, 4 vols., F. Brunet, ed., Paris.

Altomari, Donato-Antonio (1559). *De medendis humani corporis malis. Ars medica*, Lyon.

An apology for English Arminianisme... Written by O. N. heertofore of the University of Oxford (1634), n. p.

Andrewes, Lancelot (1614). *A sermon preached before His Maiestie, at Whitehall, on Easter day last,* 1614, London.

(1629). *XCVI. sermons*, London.

Aretaeus (1856). *The Extant Works of Aretaeus, the Cappadocian*, ed. and trans. Francis Adams, London.

Argenterio, Giovanni (1558). *De morbis libri XIIII*, Lyon.

Aristotle (1923). *The Politics*, trans. H. Rackham, London.

(1934). *The Nicomachean Ethics*, rev. ed., trans. H. Rackham, London.

(1936a). *Minor Works*, trans. W. S. Hett, London.

(1936b). *On the Soul, Parva Naturalia, On Breath*, trans. W. S. Hett, repr., Cambridge, Mass., and London.

(1953). *Problems*, I: trans. W. S. Hett, repr., London.

(1957). *Problems*, II, *Books XXII–XXXVIII, Rhetorica ad Alexandrum*, trans. W. S. Hett, repr., London and Cambridge, Mass.

(1961). *Parts of Animals, Movement of Animals, Progression of Animals*, trans. A. L. Peck and E. L. Forster, repr., London.

(1966). *Posterior Analytics, Topica*, trans. H. Tredennick and E. S. Forster, repr., London.

(1967). *The 'Art' of Rhetoric*, trans. J. H. Freese, repr., Cambridge, Mass.

Arnald of Villanova (1585). *Opera omnia*, Basle.

Articles agreed upon by the arch-bishops and bishops of both provinces, and the whole clergie In the convocation holden at London, in the yeere 1562 (1633), London.

Aubrey, John (1898). *'Brief Lives', chiefly of Contemporaries, set down by John Aubrey, between the years* 1669 *&* 1696, 2 vols., ed. Andrew Clark, Oxford.

Augustine (1984). *Concerning the City of God Against the Pagans*, trans. H. Bettenson, London.

Avicenna (1508). *Avicene perhypatetici philosophi: ac medicorum facile primi opera in lucem redacta*, trans. C. B. Cecilius Fabrianensis, Venice.

(1546). *Avicennae Philosophi Praeclarissimum ac Medicorum Principis. Compendium de anima. De Mahad. . . .*, Venice.

(1608). *Canon medicinae ex Gerardi Cremonensis versione, & Andreae Alpagi Belunensis castigatione. A Ioanne Costeo, & Ioanne Paulo Mongio Annotationibus. . .*, 2 vols., Venice.

Bacon, Francis (1906). *The Advancement of Learning and New Atlantis*, with a preface by Thomas Case, London.

(1985). *The Essayes or Counsells, Civill and Morall*, ed. Michael Kiernan, Oxford.

(1994). *Novum Organum, with other parts of The Great Instauration*, ed. and trans. Peter Urbach and John Gibson, Chicago and La Salle, Ill.

Bargrave, Isaac (1624). *A sermon preached before the honorable assembly of knights, cittizens, and burgesses, of the lower house of Parliament: February the last.* 1623, London.

Bartholin, Caspar (1628). *Opuscula quatuor singularia: I. De Unicornu eiusque affinibus & succedaneis. II. De Lapide nephritico, & Amuletis praecipuis. III. De Pygmaeis. IV. Consilium de studio medico*, Copenhagen.

Baxter, Richard (1696). *Reliquiae Baxteriana, or, Mr. Richard Baxters narrative of the most memorable passages of his life and times*, London.

Baynes, Roger (1577). *The praise of solitarinesse*, London.

Bernard of Gordon (1617). *Lilium medicinae Ε'ΠΤΑΦΥΛΛΟΝ*, Frankfurt.

Boccalini, Trajano (1626). *The new-found politicke Disclosing the secret natures and dispositions as well of private persons as of statesmen and courtiers*, trans. John Florio, William Vaughan, et al., London.

Bodin, Jean (1566). *Methodus, ad facilem historiarum cognitionem*, Paris.

Botero, Giovanni (1606). *A treatise, concerning the causes of the magnificencie and greatnes of cities, devided into three*, trans. Robert Peterson, London.

(1608). *Relations, of the most famous kingdoms and common-weales thorough the world*, trans. R[obert] I[ohnson], London.

(1635). *The cause of the greatnesse of cities. Three Bookes. With certaine observations concerning the sea*, trans. Sir T. H., London.

Bright, Timothy (1586). *A Treatise of Melancholie*, London.

Browne, Sir Thomas (1977). *The Major Works*, ed. C. A. Patrides, London.

Burton, Robert (1621). *The anatomy of melancholy. What it is, with all the kindes, causes, symptomes, prognostickes, and severall cures of it. In three maine partitions with their severall sections, members, and subsections. Philosophically, medicinally, historically, opened and cut up. By Democritus Junior. With a satyricall preface, conducing to the following discourse*, Oxford.

(1624). *The anatomy of melancholy ... By Democritus Junior. With a satyricall preface, conducing to the following discourse*, Oxford.

(1628). *The anatomy of melancholy ... By Democritus Junior. With a satyricall preface, conducing to the following discourse*, Oxford.

(1632). *The anatomy of melancholy ... By Democritus Junior. With a satyricall preface, conducing to the following discourse*, Oxford.

(1638). *The anatomy of melancholy ... By Democritus Junior. With a satyricall preface, conducing to the following discourse*, Oxford.

(1651). *The anatomy of melancholy ... with a satyricall preface conducing to the following discourse by Democritus junior*, Oxford.

(1977). *Robert Burton's 'Philosophaster', with an English translation of the same. Together with his other minor writings in prose and verse*, ed. and trans. Paul Jordan-Smith, New York.

(1989–2000). *The Anatomy of Melancholy*, 6 vols., eds. Thomas Faulkner, Nicolas Kiessling, and Rhonda Blair. Vols. I–III: Text; vols. IV–VI: commentary by J. B. Bamborough and Martin Dodsworth, Oxford.

Burton, William (1622). *The description of Leicester shire containing matters of antiquitye, historye, armorye, and genealogy*, London.

Caelius Aurelianus (1950). *On Acute Diseases and on Chronic Diseases*, ed. and trans. I. E. Drabkin, Chicago.

Calvin, Jean (1561). *An Admonicion against Astrology Iudiciall and other curiosities, that raigne now in the world*, trans. Goddred G[ilby], London.

(1936). *Institutes of the Christian Religion*, 2 vols., trans. John Allen, 7th edn rev. by B. B. Warfield, Philadelphia.

Carbone, Ludovico (2003). 'Five Books on Oratorical and Dialectical Invention', trans. William A. Wallace, in Jean Dietz Moss, and William A. Wallace (eds.), *Rhetoric and Dialectic in the Time of Galileo*, Washington DC.

Cardano, Girolamo (1576). *Cardanus Comforte*, trans. Thomas Bedingfield, London.

(1663). *Opera omnia*, 10 vols., ed. Carolus Sponius, Lyon.

Carpenter, Nathanael (1622). *Philosophia libera, triplici exercitationum decade proposita*, 2nd edn, Oxford.

(1625). *Geography Delineated Forth*, Oxford.

Cartwright, William (1639). *The royall slave. A tragi-comedy. Presented to the King and Queene by the students of Christ-Church in Oxford. August 30. 1636*, Oxford.

Casaubon, Meric (1999). *Generall Learning: A seventeenth-century treatise on the formation of the general scholar by Meric Casaubon*, ed. with an introduction by Richard Serjeantson, Cambridge.

Castiglione, Baldassare (1994). *The Book of the Courtier*, ed. Virginia Cox, London.

Celsus (1953–61). *De medicina*, 3 vols., trans. W. G. Spencer, London and Cambridge, Mass.

Chapelain, André le (1982). *Andreas Capellanus on Love*, ed. and trans. P. G. Walsh, London.

Charron, Pierre (1620), *Of wisdome three bookes*, trans. Samson Lennard, 2nd edn, London.

Chiodini, Giulio Cesare, [= Claudinus] (1607). *Responsiones et consultationes medicinales*, Venice.

Cicero, Marcus Tullius (1913). *De officiis*, trans. Walter Miller, London.

(1927). *Tusculan Disputations*, trans. J. E. King, London and Cambridge, Mass.

(1928). *De re publica; De legibus*, trans. Clinton Walker Keyes, London and Cambridge, Mass.

(1930). *Pro Publio Quinctio, Pro Sexto Roscio Amerino, Pro Quinto Roscio Comoedo, De Lege Agraria*, trans. J. H. Freese, London.

(1931). *De finibus bonorum et malorum*, trans. H. Rackham, London and Cambridge, Mass.

(1933). *De natura deorum, Academica*, trans. H. Rackham, London.

(1942). *De oratore Book III, De Fato, Paradoxa Stoicorum, De Partitione Oratoria*, trans. H. Rackham, London and Cambridge, Mass.

(1949). *De inventione, Topica*, ed. and trans. H. M. Hubbell, London.

(1971). *De senectute; De amicitia; De divinatione*, trans. William Armistead Falconer, London and Cambridge, Mass.

Clement of Alexandria (1867–9). *The Writings of Clement of Alexandria*, trans. William Wilson, 2 vols., Edinburgh.

Constantinus Africanus (1536). *Opera*, Basel.

Cooper, Anthony Ashley, Third Earl of Shaftesbury (1999). *Characteristicks of Men, Manners, Opinions, Times*, ed. Philip Ayres, Oxford.

Corbett, Richard (1955). *The Poems of Richard Corbett*, eds. C. Bennett and H. Trevor-Roper, Oxford.

Cornwallis, Sir Charles (1641). *A discourse of the most illustrious prince, Henry late Prince of Wales*, London.

Cornwallis, Sir William the Younger (1600). *Essayes*, London.

Cotta, John (1616), *The Triall of Witch-Craft shewing the true and right methode of the discovery*, London.

Cranfield, Nicholas, and Kenneth Fincham (eds.) (1987). *John Howson's Answers to Archbishop Abbot's Accusations at his 'Trial' before James I at Greenwich,* 10 *June* 1615, *Camden Miscellany* 29, London.

Crosse, Henry (1603). *Vertues common-wealth: or The high-way to honour*, London.

Day, Angel (1586). *The English secretorie*, London.

Death repeal'd by a thankfull memoriall sent from Christ-Church in Oxford celebrating the noble deserts of the Right Honourable, Paule, late Lord Viscount Bayning of Sudbury (1638), Oxford

Diogenes Laertius (1925). *Lives of Eminent Philosophers*, 2 vols., trans. R. D. Hicks, London.

Du Laurens, André (1599). *A Discourse of the Preservation of the Sight: of Melancholike Diseases; Of Rheumes, and of Old Age*, trans. Richard Surphlet, London.

Du Vair, Guillaume (1598). *The Moral Philosophie of the Stoicks*, trans. Thomas James, London.

Erasmus, Desiderius (1917). *The Complaint of Peace*, trans. Thomas Paynell, Chicago and London.

(1970). *The Enchiridion of Erasmus*, trans. and ed. Raymond Himelick, Gloucester, Mass.

(1985). 'De conscribendis epistolis', trans. C. Fantazzi, in *The Collected Works of Erasmus*, XXV: *Literary and Educational Writings* 3, ed. J. K. Sowards, Toronto, Buffalo, and London.

(1986). 'Moriae encomium', trans. Betty Radice, in *The Collected Works of Erasmus: Literary and Educational Writings*, V, ed. A. H. T. Levi, Toronto, Buffalo, and London.

(1997). *The Education of a Christian Prince*, ed. and trans. Lisa Jardine, Cambridge.

Fernel, Jean (1567). *Universa medicina, tribus et viginti libris absoluta*, Paris.

Ferrand, Jacques (1640). *EPOTOMANIA or a Treatise Discoursing of the Essence, Causes, Symptoms, Prognosticks, and Cure of Love or Erotique Melancholy*, trans. Edmund Chilmead, Oxford.

(1990). *A Treatise on Lovesickness*, ed. and trans. Donald A. Beecher and Massimo Ciavolella, Syracuse, NY.

Ficino, Marsilio (1576). *Opera*, Basel.

(1975). *The Letters of Marsilio Ficino*, 5 vols., trans. by members of the Language Department of the School of Economic Science, London.

(1985). *Commentary on Plato's Symposium on Love*, trans. Sears Jayne, Dallas.

(2001–). *Platonic Theology*, ed. James Hankins and trans. Michael J. B. Allen, 4 vols. (vols. 5–6 forthcoming), Cambridge, Mass.

Forset, Edward (1606). *A comparative discourse of the bodies natural and politique*, London.

Fuller, Thomas (1655). *The church-history of Britain from the birth of Jesus Christ until the year M.DC.XLVIII*, London.

(1662). *The History of the Worthies of England*, London.

Galen (1528a). *De differentiis symptomarum liber I, De causis symptomatum libri III, interprete Thoma Linacro*, Paris.

(1528b). *Definitiones medicae, Iona Philologo interprete*, Paris.

(1529). *De atra bile, liber. De tumoribus præter naturam, liber. Guinterio Ioanne Andernaco interprete*, Paris.

(1821–33). *Opera omnia*, 20 vols. in 22, ed. Carl Gottlob Kühn, Leipzig.
(1952). *On the Natural Faculties*, trans. Arthur J. Brock, London.
(1963). *On the Natural Faculties*, ed. and trans. Arthur J. Brock, Cambridge.
(1968). *On the Usefulness of the Parts of the Body*, 2 vols., ed. and trans. Margaret T. May, Ithaca.
(1969). *On the Parts of Medicine, On Cohesive Causes, On Regimen in Acute Diseases in Accordance with the Theories of Hippocrates*, ed. and trans. H. Schoene, K. Kalbfleisch, and G. Strohmaier, Berlin.
(1976). *Galen on the Affected Parts*, trans. Rudolph E. Siegel, Basel.
(1978–1984). *On the Doctrines of Hippocrates and Plato*, ed. and trans. Phillip De Lacy, 2 vols., Berlin.
(1991). *On the Therapeutic Method*, trans. R. J. Hankinson, Oxford.
(1997). *Selected Works*, trans. with an introduction by P. N. Singer, Oxford and New York.
Galilei, Galileo (1967). *Dialogue Concerning the Two Chief World Systems – Ptolemaic and Copernican, Second Day*, trans. S. Drake, Berkeley.
Gentillet, Innocent (1602). *A discourse upon the meanes of wel governing and maintaining in good peace, a kingdome, or other principalitie*, trans. Simon Patrick, London.
Guazzo, Franceso Maria (1929). *Compendium maleficarum*, ed. M. Summers, trans. E. A. Ashwin, London.
Guazzo, Stefano (1581). *The civile conversation of M. Steeven Guazzo*, trans. George Pettie, London.
Guicciardini, Francesco (1994). *Dialogue on the Government of Florence*, trans. and ed. Alison Brown, Cambridge.
Hall, Joseph (1609). *Salomons Divine Arts, of* 1. *Ethickes,* 2. *Politickes,* 3. *Oeconomicks*, London.
(1628). *The works of Joseph Hall, B. of Exceter. With a table newly added to the whole worke*, London.
Hearne, Thomas (1885–1921). *Remarks and Collections of Thomas Hearne*, eds. C. E. Doble, D. W. Rannie, and H. E. Salter, 11 vols., Oxford.
Herring, Thomas (1777). *Letters from the Late most Reverend Dr. Thomas Herring, Lord Archbishop of Canterbury, to William Duncombe, Esq.*, London.
Heylyn, Peter (1625). *Microcosmos. A little description of the great world*, 2nd edn, Oxford.
(1668). *Cyprianus anglicus*, London.
Hippocrates (1525). *Opera*, trans. M. Fabio Calvo, Rome.
(1839–61). *Oeuvres complètes*, 10 vols., ed. and trans. Emile Littré, Amsterdam.
(1931). *Hippocrates*, IV, trans. W. H. S. Jones, London.
(1962). *Hippocrates*, I, trans. W. H. S. Jones, repr., London and Cambridge, Mass.
(1978). *Hippocratic Writings*, ed. G. E. R. Lloyd, trans. J. Chadwick, W. N. Mann, I. M. Lonie, and E. T. Withington, repr., Harmondsworth.
(1990). *Pseudepigraphic Writings: Letters–Embassy–Speech from the Altar–Decree*, ed. and trans. Wesley D. Smith, Leiden.

Hobbes, Thomas (1994). *The Elements of Law, Natural and Politic*, ed. J. C. A. Gaskin, Oxford and New York.
(1996). *Leviathan*, ed. Richard Tuck, Cambridge.
Horace (1929). *Satires, Epistles, Ars Poetica*, trans. H. Rushton Fairclough, London.
Howson, John (1598). *A second sermon, preached at Paules Crosse, the 21. of May, 1598*, London.
(1602). *A sermon preached at St. Maries in Oxford, the 17. day of November, 1602*, Oxford.
Huarte Navarro, Juan (1594). *Examen Ingenios*, trans. R[ichard] C[arew], London.
Hume, David (1994). *Political Essays*, ed. Knud Haakonssen, Cambridge.
Ishâq, ibn 'Imran and Constantinus Africanus (1977). *Maqala Fi L-Malhihuliya, Libri duo de melancholia*, ed. Karl Garbers, Hamburg.
James I and VI (1598). *The true lawe of free monarchies*, Edinburgh.
(1599). *Basilikon doron*, Edinburgh.
(1603a). *Basilikon doron*, 2nd edn, Edinburgh.
(1603b). *Daemonologie*, London.
(1612). *His Majesties declaration concerning his proceedings with the States generall of the United Provinces of the Low Countreys, in the cause of D. Conradus Vorstius*, London.
(1958). *The Poems of King James VI*, Edinburgh.
Jorden, Edward (1603). *A Briefe Discourse of a Disease Called the Suffocation of the Mother*, London.
Kennett, White (1728). *A Register and Chronicle Ecclesiastical and Civil*, Vol. 1, London.
King, Henry (1657). *Poems, elegies, paradoxes, and sonnets*, London.
Kornmann, Heinrich (1610). *Linea amoris*, Frankfurt.
La Primaudaye, Pierre de (1618). *The French Academie*, trans. T. B. C., London.
Larkin, F. and Hughes, P. (eds.) (1973). *Stuart Royal Proclamations*, Oxford.
Laud, William (1695). *The history of the troubles and tryal of the Most Reverend Father in God and blessed martyr, William Laud, Lord Arch-Bishop of Canterbury*, London.
(1847–60). *The works of the Most Reverend Father in God, William Laud, D.D. sometime lord archbishop of Canterbury*, eds. William Scott and James Bliss, 7 vols., Oxford.
Laurence, Thomas (1635). *Two sermons The first preached at St Maries in Oxford July* 13. 1634, Oxford.
Leech, Humphrey (1609). *A triumph of truth*, Douai.
Lemnius, Levinus (1576). *The Touchstone of Complexions*, trans. Thomas Newton, London.
Lipsius, Justus (1594). *Sixe bookes of politickes or civil doctrine*, trans. William Jones, London.
(1595). *Two bookes of constancie*, trans. Sir John Stradling, London.
(1644). *I. Lipsii philosophia & physiologica Stoica*, Leiden.
Lleuelyn, Martin (1646). *Men-Miracles. With other Poemes*, Oxford.

Lucretius (1976). *De Rerum Natura*, trans. W. H. D. Rouse, rev. by M. F. Smith, Cambridge, Mass., and London.
Luther, Martin (1955). *Letters of Spiritual Counsel*, trans. Theodore G. Tappert, Philadelphia.
(1995). *Table Talk*, trans. William Hazlitt, London.
Machiavelli, Niccòlo (1970). *The Discourses*, trans. Leslie J. Walker, rev. Brian Richardson, London.
Manardi, Giovanni (1611). *ΙΑΤΡΟΛΓΙΑ ΕΠΙΣΤΟΛΙΚΗ sive curia medica*, Hanover.
Marlowe, Christopher (1976). *Complete Plays and Poems*, eds. E. D. Pendry and J. C. Maxwell, London.
Marsilius of Padua (1979). *Defensor Pacis*, ed. Alan Gewirth, New York.
Melanchthon, Philipp (1552). *Liber de anima, recognitus ab autore*, Wittenberg.
(1834–60). *Opera quae supersunt omnia*, eds. Carolus Gottlieb Bretschneider and H. E. Bindeil, 28 vols., Halle-Braunschweig.
Mercuriale, Girolamo (1617). *Medicina practica ... libri V*, 2nd edn, Lyon.
Milton, John (1957). *Samson Agonistes*, ed. F. T. Prince, Oxford.
Montaigne, Michel de (1603). *The Essayes, Or Morall, Politike and Millitarie Discourses*, trans. John Florio, London.
(1974). *Essais*, ed. Jean Plattard, Paris.
Montalto, Filoteo Eliano de (1614). *Archipathologia*, Paris.
More, Henry (1662). *A collection of several philosophical writings of Dr Henry More... as namely, his Antidote against atheism, Appendix to the said antidote, Enthusiasmus triumphatus, Letters to Des-Cartes, &c., Immortality of the soul, Conjectura cabbalistica*, London.
More, Thomas (1518). *De optimo reip. Statu, deque nova insula Utopia*, Basle.
(1573). *A dialogue of cumfort against tribulation*, Antwerp.
(1951). *Dialogue of Comfort Against Tribulation*, London and New York.
(1989). *Utopia*, trans. and ed. G. Logan, Cambridge.
Nichols, John (1797–1815). *The History and Antiquities of the County of Leicester*, 4 vols., London.
Oribasius (1567). *Synopseos ad Eustathium filium libros novem*, in Henricus Stephanus (ed.), *Medicae artis principes*, Paris.
Ovid (1979). *The Art of Love and Other Poems*, trans. J. H. Mozley, rev. ed. G. P. Goold, Cambridge, Mass., and London.
(1984). *Metamorphoses*, 2 vols., trans. F. J. Miller, rev. ed. G. P. Goold, Cambridge, Mass., and London.
Palmieri, Matteo (1997). 'Civil Life', trans. David Marsh, in Jill Kraye (ed.), *Cambridge Translations of Renaissance Philosophical Texts*, vol. 2: *Political Philosophy*, Cambridge.
Paracelsus (1996). *Four Treatises of Theophrastus von Hohenheim, called Paracelsus*, trans. C. Lilian Temkin, George Rosen, Gregory Zilboorg and Henry E. Sigerist, repr., Baltimore and London.
Pascal, Blaise (1976). *Pensées*, ed. Philippe Sellier, Paris.

Paul of Aegina (1567). *De re medica libri septem*, in Henricus, Stephanus (ed.), *Medicae artis principes*, Paris.

(1844–47). *The Seven Books of Paulus Aegineta*, trans. with a commentary by Francis Adams, 3 vols., London.

Peacham, Henry (1593). *The Garden of Eloquence*, 2nd edn, London.

Perkins, William (1591). *A Treatise tending unto a declaration, whether a man bee in the estate of damnation, or in the estate of grace . . .*, London.

(1606). *The Whole Treatise of the Cases of Conscience*, Amsterdam.

(1608–9). *The Workes . . . of William Perkins*, 2 vols., Cambridge.

Petrarch (2003). *Invectives*, trans. David Marsh, Cambridge, Mass., and London.

Pico della Mirandola, Gianfrancesco (1969). *Opera omnia*, 2 vols., repr., Hildesheim.

Plato (1914). *Euthyphro, Apology, Crito, Phaedo, Phaedrus*, trans. Harold North Fowler, London.

(1925). *The Statesman, Philebus*, trans. Harold North Fowler, London.

(1926). *Laws*, 2 vols., trans. R. G. Bury, London.

(1927). *Charmides, Alcibiades I and II, Hipparchus, The Lovers, Theages, Minos, Epinomis*, trans. W. R. M. Lamb, London.

(1929). *Timaeus, Critias, Cleitophon, Menexenus, Epistles*, trans. R. G. Bury, London.

(1930–5). *The Republic*, trans. Paul Shorey, 2 vols., London.

Platter, Felix (1602–3). *Praxeos medicae*, Basel.

and Cole, Abdiah, and Culpeper, Nicholas (1662). *A Golden Practice of Phisicke*, London.

Plutarch (1928). *Moralia* vol. II, trans. Frank Cole Babbitt, London.

(1961). *Moralia*, vol. IX, trans. E. Mina, Jr, F. H. Sandbach, and W. C. Helmbold, repr., Cambridge, Mass., and London.

Pontano, Giovanni. (1997). 'On the Prince', trans. Nicholas Webb, in Jill Kraye (ed.), *Cambridge Translations of Renaissance Philosophical Texts*, vol. 2: *Political Philosophy*, Cambridge.

Price, Daniel (1610). *The defence of truth against a booke falsely called The triumph of truth sent over from Arras* A.D. 1609, Oxford.

(1614). *Prince Henry his second anniversary*, Oxford.

Prynne, William (1646). *Canterburies doome*, London.

Quintilian (1920–2). *Institutio oratoria*, 4 vols., trans. and ed. H. E. Butler, London.

Reynolds, Edward (1640). *A Treatise of the Passions and Faculties of the Soule of Man*, London.

Rhazes (1544). *Opera exquisitora*, trans. Gerardus Cremonensis, Andreas Vesalius, and Albanus Torinus Vitduranus, Basle.

(1973). *Opera*, facsimile repr. of the 1544 edition, Brussels.

Rider, John (1612). *Riders dictionarie corrected, and with the addition of above five hundred words enriched*, London.

Rufus of Ephesus (1879). *Oeuvres de Rufus d'Ephèse*, ed. and trans. Ch. Daremberg and Ch. E. Ruelle, Paris.

Sacchi, Bartolomeo (1997). 'On the Prince', trans. Nicholas Webb, in Jill Kraye, (ed.), *Cambridge Translations of Renaissance Philosophical Texts*, vol. II: *Political Philosophy*, Cambridge.

Scala, Bartolomeo (1997). 'Dialogue on Laws and Legal Judgements', trans. David Marsh, in Jill Kraye (ed.), *Cambridge Translations of Renaissance Philosophical Texts*, vol. II: *Political Philosophy*, Cambridge.

Scaliger, Julius Caesar (1607). *Exotericarum exercitationum liber XV de subtilitate, ad Hieronymum Cardanum*, Frankfurt.

Seneca, Lucius Annaeus (1917–25). *Epistulae Morales*, 3 vols., trans. R. M. Gummere, London.

(1928–32). *Moral Essays*, trans. John W. Basore, 3 vols., London.

Sextus, Empiricus (1621). *Opera quae extant ... Gentiano Herveto Aurelio Interprete*, Geneva.

Shakespeare, William (1988). *The Complete Works*, eds. Stanley Wells and Gary Taylor, Oxford.

Smith, Samuel (1614). *Davids repentance, or, A plaine and familiar exposition of the 51 psalme*, London.

Sophocles (1957). *Ajax, The Women of Trachis, Electra, Philoctetes*, trans. J. Moore, M. Jameson, and D. Grene, Chicago and London.

Stafford, Anthony (1611). *Staffords Niobe: or His age of teares*, London.

Strode, William (1655). *The floating island a tragi-comedy, acted before his Majesty at Oxford, Aug. 29. 1636 By the students of Christ-Church*, London.

Tacitus, Cornelius (1591). *The ende of Nero and beginning of Galba. Fower bookes of the Histories of Cornelius Tacitus. The life of Agricola*, trans. Sir Henry Savile, London.

Thomas Aquinas (1952–62). *Summa theologiae*, ed. P. Caramello, 3 vols., Turin.

Thoresby, Ralph (1830). *The Diary of Ralph Thoresby, F.R.S.*, ed. Joseph Hunter, London.

Usener, Hermann, (ed.) (1887). *Epicurea*, Stuttgart.

Valesco da Taranta (1516). *Practica ... alias Philonius dicitur*, Lyon.

Valleriola, François (1588). *Observationum medicinalium libri sex*, Lyon.

Vallesio, Francisco (1582). *Controversiarum medicarum et philosophicarum libri decem*, Frankfurt.

Vaughan, William (1598). *Poematum libellus continens* 1. *Encomium illustrissimi herois, D. Roberti comitis Essexii.* 2. *De sphaerarum ordine tractatiunculam.* 3. *Palaemonis amores philosophicos*, London.

(1626). *The golden fleece*, London.

Victorius, Leonellus Faventinus de (1574). *Practica medicinalis*, Lyon.

Vives, Juan Luis (1555). *De anima & vita libri tres*, Lyon.

(1964). *Opera omnia*, ed. Gregorio Majansio, facsimile repr., London.

Wilson, Thomas (1553). *The arte of rhetorique*, 2nd edn, London.

Wither, George (1613). *Abuses stript, and whipt*, London.

(1614). *A Satyre: Dedicated to his Most Excellent Majestie*, London.

Wood, Anthony à (1792–6). *The History and Antiquities of the University of Oxford*, ed. John Gutch, 2 vols., Oxford.

(1815). *Athenae Oxonienses*, 2 vols., London.

Wright, Thomas (1971). *The Passions of the Minde in Generall*, facsimile of 1630 edition, with an introduction by Thomas O. Sloan, Urbana, Ill.

PRINTED SECONDARY SOURCES

Alet, Martine (2000). 'La Mélancolie dans la psycho-physiologie du début du XVIIe siècle', *Papers on French Seventeenth Century Literature* 27, 447–71.

Anglo, Sydney (1976). 'Melancholia and Witchcraft: The Debate Between Wier, Bodin, and Scot', in Alois, Gerlo (ed.), *Folie et Déraison à la Renaissance: Colloque international tenu en novembre 1973 sous le auspices de la Fédération Internationale des Instituts et Sociétés pour l'Étude de la Renaissance*, Brussels, pp. 209–22.

Archer, Ian (1988). 'The London Lobbies in the Later Sixteenth Century', *Historical Journal* 31, 17–44.

Babb, Lawrence (1951). *The Elizabethan Malady: A Study of Melancholia in English Literature from 1580 to 1642*, East Lansing.

(1959). *Sanity in Bedlam: A Study of Robert Burton's 'Anatomy of Melancholy'*, East Lansing.

Baldwin, Geoff (2001). 'Individual and Self in the Late Renaissance', *Historical Journal* 44, 341–64.

(2004). 'Reason of State and Stuart Parliaments, 1610–42', *History of Political Thought* 25, 620–41.

Ballester, Luis García (1995). '*Artifex factivus sanitatis*: Health and Medical Care in Medieval Latin Galenism', in Don Bates (ed.), *Knowledge and the Scholarly Medical Traditions*, Cambridge, 127–50.

Bamborough, J. B. (1981). 'Robert Burton's Astrological Notebook', *Review of English Studies* n.s. 32, 267–85.

(1983). 'Burton and Hemingius', *Review of English Studies* n.s. 34, 441–5.

(1989). 'Introduction', in Robert Burton, *The Anatomy of Melancholy*, eds. T. Faulkner, N. Kiessling, and R. Blair, Oxford, pp. xiii–vi.

Barbour, Reid (1998). *English Epicures and Stoics: Ancient Legacies in Early Stuart Culture*, Amherst.

Barlow, Richard G. (1973). 'Infinite Worlds: Robert Burton's Cosmic Voyage', *Journal of the History of Ideas* 34, 291–302.

Baron, Hans (1966). *The Crisis of the Early Italian Renaissance*, 2nd edn, Princeton, NJ.

Beaty, N. L. (1970). *The Craft of Dying: A Study in the Literary Tradition of the 'Ars moriendi' in England*, New Haven.

Beecher, Donald A. (1992). 'Quattrocento Views on the Eroticization of the Imagination', in Donald A. Beecher and Massimo Ciavolella (eds.), *Eros and Anteros: The Medical Traditions of Love in the Renaissance*, Toronto, pp. 49–65.

Beecher, Donald, and Ciavolella, Massimo (1990). 'Jacques Ferrand and the Tradition of Erotic Melancholy in Western Culture', in Jacques Ferrand, *A Treatise on Lovesickness*, Syracuse, NY, pp. 1–202.

(eds.) (1992). *Eros and Anteros: The Medical Traditions of Love in the Renaissance*, Toronto.

Bensly, Edward (1909). 'Robert Burton and Jacques Ferrand's *Melancholie Erotique*', *Notes and Queries* series 10, vol. 11, 286.

Bentley, Christopher (1969). '*The Anatomy of Melancholy* and Richard Whitlock's Zootomia', *Renaissance and Modern Studies* 13, 88–105.

Bernard, G. W. (1990). 'The Church of England, c. 1529–1642', *History* 75, 183–206.

Binns, J. W. (1990a). *Intellectual Culture in Elizabethan and Jacobean England: The Latin Writings of the Age*, Leeds.

(1990b). 'Elizabeth I and the Universities', in John Henry and Sarah Hutton (eds.), *New Perspectives on Renaissance Thought: Essays in the History of Science, Education, and Philosophy in Memory of Charles B. Schmitt*, London, pp. 244–52.

Blair, Ann (1997). *The Theater of Nature: Jean Bodin and Renaissance Science*, Princeton.

(2003). 'Reading Strategies for Coping With Information Overload, ca. 1550–1700', *Journal of the History of Ideas* 64, 11–28.

Blok, F. F. (1976). *Caspar Barlaeus: From the Correspondence of a Melancholic*, Amsterdam.

Boas, F. S. and Greg, W. W. (1909). 'James I at Oxford in 1605: Property Lists from the University Archives', *Malone Society Collections*, vol. 1, pt 3, Oxford.

Bossy, John (1985). *Christianity and the West*, 1400–1700, Oxford.

Bourdieu, Pierre, and Chartier, Roger (1985). 'La lecture: une pratique culturelle', in R. Chartier (ed.), *Pratiques de la lecture*, Marseilles and Paris, pp. 218–39.

Boutcher, Warren (1996). 'Vernacular Humanism in the Sixteenth Century', in Jill Kraye (ed.), *The Cambridge Companion to Renaissance Humanism*, Cambridge, pp. 189–202.

Boyce, Benjamin (1949). 'The Stoic Consolatio and Shakespeare', *Proceedings of the Modern Language Association of America* 64, 771–80.

Brann, Noel L. (2002). *The Debate Over the Origin of Genius During the Italian Renaissance: The Theories of Supernatural Frenzy and Natural Melancholy in Accord and in Conflict on the Threshold of the Scientific Revolution*, Leiden, Boston and Köln.

Bray, J. S. (1975). *Theodore Beza's Doctrine of Predestination*, Nieuwkoop.

Browne, Robert M. (1952). 'Robert Burton and the New Cosmology', *Modern Language Quarterly* 13, 131–48.

Burgess, Glenn (1992). 'The Divine Right of Kings Reconsidered', *English Historical Review* 425, 837–61.

Burke, Peter (1999). 'Erasmus and the Republic of Letters', *European Review* 7, 5–17.

Bylebyl, Jerome (1991). 'Teaching *Methodus Medendi* in the Renaissance', in Fridolf Kudlien and Richard J. Durling (eds.), *Galen's Method of Healing: Proceedings of the* 1982 *Galen Symposium*, Leiden, pp. 159–89.

Calmann, Gerta (1960). 'The Picture of Nobody: An Iconographical study', *Journal of the Warburg and Courtauld Institutes* 23, 60–104.

Canavan, Thomas (1973). 'Robert Burton, Jonathan Swift, and the Tradition of Anti-Puritan Invective', *Journal of the History of Ideas* 32, 227–42.

Céard, Jean (1976). 'Folie et demonologie au XVIe siècle', in Alois Gerlo (ed.), *Folie et Déraison à la Renaissance: Colloque international tenu en novembre* 1973 *sous le auspices de la Fédération Internationale des Instituts et Sociétés pour l'Étude de la Renaissance*, Brussels, pp. 129–48.

(1992). 'The Devil and Lovesickness: Views of 16th-century Physicians and Demonologists', in Donald A. Beecher and Massimo Ciavolella (eds.), *Eros and Anteros: The Medical Traditions of Love in the Renaissance*, Toronto, pp. 33–47.

Chapple, Ann S. (1993). 'Robert Burton's Geography of Melancholy', *Studies in English Literature,* 1500–1900 33, 99–130.

Cherchi, Paolo (1992). 'A Dossier for the Study of Jealousy', in Donald A. Beecher and Massimo Ciavolella (eds.), *Eros and Anteros: The Medical Traditions of Love in the Renaissance*, Toronto, pp. 123–34.

(1994). *Andreas and the Ambiguity of Courtly Love*, Toronto and London.

Clavero, Bartolomé (1991), *Razón de estado, razón de individuo, razón de historia*, Madrid.

Cogswell, Thomas (1989). *The Blessed Revolution: English Politics and the Coming of War,* 1621–1624, Cambridge.

(2002). 'The People's Love: The Duke of Buckingham and Popularity', in T. Cogswell, R. Cust, and P. Lake (eds.), *Politics, Religion and Popularity: Essays in honour of Conrad Russell*, Cambridge, pp. 211–34.

Colclough, David (2003). '"Better Becoming a Senate of Venice"? The "Addled Parliament" and Jacobean Debates on Freedom of Speech', in Stephen Clucas and Rosalind Davies (eds.), *The Crisis of* 1614 *and the Addled Parliament*, Aldershot, pp. 51–61.

(2005). *Freedom of Speech in Early Stuart England*, Cambridge.

Colie, Rosalie (1967). 'Some Notes on Burton's Erasmus', *Renaissance Quarterly* 20, 335–41.

Collinson, Patrick (1980). 'A Comment: Concerning the Name Puritan', *Journal of Ecclesiastical History* 31, 483–8.

(1985). 'England and International Calvinism, 1558–1640', in Menna Prestwich (ed.), *International Calvinism,* 1541–1715, Oxford, pp. 197–223.

(1987) 'The Monarchical Republic of Queen Elizabeth I', *Bulletin of the John Rylands University Library of Manchester* 69, 394–424.

(2002). '"The State as Monarchical Commonwealth": "Tudor" England', *Journal of Historical Sociology* 15, 89–95.

Comparato, Vitor Ivo (1996). 'A Case of Modern Individualism: Politics and the Uneasiness of Intellectuals in the Baroque Age', in Janet Coleman (ed.), *The Individual in Political Theory and Practice*, Oxford, pp. 149–70.

Copenhaver, Brian P. (1991). 'A Tale of Two Fishes: Magical Objects in Natural History from Antiquity through the Scientific Revolution', *Journal of the History of Ideas* 52, 373–98.

Corbett, Margery and Lightbown, Ronald (1979). *The Comely Frontispiece: The Emblematic Title-page in England,* 1550–1660, London, Henley, and Boston.

Cox-Johnson, A. (1955). 'Lambeth Palace Library 1610–1664', *Transactions of the Cambridge Bibliographical Society* 2, 105–26.

Cunningham, J. V. (1960). *Tradition and Poetic Structure*, Denver.

Cunningham, William L (1974). *Martin Opitz: Poems of Consolation in Adversities of War*, Bonn.

Curtis, Mark H. (1959). *Oxford and Cambridge in Transition,* 1558–1642*: An Essay on Changing Relations between the English Universities and English Society*, Oxford.

(1962). 'The Alienated Intellectuals of Early Stuart England', *Past and Present* 23, 25–43.

Curtius, Ernst Robert (1953). *European Literature and the Latin Middle Ages*, trans. Willard Trask, Princeton.

Curry, John T. (1901). 'A Nameless Book', *Notes & Queries* 10th series, 4, 123–4.

Cust, Richard (2002). 'Charles I and Popularity', in T. Cogswell, R. Cust, and P. Lake (eds.), *Politics, Religion and Popularity: Essays in Honour of Conrad Russell*, Cambridge, pp. 235–58.

(2004–5). 'William Burton', in H. C. G. Matthew and Brian Harrison (eds.), *The Oxford Dictionary of National Biography*, IX, Oxford, pp. 46–8.

Daston, Lorraine (1991). 'Marvelous Facts and Miraculous Evidence in Early Modern Europe', *Critical Inquiry* 18, 93–124.

and Park, Katharine (1998). *Wonders and the Order of Nature,* 1150–1750, New York.

Davies, E. T. (1950). *Episcopacy and the Royal Supremacy in the Church of England in the XVI century*, London.

Davies, Julian (1992). *The Caroline Captivity of the Church: Charles I and the Remoulding of Anglicanism,* 1625–41, Oxford.

Dear, Peter (1995). *Discipline and Experience: The Mathematical Way in the Scientific Revolution*, Chicago and London.

Delumeau, Jean (1965). *Naissance et affirmation de la Réforme*, Paris.

(1977). *Catholicism between Luther and Voltaire*, trans. Jeremy Moiser, London.

(1978). *La Peur en Occident (*XIVe*–*XVIIIe *siècles): Une cité assiégée*, Paris.

(1988). 'Prescription and Reality', in Edmund Leites (ed.), *Conscience and Casuistry in Early Modern Europe*, Cambridge, pp. 134–58.

(1990). *Sin and Fear: The Emergence of a Western Guilt Culture, 13th–18th centuries*, trans. Eric Nicholson, New York.

DeJongh, Peter Y (ed.) (1968). *Crisis in the Reformed Churches: Essays in Commencement of the Great Synod of Dort, 1618–19*, Grand Rapids.
Dent, C. M. (1983). *Protestant Reformers in Elizabethan Oxford*, Oxford.
Dewey, Nicholas (1971). 'Burton's Melancholy: A paradox disinterred', *Modern Philology* 68, 292–3.
Dieckow, Fritz (1903). *John Florios englische bersetzung der Essais Montaignes und Lord Bacons, Ben Jonsons und Robert Burtons Verhältnis zu Montaigne*, Inaugural-Dissertation, Strassburg.
Diethelm, Oskar (1971). *Medical Dissertations of Psychiatric Interest Printed Before 1750*, Basle.
Donovan, Dennis G. (1967). 'Robert Burton, Anglican Minister', *Renaissance Papers* 13, 33–40.
Eamon, William (1994). *Science and the Secrets of Nature: Books of Secrets in Medieval and Early Modern Culture*, Princeton.
Evans, Bergen (1944). *The Psychiatry of Robert Burton*, New York.
Ewing, S. Blaine (1940). *Burtonian Melancholy in the Plays of John Ford*, Princeton.
Faulkner, Thomas C. (1998). 'Robert Burton's Sources and Late Topical Revision in *The Anatomy of Melancholy*', in W. Speed Hill (ed.), *New Ways of Looking at Old Texts*, II: *Papers of the Renaissance English Texts Society, 1992–96*, Tempe, Arizona, pp. 23–9.
Feingold, Mordechai (1984). 'The Occult Tradition in the English Universities of the Renaissance: A Reassessment', in Brian Vickers (ed.), *Occult and Scientific Mentalities in the Renaissance*, Cambridge, pp. 73–94.
(1997). 'The Humanities', in Nicholas Tyacke (ed.), *The History of the University of Oxford*, IV: *Seventeenth-Century Oxford*, Oxford, pp. 211–357.
Fincham, Kenneth (1993a). 'Introduction', in K. Fincham (ed.), *The Early Stuart Church*, London, pp. 1–22.
(1993b). 'Episcopal Government, 1603–1640', in K. Fincham (ed.), *The Early Stuart Church*, Basingstoke, pp. 71–91.
(2000). 'William Laud and the Exercise of Caroline Ecclesiastical Patronage', *Journal of Ecclesiastical History* 51, pp. 69–9.
(2001). 'The Restoration of the Altars in the 1630s', *Historical Journal* 44, 919–40.
Fincham, Kenneth, and Lake, Peter (1985). 'The Ecclesiastical Policy of James I', *Journal of British Studies* 24, 169–207.
Findlen, Paula (1994). *Possessing Nature: Museums, Collecting, and Scientific Culture in Early Modern Italy*, Berkeley and London.
Fish, Stanley (1972). *Self-Consuming Artifacts: The Experience of Seventeenth-Century Literature*, London.
Frank, Robert G., Jr (1973). 'Science, Medicine and the Universities of Early Modern England: Background and Sources', *History of Science* 11, 194–216, 239–69.
Friedrich, Hugo (1991). *Montaigne*, ed. Philippe Desan, trans. Dawn Eng, Berkeley, Los Angeles, and Oxford.

Frye, Northrop (1957). *The Anatomy of Criticism*, Princeton.

Gardiner, H. M., Metcalf, R. C., and Beebe-Center, J. G. (1937). *Feelings and Emotions: A History of Theories*, New York.

Gardiner, Judith Kegan (1977). 'Elizabethan Psychology and Burton's *Anatomy of Melancholy*', *Journal of the History of Ideas* 38, 373–88.

Gowland, Angus (2000). 'Rhetorical Structure and Function in *The Anatomy of Melancholy*', *Rhetorica* 19, 1–48.

(2006). 'The Problem of Early Modern Melancholy', *Past and Present*, 191, 85–128.

Goyet, Francis (1987). 'A propos de "Ces pastissages de lieux communs" (Le Rôle des notes de lecture dans le genèse des Essais), part 2', *Bulletin de la Société des Amis de Montaigne* 7–8, 9–30.

Goyet, Francis (1996). *Le Sublime du 'lieu commun': L 'Invention rhétorique dans l'Antiquité et à la Renaissance*, Paris.

Grace, W. J. (1955). 'Notes on Robert Burton and John Milton', *Studies in Philology* 52, 578–91.

Grafton, Anthony (1991). *Defenders of the Text: The Traditions of Scholarship in an Age of Science*, 1450–1800, Cambridge, Mass., and London.

(1996). 'Humanism and the New Science', in Jill Kraye (ed.), *The Cambridge Companion to Renaissance Humanism*, Cambridge, pp. 203–23.

(2000). *Cardano's Cosmos: The Worlds and Works of a Renaissance Astrologer*, Cambridge, Mass., and London.

and Jardine, Lisa (1986). *From Humanism to the Humanities: Education and the Liberal Arts in Fifteenth- and Sixteenth-Century Europe*, London.

Grant, Edward (1978). 'Aristotelianism and the Longevity of the Medieval World View', *History of Science* 16, 93–106.

Hacking, Ian (1998). *Mad Travelers: Reflections on the Reality of Transient Mental Illnesses*, Charlottesville and London.

Hadot, Pierre (1995). *Philosophy as a Way of Life: Spiritual Exercises from Socrates to Foucault*, ed. and with an introduction by A. I. Davidson, trans. Michael Chase, London.

(1998). *The Inner Citadel: The 'Meditations' of Marcus Aurelius*, trans. Michael Chase, Cambridge, Mass., and London.

(2002). *What is Ancient Philosophy?*, trans. Michael Chase, Cambridge, Mass.

Haigh, Christopher (2003). 'A Matter of Much Contention in the Realm': Parish Controversies over Communion Bread in Post-Reformation England', *History* 88, 393–404.

Hankinson, James (1993). 'Actions and Passions: Affection, Emotion, and Moral Self-Management in Galen's Philosophical Psychology', in Jacques Brunschwig and Martha C. Nussbaum (eds.), *Passions and Perceptions: Studies in Hellenistic Philosophy of Mind. Proceedings of the Fifth Symposium Hellenisticum*, Cambridge, pp. 184–221.

Hardwick, Charles (1851). *History of the articles of religion: to which is added a series of documents from* A.D. 1536 *to* A.D. 1615; *together with illustrations from contemporary sources*, Cambridge.

Harley, David (1993). 'Spiritual Physic, Providence and English Medicine, 1560–1640', in Ole Peter Grell and Andrew Cunningham (eds.), *Medicine and the Reformation*, London and New York, pp. 101–17.

(1996). 'The Theology of Affliction and the Experience of Sickness in the Godly Family, 1650–1714: The Henrys and the Newcombes', in Ole Peter Grell and Andrew Cunningham (eds.), *Religio Medici: Medicine and Religion in Seventeenth-Century England*, Aldershot, pp. 273–92.

Harrison, Peter (2002). 'Original Sin and the Problem of Knowledge in Early Modern Europe', *Journal of the History of Ideas* 63, 239–59.

Harth, Philip (1961). *Swift and Anglican Rationalism: The Religious Background of 'A Tale of a Tub'*, Chicago.

Harvey, E. Ruth (1975). *The Inward Wits: Psychological Theory in the Middle Ages and the Renaissance*, London.

Heusser, Martin (1987). *The Gilded Pill: A Study of the Reader–Writer Relationship in Robert Burton's 'Anatomy of Melancholy'*, Tübingen.

Heyd, Michael (1984). 'Robert Burton's Sources on Enthusiasm and Melancholy: From a Medical Tradition to Religious Controversy', *History of European Ideas* 5, 17–44.

(1995). *'Be Sober and Reasonable': The Critique of Enthusiasm in the Seventeenth and Early Eighteenth Centuries*, Leiden.

Holland, Philip H. (1979). *Robert Burton's 'Anatomy of Melancholy' and Menippean Satire, Humanist and English*, unpublished PhD diss., University of London.

Hotson, Howard (2000), *Johann Heinrich Alsted, 1588–1638: Between Renaissance, Reformation and Universal Reform*, Oxford.

Hoyle, David (1986). 'A Commons Investigation of Arminianism and Popery in Cambridge on the Eve of the Civil War', *Historical Journal* 29, 419–25.

Hughes, Séan (1998). 'The Problem of 'Calvinism': English Theologies of Predestination c.1580–1630', in Susan Wabuda and Caroline Litzenberger (eds.), *Belief and Practice in Reformation England: A tribute to Patrick Collinson from His Students*, Aldershot, pp. 229–49.

Hutton, Sarah (1978). 'Thomas Jackson, Oxford Platonist, and William Twisse, Aristotelian', *Journal of the History of Ideas* 39, 635–52.

Jackson, Heather Joanna (1975). 'Sterne, Burton, and Ferriar: Allusions to the *Anatomy of Melancholy* in Volumes Five to Nine of *Tristram Shandy*', *Philological Quarterly* 54, 457–70.

Jackson, Stanley W. (1986). *Melancholia and Depression from Hippocratic Times to Modern Times*, New Haven and London.

(1989). 'Robert Burton and Psychological Healing', *Journal of the History of Medicine and Allied Sciences* 44, 160–7.

Jarcho, Saul (1970). 'Galen's Six Non-Naturals: A Bibliographical Note and Translation', *Bulletin of the History of Medicine* 44, 373–7.

Jardine, Lisa (1983). 'Lorenzo Valla: Academic Skepticism and the New Humanist Dialectic', in M. Burnyeat (ed.), *The Skeptical Tradition*, Berkeley and Los Angeles, pp. 253–86.

(1993). *Erasmus, Man of Letters: The Construction of Charisma in Print*, Princeton, NJ.

Jardine, Nicholas (1987). 'Scepticism in Renaissance Astronomy: A Preliminary Study', in Richard H. Popkin and Charles B. Schmitt (eds.), *Scepticism from the Renaissance to the Enlightenment*, Wiesbaden, pp. 83–102.

(1991). 'Demonstration, Dialectic, and Rhetoric in Galileo's *Dialogue*', in D. R. Kelley and R. H. Popkin (eds.), *The Shapes of Knowledge from the Renaissance to the Enlightenment*, Dordrecht, pp. 49–60.

Jefferson, D. W. (1952). 'Tristram Shandy and the Tradition of Learned Wit', *Essays in Criticism* 1, 225–48.

Jehasse, Jean (1980). 'Démocrite et la renaissance de la critique', *Etudes seizièmistes offertes à V.-L. Saulnier*, 41–64.

Jobe, T. H. (1976). 'Medical Theories of Melancholia in the Seventeenth and Early Eighteenth Centuries', *Clio Medica* 11, 217–31.

Joutsivuo, Timo (1999). *Scholastic Tradition and Humanist Innovation: The Concept of the Neutrum in Renaissance Medicine*, Helsinki.

Kassell, Lauren (1998). 'How to Read Simon Forman's Casebooks: Medicine, Astrology and Gender in Elizabethan London', *Social History of Medicine* 12, 3–18.

Kelley, Donald R. (1997). 'The Problem of Knowledge and the Concept of Discipline', in Donald R. Kelley (eds.), *History and the Disciplines: The Reclassification of Knowledge in Early Modern Europe*, Rochester, NY, pp. 13–27.

(2001). 'Eclecticism and the History of Ideas', *Journal of the History of Ideas* 62, 577–92.

Kiessling, Nicolas K. (1988). *The Library of Robert Burton*, Oxford.

(1990). 'Robert Burton's Will Holograph Copy', *Review of English Studies* 41, 94–101.

Klibansky, Raymond, Panofsky, Erwin, and Saxl, Fritz (1964). *Saturn and Melancholy: Studies in the History of Natural Philosophy, Religion, and Art*, Cambridge.

Kristeller, Paul Oskar (1956). 'The School of Salerno: Its Development and Its Contribution to the History of Learning', in *Studies in Renaissance Thought and Letters*, Rome, pp. 495–551.

(1976). 'Bartholomaeus, Musandinus, and Maurus of Salerno and Other Early Commentators of the 'Articella', with a Tentative List of Texts and Manuscripts', *Italia Medioevale e Umanistica* 19, 57–87.

Kusukawa, Sachiko (1995). *The Transformation of Natural Philosophy: The Case of Philip Melanchthon*, Cambridge.

Lake, Peter (1982). *Moderate Puritans and the Elizabethan Church*, Cambridge.

(1987). 'Calvinism and the English Church, 1570–1635', *Past and Present* 114, 32–76.

(1988). *Anglicans and Puritans? Presbyterianism and English Conformist thought from Whitgift to Hooker*, London.

(1991). 'Lancelot Andrewes, John Buckeridge and Avant-Garde Conformity at the Court of James I', in L. Levy Peck (ed.), *The Mental World of the Jacobean Court*, Cambridge, pp. 111–33.
(1992). 'The Laudians and the Argument from Authority', in B. Y. Kunze and D. D. Brautigan (eds.), *Court, Country and Culture*, Rochester, NY, pp. 149–76.
(1993a). 'The Laudian Style: Order, Uniformity and the Pursuit of the Beauty of Holiness in the 1630s', in Kenneth Fincham (ed.), *The Early Stuart Church, 1603–1642*, London, pp. 161–85.
(1993b). 'Defining Puritanism – Again?', in Francis J. Bremer (ed.), *Puritanism: Transatlantic Perspectives on a Seventeenth-Century Anglo-American Faith*, Boston, Mass., pp. 3–29.
(1995). 'The Moderate and Irenic Case for Religious War: Joseph Hall's *Via Media* in Context', in Susan D. Amussen and Mark A. Kishlansky (eds.), *Political Culture and Cultural Politics in Early Modern England: Essays Presented to David Underdown*, Manchester, pp. 55–83.
Lambert, Sheila (1989). 'Richard Montagu, Arminianism, and Censorship', *Past and Present* 124, 36–68.
Lawn, Brian (1963). *The Salernitan Questions: An Introduction to the History of Medieval and Renaissance Problem Literature*, Oxford.
(1993). *The Rise and Decline of the Scholastic 'Quaestio Disputata', with Special Emphasis on its Use in the Teaching of Medicine and Science*, Leiden.
Levi, A. H. T. (1964). *French Moralists: The Theory of the Passions, 1585 to 1649*, Oxford.
(2002). *Renaissance and Reformation: The Intellectual Genesis*, New Haven and London.
Lievsay, John L. (1956). 'Robert Burton's *De Consolatione*', *South Atlantic Quarterly* 55, 329–36.
Lines, David (1996). 'The Importance of Being Good: Moral Philosophy in the Italian Universities, 1300–1600', *Rinascimento* n.s. 36, 139–93.
Livingston, Donald W. (1998). *Philosophical Melancholy and Delirium: Hume's Pathology of Philosophy*, Chicago and London.
Loewenstein, Joseph (1996). 'Humanism and Seventeenth-Century English Literature', in Jill Kraye (ed.), *The Cambridge Companion to Renaissance Humanism*, Cambridge, pp. 269–93.
Lowes, John Livingston (1914). 'The Loveres Maladye of Hereos', *Modern Philology* 11, 491–546.
Lytle, Guy Fitch (1981). 'Religion and the Lay Patron in Reformation England', in Guy Fitch Lytle and Stephen Orgel (eds.), *Patronage in the Renaissance*, Princeton, pp. 65–114.
Macaulay, Rose (1931). *Some Religious Elements in English Literature*, London.
MacCaffrey, Wallace (1961). 'Place and Patronage in Elizabethan Politics', in S. T. Bindhoff, J. Hurstfield, and C. H. Williams (eds.), *Elizabethan Government and Society: Essays Presented to Sir John Neale*, London, pp. 95–126.

MacDonald, Michael (1981). *Mystical Bedlam: Madness, Anxiety, and Healing in Seventeenth-Century England*, Cambridge.

(1982). 'Religion, Social Change, and Psychological Healing in England 1600–1800', in W. J. Sheils (ed.), *The Church and Healing*, Oxford, pp. 101–25.

(1996). 'The Career of Astrological Medicine in England', in Ole Peter, Grell, and Andrew Cunningham (eds.), *Religio Medici: Medicine and Religion in Seventeenth-Century England*, Aldershot, pp. 62–90.

Mack, Peter (1993). *Renaissance Argument: Valla and Agricola in the Traditions of Rhetoric and Dialectic*, Leiden.

MacKenzie, Iain M. (2002). *God's Order and Natural Law: The Works of the Laudian Divines*, Aldershot.

Maclean, Ian (1980). *The Renaissance Notion of Woman: A Study in the Fortunes of Scholasticism and Medical Science in European Intellectual Life*, Cambridge.

(1984). 'The Interpretation of Natural Signs: Cardano's *De Subtilitate* versus Scaliger's *Exercitationes*', in Brian Vickers (ed.), *Occult and Scientific Mentalities in the Renaissance*, Cambridge, pp. 231–52.

(1992). *Interpretation and Meaning in the Renaissance: The case of law*, Cambridge.

(1999). 'Language in the Mind: Reflexive Thinking in the Late Renaissance', in Constance Blackwell and Sachiko Kusukawa (eds.), *Philosophy in the Sixteenth and Seventeenth Centuries: Conversations with Aristotle*, Aldershot, pp. 296–321.

(2000). 'Evidence, Logic, the Rule and the Exception in Renaissance Law and Medicine', *Early Science and Medicine* 5, 227–57.

(2002). *Logic, Signs and Nature in the Renaissance: The Case of Learned Medicine*, Cambridge.

Maltby, Judith (1998). *Prayer Book and People in Elizabethan and Early Stuart England*, Cambridge.

Mayer, R. (1993–4). 'Nathaniel Crouch, Bookseller and Historian: Popular Historiography and Cultural Power in Late Seventeenth-Century England', *Eighteenth-Century Studies* 27, 391–420.

McClure, George W. (1986). 'The Art of Mourning: Autobiographical Writings on the Loss of a Son in Italian Humanist Thought (1400–1461)', *Renaissance Quarterly* 39, 440–75.

(1991). *Sorrow and Consolation in the Italian Renaissance*, Princeton.

McConica, James (1965). *English Humanists and Reformation Politics under Henry VIII and Edward VI*, Oxford.

McCrea, Adriana (1997). *Constant Minds: Political Virtue and the Lipsian Paradigm in England*, 1584–1650, Toronto and London.

McCullough, Peter E. (1998a). *Sermons at Court: Politics and Religion in Elizabethan and Jacobean Preaching*, Cambridge.

(1998b). 'Making Dead Men Speak: Laudianism, Print, and the Works of Lancelot Andrewes, 1625–1642', *Historical Journal* 41, 401–24.

McCutcheon, Elizabeth (1998). 'Robert Burton/Democritus Junior', *Moreana: Mélanges Miller: Studies in Honor of Clarence H. Miller*, eds. Katherine Gardiner-Rodgers and Stephen Merriam, vol. 35, 55–74.
McVaugh, Michael (1990). 'The Nature and Limits of Medical Certitude at Early Fourteenth-Century Montpellier', *Osiris* n.s. 6, 62–84.
Ménager, Daniel (1995). *La Renaissance et le rire*, Paris.
Mendle, Michael (1993). 'Parliamentary Sovereignty: A Very English Absolutism', in N. Phillipson and Q. Skinner (eds.), *Political Discourse in Early Modern Britain*, Cambridge, pp. 97–119.
Mennecke-Haustein, Ute (1989). *Luthers Trostbriefe*, Gütersloh.
Merritt, J. F. (1998). 'Puritans, Laudians and the Phenomenon of Church-Building in Jacobean London', *Historical Journal* 41, 935–60.
Michael, Emily (2000). 'Renaissance Theories of Body, Soul, and Mind', in John P. Wright and Paul Potter (eds.), *Psyche and Soma: Physicians and metaphysicians on the mind–body problem from Antiquity to Enlightenment*, Oxford, pp. 147–73.
Midelfort, H. C. Erik (1996). 'Religious Melancholy and Suicide: On the Reformation Origins of a Sociological Stereotype', in Andrew Weiner and Leonard Kaplan (eds.), in *Graven Images*, III: *Madness, Melancholy and the Limits of the Self*, Madison, pp. 41–56.
Miles, Leland (1965/66). 'Boethius and Thomas More's Dialogue of Comfort', *English Language Notes* 3, 97–101.
Miller, John (1997). 'Plotting a Cure: The Reader in Robert Burton's *Anatomy of Melancholy*', *Prose Studies* 20, 42–71.
Miller, Peter N. (2000). *Peiresc's Europe: Learning and Virtue in the Seventeenth Century*, New Haven and London.
Milton, Anthony (1995). *Catholic and Reformed: The Roman and Protestant Churches in English Protestant Thought*, Cambridge.
(1993). 'The Church of England, Rome, and the True Church: The demise of a Jacobean Consensus', in Kenneth Fincham (ed.), *The Early Stuart Church*, Basingstoke, pp. 187–210.
(2002). 'The Creation of Laudianism: A New Approach', in T. Cogswell, R. Cust, and P. Lake (eds.), *Politics, Religion and Popularity: Essays in honour of Conrad Russell*, Cambridge, pp. 162–84.
Morford, M. (1991). *Stoics and Neostoics: Rubens and the Circle of Justus Lipsius*, Princeton, NJ.
(1993). 'Tacitean Prudentia and the Doctrines of Justus Lipsius', in T. J. Luce and A. J. Woodman (eds.), *Tacitus and the Tacitean Tradition*, Princeton, pp. 129–51.
Moss, Ann (1996). *Printed Commonplace-Books and the Structuring of Renaissance Thought*, Oxford.
Mueller, William R. (1949). 'Robert Burton's Frontispiece', *Publications of the Modern Language Association of America* 64, 1074–88.
Muller, Richard (1986). *Christ and the Decree: Christology and Predestination in Reformed Theology from Calvin to Perkins*, Durham, NC.

Muslow, Martin (2004). 'Ambiguities of the Prisca Sapientia in Late Renaissance Humanism', *Journal of the History of Ideas* 65, 1–13.

Neale, J. E. (1953). *Elizabeth and her Parliaments*, 2 vols., London.

Nelson, Eric (2003). *The Greek Tradition in Republican Thought*, Cambridge.

Nelson, John Charles (1958). *Renaissance Theory of Love: The Context of Giordano Bruno's 'Eroici furori'*, New York.

Neugebauer, Richard (1979). 'Medieval and Early Modern Theories of Mental Illness', *Archives of General Psychiatry* 36, 477–83.

Niebyl, Peter H. (1971). 'The Non-Naturals', *Bulletin of the History of Medicine* 45, 486–92.

Nochimson, Richard L. (1974). 'Studies in the Life of Robert Burton', *Yearbook of English Studies* 4, 85–111.

Norbrook, David (1984). *Poetry and Politics in the English Renaissance*, London.

Nussbaum, Martha Craven (1993). 'Poetry and the Passions: Two Stoic Views', in Jacques Brunschwig and Martha C. Nussbaum (eds.), *Passions and Perceptions: Studies in Hellenistic Philosophy of Mind. Proceedings of the Fifth Symposium Hellenisticum*, Cambridge, pp. 97–149.

Nutton, Vivian (1981). 'Medicine in the Age of Montaigne', in Keith Cameron (ed.), *Montaigne and His Age*, Exeter, pp. 15–25.

(1988a). '*De Placitis Hippocratis et Platonis* in the Renaissance', in Paola Manuli and Mario Vegetti (eds.), *Le Opere Psicologiche di Galeno: Atti terzo colloquio Galenice Internazionale Pavia,* 10–12 *settembre* 1986, Naples, pp. 281–309.

(1988b). '"Prisci dissectionum professores": Greek Texts and Renaissance Anatomists', in A. Dionisotti, A. T. Grafton, and J. Kraye (eds.), *The Uses of Greek and Latin*, London, pp. 111–26.

(1989). 'Hippocrates in the Renaissance', *Sudhoffs Archiv*, Beiheft 27, 420–39.

(1990). 'The Anatomy of the Soul in Early Renaissance Medicine', in G. R. Dunstan (ed.), *The Human Embryo: Aristotle and the Arabic and European Traditions*, Exeter, pp. 136–57.

(1991). 'Style and Context in the Method of Healing', in Fridolf Kudlien and Richard J. Durling (eds.), *Galen's Method of Healing: Proceedings of the* 1982 *Galen Symposium*, Leiden, pp. 1–25.

(1993). 'Wittenberg Anatomy', in Ole Peter Grell and Andrew Cunningham (eds.), *Medicine and the Reformation*, London and New York.

O'Callaghan, Michelle (2000). *The 'Shepheards Nation': Jacobean Spenserians and Early Stuart political Culture,* 1612–1625, Oxford.

Olivieri, Grazia Tonelli (1991). 'Galen and Francis Bacon: Faculties of the Soul and the Classification of Knowledge', in Donald R. Kelley and Richard H. Popkin (eds.), *The Shapes of Knowledge from the Renaissance to the Enlightenment*, Dordrecht, pp. 61–81.

Olson, Glending (1982). *Literature as Recreation in the Later Middle Ages*, Ithaca and New York.

Osler, William (1926). 'The Library of Robert Burton', *Oxford Bibliographical Society Proceedings and Papers* 1, 182–90.

Ottosson, Per-Gunnar (1984). *Scholastic Medicine and Philosophy: A Study of the Commentaries on Galen's Tegni (ca. 1300–1450)*, Naples.

Parrish, John M. (1997). 'A New Source for More's Utopia', *Historical Journal* 40, 493–8.

Peck, Linda Levy (1981). 'Court Patronage and Government Policy: The Jacobean Dilemma', in Guy Fitch Lytle and Stephen Orgel (eds.), *Patronage in the Renaissance*, Princeton, pp. 27–46.

(1990). *Court Patronage and Corruption in Jacobean England*, Boston, Mass., and London.

Peltonen, Markku (1995). *Classical Humanism and Republicanism in English Political Thought*, 1570–1640, Cambridge.

(2002). 'Citizenship and Republicanism in Elizabethan England', in Quentin Skinner and Martin Van Gelderen (eds.), *Republicanism: A Shared European Heritage*, I: *Republicanism and Constitutionalism in Early Modern Europe*, Cambridge, pp. 85–106.

Pigeaud, Jackie (1992). 'Reflections on Love-Melancholy in Robert Burton', in Donald A. Beecher and Massimo Ciavolella (eds.), *Eros and Anteros: The Medical Traditions of Love in the Renaissance*, Toronto, pp. 211–31.

Pigman, G. W., III (1985). *Grief and English Renaissance Elegy*, Cambridge.

Pittion, J.-P. (1987). 'Scepticism and Medicine in the Renaissance', in Richard H. Popkin and Charles B. Schmitt (eds.), *Scepticism from the Renaissance to the Enlightenment*, Wiesbaden, pp. 103–32.

Pocock, J. G. A. (1985). 'The History of British Political Thought: The Creation of a Center', *Journal of British Studies* 24, 283–310.

(1999–2003). *Barbarism and Religion*, 3 vols., Cambridge.

Porter, H. C. (1958). *Reformation and Reaction in Tudor Cambridge*, Cambridge.

and Thomson, D. F. S. (eds.), *Erasmus and Cambridge*, Toronto.

Rather, L. J. (1968). 'The 'Six Things Non-Natural': A Note on the Origins and Fate of a Doctrine and a Phrase', *Clio Medica* 3, 337–47.

Remer, Gary (1996). *Humanism and the Rhetoric of Toleration*, University Park.

Renaker, David (1979). 'Robert Burton's Palinodes', *Studies in Philology* 76, 162–81.

Richardson, R. C. (1972). *Puritanism in North-West England*, Manchester.

Rosen, George (1969). *Madness in Society: Chapters in the Historical Sociology of Mental Illness*, New York.

Rütten, Thomas (1992). *Demokrit-Lachender Philosoph und Sanguinischer Melancholiker: Eine pseudohippokratische Geschichte*, Leiden.

(1993). 'Pseudohippokrates, Marco Fabio Calvo und Robert Burton. Zur Rezeptionsgeschichte eines antiken Textes', in R. Kinsky (ed.), *Offenheit und Interesse: Studien zum 65. Geburtstag von Gerhard Wirth*, Amsterdam, pp. 31–43.

Sage, E. (1918). *The Pseudo-Ciceronian 'Consolatio'*, Chicago.

Salmon, J. H. M. (1989). 'Stoicism and Roman Example: Seneca and Tacitus in Jacobean England', *Journal of the History of Ideas* 50, 199–225.

Schleiner, Winfried (1991). *Melancholy, Genius and Utopia in the Renaissance*, Wiesbaden.

Schmitt, Charles B. (1983). *Aristotle and the Renaissance*, Cambridge, Mass.

(1985). 'Aristotle among the Physicians', in A. Wear, R. K. French, and I. M. Lowie (eds.), *The Medical Renaissance of the Sixteenth Century*, Cambridge, pp. 1–15.

Schoeck, Richard J. (1984). 'Sir Thomas Browne and the Republic of Letters', *English Language Notes* 19, 299–312.

Screech, M. A. (1983). *Montaigne and Melancholy: The Wisdom of the Essays*, London.

Selig, Sharon Cadman (1996). *Generating Texts: The Progeny of Seventeenth-Century Prose*, Charlottesville and London.

Sena, John F. (1973). 'Melancholic Madness and the Puritans', *Harvard Theological Review* 66, 239–309.

Serjeantson, Richard W. (1998). *Testimony, Authority and Proof in Seventeenth-Century England*, unpublished PhD diss., University of Cambridge.

Sharpe, Kevin M. (1981). 'Archbishop Laud and the University of Oxford', in Valerie Pearl, Blair Worden, and H. Lloyd Jones (eds.), *History and Imagination: Essays in Honour of Hugh Trevor-Roper*, London, pp. 146–64.

(1992). *The Personal Rule of Charles I*, New Haven and London.

Shiflett, Andrew (1998). *Stoicism, Politics and Literature in the Age of Milton*, Cambridge.

Shriver, Frederick (1970). 'Orthodoxy and Diplomacy: James I and the Vorstius Affair', *English Historical Review* 85, 449–74.

Siegel, Rudolph E. (1968). *Galen's System of Physiology and Medicine: An Analysis of His Doctrines and Observations on Bloodflow, Respiration, Humors and Internal Diseases*, Basle and New York.

(1971). 'Melancholy and Black Bile in Galen and Later Writers', *Bulletin of the Cleveland Medical Library* 18, 10–20.

(1973). *Galen on Psychology, Psychopathology, and Functions and Diseases of the Nervous System*, Basle.

Simon, Jean Robert (1964). *Robert Burton et 'l 'anatomie de la mélancholie'*, Paris.

Sinclair, H. M. (1974). 'Oxford Medicine', in Allen G. Debus (ed.), *Medicine in Seventeenth-Century England: A Symposium Held at UCLA in Honor of C. D. O'Malley*, Berkeley, pp. 371–93.

Siraisi, Nancy G. (1981). *Taddeo Alderotti and his Pupils: Two Generations of Italian Medical Learning*, Princeton, NJ.

(1987). *Avicenna in Renaissance Italy: The 'Canon' and Medical Teaching in Italian Universities after* 1500, Princeton.

(1990a). *Medieval and Renaissance Medicine: An introduction to Knowledge and Practice*, Chicago and London.

(1990b). 'Giovanni Argenterio and Sixteenth Century Medical Innovation: Between Princely Patronage and Academic Controversy', in M. McVaugh and N. Siraisi (eds.), *Renaissance Medical Learning: Evolution of a tradition, Osiris*, 2nd ser., 6, 161–80.

(1990c). 'Medicine, Physiology and Anatomy in Early Sixteenth-Century Critiques of the Arts and Sciences', in John Henry and Sarah Hutton (eds.), *New Perspectives on Renaissance Thought: Essays in the History of Science, Education, and Philosophy in Memory of Charles B. Schmitt*, London, pp. 214–29.
(1997). *The Clock and the Mirror: Girolamo Cardano and Renaissance Medicine*, Princeton.
(2000). 'Anatomising the Past: Physicians and History in Renaissance Culture', *Renaissance Quarterly* 53, 1–30.
(2001). *Medicine and the Italian Universities*, 1250–1600, Leiden.
(2003). 'History, Antiquarianism, and Medicine: The Case of Girolamo Mercuriale', *Journal of the History of Ideas* 64, 231–51.
Skinner, Quentin (1978). *The Foundations of Modern Political Thought*, 2 vols., Cambridge.
(1988). 'Political Philosophy', in C. B. Schmitt and Q. Skinner (eds.), *The Cambridge History of Renaissance Philosophy*, Cambridge, pp. 389–452.
(1998). *Liberty before Liberalism*, Cambridge.
Smith, Wesley D. (1979). *The Hippocratic Tradition*, Ithaca and London.
Smuts, R. Malcolm (1981). 'The Political Failure of Stuart Cultural Patronage', in Guy Fitch Lytle and Stephen Orgel (eds.), *Patronage in the Renaissance*, Princeton, pp. 165–87.
(1987). *Court Culture and the Origins of a Royalist Tradition in Early Stuart England*, Philadelphia.
Sommerville, Johann P. (1996). 'English and European Political Ideas in the Early Seventeenth Century: Revisionism and the Case of Absolutism', *Journal of British Studies* 35, 168–90.
Stachniewski, John (1991). *The Persecutory Imagination: English Puritanism and the Literature of Religious Despair*, Oxford.
Starobinski, Jean (1960). *Histoire du traitement de la mélancolie des origines à* 1900. *Acta psychosomatica* 3, Basel.
(1962). 'La Mélancolie de L'Anatomiste', *Tel Quel* 10, 21–9.
(1985). *Montaigne in Motion*, trans. Arthur Goldhammer, Chicago and London.
Stone, M. W. F. (2000). 'The Adoption and Rejection of Aristotelian Moral Philosophy in Reformed "Casuistry"', in Jill Kraye and M. W. F. Stone (eds.), *Humanism and Early Modern Philosophy*, London and New York, pp. 59–90.
Taylor, Charles (1989). *Sources of the Self: The Making of the Modern Identity*, Cambridge.
Thrush, Andrew (2003). 'The Personal Rule of James I, 1611–1620', in Thomas Cogswell, Richard Cust, and Peter Lake (eds.), *Politics, Religion and Popularity in Early Stuart Britain: Essays in Honour of Conrad Russell*, Cambridge, pp. 84–102.
Todd, Margo (1987). *Christian Humanism and the Puritan Social Order*, Cambridge.

Traister, Barbara (1976). 'New Evidence about Burton's Melancholy?', *Renaissance Quarterly* 29, 66–70.

Trevor-Roper, Hugh (1987). *Catholics, Anglicans and Puritans: Seventeenth Century Essays*, London.

Trinkaus, Charles (1940). *Adversity's Noblemen: The Italian Humanists on Happiness*, New York.

Tuck, Richard (1993a). 'The Civil Religion of Thomas Hobbes', in N. Phillipson and Q. Skinner (eds.), *Political Discourse in Early Modern Britain*, Cambridge, pp. 120–38.

(1993b). *Philosophy and Government*, 1572–1651, Cambridge.

Tucker, G. Hugo (1997). 'Mantua's "Second Virgil": Du Bellay, Montaigne and the Curious Fortune of Lelio Capilupi's *Centones ex Virgilio* Romae, 1555', in G. Tournoy and D. Sacré (eds.), *Ut Granum Sinapis: Essays on Neo-Latin Literature in Honour of Jozef Ijsewijn*, Supplementa Humanistica Lovaniensia 12, Leuven, pp. 264–91.

Tyacke, Nicholas (1978). 'Science and Religion at Oxford before the Civil War', in David Pennington and Keith Thomas (eds.), *Puritans and Revolutionaries: Essays in Seventeenth-Century History Presented to Christopher Hill*, Oxford, pp. 73–93.

(1987a). *Anti-Calvinists: The Rise of English Arminianism c.* 1590–1640, Oxford.

(1987b). 'The Rise of Arminianism Reconsidered', *Past and Present* 115, 201–29.

(1993). 'Archbishop Laud', in Kenneth Fincham (ed.), *The Early Stuart Church*, Basingstoke, pp. 51–70.

(1997). 'Religious Controversy', in N. Tyacke (ed.), *The History of the University of Oxford* IV: *Seventeenth-Century Oxford*, Oxford, pp. 569–619.

(2000). 'Lancelot Andrewes and the Myth of Anglicanism', in Peter Lake and Michael Questier (eds.), *Conformity and Orthodoxy in the English Church, c.*1500–1660, Woodbridge, pp. 5–53.

Ullmann, Manfred (1978). *Islamic Medicine*, Edinburgh.

Valadez, Frances (1974). 'Anatomical Studies at Oxford and Cambridge', in Allen G. Debus (ed.), *Medicine in Seventeenth-Century England: A Symposium held at UCLA in honor of C. D. O'Malley*, Berkeley, pp. 393–420.

Van der Eijk, Philip J. (1990). 'Aristoteles über die Melancholie', *Mnemosyne* 43, 33–72.

Veith, Ilza (1976). 'Elizabethans on Melancholia', *Journal of the American Medical Association* 212, 127–31.

Vicari, E. Patricia (1989). *The View from Minerva's Tower: Learning and Imagination in 'The Anatomy of Melancholy'*, Toronto.

Vickers, Brian (1992). 'Critical Reactions to the Occult Sciences during the Renaissance', in E. Ullmann-Margalit (ed.), *The Scientific Enterprise*, Dordrecht, pp. 43–92.

Viroli, Maurizio (1992). *From Politics to Reason of State*, Cambridge.

Wack, Mary Frances (1986). 'Imagination, Medicine, and Rhetoric in Andreas Capellanus' *De Amore*', in Arthur Groos (ed.), *Magister Regis: Studies in honor of Robert Earl Kaske*, New York, pp. 101–15.

(1990). *Lovesickness in the Middle Ages: The 'Viaticum' and its Commentaries*, Philadelphia.

(1992). 'From Mental Faculties to Magical Philters: The Entry of Magic into Academic Medical Writing on Lovesickness, 13th–17th Centuries', in Donald A. Beecher and Massimo Ciavolella (eds.), *Eros and Anteros: The Medical Traditions of Love in the Renaissance*, Toronto, pp. 9–31.

Waquet, Françoise (1990). 'Qu'est-ce que la République des Letters? Essai de Sémantique Historique,' *Bibliothèque de l 'École des Chartes* 147, 475–8.

Wear, Andrew (1995). 'Epistemology and Learned Medicine in Early Modern England', in Don Bates (ed.), *Knowledge and the Scholarly Medical Traditions*, Cambridge, pp. 151–73.

Weber, Wolfgang (1995). '"What a Good Ruler Should Not Do": Theoretical Limits of Royal Power in European Theories of Absolutism, 1500–1700', *Sixteenth Century Journal* 26, 897–915.

Webster, Charles (1975). *The Great Instauration: Science, Medicine and Reform 1626–1660*, London.

Wenzel, Siegfried (1967). *The Sin of Sloth: Acedia in Medieval Thought and Literature*, Chapel Hill.

White, Peter (1992). *Predestination, Policy and Polemic: Conflict and Consensus in the English Church from the Reformation to the Civil War*, Cambridge.

Williamson, George (1933). 'The Restoration Revolt against Enthusiasm', *Studies in Philology* 30, 571–603.

Wood, Neal (1968). 'Some Common Aspects of the Thought of Seneca and Machiavelli', *Renaissance Quarterly* 21, 11–23.

Yates, Francis A. (1934). *John Florio: The Life of an Italian in Shakespeare's England*, Cambridge.

Young, M. B. (1997). *Charles I*, London.

Index

Abbot, George 153, 289
Abbot, Robert 152
absolutism 195, 203, 215, 217–8
acedia 69
Acontius, Jacobus 144
Agrippa, Cornelius 25–6, 95, 118
  De occulta philosophia
  on medicine 102–4
Airay, Henry 151
Alba 6, 287
Alexander of Tralles
  on mania and melancholy 71
Alsted, Johann Heinrich 29, 42
An Apology of English Arminianisme 153
Andreae, Johann Valentin 263
Andrewes, Lancelot 145, 147, 149, 151
Anglicanism 141
Aretaeus of Cappadocia 126
  on mania and melancholy 71
aristocracy, see Nobility
Aristotelianism
  in epistemology 36, 112–3
  in ethics and politics 58, 82, 207, 210, 211, 235, 271
  in human physiology 36, 44, 45, 49
  in logic 57, 73
  in natural philosophy 41, 123
  in poetics 138
  in psychology 48, 58, 65–8, 87–8, 109, 123, 271
  in religion 70, 123
Aristotle 15, 44, 54, 88, 208, 230, 234, 239
  Nicomachean Ethics 38, 207
  on bodily heat 44
  on emotional madness 65–6
  Politics 207
Aristotle, Ps.-
  Problems 78, 90
Arminianism
  and the English Church 147–9, 151–7, 199–200
  discussed in the *Anatomy* 185–9
  Robert Burton's attitude towards 190–2, 199–200
Arminius, Jacobus 147, 155, 200
Arnald of Villanova 66
Arnisaeus, Henning 229
Apollo 128
Aquinas, Thomas 26
Ascham, Roger 246
astrology 52–3, 80, 89–91, 300
atheism 70, 160, 183, 226, 262, 301
Augustine 120, 125, 174, 192, 231
Augustinianism 3, 15, 67, 68, 70, 121, 124, 160, 166, 174, 181, 201–2, 271
Averroës 41, 116
Avicenna 37, 59, 66, 69, 88
  on emotions and spirits 49
  on imagination 52, 88
  on melancholy and demonic possession 86
  on melancholy and mania 71
  on *spiritus* 48
  on the different forms of melancholy 63
  on the primary and secondary humours 44

Bacon, Francis 214, 235, 247, 249, 263
  on civil religion 195–7
  on medicine 103
  on superstition 162
Bancroft, John 6, 154, 288
Bancroft, Richard 158
Bargrave, Isaac 173
Baro, Peter 151
Barrett, William 151
Baxter, Richard 175
  The Signs and Causes of Melancholy 298
Baynes, Roger 260
Beniveni, Domenico 41
Berkeley, George 6, 274, 291
Bernard of Gordon 66, 133
Bert, Pieter 155
Berthelet, Thomas 246

Beza, Theodore 145, 178, 183, 188
black bile 14, 59, 63–4, 76, 109
  and imagination 87, 88
  and prophetic inspiration 87
  and madness 70–1
  and 'vulgar' love 91
  as *balneum diaboli* 86
  as material cause of melancholy 76
  counteraction of 75
  effects of 46, 63–5, 77–9
  evacuated through laughter 137, 138
  in 'adust' form 63, 64
  in fear and sadness 49
  in the melancholic complexion 46, 70–1
  preponderant in autumn 52
  qualities of 44, 46
  studied by Democritus 283
Boccalini, Trajano
  Ragguagli di Parnasso 218, 242, 262
Bodin, Jean 144, 215
  on division 57
body
  Aristotelian conception of 44
  body politic 196, 215, 223–8, 233–8, 241–2
  Galenic conception of 44–5, 47–8
  Hippocratic conception of 44, 52
  Neo-Galenic conception of 45–53
Boethius 250
Botero, Giovanni 217
  quoted and used in the *Anatomy* 31, 226, 229, 234, 235, 237, 241–2
Bottoni, Alberto 62
Bridges, Gabriel 153
Bright, Timothy 140, 175–6
Brooke, Christopher 220, 247
Browne, Thomas 53, 190
  on melancholy and demonic possession 87
Browne, William 220, 261
Buckeridge, John 145
Buckingham, George Villiers, duke of 148, 169, 220, 221, 233, 247
Bullinger, Heinrich 186
Burton, Ralph 5
Burton, Robert
  born 5
  career at Oxford 5–7
  library of 7–8, 151, 200, 243
  pursuit of patronage 6, 287–91
  rumoured suicide 300–1
Burton, William 5, 192
Burton, William (d. 1461) 168

Cadiz expedition 143, 169
Calvin, Jean 174, 178, 183, 187
Calvinism 143
  and despair 174–92
  and predestination 175–92
  and scepticism 27
  discussed in the *Anatomy* 163–4
  idea of conscience 179–81, 183, 213
  in Oxford 151–4, 288
  in the English Church 145–58, 199–200
  Robert Burton's attitude towards 170–3, 190–3, 202
Calvo, Fabio 9, 13
Cambridge, University of
  Christ's College 19
  Emmanuel College 296
  predestinarian dispute in 151, 153
  Trinity College 147
Campanella, Tomasso 263
Canonieri, Pietro-Andrea 106
Capella, Martianus 106
Cardano, Girolamo 39, 50, 75, 83
  Contradicentrium medicorum liber 37, 83, 105, 135
  De consolatione 250, 251
  Hippocratic medical method of, 38–9, 105
  Occultist medicine of 41, 90, 93
Carleton, George
  Αστρολογομανια: The madnesse of astrologers 8
Carpenter, Nathanael 297–8
Cartwright, William 195, 215
Casaubon, Meric
  on 'generall learning' 95
  Treatise concerning enthusiasme, A 298
Case, John 248
Cassander, Georg 144
Castellio, Sebastian 144
Castiglione, Baldassare 31
  on erotic melancholy 91–2
Catholicism, Roman
  and St. John's College, Oxford 152
  as 'superstition' 140, 160–2
  attitude of James I towards 146
  Buckingham suspected of 143
  Charles I and his court suspected of 143, 149, 223
  English Protestant hostility towards 143, 145, 146, 150, 161–2, 223, 243
  in the family of Robert Burton 5, 169–70
  James I suspected of 142, 222
  recusancy 146
  Reform movement of 17
  Robert Burton's view of 163, 169–70, 172, 199
Cato, Marcus Porcius 234
Celsus 71
cento, the 116–8, 135, 245, 277, 299

Charles I 6
and anti-Calvinism 148–9
and contemporary concerns about favouritism 220–1
ecclesiastical policies of 149–51
monarchical rule of 222, 223
on universities 248
Robert Burton's view of 268
Charron, Pierre 249, 255–7
Cheke, John 246
Chillingworth, William 145
Chilmead, Edmund 67, 117, 130
China 196, 237–8, 265
Chiodini, Giulio Cesare 1
Chytraeus, David 200
Cicero, Marcus Tullius 241
Consolatio seu de luctu minuendo 2, 250
De legibus 228
De officiis 210
on civic activity 207, 208, 210
on civil laws 211
on melancholy and *furor* 71
on psychological freedom 211
on religion 165
Tusculanae disputationes 14
civic activity 11, 207, 209, 210, 214, 216, 241, 253
and patronage 260, 267–9
criticised by Montaigne 255
Joseph Hall on 259
civic greatness 167, 217, 233–8, 265
Clapmar, Arnold 229
Clerk, John 246
Coke, John 288
Colet, John 166
commerce 217, 234–7, 240–2
complexion, complexions 45–6
and astral causes 90
and emotions 49, 85–7
and erotic desire 66
and therapeutics 75–6
complexionate and pathological melancholy 59–60, 70–1
complexionate melancholy and demonic possession 85–7
diverse effects of 111
Galen on 45
in the category of *res naturales* 73
medieval theories of 45–6
predisposing to love melancholy 77
variations of 84
conformism, religious 144, 149, 166, 193
and nonconformism 145, 147
avant-garde 145–7, 149, 170–3, 192, 193
Calvinist 145, 158, 173, 192
James I on 146–7
consolation, consolations 249–54
Cicero, *Consolatio seu de luctu minuendo* 2, 250
'Conslatory Digression' in *The Anatomy of Melancholy* 81, 124, 179, 232, 266–75, 285–7
spiritual consolation in *The Anatomy of Melancholy* 181–5, 190–2
contemplation 253
Anthony Stafford on 260
classical justifications of 207, 209–10
in the pseudo-Hippocratic *Letter to Damagetes* 11
Joseph Hall on 257–9
Justus Lipsius on 255
Michel de Montaigne on 255–6
Pierre Charron on 256
Robert Burton's attitude towards 16, 241, 275, 282–5
Roger Baynes on 260
spiritual contemplation 202, 257–9
Stefano Guazzo on 257
Cooke, Anthony 246
Corbett, Richard 153, 169
Cornwallis, William 220
Cotton, Robert 247
counsel 205, 208, 210, 213, 215, 219–23, 233, 234, 246–9, 260, 276–81
Coverdale, Miles 246
Cox, Richard 246
Crosse, Henry 260
Crouch, Nathaniel 296
Curione, Celio Secondo 186, 187
curiosity 19–20, 26, 120, 156, 177–9, 184, 198–9
Cynicism 9, 11–3, 19, 282

D' Abano, Pietro 37
definition, definitions
of love and love melancholy 68
of jealousy 69
of the disease of melancholy 57–65, 126
Democritus, in the pseudo-Hippocratic *Letter to Damagetes* 9–16, 21, 137–8, 206, 276, 282–5, 292–3, 299
demonology 18, 50, 52, 69, 85–9, 118–20
demons 50, 69, 72, 85–9, 104, 119–20
despair 69, 81, 159, 251, 266, 301
and predestination 174–92, 200–3
diagnosis 46, 72, 73, 96
of the disease of melancholy 72–4, 76–82, 85–92
Dino del Garbo 66
Diogenes Laertius
Lives of Eminent Philosophers 9

Diogenes the Cynic 12
Divine fury 69
division 56–61
  and the definition of the disease of melancholy 58–62
  of the disease of melancholy 72–5
  of the kinds of love 67, 68
  Jean Bodin on 57
  Michel de Montaigne on 102
Dort, Synod of 147, 173, 180, 187, 199
Du Laurens, André 1, 61
  on melancholic inspiration 78
  on melancholy as complexion and disease 70
  on occult pathogens 51
  on the definition of dotage 62
  on the melancholic imagination
Du Vair, Guillaume 253–4
Duppa, Brian 153, 288
Dürer, Albrecht 78

Egerton, Thomas 248
Eliot, John
  The survay or topographical description of France 8
Elizabeth I 246
Elyot, Thomas 246
emotions, see passions
encyclopedism 7, 41, 42, 44
  in *The Anatomy of Melancholy* 28–9, 33, 44, 55, 95, 98, 116, 118, 121–2, 133, 135–6, 296–7
enthusiasm 159, 160, 162, 298–9
envy, see passions, jealousy
Epictetus 253
Epicureanism
  as moral philosophy 11–2, 128, 255, 256, 283, 292
  as synonym for atheistic vice 226, 228, 233, 267, 274
epidemic of melancholy 1–2, 16–8
Erasmus, Desiderius 19–21, 29, 31, 186, 214
  De conscribendis epistolis 250
  Moriae encomium 15, 16, 19–21, 197, 232
  on idleness 237
  on Origen 186
  on tyranny 212
  on warfare 166–8
  practical spirituality of 122
Erastus, Thomas 89, 93, 95, 118
erotomania, see melancholy
Essex, Robert Devereux, third earl of 218, 221, 247, 289
ethics, see humanism, Epicureanism, passions, Stoicism

Exeter, Frances Cecil, Frances, Countess Dowager of 6, 274

Faunt, Anthony 5
Faunt, Arthur 5
Faunt, Dorothy 5
Fell, Samuel 154, 288
Fernel, Jean 50
  on knowledge of causes 72
  on sympathy 51
Ferrand, Jacques
  on occult therapies 93
  Traité de l' essence et guérison de l'amour ou melancholie erotique 59, 67, 82, 117–8, 127–33
Ficino, Marsilio 41
  on earthly and heavenly love 67, 160
  on erotic melancholy 91–2
  on genial melancholy 90, 210
  on imagination 52
  on occult therapies 93
  on scholarly melancholy 80
  on *spiritus* 51
  on the body-soul relationship 49
  Theologia Platonica de immortalitate animarum 42, 49, 89
Filefo, Francisco 251
Florio, John 242, 272
Ford, John 295
Forman, Simon 6
Forset, Edward
  A Comparative Discourse of the Bodies Natural and Politique 225–6
Foxe, John
  Acts and Monuments 161
Fracastoro, Girolamo 51
France 142, 143, 164, 168, 197, 239, 248, 253
freedom
  from passions 13–7, 208–12, 214, 233, 241, 254–7, 271, 273–5
  of speech; 219–23, 260–2, 269, 275–85; see also: counsel
  of will; 178, 185, 192, 200–1, 256, 290; see also: Arminianism, predestination
Fregoso, Giovan Battista
  Anteros, sive tractatus contra amorem 67
frenzy; 59, 61; see also: divine fury
Frewen, Accepted 289
Fuller, Thomas 24, 95, 176, 257

Galen 36, 37, 41, 44, 54, 59, 116
  De placitis Hippocratis et Platonis 40
  De locis affectis 54, 61, 62, 64
  De methodo medendi 57, 72

De symptomatum causis 65, 74, 77
Ars medica 75
on diagnosis and prognosis 73, 96
on division 57
on emotions 47–8
on health and sickness 44–5
on occult properties 92–3
on the affected part in melancholy 64
on the body-soul relationship 47–8
on the definition of disease 57
on the definition of melancholy 61
on the fluctuation of complexions 46
on the psychological symptoms of melancholy 65
on the therapy of disease 72, 75, 96
Galen, Ps.-
Introductio, seu medicus 38
Definitiones medicae
Galenism, neo-
and logic 56–8
and occultism 50–3, 85–96
conception of body and soul 43–9
definition of the disease of melancholy 63–5, 70–1
diagnosis in 72–4
diagnostics of melancholy in 76–82
Francis Bacon on 103
humanism and 35–40, 96
in seventeenth-century Oxford 54
love melancholy in 65–7
Michel de Montaigne on 102
relationship with Christian ethics 40–3, 123–34, 159
religious melancholy in 69
scholasticism and 35–40, 96
therapeutics in 74–6, 81–2
therapeutics of melancholy in 78–9
Gardiner, Richard 154
genius, genial melancholy 77–8, 90–1, 210
Gentillet, Innocent 230
geography 31, 83, 217, 226, 233–8, 242
Giovanni da Ravenna 251
Goodwin, William 153
'Great Tew Circle', the 145, 189
grace, see predestination
Gregory, Edmund
Historical Anatomy of Christian Melancholy 298
Grotius, Hugo 165
Guazzo, Stefano
La civil conversazione 210, 257

Hall, Joseph 146, 199, 219
on courtiers 214
on laughter 292
on monarchy 213
Stoic moral psychology of 257–9
Haly Abbas 66
Harrington, James 196
Hawkins, Thomas
Hearne, Thomas 291
Heinsius, Daniel 13
hellebore 79, 108, 116
Hemmingsen, Niels 182, 191–2
Henry, Prince of Wales 222, 247, 260
Henry VIII 246
Heraclitus, as 'weeping philosopher' 137, 284, 292, 299
Heraclitean lamentation 132, 134, 137, 284, 292–3
'heroic' love, see melancholy
Heylyn, Peter 151, 152, 156, 158, 288
Hippocratics, the 37, 44, 54, 59, 83
Aphorisms 38, 79, 83
Epidemics 73
Prognostics 74
on diagnosis 73
on melancholic fear and sorrow 79
on melancholy and nervous diseases 71
on mental exertion 80
on prognosis 73
on the bodily humours 44
On the Sacred Disease 87
on the seasonal variation of humours 52
on therapy 75
Hippocrates, Ps.-
De atra bilis agitatione melancholiave 54
Letter to Crateuas 127
Letter to Damagetes, The 9–16, 137–8, 240, 241
Hippocratism, in Renaissance medicine, 38–40, 75, 103
in *The Anatomy of Melancholy* 55–6, 83–4, 100, 105, 108–9, 123, 124, 135
history
of the church 158, 161, 163–5, 172, 196
and humanist historicism 39, 84, 100–2, 104–5, 107, 108
historical argument in *The Anatomy of Melancholy* 106–8, 127, 164–5, 233, 237
medical case-histories 38, 84, 103
Hobbes, Thomas 23, 196, 202
Holdsworth, Richard 296
Hooker, Richard 145
On the Laws of Ecclesiastical Polity 144
Howson, John 151–3
Huarte Navarro, Juan 40
humanism, classical 9, 14, 23, 54
and 'civil religion' 195–7, 204

humanism, classical (cont.)
and dialectic 24, 95
and encyclopaedic learning:, see encyclopedism
and history, see history
and medicine 39–43, 54, 96, 100–9
and moral philosophy/psychology 11–5, 17–9, 56, 123, 127, 177, 201–3, 206–12, 223–33
and occultism 52, 88, 89, 93, 94
and politics 195–7, 205–15, 223–33, 238–40, 246–9, 260–71, 275–81
and 'practical' vernacular humanism 29–31
and 'reason of state' 216–9, 229–31
and religious toleration 144–5, 164–6, 186, 204
and rhetoric 24, 25, 28, 113, 124
and scholasticism 19–28, 34–5, 56, 99–100, 115–22, 135, 197–200, 203–4
and the European *respublica literaria* 29–31
Christian humanism 19–21, 27, 31, 99, 166–9, 194, 197–201, 204, 253–61, 271–5, 281–7, 292–3
Hume, David 299
humours
and adust melancholy 126
and complexions 45–6, 75
and demonic interference 86
and emotions 49
as one of the *res naturales* 73
Avicenna on 44
in Hippocratic theory 44
in Galenic theory 44–5, 47, 133
in neo-Galenic therapeutics 75–6, 252
in the Neoplatonic conception of 'vulgar' love 91–2
see also: black bile
Hunnius, Aegidius 200

idleness
and the nobility 133, 210, 266–7, 278
and writing 2–27, 136, 299
as a cause of melancholy 2, 3, 80, 81, 123, 133, 136, 191, 300
in the 'melancholic' body politic 233, 234, 236–7, 240–2
imagination 43, 51–2, 79, 252
and erotic desire 66–7, 81, 128, 130
as affected part in melancholy 3, 61, 62, 77, 80, 81, 86, 176, 183–4
as medium for occult influence on the body 51–2, 85–9, 183–4
Isidore, of Seville 42
Jackson, Thomas 153, 157, 203–4
James I 6, 164, 219–21
mentioned in the *Anatomy* 236, 268
on courtiers 214, 221
on law and reason 211
on monarchy 213–4, 222–3
on neostoicism 219
pacifism of 142, 167
patronage of 247
theology and ecclesiology of 146–7, 149, 159
Jerome, Saint 42
Johnson, Robert 217
Joubert, Laurent
Erreurs populaires au fait de la médecine et regime de santé 37

Keckermann, Bartholomaeus 42
Kennett, White 300
King, Henry 295
King, John 153
Kornmann, Heinrich
Linea amoris 82, 92
Krämer, Heinrich
Malleus maleficarum 88, 89
Kromer, Marcin 229

Lake, Thomas 220
Laud, William 148–51, 270, 288–9
Laudianism 149
laughter 64, 126, 266, 292
of Democritus, see Democritus
Laurence, Thomas 156, 157
law, laws
civil 144, 208, 210–2, 215, 217, 218, 227, 238, 240, 244, 245, 256, 280–1
divine 161, 174, 179, 215
natural 144, 211, 215
Lawyers 227, 244, 245, 264, 269
Leech, Humphrey 152
Lemnius, Levinus
De habitu et constitutione corporis 175
on *spiritus* 48, 51
Leone Ebreo 67, 68
Letter to Damagetes, The, see Hippocrates, Ps.-
liberty, see freedom
Lipsius, Justus 249, 253
De constantia libri duo 13, 216, 254–5, 283
Manuductio ad Stoicam philosophiam 282
on classical views of religion 195
on dispassionate wisdom 282
on monarchy and counsel 222
on moral virtue and politics 216, 217, 224
on Tacitus 218, 243
Politicorum sive civilis doctrinae libri sex 24, 30, 195, 216, 222, 230
Stoic moral psychology of 254–5
Lleuelyn, Martin 301

Lombard, Peter 26
love, see passions
love melancholy, see melancholy, the complexion of
Lucretius 65, 128, 197
Lupset, Thomas 246
Luther, Martin 155, 159, 174, 175, 178
Lutheranism 42, 163–4, 173, 178, 179
  and anti-Calvinism/Arminianism 155–7, 175, 176, 182, 184–6, 191–2, 200–1

Machiavelli, Niccol
  on civil religion 144, 195, 196, 229
  on politics and ethics 216, 230
  quoted in the *Anatomy* 162, 196, 229, 230, 239
Madan, Falconer 117
madness, see melancholy
Manardi, Giovanni 78
mania 13, 59, 61, 71, 81, 126–7
Marlowe, Christopher
  Doctor Faustus 178
Mars
Marshall, William 246
medicine
  and ethics and theology 40–3, 122–34, 159–60, 166, 175–6, 179
  and physicians, Robert Burton's view of 21–2, 103–7
  and politics 225–6, 241–2
  as *ars* or *scientia* 35–40
  humanist critiques of 100–9, 115–22
melancholy, the complexion of, see complexion
melancholy, the disease of
  and madness 13–6, 59, 64–7, 69, 71–2, 74, 125–7, 141, 224–5, 286
  as a species of *delirium* 14, 59, 61–2, 66–72
  caused by reading about melancholy 4
  causes of 2, 58, 63–4, 68, 70, 72–3, 76–7, 79–80, 83, 85–92, 123–7, 133, 160–1, 176–81
  kinds or species of; 63–70, 110, 114; see also: genius, genial melancholy
  love melancholy 65–70, 79–83, 88–9, 91–2, 117–9, 127–33, 160, 286, 295
  prognostics of 74, 81, 82, 112
  religious melancholy 69–70, 95, 139–40, 158–66, 170–1, 174–92, 202–3, 298–9
  symptoms of 58, 61–2, 64–5, 70, 71, 74, 76–8, 80–1, 87, 90, 111–4, 121–2, 127–8, 131, 134, 159, 162, 177, 224, 227, 233–4, 236–7, 286
  therapy of 2–4, 74–6, 78–9, 81–2, 93–4, 103, 112, 116, 123–5, 130, 136–8, 165–6, 171, 181–5, 190–2, 202–3, 257, 266, 271, 274, 285–7, 299–300
Melanchthon, Philipp 1, 42, 90, 99
  De anima 42, 43, 51, 64
  Lutheranism of 200–1
  on different forms of melancholy 64
  on grace and salvation 155
  on *spiritus* 51
Menippus 12
Mercuriale, Girolamo 1, 95
  on astral causation of disease 90
Mercury 90
Mersenne, Marin
  Quaestiones celeberrimae in Genesim 95
Middlesex, Lionel Cranfield, Earl of 6, 289
Milton, John 19
mixed constitution 114, 149, 212, 238–40
monopolies 240
monarchy; 149, 207, 208, 211–5, 219–23, 225, 227–9, 231–3, 238, 239, 241; see also: absolutism
  and Church 144, 150, 195
Montagu, Richard 148, 149, 153, 172
Montaigne, Michel de 3, 25, 249
  on consolation and diversion 252–3
  on contemplation and activity 255–6, 283
  on Democritus and Heraclitus 284, 292
  on medical knowledge and practice 102, 113
  on reading and writing 136, 272, 299
  on vice and politics 216, 217
  scepticism of 25, 102, 115, 136
Montalto, Eliano 61
moral philosophy, see humanism, Epicureanism, passions, Stoicism
More, Henry
  Enthusiasmus Triumphatus 298
More, Thomas 31, 241, 246
  critique of warfare 166
  Dialogue of Comfort against Tribulation 251, 252, 271
  on idleness and nobility 237
  on passions and freedom 211
  quoted in the *Anatomy* 240
  Utopia 211, 237, 249, 263, 265

Napier, Richard 90, 295
negotium, see civic activity
Netherlands, the 144–5, 147, 164, 237, 248, 253
  Mobility 237
  and idleness 210, 237, 266
  and love melancholy 133
  and patronage 267–71, 275, 291
  vera nobilitas 209, 210, 224, 238, 265
'non-naturals', the six 46, 73, 75, 77–9, 81, 123–5, 266
Northampton, Henry Howard, earl of 220, 247

occultism 41, 50–3, 85–96
and humanism 52, 88, 89, 93, 94
and the imagination 51–2, 85–9, 183–4
Origen 186
otium, see contemplation
Ovid 65, 128
Oxford, university of 7, 54, 67, 94, 151–4, 192, 195, 248, 270, 288–9, 297
All Souls College 156
Brasenose College 5
Christ Church 6, 7, 152, 195, 215, 287, 288
Corpus Christi College 153
Exeter College 297
Merton College 5
St John's College 152

Pace, Richard 246
Palmieri, Matteo
on civil virtues 209
Paracelsianism 53, 93
Paracelsus 53, 88, 93, 95, 160
Parsons, Robert 245
Pascal, Blaise 3
passions 16–9, 41, 43, 46–9, 59–60, 62, 73, 81, 99
and madness/vice 10–6, 123, 125–34, 159, 281–7, 292–3
and politics 17–8, 208–16, 222–33, 246–9, 253–60, 262
and the therapy of melancholy –203, 78, 81–2, 93, 123–4, 130, 136–8, 181, 202–3, 249–53, 266, 271–5, 281–7
anger 14, 46, 49, 65, 79, 126, 138, 167, 212, 284, 292
as pathological causes 47–9, 79–80, 124–7, 133
as symptoms of melancholy –203, 77, 122, 202–3
fear 3, 14, 15, 46, 48–9, 59, 61–2, 64, 69, 70, 77, 79, 88, 116, 126, 137, 159, 161, 174–5, 177, 181, 202
in Christian theology and spirituality 66, 67, 78, 123, 124, 134, 159, 166–9, 271, 292–3, 298–9
jealousy, envy 3, 10, 14, 30, 68–9, 122, 212, 271, 284
Joy 48, 49, 77, 126
love, see love melancholy, religious melancholy
sadness 2, 14, 15, 46, 49, 59–62, 69, 70, 77, 79, 116, 126, 137, 159, 174–5, 251, 284, 287, 292, 299; see also: despair
patronage 150, 219–23, 233, 239, 249, 259–61, 264–83, 287–94
Paul of Aegina
on melancholy and demonic possession 85
on the definition of melancholy 61
Paynell, Thomas 246
Peacham, Henry 251
Peletier, Jacques
De conciliatione locorum Galeni, sectiones duae 37
Perkins, William 176, 178, 180, 183, 184, 187, 191
Petrarch, Francesco 23, 127–8, 250, 251
on medicine and physicians 100–1, 105, 106
Peterson, Robert 217
Philosophaster 6–7, 26, 28
phrenitis, see frenzy
Pico della Mirandola, Gianfrancesco 25
on physiology 101–2
Pico della Mirandola, Giovanni 89
Disputationes adversus astrologiam divinatricem 53, 90
Plato 207, 208
Charmides 41, 124
Laws 134, 237, 241
on mental exertion 80
Phaedrus 65
Philebus 67
Republic 237
Timaeus 80, 133
Platonism, neo- 91, 128, 129, 133, 180, 1035, 185, 1031, 4335, 4336, 833, 2118, 401, 4337, 2130, 4338, 737, 737; see also: divine fury, genius, genial melancholy
Platter, Felix 69, 140
Pliny, the Elder 106, 165
Plutarch 165, 271
Plutarch, Ps.-
Consolation to Apollonius 250
Pomponazzi, Pietro 28, 93
De immortalitate animae 28, 40
De incantationibus 88, 89, 93
Pontano, Giovanni 212
Porphyry 57
Pucci, Francesco 151
predestination 145–9, 151–7, 174–92, 198–203; see also: Arminianism, despair
Price, Daniel 222
Prideaux, John 153, 288
prognosis 52, 73–4, 81, 82, 96, 112
prophecy 78, 87, 150, 160, 162, 301; see also: enthusiasm, divine fury
Prynne, William 203
psychology, see soul
Ptolemy, Claudius
Tetrabiblos 52
puritanism 31, 141, 142, 144–7, 150, 151, 153, 154, 158, 159, 172, 176, 180, 191, 203, 288, 297–9; see also: Calvinism
Robert Burton's view of, 140, 160, 162, 164, 170, 171, 179, 184, 192, 202, 203, 239

Ravis, Thomas 153
Ré expedition 143, 169
reason of state 216–9, 229–31, 242;
see also: neostoicism, Tacitism
republicanism 195, 207, 210, 212–3, 215, 218,
238–41, 264; see also: civic activity, mixed
constitution
Rhazes 53, 66
rhetoric; 24, 124, 128, 130–3, 226, 234, 250–2,
286; see also: humanism
Ricci, Matteo 265
Rosicrucianism 116, 140, 238, 244, 261–2
Rowlands, Samuel
Democritus, or Doctor Merry-Man his Medicines, Against Melancholy Humours 137
Rufus of Ephesus 54, 64, 75

Sabbatarianism 150, 162, 171
Sacchi, Bartolomeo
De principe 209
Salerno, School of 37
Salisbury, Robert Cecil, earl of 247
Sallust 228
Salutati, Coluccio 250
Sassonia, Ercole 61, 62, 69
satire 8–16, 19–26, 197–8, 260–1, 266–71, 284,
292; see also: Democritus, laughter,
Philosophaster
and freedom of speech 260, 261, 275–81
anti-medical satire 100–22
Saturn 90
Savile, Henry 218
Scala, Bartolomeo
De legibus et iudiciis dialogus 211, 212
scepticism 25–6, 101–2, 104, 115, 252–3, 256, 298,
300
Academic Scepticism 27
and theology 27, 120, 121, 144, 156–7, 165–6,
185, 200, 201
in *The Anatomy of Melancholy* 24–9, 84, 87,
93–4, 104–7, 135–6, 165–6, 185, 200, 201,
262, 285
Pyrrhonian Scepticism 12, 122
scholasticism 19–20, 26, 28, 58, 116–22;
see also: humanism
and medicine 22, 37–40, 96, 100–2, 117, 132
and theology 22, 156–7, 172, 178, 184, 187, 203,
285, 298
Scot, Reginald 87
Scott, Thomas 243
Seneca, Lucius Annaeus 165, 195, 241, 250, 253,
255
Apocolocyntosis 277
De brevitate vitae 13
De ira 13
De otio 264
on monarchy 208, 212
on *negotium* 274
Sennert, Daniel 42
Severinus, Petrus 22
Sextus Empiricus 89, 122
Seyssel, Claude de 239
Shaftesbury, Anthony Ashley Cooper, third earl
of
Characteristicks of Men, Manners, Opinions, Times 299
Simpson, Edward 147
Smith, Thomas 215, 239, 246
solitude 3, 11, 80, 191, 210, 255–7, 260, 283, 284,
300; see also: contemplation
Somerset, Robert Carr, earl of 220, 247
Sophocles 65
Soranus of Ephesus 59
soul
and humanist ethics 9–19, 82, 99, 127, 206–12,
249–60, 266, 271–5, 281–5
and humanist politics 206–20, 222–8, 241,
253–60, 292–3
and the therapy of melancholy 81–2, 99,
123–5, 127, 136–8, 202–3, 249–53, 266,
271–5, 285–7
Aristotelian conception of 41, 48, 49, 65–6,
87–8, 109
Galenic conception of 44, 47–8
effects of melancholy on 62, 66–7, 76–8
effects on body in melancholy 79–81, 124–5
in Christian theology 15–7, 42, 66, 124,
159–61, 174–6, 200–1
medieval Arabic conception of 48, 52
neo-Galenic conception of 40–3, 46, 48–9,
51–2, 109, 123
Platonic conception of 48, 67, 82; see also:
divine fury, passions, despair
Spain 142–3, 146, 167–9, 236, 243
'Spenserian' poets, the 220, 247, 260–1
Sprenger, Jakob
Malleus maleficarum 88, 89
Stafford, Anthony 247, 260
Starkey, Thomas 246
Steevens, George 297
Stoicism 19, 51, 126, 128, 167, 225
and humanist ethics 252, 283, 284
and humanist politics 207–9, 211
in the *Anatomy of Melancholy* 11–5, 166–9, 223,
227–30, 266, 271–5, 281–5, 292
neo-Stoicism 18, 216, 218–9, 224, 253–61, 282
Stringer, Philip 6
Strode, William 195, 215, 288
suicide 77, 81, 82, 112, 181, 300–1

Swift, Jonathan
Tale of a Tub, A 299
Sydenham, Thomas 38

Tacitism 218–20, 222, 223, 229–31, 260–1
Tacitus, Cornelius 216, 218, 243
Tasso, Torquato 69
temperament, see complexion
theology 15, 19, 70, 81
and medicine 40–3, 51, 53, 67, 99, 104, 123–34
see also: Arminianism, Augustinianism, Calvinism, Catholicism, Roman, Lutheranism
therapeutics 46, 74–6
Thirty Years War, the 141–3
Thoresby, Ralph 299
tristitia; 123, 174; see also: despair, passions, sadnes
tyranny 211–2, 218, 221, 223, 227–8, 230

Ursinus, Zacharias 187
utopia, utopianism 197, 238–41, 249, 261–5, 276–7, 281, 291, 293–4

Valla, Lorenzo 24
Valleriola, François 98
Valles, Francisco
Controversiarum medicarum et philosophicorum libri decem 37
Varchi, Benedetto 69
Vaughan, William 199–200, 220, 227, 242–5
Venice 238, 239
Vesalius, Andreas 58
vital heat 45–6, 49, 81
Vives, Juan Luis 20, 31, 166
De anima et vita 40, 43, 125
De causis corruptarum artium 102, 122
on medical reform 102
Vorstius, Conrad 146, 155

Walther, Rudolph 186
war, Robert Burton's view of 166–9, 234–5
Wecker, Johannes Jacob 50
West, Richard 130
Weyer, Johann 87–9, 118
White, Francis 148, 149, 158
Whitlock, Richard
Zootomia, or, Observations on the Present Manners of the English 297
will, freedom of, see freedom
Willet, Andrew
De anime natura et viribus quaestiones quaedam 37
witchcraft 18, 85, 87–9, 116, 125
Wither, George 220, 247, 261, 281
Wood, Anthony 24, 95, 172, 189, 296, 300
Wortels, Abraham 106
writing and melancholy 2–4, 135–8, 281–7, 292–4, 299–300

Zanchi, Girolamo 187
Zwingli, Ulrich 159, 186

IDEAS IN CONTEXT

Edited by QUENTIN SKINNER and JAMES TULLY

1. RICHARD RORTY, J. B. SCHNEEWIND and QUENTIN SKINNER (eds.)
Philosophy in History
Essays in the Historiography of Philosophy
pb: 0 521 27330 7

2. J. G. A. POCOCK, *Virtue, Commerce and History*
Essays on Political Thought and History, Chiefly in the Eighteenth Century
pb: 0 521 27660 8

3. M. M. GOLDSMITH, *Private Vices, Public Benefits*
Bernard Mandeville's Social and Political Thought
hb: 0 521 30036 3

4. ANTHONY PAGDEN (ed.), *The Languages of Political Theory in Early Modern Europe*
pb: 0 521 38666 7

5. DAVID SUMMERS, *The Judgment of Sense*
Renaissance Nationalism and The rise of Aesthetics
pb: 0 521 38631 4

6. LAURENCE DICKEY, *Hegel: Religion, Economics and the Politics of Spirit, 1770–1807*
pb: 0 521 38912 7

7. MARGO TODD, *Christian Humanism and the Puritan Social Order*
pb: 0 521 89228 7

8. LYNN SUMIDA JOY, *Gassendi the Atomist*
Advocate of History in an Age of Science
pb: 0 521 52239 0

9. EDMUND LEITES (ed.), *Conscience and Casuistry in Early Modern Europe*
pb: 0 521 52020 7

10. WOLF LEPENIES, *Between Literature and Science: The Rise of Sociology*
pb: 0 521 33810 7

11. TERENCE BALL, JAMES FARR and RUSSELL L. HANSON (eds.)
Political Innovation and Conceptual Change
pb: 0 521 35978 3

12. GERD GIGERENZER *et al.*, *The Empire of Chance*
How Probability Changed Science and Everyday Life
pb: 0 521 39838 X

13. PETER NOVICK, *That Noble Dream*
The 'Objectivity Question' and the American Historical Profession
hb: 0 521 34328 3 pb: 0 521 35745 4

14. DAVID LIEBERMAN, *The Province of Legislation Determined*
Legal Theory in Eighteenth-Century Britain
hb: 0 521 24592 3 pb: 0 521 52854 2

15. DANIEL PICK, *Faces of Degeneration*
A European Disorder, c. 1848–c. 1918
pb: 0 521 45753 X

16. KEITH BAKER, *Inventing the French Revolution*
Essays on French Political Culture in the Eighteenth Century
pb: 0 521 38578 4

17. IAN HACKING, *The Taming of Chance*
hb: 0 521 38014 6 pb: 0 521 38884 8

18. GISELA BOCK, QUENTIN SKINNER and MAURIZIO VIROLI (eds.)
Machiavelli and Republicanism
pb: 0 521 43589 7

19. DOROTHY ROSS, *The Origins of American Social Science*
pb: 0 521 42836 X

20. KLAUS CHRISTIAN KOHNKE, *The Rise of Neo-Kantianism*
German Academic Philosophy between Idealism and Positivism
hb: 0 521 37336 0

21. IAN MACLEAN, *Interpretation and Meaning in the Renaissance*
The Case of Law
hb: 0 521 41546 2

22. MAURIZIO VIROLI, *From Politics to Reason of State*
The Acquisition and Transformation of the Language of Politics 1250–1600
hb: 0 521 41493 8

23. MARTIN VAN GELDEREN, *The Political Thought of the Dutch Revolt 1555–1590*
hb: 0 521 39204 7 pb: 0 521 89163 9

24. NICHOLAS PHILLIPSON and QUENTIN SKINNER (eds.)
Political Discourse in Early Modern Britain
hb: 0 521 39242 X

25. JAMES TULLY, *An Approach to Political Philosophy: Locke in Contexts*
hb: 0 521 43060 7 pb: 0 521 43638 9

26. RICHARD TUCK, *Philosophy and Government 1572–1651*
pb: 0 521 43885 3

27. RICHARD R. YEO, *Defining Science*
William Whewell, Natural Knowledge and Public Debate in Early Victorian Britian
hb: 0 521 43182 4 pb: 0 521 54116 6

28. MARTIN WARNKE, *The Court Artist*
The Ancestry of the Modern Artist
hb: 0 521 36375 6

29. PETER N. MILLER, *Defining the Common Good*
Empire, Religion and Philosophy in Eighteenth-Century Britain
hb: 0 521 44259 1

30. CHRISTOPHER J. BERRY, *The Idea of Luxury*
A Conceptual and Historical Investigation
pb: 0 521 46691 1

31. E. J. HUNDERT, *The Enlightenment's 'Fable'*
Bernard Mandeville and the Discovery of Society
hb: 0 521 46082 4

32. JULIA STAPLETON, *Englishness and the Study of Politics*
The Social and Political Thought of Ernest Barker
hb: 0 521 46125 1

33. KEITH TRIBE, *Strategies of Economic Order*
German Economic Discourse, 1750–1950
hb: 0 521 46291 6

34. SACHIKO KUSUKAWA, *The Transformation of Natural Philosophy*
The Case of Philip Melancthon
hb: 0 521 47347 0

35. DAVID ARMITAGE, ARMAND HIMY and QUENTIN SKINNER (eds.)
Milton and Republicanism
hb: 0 521 55178 1 pb: 0 521 64648 0

36. MARKKU PELTONEN, *Classical Humanism and Republicanism in*
English Political Thought 1570–1640
hb: 0 521 49695 0

37. PHILIP IRONSIDE, *The Social and Political Thought of Bertrand Russell*
The Development of an Aristocratic Liberalism
hb: 0 521 47383 7

38. NANCY CARTWRIGHT, JORDI CAT, LOLA FLECK and THOMAS E. UEBEL
Otto Neurath: Philosophy between Science and Politics
hb: 0 521 45174 4

39. DONALD WINCH, *Riches and Poverty*
An Intellectual History of Political Economy in Britain, 1750–1834
pb: 0 521 55920 0

40. JENNIFER PLATT, *A History of Sociology Research*
Methods in America

41. KNUD HAAKONSSEN (ed.), *Enlightenment and Religion*
Rational Dissent in Eighteenth-Century Britain
hb: 0 521 56060 8

42. G. E. R. LLOYD, *Adversaries and Authorities*
Investigations into Ancient Greek and Chinese Science
hb: 0 521 55331 8 pb: 0 521 55695 3

43. ROLF LINDNER, *The Reportage of Urban Culture*
Robert Park and the Chicago School
hb: 0 521 44052 1

44. ANNABEL BRETT, *Liberty, Right and Nature*
Individual Rights in Later Scholastic Thought
hb: 0 521 56239 2 pb: 0 521 54340 1

45. STEWART J. BROWN (ed.), *William Robertson and the Expansion of Empire*
hb: 0 521 57083 2

46. HELENA ROSENBLATT, *Rousseau and Geneva*
From the First Discourse *to the* Social Contract, *1749–1762*
hb: 0 521 57004 2

47. DAVID RUNCIMAN, *Pluralism and the Personality of the State*
hb: 0 521 55191 9

48. ANNABEL PATTERSON, *Early Modern Liberalism*
hb: 0 521 59260 7

49. DAVID WEINSTEIN, *Equal Freedom and Utility*
Herbert Spencer's Liberal Utilitarianism
hb: 0 512 62264 6

50. YUN LEE TOO and NIALL LIVINGSTONE (eds.), *Pedagogy and Power*
Rhetorics of Classical Learning
hb: 0 521 59435 9

51. REVIEL NETZ, *The Shaping of Deduction in Greek Mathematics*
A Study in Cognitive History
hb: 0 521 62279 4 pb: 0 521 54120 4

52. MARY MORGAN and MARGARET MORRISON (eds.),
Models as Mediators
Perspectives on Natural and Social Science
hb: 0 521 65097 6 pb: 0 521 65571 4

53. JOEL MICHELL, *Measurements in Psychology*
A Critical History of a Methodological Concept
hb: 0 521 62120 8

54. RICHARD A. PRIMUS, *The American Language of Rights*
hb: 0 521 65250 2

55. ROBERT ALUN JONES, *The development of Durkheim's Social Realism*
hb: 0 521 65045 3

56. ANNE MCLAREN, *Political Culture in the Reign of Elizabeth I*
Queen and Commonwealth 1558–1585
hb: 0 521 65144 1

57. JAMES HANKINS (ed.), *Renaissance Civic Humanism Reappraisals and Reflections*
hb: 0 521 78090 X pb: 0 521 54807 1

58. T. J. HOCHSTRASSER, *Natural Law Theories in the Early Enlightenment*
hb: 0 521 66193 5

59. DAVID ARMITAGE, *The Ideological Origins of the British Empire*
hb: 0 521 59081 7 pb: 0 521 78978 8

60. IAN HUNTER, *Rival Enlightenments*
Civil and Metaphysical Philosophy in Early Modern Germany
hb: 0 521 79265 7

61. DARIO CASTIGLIONE and IAIN HAMPSHER-MONK (eds.)
The History of Political Thought in National Context
hb: 0 521 78234 1

62. IAN MACLEAN, *Logic, Signs and Nature in the Renaissance*
The Case of Learned Medicine
hb: 0 521 80648 8

63. PETER MACK, *Elizabethan Rhetoric Theory and Practice*
hb: 0 521 81292 5

64. GEOFFREY LLOYD, *The Ambitions of Curiosity*
Understanding the World in Ancient Greece and China
hb: 0 521 81542 8 pb: 0 521 89461 1

65. MARKKU PELTONEN, *The Duel in Early Modern England*
Civility, Politeness and Honour
hb: 0 521 82062 6

66. ADAM SUTCLIFFE, *Judaism and Enlightenment*
hb: 0 521 82015 4

67. ANDREW FITZMAURICE, *Humanism and America*
An Intellectual History of English Colonisation, 1500–1625
hb: 0 521 82225 4

68. PIERRE FORCE, *Self-Interest before Adam Smith*
A Genealogy of Economic Science
hb: 0 521 83060 5

69. ERIC NELSON, *The Greek Tradition in Republican Thought*
hb: 0 521 83545 3

70. HARRO HOPEL, *Jesuit Political Thought*
The Society of Jesus and the State, c1540–1640
hb: 0 521 83779 0

71. MIKAEL HORNQVIST, *Machiavelli and Empire*
hb: 0 521 83945 9

72. DAVID COLCLOUGH, *Freedom of Speech in Early Stuart England*
hb: 0 521 84748 6

73. JOHN ROBERTSON, *The Case for the Enlightenment Scotland and Naples 1680–1760*
hb: 0 521 84787 7

74. DANIEL CAREY, *Locke, Shaftesbury, and Hutcheson Contesting Diversity in the Enlightenment and Beyond*
hb: 0 521 84502 5

75. ALAN CROMARTIE, *The Constitutionalist Revolution in England Commonwealth, Common Law and Reformation*
hb: 0 521 78269 4

76. HANNAH DAWSON, *Locke, Language and Early Modern Philosophy*
hb: 0 521 85271 4

77. CONAL CONDREN, STEPHEN GAUKROGER and IAN HUNTER (eds) *The Philosopher in Early Modern Europe The Nature of a Contested Identity*
hb: 0 521 8666464

78. ANGUS GOWLAND, *The Worlds of Renaissance Melancholy Robert Burton in Context*
hb: 0 521 86768 1

Lightning Source UK Ltd.
Milton Keynes UK
UKHW011121230819
348459UK00024B/612/P

9 781107 403017